Rethinking
the
Western
Tradition

*The volumes in this series
seek to address the present debate
over the Western tradition
by reprinting key works of
that tradition along with essays
that evaluate each text from
different perspectives.*

Questions on Love and Charity

Summa Theologiae, Secunda Secundae, Questions 23–46

THOMAS AQUINAS

Edited, Translated, and with an
Introduction by
Robert Miner
with essays by
Jeffrey A. Bernstein
Dominic Doyle
Mark D. Jordan
Robert Miner
Sheryl Overmyer

Yale
UNIVERSITY PRESS

New Haven and London

Published with assistance from
the foundation established in memory of
Philip Hamilton McMillan of the Class of 1894, Yale College.

Yale University Press books may be purchased in quantity for educational,
business, or promotional use. For information, please e-mail sales.
press@yale.edu (U.S. office) or sales@yaleup.co.uk (U.K. office).

Set in Times Roman type by Newgen North America.
Printed in the United States of America.

ISBN 978-0-300-19541-5 (paperback : alk. paper)
Library of Congress Control Number: 2015947983

A catalogue record for this book is available from the British Library.

This paper meets the requirements of ANSI/NISO Z39.48–1992 (Permanence of Paper).

10 9 8 7 6 5 4 3 2 1

Contributors

Jeffrey A. Bernstein is Associate Professor of Philosophy at the College of the Holy Cross.

Dominic Doyle is Associate Professor of Systematic Theology at Boston College.

Mark D. Jordan is Andrew W. Mellon Professor of Christian Thought at the Harvard Divinity School.

Robert Miner is Professor of Philosophy in the Honors College at Baylor University.

Sheryl Overmyer is Assistant Professor of Catholic Studies at DePaul University.

Contents

List of Abbreviations   xiv

Introduction: Reading Thomas on Charity in the *Summa of Theology*
    Robert Miner   1

Summa of Theology, Secunda Secundae, Questions 23–46 on Charity,
with the Opposed Vices, Precepts, and Gift

Question 23. Charity in Itself   21
    Article 1. Whether charity is friendship.   21
    Article 2. Whether charity is something created in the soul.   24
    Article 3. Whether charity is a virtue.   26
    Article 4. Whether charity is a special virtue.   28
    Article 5. Whether charity is one virtue.   30
    Article 6. Whether charity is the most excellent of the virtues.   31
    Article 7. Whether there can be any true virtue without charity.   33
    Article 8. Whether charity is the form of the virtues.   36

Question 24. The Subject of Charity   38
    Article 1. Whether the will is the subject of charity.   38
    Article 2. Whether charity is caused in us by infusion.   40
    Article 3. Whether charity is infused according to the quantity
        of natural things.   41
    Article 4. Whether charity can be increased.   43
    Article 5. Whether charity is increased by addition.   45
    Article 6. Whether charity is increased by any particular act
        of charity.   48
    Article 7. Whether charity is increased to infinity.   49
    Article 8. Whether charity can be completed in this life.   51
    Article 9. Whether three steps of charity are appropriately
        distinguished.   53

Article 10. Whether charity can be decreased.   55
Article 11. Whether charity once possessed can be lost.   58
Article 12. Whether charity is lost by a single act of mortal sin.   61

Question 25. The Object of Charity   65
Article 1. Whether the love of charity stops at God, or also
    extends to our neighbor.   65
Article 2. Whether charity should be loved out of charity.   67
Article 3. Whether even irrational creatures should be loved
    out of charity.   69
Article 4. Whether a person loves himself out of charity.   70
Article 5. Whether a person should love his own body out of
    charity.   72
Article 6. Whether sinners should be loved out of charity.   73
Article 7. Whether sinners love themselves.   76
Article 8. Whether it is necessary for charity that enemies
    are loved.   78
Article 9. Whether it is necessary for charity that a person
    show the signs or effects of love to his enemy.   80
Article 10. Whether we should love the angels out of charity.   82
Article 11. Whether we should love the demons out of charity.   83
Article 12. Whether the four things that should be loved out
    of charity are inappropriately enumerated.   85

Question 26. The Order of Charity   87
Article 1. Whether there is an order in charity.   87
Article 2. Whether God should be loved more than
    one's neighbor.   88
Article 3. Whether a person should out of charity love God
    more than himself.   90
Article 4. Whether a person should out of charity love himself
    more than his neighbor.   92
Article 5. Whether a person should love his neighbor more
    than his own body.   94
Article 6. Whether one neighbor should be loved more than
    another.   95
Article 7. Whether we should love our better neighbors more
    than our closely connected ones.   97
Article 8. Whether one who is connected to us by carnal origin
    should be loved most of all.   100

Article 9. Whether out of charity a person should love his child
more than his father.   102
Article 10. Whether a person should love his mother more than
his father.   104
Article 11. Whether a man should love his wife more than his
father or mother.   106
Article 12. Whether a person should love his benefactor more
than his beneficiary.   107
Article 13. Whether the order of charity remains in the
homeland.   109

Question 27. The Principal Act of Charity, Which Is Love   113
Article 1. What is more proper to charity, being loved or loving.   113
Article 2. Whether loving, so far as it is charity's act, is nothing
other than goodwill.   115
Article 3. Whether God is loved out of charity on account of
himself.   117
Article 4. Whether in this life God can be loved without
mediation.   119
Article 5. Whether God can be loved wholly.   121
Article 6. Whether in divine love some measure should be
observed.   122
Article 7. Whether loving an enemy is more meritorious than
loving a friend.   125
Article 8. Whether loving our neighbor is more meritorious
than loving God.   127

Question 28. On Joy   129
Article 1. Whether joy is an effect of charity in us.   129
Article 2. Whether the spiritual joy that is caused by charity
receives an admixture of sorrow.   131
Article 3. Whether the spiritual joy that is caused by charity
can be full in us.   132
Article 4. Whether joy is a virtue.   134

Question 29. On Peace   137
Article 1. Whether peace is the same as concord.   137
Article 2. Whether all things desire peace.   139
Article 3. Whether peace is a proper effect of charity.   141
Article 4. Whether peace is a virtue.   143

Question 30. On Mercy   145
  Article 1. Whether an evil is properly the motive of mercy.   145
  Article 2. Whether a defect on the part of the one who is
      merciful is the reason for being merciful.   147
  Article 3. Whether mercy is a virtue.   149
  Article 4. Whether mercy is the greatest of the virtues.   152

Question 31. On Doing Good   154
  Article 1. Whether doing good is an act of charity.   154
  Article 2. Whether good should be done to everyone.   156
  Article 3. Whether more good should be done to those who are
      more connected to us.   157
  Article 4. Whether doing good is a special virtue.   160

Question 34. On Hatred   162
  Article 1. Whether anyone can hate God.   162
  Article 2. Whether hatred of God is the greatest of sins.   164
  Article 3. Whether all hatred of one's neighbor is a sin.   165
  Article 4. Whether hatred of one's neighbor is the gravest
      of the sins that are committed against one's neighbor.   167
  Article 5. Whether hatred is a capital vice.   168
  Article 6. Whether hatred arises from envy.   170

Question 35. On Acedia   173
  Article 1. Whether acedia is a sin.   173
  Article 2. Whether acedia is a special vice.   176
  Article 3. Whether acedia is a mortal sin.   177
  Article 4. Whether acedia should be set down as
      a capital vice.   179

Question 36. On Envy   183
  Article 1. Whether envy is sorrow.   183
  Article 2. Whether envy is a sin.   185
  Article 3. Whether envy is a mortal sin.   188
  Article 4. Whether envy is a capital vice.   190

Question 37. On Discord   193
  Article 1. Whether discord is a sin.   193
  Article 2. Whether discord is the daughter of vainglory.   195

Question 38. On Contention   198
 Article 1. Whether contention is a mortal sin.   198
 Article 2. Whether contention is the daughter of vainglory.   201

Question 39. On Schism   203
 Article 1. Whether schism is a special sin.   203
 Article 2. Whether schism is a graver sin than faithlessness.   205
 Article 3. Whether schismatics have any power.   208
 Article 4. Whether it is appropriate to punish schismatics by
   excommunication.   210

Question 40. On War   212
 Article 1. Whether to make war is always a sin.   212
 Article 2. Whether it is lawful for clerics and bishops to fight.   215
 Article 3. Whether in wars it is lawful to lay ambushes.   218
 Article 4. Whether it is lawful to make war on feast days.   219

Question 41. On Quarreling   221
 Article 1. Whether quarreling is always a sin.   221
 Article 2. Whether quarreling is the daughter of anger.   223

Question 42. On Sedition   226
 Article 1. Whether sedition is a special sin, distinct from
   other sins.   226
 Article 2. Whether sedition is always a mortal sin.   227

Question 43. On Scandal   230
 Article 1. Whether scandal is inappropriately defined
   as "something said or done less rightly, bringing an
   occasion of ruin."   230
 Article 2. Whether scandal is a sin.   233
 Article 3. Whether scandal is a special sin.   235
 Article 4. Whether scandal is a mortal sin.   237
 Article 5. Whether passive scandal can fall upon even those
   who are perfect.   238
 Article 6. Whether active scandal can be found in
   perfect men.   240
 Article 7. Whether spiritual goods should be given up on
   account of scandal.   241

Article 8. Whether temporal things should be given up on
    account of scandal.   245

Question 44. The Precepts of Charity   248
    Article 1. Whether a precept should be given about charity.   248
    Article 2. Whether two precepts should have been given.   250
    Article 3. Whether two precepts of charity suffice.   252
    Article 4. Whether it is appropriately commanded that God
        should be loved with one's whole heart.   254
    Article 5. Whether it is appropriately added "and with your
        whole soul and with your whole strength," etc.   256
    Article 6. Whether this precept about the love of God can be
        kept *in via.*   257
    Article 7. Whether the precept about the love of one's neighbor
        is given appropriately.   259
    Article 8. Whether the order of charity falls under a precept.   261

Question 45. The Gift of Wisdom   263
    Article 1. Whether wisdom should be counted among the gifts
        of the Holy Spirit.   263
    Article 2. Whether wisdom is in the intellect, as in its subject.   265
    Article 3. Whether wisdom is only speculative, or
        also practical.   267
    Article 4. Whether wisdom can be without grace, and with
        mortal sin.   269
    Article 5. Whether wisdom is in everyone who has grace.   270
    Article 6. Whether the Seventh Beatitude corresponds to the
        gift of wisdom.   272

Question 46. On Folly, Which Is Opposed to Wisdom   276
    Article 1. Whether folly is opposed to wisdom.   276
    Article 2. Whether folly is a sin.   278
    Article 3. Whether folly is the daughter of lust.   279

Essays
    Some Paradoxes in Teaching Charity   283
        Mark D. Jordan
    Disagreeing in Charity: Learning from Thomas Aquinas   299
        Robert Miner

Is Charity the Holy Spirit? The Development of Aquinas's
Disagreement with Peter Lombard   313
Dominic Doyle
Righteousness and Divine Love: Maimonides and Thomas
on Charity   336
Jeffrey A. Bernstein
Grace-Perfected Nature: The Interior Effect of Charity in Joy,
Peace, and Mercy   355
Sheryl Overmyer

Works Cited   373

Scriptural Citations   374

Nonscriptural Citations   384

Abbreviations

Textual Divisions of the *Summa of Theology* and Other Writings

1a	The *Prima Pars* (First Part) of the *Summa*
1a2ae	The *Prima Secundae* (First Part of the Second Part) of the *Summa*
2a	The *Secunda Pars* (Second Part) of the *Summa*
2a2ae	The *Secunda Secundae* (Second Part of the Second Part) of the *Summa*
3a	The *Tertia Pars* (Third Part) of the *Summa*
a./aa.	Article/Articles
ad 1, ad 2	Reply to an opening argument
arg	Opening argument ("objection")
bk.	Book
chap.	Chapter
corp	Body or "response" of an Article
d.	Distinction
pr	Prologue of a Part or a Question
pt.	Part
q./qq.	Question/Questions
sect.	Section
sc	Argument to the contrary (*sed contra*)

Other Abbreviations

can.	Canon
col.	Column
ep.	Epistle
hom.	Homily
serm.	Sermon
tr.	Tract

Introduction

Reading Thomas on

Charity in the *Summa of Theology*

ROBERT MINER

Thomas as Educator

Thomas Aquinas's unfinished masterwork, the *Summa of Theology,* is known for its dispassionate posing of questions, not to mention its considered distinctions and measured judgments. Written in a tranquil, almost colorless Latin, the *Summa* hardly seems to qualify as an "incendiary" work. Yet it has provoked incendiary reactions. There is the legend of Martin Luther throwing the book into the flames.[1] A tireless proponent of freedom of the press, Voltaire did not burn the work, but his judgment of the *Summa*'s afterlife might be described as incendiary: "The *Summa* of St. Thomas has produced two thousand fat volumes of theology, and the same family of little worms that have fed upon the mother continue to feed upon the children."[2] At the other extreme, there has been no shortage of triumphalist admirers of the *Summa,* praising Thomas in the most imperialistic terms, along with the "Scholasticism" he ostensibly represents. To quote the introduction to the *Summa*'s first English translation: "Scholasticism is Metaphysics. Modern science is anything else: Mechanics, Chemistry, Biology, everything that ends in sense. Metaphysics will return to popular favour when Scholasticism with its characteristic *word* returns to power."[3]

Why should a text with a surface as tranquil as the *Summa of Theology* provoke such unbalanced reactions? Do we find an answer in the externals of Thomas's life? The bare facts can be stated briefly.[4] Thomas Aquinas (1225–1274)[5] was a Dominican friar, teacher, and author. Coming from an aristocratic family in southern Italy, he defied his family's wishes and joined the Dominican order (founded a decade before he was born) at the age of nineteen. In Paris and Cologne, he studied under Albert Magnus, becoming a "master of the sacred page" at the University of Paris in 1256, at the same time as his Franciscan contemporary Bonaventure. Thomas traveled across Europe, preaching sermons, teaching courses, and overseeing houses of study in Paris, Orvieto, Rome, and Naples. He composed works in multiple genres: not only *Summas,* but also prayers and hymns, a dozen expositions of Aristotle, and still more commentaries on Scripture. Near the end of 1273, he seems to have experienced a vision,[6] leaving his masterwork unfinished. He died three months later.

The externals of Thomas's life reassert the question: Why should the texts of a Dominican priest known more for his mild equanimity than his rhetorical brilliance arouse responses that range from indignant rejection to virtual idolatry? Beneath the surface of Thomas's unflashy prose, we can discern an extraordinarily powerful voice – the voice of a teacher who wants to persuade his readers. But to persuade them to do what? "To submit to the decrees of Roman Catholicism," incendiary partisans would have us think. But can this be Thomas's real aim? In the Prologue of the *Summa,* Thomas indicates his frustration with the dominant modes of theological teaching. Newcomers to Christian theology, he says, get worn down by endless repetition of the same things – a dulling monotony that produces "distaste and confusion in the souls of students." Or they find themselves addressed in a way that does not even try to distinguish their real needs from their sham needs. The principle of teaching is extrinsic, "according to what the exposition of books used to require, or according to what some occasion for disputing a question would provide" (1a pr).[7] No suitable "order of learning" enters the picture. This ensures a proliferation of "useless questions, articles, and arguments." Even if true things are conveyed through these questions, articles, and arguments, they are not taught efficaciously. They do nothing to lead "newcomers" closer to what Thomas regards as the ideal condition of the human being – the condition of "blessedness" (*beatitudo*).

Thomas writes the *Summa* as a teacher who cares about people and their progress toward blessedness. He arranges the work according to a conception of the "order of learning," an order reflecting what he judges to be most necessary and most effective in addressing the needs of newcomers. This arrangement has not always been respected. It is routinely violated by those who plunder the *Summa,* taking its words as proof-texts for their own notions, often adopted well before the discovery of Thomas. But, one might ask, might a similar charge be brought against the present edition? The charge has some force, since the fullest respect for Thomas's order of learning would require one to begin at the beginning. The present edition – a selection of Questions taken from the second subdivision of the Second Part of the *Summa* – seems to flout this requirement. Is it not also a violent excerpting of Thomas's texts? Does it not succumb to Montaigne's jab: "Every abridgment of a good book is a stupid abridgment"?[8]

To this charge, it may readily be granted that an ideal reader would encounter the questions on charity only after having read and assimilated the preceding Questions. But most of us cannot be ideal readers. We tend to meet Thomas where we are, as we are. Not many who desire greater familiarity with Thomas's thinking about moral topics are in a position to undertake the demanding task of reading the *Summa* whole. Some give up reading Thomas at all, resorting to summaries or abstracts of the "philosophy of Aquinas." These are misleading for a host of reasons, not least because they rarely question the dubious assumption that Thomas writes autonomous philosophy (as distinct from making use of philosophy within theology).[9] Even when they are not driven by agendas of their own, summaries are necessarily a poor substitute for Thomas's own writing. Rarely does one see Thomas through the grille of apologetic renditions or academic expositions, at least when taken as substitutes for the texts.

The present edition of Thomas is intended to meet the needs of those who want a substantial introduction to his thinking about moral topics, but who are unable to drop everything and start reading the *Summa* from the beginning. It does not resort to summary or paraphrase. Rather, it selects for translation a sequence of Questions that lies at the heart of the *Summa*'s moral teaching. These are the questions on charity in the *Secunda Secundae* (hereafter 2a2ae). (For reasons of space, Questions 32 and 33 on works of mercy and fraternal correction are not included. My translations of these Questions are available online at a Yale University Press website [yalebooks.com/aquinasloveand charity] for this volume.) Why these particular Questions? Why not others? Certainly other clusters of Questions from the *Summa* are worth reading. They too merit, and have sometimes found, fresh translations. But for those interested in ethics as conceived by Thomas–or simply in the *Summa* itself–the questions on charity stand out. Thomas does not regard charity simply as one virtue among others. It is, he says, the "mother and root of all the virtues" (1a2ae 62.4 corp). To understand any of the other virtues in isolation from its root in charity is to uproot it–and thereby to misunderstand it.

The Moral Part of the *Summa*

The premise of this edition is simply stated. Those new to Thomas can read the questions on charity in the 2a2ae with pleasure and profit, confident that they are encountering an integral teaching about the highest

virtue, as Thomas sees it. But they should not forget that what they encounter is part of a larger whole, whose main contours the attentive reader
will want to keep in mind. In the most economical fashion, Thomas states
the *Summa*'s plan early in the *Prima Pars:* "We shall first treat of God;
second, of the rational creature's motion toward God; third, of Christ, who
so far as he is man, is for us a way (*via*) for tending toward God" (1a 2 pr).
In the *Prima Pars,* Thomas begins with God and moves to creation and
creatures, considered as proceeding from a divine origin. In the lexicon of
Latin Neoplatonism, the motion is an *exitus.* Of the many things that ema-
nate from the divine origin in this *exitus,* Thomas selects one for special
consideration in the *Secunda Pars:* the "rational creature." Inverting the
direction of the First Part, the Second Part treats "the motion of the rational
creature to God"–a return (*reditus*). There has been some debate about
the application of the *exitus/reditus* schema to the *Summa.*[10] However one
judges this debate, the *exitus/reditus* schema makes a good starting point
for grasping the macroscopic rhythms of the *Summa*'s first two parts. In the
Tertia Pars, Thomas turns to the Incarnation of Christ and the sacraments.
He breaks off abruptly in the middle of the questions on penance, leaving
the *Summa* unfinished.

The *Secunda Pars* of the *Summa* treats the rational creature's motion
toward God, considered under the aspect of blessedness. It is appropriately
known as the *pars moralis,* or "moral part," of the *Summa.* Thomas carefully positions it between the *Prima Pars*'s discourse on God and creation
and the *Tertia Pars*'s treatment of Christ. Mark Jordan proposes that the
Summa's structure can be seen as "enframing the study of Christian moral
life between a theology that issues in cosmology and a Christology that issues in an ecclesiology."[11] Habitually and sloppily, we speak of Thomas's
"moral theology"–a phrase that appears nowhere in his texts. Should we
persist in this questionable habit, we ought to do so with caution. By its
very structure, the *Summa* rejects the possibility of treating *moralia* as if
they were free-standing. In placing the *pars moralis* right in the middle of
the *Summa,* Thomas simultaneously privileges moral discourse and indicates its essentially "in-between" character. Moral topics must be treated.
But in the ideal case, inquiry would neither originate nor terminate with
straightforwardly "moral" questions.

The *Secunda Pars,* though not fully intelligible when abstracted from
the *Summa*'s other two Parts, has a plan of its own. Thomas identifies the
structuring principle most clearly in the Prologue of the 2a2ae. The first
subdivision, the *Prima Secundae* (hereafter 1a2ae), is a "consideration in
general of virtues and vices and of the other things belonging to moral

matters" (2a2ae pr). Thomas begins the 1a2ae with Questions about the end (*finis*) of human life, blessedness. From there, he moves backwards (so to speak), treating two categories in order of their nearness to the end. First, he considers the *actus* by which a person moves (or is moved) closer to the end. These include acts of the will, along with acts that humans have in common with other animals, the "passions of the soul" (*passiones animae*). Second, he considers the *principia,* the "starting points" from which acts spring. Some of these are "intrinsic," existing within an agent. These are "habits," which may lead the human agent toward blessedness (virtues) or away from it (vices). Others are "extrinsic," existing outside the human agent in the forms of law and the free gift of grace. The 1a2ae is a sonata with three movements: the end, the acts tending toward the end, and the starting points of these acts.

Because the 1a2ae treats large categories in a general manner, its usefulness is strictly limited. "Universal moral discourses are less useful, in that actions are about particular things," Thomas writes in the 2a2ae's Prologue. He regards the *sermones morales universales* of the 1a2ae not as an end in themselves, but as propaedeutic to the more particularized treatment of moral matters to come in the 2a2ae. Universal moral discourses are needed, but chiefly to prepare readers for instruction in the particular virtues that are most potent for moving them toward the goal of blessedness. The point is not that readers of the 2a2ae should view the 1a2ae as a ladder to be thrown away after they have climbed up on it. On the contrary, throughout the 2a2ae Thomas will refer readers back to explanations given in the 1a2ae. But the universal moral discourse of the 1a2ae, though not dispensable, is essentially preparatory. It serves as an incubator for the treatment of particular virtues that constitutes the 2a2ae.

Thomas inherits a bewildering variety of texts on moral matters. These texts treat a swarm of virtues, perhaps more than one swarm. Thomas knows that if he is to avoid merely replicating the defects about which the *Summa*'s Prologue complains, he must reduce this swarming multiplicity to a convincing order. The achievement of the 2a2ae is to perform just this reduction. Thomas considers many virtues in the 2a2ae; he leads all of them back to seven. These are the three virtues mentioned by Paul at 1 Corinthians 13, along with the four virtues taken as primary by Plato's *Republic,* as well as by Cicero and some patristic writers. The 2a2ae begins with the "theological virtues" of faith, hope, and charity. Only after treating charity does the 2a2ae take up the four "cardinal virtues." The order in which Thomas considers these mirrors the hierarchy of the human soul's powers. These are the intellect (perfected by prudence), the will (perfected by justice), and the sensitive appetite, in which Thomas distinguishes an "irascible power" (perfected by courage) and a "concupiscible power" (perfected by temperance). Structurally, charity is the hinge connecting the 2a2ae's treatment of the theological virtues to its consideration of the cardinal virtues.

Beyond reducing the virtues to seven, the *Summa*'s other great structural innovation is a schema used throughout the 2a2ae. The schema has four elements: a particular virtue, its opposed vices, the corresponding gifts, and associated precepts. This fourfold schema gives Thomas a "more concise and rapid path (*via*) of consideration," as he says in the Prologue of the 2a2ae. It enables him to avoid the "*frequens repetitio*" lamented at the beginning of the *Summa*. Rather than "say the same thing many times over" (2a2ae pr), as a sequential treatment of every virtue, vice, gift, and precept seems to require, Thomas places the accent on the dominant good, the master virtue. He then treats other phenomena as they appear in the light of this good. For Thomas, this constitutes a large improvement on previous treatments – an improvement at once more truthful, concise, and pedagogically appropriate.

The Structure of *Summa* 2a2ae 23–46

As one can see from Question 23's Prologue, Thomas subdivides the treatment of "charity itself" into five parts:

1. Charity itself (Questions 23–24)
2. The object of charity (Questions 25–26)
3. The acts and effects of charity (Questions 27–33)
4. The vices opposed to charity (Questions 34–43)
5. The precepts of charity (Question 44)

The first two parts have a common feature. Each treats topics too large for a single Question. Each demands a "twofold consideration," Thomas says. So "charity itself" requires not only a treatment of charity "in itself" (Question 23), but also a treatment in relation to its subject – its seat in the human soul (Question 24). Similarly, the "object" of charity requires one Question (Question 25) to clarify its constituent parts and another (Question 26) to set out and justify the "order" in which these things should be loved (the "*ordo caritatis*": God, self, neighbor).

The third part marks a transition from the virtue to what springs from it, "acts and effects." First among these is charity's principal act, the love that

Thomas calls *dilectio* (Question 27). This love is both an effect of a habit and a causal power in its own right. It brings about three "inward" effects: joy (*gaudium*, Question 28), peace (*pax*, Question 29), and mercy (*misericordia*, Question 30). These inward effects radiate outward, generating three exterior effects that Thomas arranges in yet another deployment of the general/particular distinction that pervades the 2a2ae. These are "doing good" (*beneficientia* as the most general outward effect, Question 31), works of mercy (*eleemosynae*, Question 32), and fraternal correction (*correctio fraterna*, as a particular work of mercy, Question 33). That mercy should be directly followed by beneficence is not accidental. Mercy is the link between the deepest inward effect of charity and its first outward effect. Also worth noting is the placement of mercy. Of the Questions on "charity itself," mercy lies at the very center of the consideration's middle part. It is the only inward effect of charity that Thomas expressly describes as a virtue. Mercy is not just any virtue, he says, but the highest of the virtues by which we are related to our neighbor (30.4 corp). Perhaps for this reason he inscribes *misericordia* into the heart of the questions on charity.

The structure of the fourth part is remarkable in several ways. Here Thomas considers ten vices opposed to charity. He begins with the vice opposed to charity's principal act, treating hatred (*odium*, Question 34) as contrary to the act of love. He proceeds by considering acedia (Question 35) and envy (*invidia*, Question 36) as modes of sorrow, standing contrary to charity's first inward effect, joy. He moves to the vices opposed to charity's second inward effect, peace. Then and now, the vices that oppose peace are numerous. In his first statement of the plan for this section, Thomas mentions only discord and schism (Question 34, Prologue). But in the treatment actually given, the reader finds six vices opposed to peace. The first two are discord (*discordia*, Question 37), a vice of the heart, and contention (*contentio*, Question 38), a vice of the lips. The next four are unpeaceful deeds: schism (*schisma*, Question 39), war (*bellum*, Question 40), quarreling (*rixa*, Question 41), and sedition (*seditio*, Question 42).

In view of the pattern established so far, we would expect Thomas now to consider the vice opposed to charity's third interior effect, mercy. Here Thomas frustrates the expectation. He breaks the pattern, conspicuously failing to include a Question on any vice opposed to mercy. Instead, he moves directly to scandal (Question 43), a vice opposed to charity's first outward effect, beneficence. Thomas continues to defy expectations by deciding not to include Questions on vices opposed to the second and third outward effects (works of mercy and fraternal correction). Rather, he simply brings the treatment of opposed vices to a halt. Thomas moves to Question 44 on the precepts (*praecepta*), the fifth and final part of the questions on charity itself, before concluding with the Question on the gift of wisdom (*sapientia,* Question 45) and its contrary, folly (*stultitia,* Question 46).

Reading an Article of the *Summa*

More could be said about the structure of Questions 23–46 of the 2a2ae. But let us turn to the task of closely reading a single Article within a Question. Because careful attention to individual Articles is the foundation upon which good readings of the *Summa* are built, the plan common to any Article of the *Summa* deserves special attention. Typically there are five sections.

1. The first is the "query" posed by an Article, for example, "Whether charity is friendship" (23.1). Because the manuscripts do not show that Thomas himself placed the query's words at the head of each Article, the present edition encloses these words in brackets. (Headings of Questions also appear in brackets, for the same reason.) The query's words are not for that reason arbitrary. They echo the brief descriptions of Articles that Thomas gives in a Question's Prologue. In the typical case, the query begins with the word "whether" (*utrum*). Neither completely open-ended nor entirely obvious, the query admits of resolution in a limited number of ways.

2. The second section invariably begins with the words "IT SEEMS that" (*videtur quod*). It introduces anywhere from two to six (but most often three) distinct arguments. For the most part, these are not "objections" to be defeated or vanquished. They are better understood as dialectical arguments, rehearsed for the sake of showing just how an appearance presents itself. This appearance – the initial "look" of the matter – typically contains some truth.

3. The third section invariably begins with the words "BUT TO THE CONTRARY" (*sed contra*). No section of an Article from the *Summa* is so persistently misunderstood as the *sed contra*. Thomas never proposes the *sed contra* as though it were a satisfying argument. He does not suppose it capable of defeating the arguments contained in the *videtur quod*. Rather, he understands the function of the *sed contra* in a minimalist manner. Its job is to set forth a counterappearance, a way of answering the question that diverges from the opening set of appearances. Frequently the *sed contra* cites an authority. Often it supplies a quotation; in some cases, there is

only a bare reference. Or it may state an argument invented by Thomas, without furnishing a textual precedent. Whatever the case, the aim of the *sed contra* is always to show that the query that begins the Article is a genuine question. In the words of Thomas's predecessor, Gilbert of Poitiers (1075–1174): "Not every contradiction makes a question . . . , but where both sides appear to have arguments, there you have a question."[12]

4. In the play of appearance and counterappearance, set before the reader *ad oculos,* how can a truthful determination be made? What would such a determination look like? Answering these questions is the function of an Article's fourth section, invariably introduced by the phrase "I ANSWER THAT IT SHOULD BE SAID THAT [*respondeo dicendum*]." The apparent redundancy can be understood as evoking the activity of a theological *magister,* playing his appointed role in the *determinatio* of a disputed question. In the fourth section of an Article – sometimes called its "body" or "response" – Thomas gives a determination. His most characteristic impulse in the *Summa* is to combine adequacy with brevity.

5. The final section of an Article in the *Summa* contains "Replies" to the opening arguments – and occasionally to the *sed contra* as well. Often Thomas shows how an argument advanced in the *videtur quod* involves partial quotation, poor inference, incomplete reasoning, insufficient attention to context, conflation of a term's different senses, or some other intellectual vice. Thomas knows, however, that any argument sufficiently powerful to generate an appearance is unlikely to contain only falsehood. Therefore, the Replies attempt both to show what has gone wrong and to preserve whatever truth among the appearances can be preserved. Most Articles include this fifth section, but a minority of them do not. Sometimes Thomas decides that the previous section has said enough to address the opening arguments. No formula exists here, save for his pedagogical judgment.

In virtually every Article of the *Summa,* the reader finds Thomas citing and quoting other authors – his "authorities." Medieval *auctoritates* should not be confused with "authorities" in a modern sense. *Auctoritates* are not sources to be unconditionally deferred to; they are not authors whose every word should be taken for truth. Rather, as Mark Jordan observes, an *auctoritas* is a "textual precedent deserving attention."[13] Throughout the questions on charity, Thomas deploys a number of *auctoritates.* These fall into one of three main groups:

Scripture, along with various *Glossae.* The questions on charity contain almost 160 references to the Old Testament, along with nearly 300 citations to the New Testament. Matthew receives more citations than the other

Gospels combined. Quotations from the Pauline letters regularly appear; 1 Corinthians is perhaps the most visible. Of the so-called general epistles, the most prominent is 1 John.

Pagan authors. These include Cicero and Sallust, along with Aristotle, the pagan philosopher to whom Thomas alludes most frequently. The questions on charity contain about 150 references to Aristotle. The Aristotelian text Thomas cites most often is the *Nicomachean Ethics,* followed by the *Rhetoric* (with a third as many references).

Patristic authors. The patristic author to whom Thomas refers most extensively (by far) is Augustine. The questions on charity mention no fewer than twenty-nine of his works. Other patristic authors he quotes with some frequency are Gregory the Great, Pseudo-Dionysius, Jerome, Isidore of Seville, and John of Damascus. Appearing less often are Ambrose, the author known as "Ambrosiaster" or "pseudo-Ambrose," Basil the Great, John Chrysostom, and John Cassian.

The *Summa* may be read in part as Thomas's ongoing dialogue with the philosophical and theological precedents known to him. For any given topic, readers may wish to attend closely to his use of these precedents, asking why he chooses the authorities he does, what use he makes of them, where he amplifies or departs from them, and how he subjects them to correction or revision. Readers who ask questions of this sort, while also examining the details and merits of particular arguments (the two approaches are not incompatible), will be well equipped to discover for themselves what is distinctive in Thomas's approach to the topic.

Note on the Translation and Texts

Translating Thomas poses multiple challenges, not least of which is that his Latin conveys many things in few words. Often the translator is faced with an unhappy choice between (1) attempting to emulate Thomas's style by using few words, while risking a significant loss of clarity, and (2) using more words for the sake of added clarity, while creating a rhetorical effect alien to Thomas. This translation has attempted a compromise between these extremes. How could it do otherwise? As Mark Jordan remarks, no translation of Thomas into English can simultaneously preserve "his rhythm, his brevity, his simplicity, his precision, and his fidelity to traditional vocabularies."[14]

To meet the challenges posed by Thomas's use of gendered language, I have not followed any rigidly consistent policy. Generally speaking, pronouns used for God are masculine. Accurately representing Thomas's practice here, however offensive some readers may find it, seems better than concealing it by aggressive translation. For *homo* and *aliquis* I have typically opted for "human being" or "someone" or "person" (trusting the reader *not* to hear Trinitarian echoes in the latter). There are exceptions – for instance, at 26.11, where Thomas clearly uses *homo* to refer to a biologically gendered male in relation to his wife.

In the questions on charity, Thomas draws upon multiple vocabularies, often bringing them into a coherent relation. An English translation can hope for only partial success in capturing this side of the *Summa*. Below are some notes on a few of the more significant terms.

Caritas. This term is uniformly rendered as "charity." That "charity" is the best translation of *caritas* is not obvious. The English word "charity" has acquired somewhat narrow connotations that simply do not apply to the medieval *caritas*. Numerous readers of English translations of the Bible know Paul to speak at 1 Corinthians 13:13 of "faith, hope, and *love*." Many speak about their gratitude for receiving divine love, or the love of a neighbor; not so many speak of "charity" in the same way. For Thomas, to speak of *caritas* is entirely (though not uniquely) appropriate in these contexts. For readers of English (as well as other modern languages), uses of "charity" in these same contexts may seem oddly stilted or narrow. One can thus make a very strong case for translating *caritas* as "love."

Despite the strength of this case, I have nonetheless opted for "charity." The principal reason is that for Thomas *caritas* picks out a species within a genus, the broader genus named by *amor* (see 1a2ae 26.4). Translating both terms as "love" would obscure both the distinction and the relation between *caritas* and *amor.*

Acedia. This names the first of two vices that are directly opposed to the joy that charity brings. Sometimes English speakers know the vice as "sloth." But "sloth" is not a suitable translation, since *acedia* is compatible with (and sometimes promotes) busy diversion. "Despair" is perhaps better than "sloth." But translating *acedia* as "despair" risks conflating *acedia* with the condition that Thomas calls *desperatio*. Since these and other possibilities (e.g., "spiritual apathy") are so problematic, I have opted to let *acedia* stand as "acedia."

Beatitudo. Some readers will know this term as "happiness," since *beatitudo* is used to translate *eudaimonia* by the Latin Aristotle that Thomas knew. But "happiness" as heard by most English speakers today falls short of the condition that Thomas means to indicate. This is more adequately conveyed as "beatitude" or "blessedness" (Latin *beatus* = "blessed"). In the translation, *beatitudo* appears uniformly as "blessedness."

Communicatio. This term is extraordinarily difficult to translate. It has a range of meanings, including "sharing," "participation," "diffusion," and "living in common." Though I have opted for "sharing," the reader should be open to hearing each of these meanings whenever Thomas uses the term.

Misericordia. This term is sometimes translated as "pity," "sympathy," or "compassion." "Pity" has associations for contemporary English speakers that Thomas does not intend. "Sympathy" and "compassion" should be reserved for *compassio,* a term Thomas also uses. Accordingly, I have rendered *misericordia* as "mercy."

Patria. "Heaven" is one possibility, but Latin has another word (*caelum*) that is more aptly and literally translated as "heaven." Another possibility is "fatherland," which has the advantage of preserving the connection to *pater* ("father"). This advantage, however, is offset by the repulsive connotations carried by the term after the Second World War. Accordingly, *patria* is uniformly rendered by "homeland" (a term not without its own defects).

Perfectus. More often than not, I have rendered *perfectus* as "complete." The English term "perfect" has connotations of "faultless," as well as other moralistic resonances not necessarily shared by *perfectus*. The sense of *perfectus* (*per* + *facere*) is often "thoroughly made" or "fully achieved." No single policy for *perfectus,* however, is desirable. Some contexts (e.g., 43.6) seem to call for "perfect" rather than "complete."

Praeceptum. I uniformly use "precept" rather than "commandment," which is best reserved for *mandatum*. One should always hear in *praeceptum* the echoes of "teaching," as suggested by its connection to *praecipere,* "to teach" or "to instruct."

Principium. Often the literal translation "principle" is misleading. For Thomas, a *principium* is not typically a "rule" or "guideline" or "conviction" (to name some different senses that "principle" takes in English). Most characteristically, it refers to what is "first" (*princeps*), whether in a logical or temporal sequence. In some cases, I have translated it as "source" or "origin."

Ratio. Like *principium,* this term bears a wide range of meanings, many of which may be intended simultaneously. It can take any or all of the following senses: "aspect," "notion," "account," "definition," "formula," "essence," "argument," "reasoning," "cause," "nature," and "character." Different contexts demand different translations; here, no uniform policy is possible. When any single term seems particularly unsatisfying, I have flagged occurrences of *ratio* with a parenthetical reference.

There is still no text of the *Summa* that has been edited to the standards of a modern critical edition. Enthusiasts for the "Leonine" edition of Thomas's *opera omnia* (commissioned by Pope Leo XIII; the first volume appeared in 1882) will sometimes speak of its version of the *Summa* (volumes 4–12) as "the critical edition." This way of speaking is understandable, since the Leonine *Summa* does take account of readings from multiple manuscripts – specifically, eleven manuscripts housed at the Vatican Library. But these eleven are only a small portion of the surviving manuscripts. This holds particularly for the 2a2ae, which was the most widely copied part of the *Summa.* According to J. N. Hillgarth, more than 286 manuscripts of the 2a2ae survive.[15] Because the Leonine edition makes use of less than 4 percent of these manuscripts, its version of the 2a2ae stands at a considerable distance from the standards of a modern critical edition.

In preparing this translation, I have used both the Leonine edition and the edition of the *Summa* published by a team of Dominicans in Ottawa from 1941 to 1945. Readers of Thomas owe a large debt to the Ottawa Dominicans. The Ottawa *Summa* is a reprint of the 1570 "Piana" edition of the *Summa.* Because the *editio Piana* was derived from a set of manuscripts that is not identical to the group used for the Leonine, its text offers a useful comparison. Moreover, the Ottawa edition contains a valuable editorial apparatus, featuring helpful cross-references to other parts of the *Summa,* as well as generally reliable (but now outdated) references to the texts of Thomas's authorities. It indicates many (but not all) of the differences between the Piana text and the Leonine text. My general practice has been to translate from the Leonine edition, but not without close comparison with the Piana text (as it appears in the Ottawa edition).

Throughout the *Summa,* Thomas cites a wide range of texts. Whenever possible, a footnote provides a reference to a modern critical edition of a cited text. Rather than refer to existing English translations of these texts, I have translated Thomas's Latin quotations directly into English. The reason is that English translations of ancient texts may adopt, for perfectly good reasons of their own, conventions that are foreign to Thomas. My practice of translating directly from the *Summa*'s Latin extends to Thomas's scriptural citations. Numbering of Psalms follows the Vulgate, rather than that of modern editions. (The modern equivalent can usually be had by adding "1" to the Vulgate numbering.)

Five Interpretive Essays

The essays that follow the translated text have been written for this volume. They offer diverse but thematically connected approaches to reading Thomas on charity. Mark D. Jordan's "Some Paradoxes in Teaching Charity" begins by drawing a series of incisive contrasts between Thomas's theology of love and the (still-influential) work of Anders Nygren, *Agape and Eros*. Nygren embarks upon a determined separation of *agapē* from *eros*. Thomas sets himself the quite different task of "judging the relative adequacy of traditional languages about a divine gift." If charity is a divine gift, what does Thomas hope to add to it by writing questions? Posing this query, Jordan constructs an answer that focuses in detail on three features of Thomas's moral pedagogy. These are exhortation, admonition, and "the persuasion of loving vision." This latter category, Jordan shows, includes both Thomas's "visual physics of love," as expressed in the 2a2ae's questions on charity, and a particular use of Gospel narrative, found most vividly in the *Tertia Pars*. In this way, Jordan not only gives a subtle and provocative reading of Questions from the 2a2ae, but also effectively ushers the reader into the *Summa*'s comparatively neglected third part.

In keeping with Jordan's view that Thomas offers a moral pedagogy worth considering, my essay, "Disagreeing in Charity: Learning from Thomas Aquinas," asks what we might learn from Thomas about disagreeing rationally and in charity. Beginning with his account in the 2a2ae of two vices opposed to charity – contention and discord – I show how contentious speech arises from discord between persons, which itself is grounded in a prior discord within a person. As Thomas sees it, such internal discord is not rooted in the tendency to love oneself too much. It springs, rather, from a failure to love oneself, in the most charitable and rational sense of loving. How does Thomas's own zest for disputation, not to mention his apparent doctrinal rigidity, square with my claim that his pedagogy contains a persuasive teaching about the nature of reasonable and charitable disagreement? In the two final sections of my essay, I take up these questions.

Dominic Doyle adopts an approach that differs from (but does not exclude) those taken by Jordan and myself. His essay "Is Charity the Holy Spirit? The Development of Aquinas's Disagreement with Peter Lombard" features a "developmental" way of reading Thomas, one that attends to the successive articulations of an idea in texts early, middle, and late.[16] If Thomas values rational and charitable disagreement, we should expect his engagement with other authors to model such disagreement. Is this expectation met? Doyle addresses the question by tracing the unfolding of

Thomas's teaching over time. His essay considers a sustained disagreement that Thomas conducts with his predecessor Peter Lombard. Is charity simply identical with the Holy Spirit? Lombard says yes, Aquinas says no. Beginning with Thomas's early commentary on Peter Lombard's *Sentences,* Doyle moves to his second (and ultimately abandoned) *Sentences* commentary. His essay concludes with a comparison between Thomas's two later presentations of charity: a "disputed question" on *caritas* and the teaching of the 2a2ae. In taking a developmental approach, Doyle seeks both to illuminate a key text of the *Summa*'s treatment of charity and to show Thomas's mind in motion.

Jeffrey A. Bernstein adds a comparative dimension to the interpretive essays with "Righteousness and Divine Love: Maimonides and Thomas on Charity." He does so by placing Thomas in dialogue with Moses Maimonides, the medieval Jewish thinker whose writings Thomas knew in translation and held in high regard. Bernstein compares and contrasts Thomas's understanding of charity as an "infused" virtue with Maimonides's conception of charity (*tzedakah*) as the virtue of righteousness, "the capacity for which belongs (in principle) to all human beings naturally." Bernstein shows how reading Maimonides and Thomas together has the power to expand and sharpen our sense of the possible relations between law and faith, justice and mercy, nature and grace. Bernstein makes no attempt to resolve the questions. Rather, he aims to show how distinct religious traditions formulate the questions differently, yet without precluding genuine dialogue between these traditions.

As the first words of its title indicate, Sheryl Overmyer's contribution, "Grace-Perfected Nature: The Interior Effect of Charity in Joy, Peace, and Mercy," explicitly takes up a theme of Bernstein's essay: the relation between nature and grace. Overmyer seeks to illuminate the role played by charity's three inward effects – joy, peace, and mercy – in what Thomas understands as the perfecting of nature by grace. Overmyer's discussion gives special attention to the distinction between "complete" and "incomplete" peace, as well as to the status of mercy as both gift and virtue. She also touches on the vices that are opposed to charity, focusing particularly on acedia, envy, and war. As an instance of the dialogue between traditions mentioned in Bernstein's essay, one might juxtapose an imperative quoted by Bernstein – "In a world devoid of humans, become human" – with Overmyer's conclusion that charity does not make us "other" than we are, but enables us to become "more human."

The interpretive essays are intended for the benefit of beginning and advanced readers alike. They should not, of course, be used as substitutes for the primary text. Those new to reading the *Summa* may wish to set the interpretive essays to one side. Later they may discover in them an impetus for a second or third engagement with the primary text, read anew in light of the questions the essays provoke.

NOTES

1. The legend is not strictly true. Luther did not actually burn the *Summa* in the marketplace at Wittenberg. According to Joseph Pieper, this was only because he could not find anyone "willing to part with his copy" (*The Silence of St. Thomas* [South Bend, IN: St. Augustine's Press, 1999], 33).

2. Voltaire, *Philosophical Dictionary,* closing words of the entry on "Books." See *The Portable Voltaire,* ed. B. R. Redman (London: Penguin, 1977), 92.

3. The *"Summa Theologica" of St. Thomas Aquinas,* Part I, First Number (London: R. & T. Washbourne, 1911), xlvii.

4. For more than summary, the standard biographies in English are (1) Jean-Pierre Torrell, O.P., *Saint Thomas Aquinas: Volume 1, The Person and His Work,* trans. Robert Royal (Washington, DC: Catholic University of America Press, 1996); (2) James Weisheipl, O.P., *Friar Thomas d'Aquino: His Life, Thought and Works* (Washington, DC: Catholic University of America Press, 1983); and (3) Simon Tugwell, O.P., *Albert & Thomas: Selected Writings* (New York: Paulist Press, 1988), 201–344. A more recent biographical sketch, less documentarian and more meditative, is Denys Turner, *Thomas Aquinas: A Portrait* (New Haven, CT: Yale University Press, 2013).

5. Thomas's birth year is a matter of some uncertainty. Though some put his birth in 1224, the current consensus seems to be 1225. Tugwell argues vigorously for 1226 (*Albert & Thomas,* 201, 296n45, 304n121).

6. The hagiographical accounts emphasize this point, as one might expect. But even some very sympathetic to Thomas have wanted to deromanticize his final months. After December 1273, Tugwell (*Albert & Thomas*) says, he was "obviously a sick and rather helpless man" (233); once he could no longer write, "he was evidently frustrated and confused" (267).

7. Citations to the *Summa* are parenthetical references, cited by Part, Question, Article, and part of Article. When I do not mention a Part, the reference is to the 2a2ae.

8. Montaigne, *Essais* III.8 ("Of the Art of Discussion"), in Michel de Montaigne, *The Complete Works* (New York: Everyman's Library, 2003), 872.

9. See Mark D. Jordan, "Philosophy in a *Summa of Theology,*" in *Rewritten Theology: Aquinas After His Readers* (Oxford: Blackwell, 2006), 155.

10. The reader who most influentially locates the *exitus/reditus* schema as a key to the *Summa*'s plan is M.-D. Chenu. See Chenu, *Toward Understanding St. Thomas* (Chicago: Regnery, 1964), 310–17. For a critique of Chenu's application of *exitus/reditus* to the *Summa,* see Rudi Te Velde, *Aquinas on God: The "Divine Science" of the Summa Theologiae* (Burlington, VT: Ashgate, 2006), 11–18.

11. Mark D. Jordan, *On Faith: "Summa theologiae," Part 2–2, Questions 1–16 of St. Thomas Aquinas,* Introduction (Notre Dame: University of Notre Dame Press, 1990), 9.

12. Gilbert of Poitiers, *Commentary on Boethius's "De Trinitate,"* quoted in Bernard McGinn, *Thomas Aquinas's "Summa Theologiae": A Biography* (Princeton, NJ: Princeton University Press, 2014), 13.

13. Mark D. Jordan, "Thomas's Alleged Aristotelianism *or* Aristotle among the Authorities," in *Rewritten Theology,* 64.

14. Mark D. Jordan, Introduction to *On Faith,* 18.

15. J. N. Hillgarth, "Who Read Thomas Aquinas?," in *The Etienne Gilson Lectures on Thomas Aquinas,* ed. James P. Reilly (Toronto: PIMS, 2008), 48.

16. While privileging the *Summa* as the appropriate text for beginners, Doyle's contribution allows the reader a good way into two other texts by Thomas on charity. Both have found excellent recent translations. These are St. Thomas Aquinas, *On Love and Charity: Readings from the "Commentary on the Sentences of Peter Lombard,"* trans. Peter Kwasniewski, Thomas Bolin, and Joseph Bolin (Washington, DC: Catholic University of America Press, 2008); and Thomas Aquinas, *Disputed Questions on Virtue,* trans. Jeffrey Hause and Claudia Murphy (Indianapolis, IN: Hackett, 2010).

*Summa of Theology,
Secunda Secundae,*
Questions 23–46
on Charity, with
the Opposed Vices,
Precepts, and Gift

[Charity in Itself]

One should next consider charity. And first, charity itself; second, the gift of wisdom corresponding to it. Regarding the first, one should consider five things: first, charity itself; second, the object of charity; third, its acts; fourth, its opposed vices; fifth, the precepts belonging to it.

About the first point, there is a twofold consideration: first, a consideration of charity in itself, according to its own nature; second, a consideration of charity by comparison to its subject. Regarding the first, eight queries are raised. (1) Whether charity is friendship. (2) Whether it is something created in the soul. (3) Whether it is a virtue. (4) Whether it is a special virtue. (5) Whether it is one virtue. (6) Whether it is the greatest of the virtues. (7) Whether there can be any true virtue without it. (8) Whether it is the form of the virtues.

Article 1. [Whether charity is friendship.]

One proceeds in this way to the first query. IT SEEMS that charity is not friendship.

[1] "Nothing is so proper to friendship as living with a friend," as the Philosopher says in *Ethics* 8.[1] But charity is from man toward God and the angels, whose converse (*conversatio*) is not with human beings, as Daniel 2 says.[2] Therefore charity is not friendship.

[2] Furthermore, there is no friendship without love in return (*reamatio*), as said in *Ethics* 8.[3] But charity is had even toward enemies,

---

1. Aristotle, *Nicomachean Ethics* bk.8 chap.5 (1157b19).
2. Daniel 2.11.
3. Aristotle, *Nicomachean Ethics* bk.8 chap.2 (1155b28). *Reamatio* is an uncommon term in medieval Latin, hardly appearing in any medieval author before Thomas. The term does appear in the Latin Aristotle, where it renders Aristotle's "*antiphilēsis.*"

according to Matthew 5: "Love your enemies."[4] Therefore charity is not friendship.

[3] Furthermore, there are three species of friendship, according to the Philosopher in *Ethics* 8, namely friendship of pleasure, friendship of utility, and friendship based on what is noble.[5] But charity is not friendship of utility or pleasure, for as Jerome says in his letter to Paulinus, which is placed at the beginning of the Bible: "There is a true intimacy, sealed by Christ himself, where men are brought together not by interest in familiar things, not by the mere presence of bodies, not by crafty and flattering adulation, but by the fear of God and the study of divine Scriptures."[6] Likewise, charity is not friendship based on what is noble, since by charity we love even sinners. But friendship based on what is noble exists only with the virtuous, as is said in *Ethics* 8.[7] Therefore charity is not friendship.

BUT TO THE CONTRARY there is what John 15 says, "Now I will not call you servants, but my friends."[8] But this was not said to them except by reason of charity. Therefore charity is friendship.

I ANSWER THAT IT SHOULD BE SAID that according to the Philosopher in *Ethics* 8,[9] not every love has the aspect (*ratio*) of friendship, but only the love that comes with goodwill – that is, when we love someone so that we will him a good. If, however, we do not will some good to the things that are loved, but rather we will some good of theirs for ourselves, as when we are said to love wine or a horse or something else like this, then there is no love of friendship (*amor amicitiae*), for it is ridiculous to say that someone has friendship with wine or a horse. But goodwill does not suffice for the notion (*ratio*) of friendship. A certain mutual love (*amatio*) is also required, since a friend is a friend to [another] friend. Now such mutual goodwill is founded upon a sharing of some kind (*aliqua communicatio*).[10]

---

4. Matthew 5.44.

5. Aristotle, *Nicomachean Ethics* bk.8 chap.3 (1156a7); bk.8. chap.2 (1155b21).

6. Jerome, *Epistulae* ep.53 (PL 22:540; CSEL 54:442.5–443.1–4).

7. Aristotle, *Nicomachean Ethics* bk.8 chap.4 (1157a18).

8. John 15.15.

9. Aristotle, *Nicomachean Ethics* bk.8 chap.2 (1155b31).

10. *Communicatio* is an important term for the questions on charity. No single English rendering is able to capture all of its nuances.

Since, therefore, there is a sharing of some kind between man and God, according as God shares his blessedness with us, it is necessary that upon this sharing some friendship be founded. About this sharing 1 Corinthians 1 says, "Faithful God, by whom you are called into the fellowship (*societas*) of his Son."[11] Now love founded upon this sharing is charity. So it is clear that charity is a certain friendship of man with God.

[1] TO THE FIRST ARGUMENT, THEREFORE, IT SHOULD BE SAID that the life of man is twofold. One life is exterior, according to sensible and bodily nature. According to this life, we have no sharing or converse (*conversatio*) with God and the angels. Another life, however, is the spiritual life of man according to mind. And according to this life, we have converse both with God and with the angels. Incompletely, to be sure, in the present state, so that Philippians 3 says, "Our converse is in heaven."[12] But this converse will be completed in our homeland (*patria*) when his servants shall serve God and see his face, as said in Revelation, final chapter.[13] And thus we have incomplete charity here, but in our homeland it shall be completed.

[2] To the second it should be said that friendship extends to a person in two ways. In one way, with respect to oneself – and in this way friendship never extends to anyone except a friend. In another way, it extends to one person with respect to another person. For instance, if a person has a friendship with some man, he loves everyone who belongs to that man, be they sons or slaves or others connected to him in some manner, on account of the friendship. And the love of a friend can be so great that for the friend's sake, all those who belong to him are loved, even if they hurt us or hate us. And in this way the friendship of charity extends even toward enemies, whom we love out of charity as ordered to God, with whom the friendship of charity is principally had.

[3] To the third it should be said that there is no friendship based on what is noble, unless it is with someone virtuous as the principal person – while those connected to him are loved for his sake, even if they are not virtuous. And in this way charity, which most of all is friendship based on what is noble, extends to sinners, whom we love out of charity on account of God.

11. 1 Corinthians 1.9.
12. Philippians 3.20.
13. Revelation 22.3, 4.

Article 2. [Whether charity is something created in the soul.]

One proceeds in this way to the second query. IT SEEMS that charity is not something created in the soul.

[1] In *On the Trinity* 8, Augustine says: "He who loves his neighbor, it follows that he loves love itself. Now God is love. It follows, therefore, that he loves God especially."[14] And in *On the Trinity* 15 he says: "Just as it was said, 'God is charity,' so it is said, 'God is spirit.'"[15] Therefore charity is not something created in the soul, but is God himself.

[2] Furthermore, God is the life of the soul spiritually, just as the soul is the life of the body, according to Deuteronomy 30: "He is your life."[16] But the soul gives life to the body through itself. Therefore God gives life to the soul through himself. Now he gives life to the soul through charity, according to 1 John 3: "We know that we have passed from death to life, because we love the brethren."[17] Therefore God is charity itself.

[3] Furthermore, nothing created is of infinite power (*virtus*), but rather every creature is vanity (*vanitas*). Now charity is not vanity, but is rather repugnant to vanity, and is of infinite power, since it leads the human soul toward an infinite good. Therefore charity is not something created in the soul.

BUT TO THE CONTRARY there is what Augustine says in *On Christian Doctrine*, Book 3: "I call 'charity' the motion of the mind toward enjoying God for God's own sake."[18] But a motion of the mind is something created in the soul. Therefore charity is also something created in the soul.

I ANSWER THAT IT SHOULD BE SAID that the Master has thoroughly investigated this question in *Sentences,* Book 1, Distinction 17.[19]

---

14. Augustine, *De trinitate* bk.8 chap.7 sect.10 (PL 42:957; CCSL 50: 285.31–34).

15. Augustine, *De trinitate* bk.15 chap.17 sect.27 (PL 42:1080; CCSL 50A: 502.22–23). The allusion is to 1 John 4.16 and John 4.24.

16. Deuteronomy 30.20. Compare Augustine, *Confessiones* bk.10 chap.6 sect.10 (PL 32:783; CCSL 27:160.60).

17. 1 John 3.14.

18. Augustine, *De doctrina christiana* bk.3 chap.10 sect.16 (PL 34:72; CCSL 32:87.1–2).

19. Peter Lombard, *Sententiae* bk.1 d.17 chap.1 (Grottaferrata 1:142).

He proposes that charity is not something created in the soul, but is the Holy Spirit itself inhabiting the mind. Nor is it his intention to say that the motion of love by which we love God is the Holy Spirit itself, but that this motion of love is from the Holy Spirit not by means of some habit, as other virtuous acts are from the Holy Spirit by means of the habits of other virtues, such as the habit of hope or faith or any of the other virtues. And this he said on account of the excellence of charity.

But if one considers the matter rightly, this would rather redound to the detriment of charity. For the motion of charity does not proceed from the Holy Spirit moving the human mind so that the human mind is only moved and is in no way the principle of this motion, as when a body is moved by some exterior mover. For this is contrary to the character of the will, whose principle must be in itself, as was said above.[20] So it would follow that to love would not be voluntary – which entails a contradiction, since love by its very notion implies that it is an act of the will. Likewise it cannot be said that the Holy Spirit moves the will to the act of loving as an instrument is moved. Even if it be the principle of an act, an instrument still does not have it in itself either to act or not to act. For in this way the aspect of the voluntary would be destroyed, and the aspect of merit would be excluded, since as attested above[21] the love of charity is the root of meriting. Rather, it is necessary that the will be moved by the Holy Spirit toward loving in this way – that the will itself also bring about this act [of loving].

Now no act is completely produced by some active power, unless the act has a natural affinity to the power by some form that is the principle of action. So that God, who moves all things to their due ends, has given to particular things the forms by which they are inclined to ends determined for them by God, and accordingly "he disposes all things sweetly," as is said in Wisdom 8.[22] Now it is clear that charity's act exceeds the nature of the will's power. Therefore unless some form be superadded to the natural power through which it is inclined to an act of love, charity's act would be more incomplete than natural acts and acts of the other virtues, nor would it be easy or pleasurable. But this is clearly false, since no virtue has so great an inclination to its own act as charity, nor does any virtue work so pleasurably. So it is especially necessary that for charity's act there exists in us some habitual form, superadded to the natural power, inclining that power to charity's act, making it work promptly and pleasurably.

20. *Summa* 1a2ae q.6 a.1.
21. *Summa* 1a2ae q.114 a.4.
22. Wisdom 8.1.

[1] TO THE FIRST ARGUMENT, THEREFORE, IT SHOULD BE SAID that the divine essence itself is charity, just as wisdom is, and just as goodness is. So that just as we are called good by the goodness that is God, and wise by the wisdom that is God – since the goodness by which we are formally good is a certain participation in divine goodness, and the wisdom by which we are formally wise is a certain participation in divine wisdom – thus even the charity by which we formally love our neighbor is a certain participation in divine charity. For this way of speaking is customary with the Platonists, with whose teachings Augustine was imbued. Those who have failed to attend to his words have taken it as an occasion for erring.

[2] To the second it should be said that God is effectively the life both of the soul through charity, and of the body through the soul, but charity is formally the life of the soul, as the soul is the life of the body. So from this it can be concluded that just as the soul is immediately united to the body, so charity is to the soul.

[3] To the third it should be said that charity works formally. Now the efficacy of a form is according to the power of the agent who induces the form. And so it is clear that charity is not vanity,[23] but brings about an infinite effect as it joins the soul to God, by justifying it. This demonstrates the infinity of divine power (*virtus divina*), which is the author of charity.

Article 3. [Whether charity is a virtue.]

One proceeds in this way to the third query. IT SEEMS that charity is not a virtue.

[1] Charity is a certain friendship. But friendship is not set down as a virtue by the Philosopher, as is clear from the *Ethics*,[24] in which it is counted neither among the moral virtues nor among the intellectual. Therefore neither is charity a virtue.

[2] Furthermore, "virtue is the last thing (*ultimum*) of a power," as is said in *On the Heavens,* Book 1.[25] But charity is not the last thing – rather, joy and peace are. Therefore it seems that charity is not a virtue, but joy and peace are.

23. Some versions read "charity is not infinite."
24. Aristotle, *Nicomachean Ethics* bk.8 chap.1 (1155a3).
25. Aristotle, *On the Heavens* 1.11 (281a11).

[3] Furthermore, every virtue is a certain accidental habit. But charity is not an accidental habit, since it is nobler than the soul itself. But no accident is more noble than its subject. Therefore charity is not a virtue.

BUT TO THE CONTRARY there is what Augustine says, in his book *On the Morals of the Catholic Church:* "Charity is the virtue that, when our affection is most correct, joins us to God, by which we love him."[26]

I ANSWER THAT IT SHOULD BE SAID that human acts have goodness according as they are regulated by a due rule and measure. And so human virtue, which is the principle of all good acts of a human being, consists in arriving at the rule of human acts. This is twofold, as was said above – human reason and God himself.[27] So that just as moral virtue is defined by what is in accord with right reason, as is clear in *Ethics* 2,[28] so also to arrive at God constitutes the notion (*ratio*) of virtue, as also was said above regarding faith and hope.[29] So charity arrives at God, since it joins us to God, as is clear from the authority of Augustine that was cited. Consequently, charity is a virtue.

[1] TO THE FIRST ARGUMENT, THEREFORE, IT SHOULD BE SAID that the Philosopher in *Ethics* 8 does not deny that friendship is a virtue but says that it is "a virtue or is accompanied by virtue."[30] For it can be said that it is a moral virtue as regards actions that are directed to another, yet under a different aspect than justice. For justice is about actions that are directed to another under the aspect of legal duty, whereas friendship concerns actions under the aspect of a certain friendly or moral duty – or rather under the aspect of benefits freely given, as is clear from the Philosopher in *Ethics* 8.[31] Yet it can be said that friendship is not a virtue *per se,* distinct from the other virtues. For it does not have the nature of the praiseworthy and the noble except from its object, since it is founded on the nobility of the virtues. This is clear for the reason that not every friendship has the character of the praiseworthy and noble, as is clear in friendship of

26. Augustine, *De moribus ecclesiae Catholicae* bk.1 chap.11 sect.19 (PL 32: 1319; CSEL 90:23.7–9), condensed.
27. *Summa* 2a2ae q.17 a.1.
28. Aristotle, *Nicomachean Ethics* bk.2 chap.6 (1107a1).
29. *Summa* 2a2ae q.4 a.3; q.17 a.1.
30. Aristotle, *Nicomachean Ethics* bk.8 chap.1 (1155a3).
31. Aristotle, *Nicomachean Ethics* bk.8 chap.13 (1162b21).

pleasure and utility. So virtuous friendship is something that follows upon the virtues,[32] rather than a virtue itself. Nor is this like charity, which is not founded principally upon human virtue, but upon divine goodness.

[2] To the second it should be said that it belongs to the same virtue to love someone and to rejoice over him, since joy follows love, as attested above when we treated the passions.[33] And so love is set down as a virtue, rather than joy, which is an effect of love. Moreover, the "last thing" that is supposed in the notion of virtue does not denote an order of effect, but rather an order of a certain excess, over and beyond – as a hundred pounds exceed sixty.

[3] To the third it should be said that every accident according to its be-ing (*esse*) is below substance, since substance is being through itself (*ens per se*), whereas accident is being in another. But according to the nature of its species, a certain accident that is caused by the principles of its subject is more unworthy of the subject, just as an effect is in relation to its cause. Now an accident that is caused by participation in another higher nature is worthier than the subject, so far as there is a likeness to a higher nature, as light is to the transparent. And in this way charity is worthier than the soul, so far as it is a certain participation in the Holy Spirit.

Article 4. [Whether charity is a special virtue.]

One proceeds in this way to the fourth query. IT SEEMS that charity is not a special virtue.

[1] Jerome says: "So as to encompass concisely a definition of every virtue – virtue is charity, by which God and neighbor are loved."[34] And Au-gustine says, in *On the Morals of the Catholic Church,* that "virtue is the order of love."[35] But no special virtue is set down in the definition of virtue in general. Therefore charity is not a special virtue.

[2] Furthermore, what extends to the works of all the virtues cannot be a special virtue. But charity extends to the works of all the virtues, accord-

32. Some versions read "follows upon a virtue."

33. *Summa* 1a2ae q.25 a.2.

34. Though Thomas cites Jerome, the actual text seems to be Augustine, *Epistu-lae* ep.167 to Jerome chap.15 (PL 33:739; CSEL 44:602.10–12).

35. Thomas refers incorrectly to *De moribus ecclesiae catholicae.* The phrase actually appears in Augustine, *De civitate Dei* bk.15 chap.22 (PL 41:467; CCSL 48:488.33–34).

ing to 1 Corinthians 13: "Charity is patient, charity is kind," etc.[36] It even extends to all human works, according to the last chapter of 1 Corinthians: "Let all your works be done in charity."[37] Therefore charity is not a special virtue.

[3] Furthermore, precepts of the law correspond to the acts of the virtues. But Augustine, in his *On the Perfection of Human Justice,* says that "'You shall love' is a general commandment, and 'You shall not covet' a general prohibition."[38] Therefore charity is a general virtue.

BUT TO THE CONTRARY nothing general is counted with what is special. But charity is counted with the special virtues, namely faith and hope, according to 1 Corinthians 13: "Now only these three remain: faith, hope, charity."[39] Therefore charity is a special virtue.

I ANSWER THAT IT SHOULD BE SAID that acts and habits are specified by their objects, as is clear from what was said above.[40] Now the proper object of love is the good, as was attested above.[41] And thus where there is a special aspect of good, so there is a special aspect of love. Now the divine good, so far as it is the object of blessedness, has a special aspect of good. And thus the love of charity, which is the love of this good, is a special love. So that charity is a special virtue.

[1] TO THE FIRST ARGUMENT, THEREFORE, IT SHOULD BE SAID that charity is placed in the definition of every virtue, not because it is every virtue essentially, but because all the virtues somehow depend upon it, as will be said below.[42] Just as prudence is also placed in the definition of the moral virtues, as is clear in *Ethics* 2 and 6, because the moral virtues depend on prudence.[43]

[2] To the second it should be said that the virtue or art to which the ultimate end belongs, commands the virtues or arts to which the other

36. 1 Corinthians 13.4.
37. 1 Corinthians 16.14.
38. Augustine, *De perfectione justitiae hominis* chap.5 sect.11 (PL 44:297; CSEL 42:10.15–16).
39. 1 Corinthians 13.13.
40. *Summa* 1a2ae q.18 a.2; q.54 a.2.
41. *Summa* 1a2ae q.27 a.1.
42. In Article 7 of this Question.
43. Aristotle, *Nicomachean Ethics* bk.2 chap.6 (1107a1); bk.6 chap.13 (1144b26).

secondary ends belong, just as the military arts command the equestrian, as is said in *Ethics* 1.[44] And thus, since charity has for its object the ultimate end of human life, namely eternal blessedness, it thus extends to the acts of all of human life by way of command, but not as directly eliciting all the acts of the virtues.

[3] To the third it should be said that the precept on loving is called a "general command" because the other precepts are traced back to it as to an end, according to 1 Timothy 1: "The end of the precept is charity."[45]

Article 5. [Whether charity is one virtue.]

One proceeds in this way to the fifth query. IT SEEMS that charity is not one virtue.

[1] Habits are distinguished according to their objects. But the objects of charity are two, God and neighbor, which stand at an infinite distance from one another. Therefore charity is not one virtue.

[2] Furthermore, different aspects of an object diversify a habit, even if the object is really the same, as is clear from what was said above.[46] But the reasons for loving God are many, since we are debtors from each of the benefits that we gain from his love. Therefore charity is not one virtue.

[3] Furthermore, friendship with one's neighbor is included under charity. But the Philosopher, in *Ethics* 8, sets down different kinds of friendship.[47] Therefore charity is not one virtue, but is multiplied in different species.

BUT TO THE CONTRARY as God is the object of faith, so he is [the object] of charity. But faith is one virtue, on account of the unity of divine truth, according to Ephesians 4, "one faith."[48] Therefore charity is also one virtue, on account of the unity of divine goodness.

I ANSWER THAT IT SHOULD BE SAID that charity, as said above,[49] is a certain friendship of man with God. Now in one way, different kinds of friendship are taken according to a difference in end, and accordingly are

44. Aristotle, *Nicomachean Ethics* bk.1 chap.1 (1094a12).
45. 1 Timothy 1.5.
46. *Summa* 2a2ae q.17, a.6; *Summa* 1a2ae q.54 a.2.
47. Aristotle, *Nicomachean Ethics* bk.8 chap.3 (1156a7).
48. Ephesians 4.5.
49. In Article 1 of this Question.

called the three kinds of friendship, namely friendship of utility, friendship of pleasure, and friendship based on what is noble. In another way, different kinds of friendship are understood according to a difference between the sharings (*communicationes*) upon which the friendships are founded – as one kind of friendship is between those related by blood, and another kind is between fellow citizens and pilgrims. Of these two kinds, one is founded upon a natural sharing; the other upon a political sharing, or that between pilgrims, as is clear from the Philosopher in *Ethics* 8.[50] Now charity cannot be divided into several parts in either of these ways. For the end of charity is one, namely divine goodness. It is also one sharing of eternal blessedness, upon which this friendship is founded. So it remains that charity is one virtue simply (*simpliciter*), not distinguished into several kinds.

[1] TO THE FIRST ARGUMENT, THEREFORE, IT SHOULD BE SAID that this reason would hold if God and neighbor were equally objects of charity. This, however, is not true, since God is the principal object of charity, whereas our neighbor is loved out of charity on account of God.

[2] To the second it should be said that by charity God is loved on account of himself. So that charity principally observes only one reason for loving, namely the divine goodness, which is his substance, according to the Psalm, "Give thanks to the Lord, for he is good."[51] Now the other reasons induced for loving, or making one indebted to his love, are secondary and follow upon the first.

[3] To the third it should be said that human friendship, of which the Philosopher is speaking, has a different end and a different sharing. This has no place in charity, as was said.[52] And so there is no similar reasoning.

Article 6. [Whether charity is the most excellent of the virtues.]

One proceeds in this way to the sixth query. IT SEEMS that charity is not the most excellent of the virtues.

[1] The higher the power, the higher its virtue, just as its work is higher. But the intellect is higher than the will and directs it.[53] Therefore

---

50. Aristotle, *Nicomachean Ethics* bk.8. chap.12 (1161b11).
51. Psalm 105.1.
52. In the body of this Article.
53. Some versions read "because it directs it."

faith, which is in the intellect, is more excellent than charity, which is in the will.

[2] Furthermore, that by which another thing works seems to be lower than it, just as a servant by whom a master works is lower than the master. But "faith works by love," as attested in Galatians 5.[54] Therefore faith is more excellent than charity.

[3] Furthermore, that which has its being from addition to another thing seems to be more complete. But hope seems to have its being from addition to charity, for charity's object is the good, whereas hope's object is the arduous good. Therefore hope is more excellent than charity.

BUT TO THE CONTRARY there is what is said in 1 Corinthians 13, "The greatest of these is charity."[55]

I ANSWER THAT IT SHOULD BE SAID that, since the good in human acts is observed to the extent that it is regulated by a due rule, it is necessary that human virtue – the principle of good acts – consists in adhering to the rule of human acts. The rule of human acts, as was said above,[56] is twofold, namely human reason and God. But God is the first rule by which even human reason should be regulated. And so the theological virtues, which consist in adhering to this first rule, since their object is God, are more excellent than the moral or intellectual virtues, which consist in adhering to human reason. Because of this, it is necessary that even among the theological virtues themselves, the one that adheres to God more is preferable. Now what exists through itself is always greater than what exists through another. Faith and hope do adhere to God, according as either knowledge of the true or attainment of the good come forth from him to us. But charity adheres to God himself, so that it may stop at God himself, and not so that something else may come forth from him to us. And so charity is more excellent than faith and hope – and consequently than all the other virtues. Just as prudence, which adheres to reason in itself, is more excellent than the other moral virtues, which adhere to reason according as by it, a mean is established in human actions and passions.

[1] TO THE FIRST ARGUMENT, THEREFORE, IT SHOULD BE SAID that the intellect's work is completed when what is understood is

---

54. Galatians 5.6.
55. 1 Corinthians 13.13.
56. In Article 3 of this Question. See also *Summa* 2a2ae q.17 a.1.

in the one who understands. And so the nobility of intellectual work is observed according to the intellect's measure. Now the will's work, and that of every appetitive power, is completed by the inclination of a desiring being toward a thing, as toward an end. Thus the dignity of appetitive work is observed according to the thing that is the work's object. Now things that are below the soul exist in the soul in a nobler way than they are in themselves, since what is contained is in the container according to the mode of the container, as attested by the *Book of Causes*.[57] But things that are above the soul exist in themselves in a nobler way than they exist in the soul. And so regarding things that are below us, cognition is nobler than love, which is why the Philosopher in *Ethics* 10 prefers the intellectual virtues to the moral virtues.[58] But regarding things that are above us, love–and chiefly love of God–is to be preferred to cognition. And so charity is more excellent than faith.

[2] To the second it should be said that faith does not work by love as by an instrument–in the way that a master works by his slave–but rather by its own form. And so the argument does not follow.

[3] To the third it should be said that the same good is the object of charity and of hope, but that charity denotes union with that good, whereas hope denotes a certain distance from it. And so charity does not look to the good as arduous, as hope does, for what is already united[59] does not have the aspect of the arduous. From this it appears that charity is more complete than hope.

Article 7. [Whether there can be any true virtue without charity.]

One proceeds in this way to the seventh query. IT SEEMS that there can be some true virtue without charity.

[1] It is proper to virtue to produce a good act. But those who do not have charity perform some good acts, as when they clothe the naked, feed the hungry, and do like things. Therefore without charity there can be some true virtue.

---

57. *Liber de causis* chap.11 sect.106–7. (Compare *The Book of Causes,* trans. Dennis Brand [Milwaukee: Marquette University Press, 1984], 30.)

58. Aristotle, *Nicomachean Ethics* bk.10 chap.7 (1177a12) and bk.10 chap.8 (1178a9).

59. Some versions read "already one."

[2] Furthermore, charity cannot be without faith, for it proceeds "from a faith unfeigned," as the Apostle says, 1 Timothy 1.[60] But in the unfaithful there can be true purity, as long as they curb desire, and true justice, as long as they judge rightly. Therefore there can be true virtue without charity.

[3] Furthermore, knowledge (*scientia*) and art are certain virtues, as is clear from *Ethics* 6.[61] But such are found in sinful human beings who do not have charity. Therefore there can be true virtue without charity.

BUT TO THE CONTRARY there is what the Apostle says, 1 Corinthians 13, "If I should distribute all my goods to feed the poor, and if I should deliver my body to be burned, but have not charity, it profits me nothing."[62] But true virtue profits much, according to Wisdom 8: "She teaches temperance and justice, prudence and virtue, than which nothing is more useful in life for human beings."[63] Therefore without charity there can be no true virtue.

I ANSWER THAT IT SHOULD BE SAID that virtue is directed to the good, as was attested above.[64] Now the good is principally an end, for things that are for the end are not called "good" except as ordered to the end. Therefore just as the end is twofold – one ultimate and the other proximate – so also is the good twofold: one is ultimate, the other proximate and particular. The ultimate and principal good of man is the enjoyment of God, according to the Psalm: "It is good for me to adhere to God."[65] Man is directed to this good by charity. The secondary and, as it were, particular good of man can be twofold – one that is in fact true good, so far as it can in itself be ordered to the principal good, which is the ultimate end. The other, however, is apparent rather than true good, since it leads a person away from the final good.

Therefore it is clear that true virtue simply (*simpliciter*) is that which directs a person to the principal human good, as the Philosopher says also in *Physics* 7: virtue is a "disposition of what is complete to the best."[66] And in this way there can be no true virtue without charity. But if virtue

---

60. 1 Timothy 1.5.
61. Aristotle, *Nicomachean Ethics* bk.6 chap.3 (1139b15).
62. 1 Corinthians 13.3.
63. Wisdom 8.7.
64. *Summa* 1a2ae q.55, a.4.
65. Psalm 72.28.
66. Aristotle, *Physics* bk.7 chap.3 (246a13).

is taken according as it is ordered to some particular end, then something can thus be called virtue without charity, so far as it is directed to some particular good.

But if that particular good is not a true good, but rather an apparent good, then the virtue that is also ordered to this good would not be true virtue, but a false likeness of virtue. Just as "the prudence of misers, by which they think out different kinds of small or petty gains, is not true virtue; nor is the justice of misers, by which they scorn the property of others through fear of heavy punishment; nor is the temperance of misers, by which they curb their appetite for expensive luxuries; nor is the fortitude of misers, by which, as Horace remarks, 'they brave the sea, cross mountains, and go through fire to flee poverty,'" as Augustine says in *Against Julian* 4.[67] If in fact the particular good is a true good, such as the preservation of a city or something like that, then it would indeed be true virtue, but incomplete, unless it be referred to the final and complete good. And accordingly, there can be no true virtue simply (*simpliciter*) without charity.

[1] TO THE FIRST ARGUMENT, THEREFORE, IT SHOULD BE SAID that the act of someone who lacks charity can be twofold. One is according to that which lacks charity, as when a person does something ordered to that by which he lacks charity. And such acts are always evil, as Augustine says in *Against Julian* 4,[68] so that an unfaithful act, so far as it is unfaithful, is always sinful, even if he were to clothe the naked or do something else of this sort, while directing it to the end of his unfaithfulness. Another act can lack charity – not according to that which lacks charity, but according as it possesses some other gift of God, whether faith or hope or even some good of nature, which is not wholly taken away by sin, as was said above.[69] And according to this there can be some act without charity that is good in its kind – yet not completely good, since it is missing a due order to the ultimate end.

[2] To the second it should be said that since the end is to things practical as the beginning (*principium*) is to things speculative, there cannot simply (*simpliciter*) be true knowledge (*scientia*) if a right estimation of the first and indemonstrable principle is missing – just as there cannot simply

67. Augustine, *Contra Julianum* bk.4 chap.3 sect.19 (PL 44:748). The reference is to Horace, *Epistles* 1.46.
68. Augustine, *Contra Julianum* bk.4 chap.3 sect.25 (PL 44:750–51).
69. *Summa* 2a2ae q.10 a.4. See also *Summa* 1a2ae q.85 a.2.

be true justice or true purity if a due order to the end is missing. This order is through charity, however well disposed a person is concerning other things.

[3] To the third it should be said that knowledge (*scientia*) and art of their own nature (*ratio*) imply an order to some particular good, but not to the ultimate end of human life. This is unlike the moral virtues, which make human beings good simply (*simpliciter*), as was said above.[70] And so there is no similar reasoning [about the two].

Article 8. [Whether charity is the form of the virtues.]

One proceeds in this way to the eighth query. IT SEEMS that charity is not the form of the virtues.

[1] The form of some thing is either an exemplar form or an essential form. But charity is not an exemplar form of the other virtues, since it would thus be necessary for the other virtues to be of the same kind as charity. Likewise, it is not an essential form of the other virtues, since if it were it would not be distinguished from the others. Therefore in no way is charity the form of the virtues.

[2] Furthermore, charity is related to the other virtues as to their root and foundation, according to Ephesians 3: "Rooted and founded in charity."[71] Now the root or foundation does not have the aspect of a form, but rather the aspect of matter, since it is the first part in generation. Therefore charity is not the form of the virtues.

[3] Furthermore, the form and end and efficient cause do not coincide in number, as is clear from *Physics* 2.[72] But charity is called the end and mother of the virtues. Therefore it should not be called the form of the virtues.

BUT TO THE CONTRARY Ambrose says that charity is the form of the virtues.[73]

---

70. *Summa* 1a2ae q.56 a.3.
71. Ephesians 3.17.
72. Aristotle, *Physics* bk.2 chap.7 (198a24).
73. Though Thomas names Ambrose, the source seems to be the author known since Erasmus as "Ambrosiaster." See Ambrosiaster, *In epistolam B. Pauli ad Corinthos Primam* chap.8, on 1 Corinthians 8.2 (PL 17:226C–D).

I ANSWER THAT IT SHOULD BE SAID that in morals the form of an act is observed primarily from the perspective of the end. The reason for this is that the principle of moral acts is the will, whose object and, as it were, form (*quasi forma*) is the end. Now the form of an act always follows upon the form of an agent. So it is necessary that in morals, that which gives an act an ordering to the end should also give it form. Now it is clear, according to the things previously said,[74] that by charity the acts of all the other virtues are ordered to the ultimate end. And according to this very ordering, charity gives form to the acts of all the other virtues. To this extent it is called the form of the virtues, for the virtues themselves are also so-called in their order to formed acts.

[1] TO THE FIRST ARGUMENT, THEREFORE, IT SHOULD BE SAID that charity is said to be the form of all the virtues – not indeed exemplarily or essentially, but rather effectively – namely, so far as it imposes form on all of them, according to the way mentioned previously.[75]

[2] To the second it should be said that charity is compared to a foundation or root so far as from it all the other virtues are sustained and given nutrition, and not according to the aspect by which a foundation or root has the aspect of a material cause.

[3] To the third it should be said that charity is called the end of the other virtues, since it orders all the other virtues to its own end. And because a mother is she who conceives in herself from another, charity is called the mother of the other virtues – since out of her desire (*appetitus*) for the ultimate end, she conceives the acts of the other virtues by commanding them.

---

74. In Article 7 of this Question.
75. In the body of this Article.

[The Subject of Charity]

One should next consider charity in relation to its subject. Regarding this point twelve queries are raised. (1) Whether charity is in the will as in its subject. (2) Whether charity is caused in a human being from preceding acts or from divine infusion. (3) Whether it is infused according to the capacity of natural things. (4) Whether it is increased in the person who has it. (5) Whether it is increased by addition. (6) Whether it is increased by any particular act. (7) Whether it is increased to infinity. (8) Whether charity-of-the-way (*caritas viae*) can be complete. (9) On the different steps of charity. (10) Whether charity can be decreased. (11) Whether charity once possessed can be lost. (12) Whether it is lost by one act of mortal sin.

Article 1. [Whether the will is the subject of charity.]

One proceeds in this way to the first query. IT SEEMS that the will is not the subject of charity.

[1] Charity is a certain kind of love. But "love," according to the Philosopher, "is in the concupiscible power."[1] Therefore charity is in the concupiscible power, and not in the will.

[2] Furthermore, charity is the most principal of the virtues, as was said above.[2] But the subject of virtue is reason (*ratio*). Therefore it seems that charity is in reason, and not in the will.

[3] Furthermore, charity extends to all human actions, according to the last chapter of 1 Corinthians: "Let all your works be done in charity."[3] But the principle of human actions is free decision. Therefore it seems that charity is especially in free decision as in its subject, and not in the will.

---

1. Aristotle, *Topics* bk.2 chap.7 (113b2).
2. In Question 23, Article 6.
3. 1 Corinthians 16.14.

BUT TO THE CONTRARY charity's object is the good, which is also the will's object. Therefore charity is in the will as in its subject.

I ANSWER THAT IT SHOULD BE SAID that appetite is two-fold – namely, sensitive and intellectual appetite, which is called "will," as attested in the *Prima Pars.*[4] The object of both is the good, but in different ways. For the object of the sensitive appetite is good apprehended by the senses; the object of the intellectual appetite, or the will, is the good under the aspect of good in general, so far as it is apprehensible by intellect. Now the object of charity is not some sensible good, but divine good, which is known by intellect alone. And so the subject of charity is not the sensitive appetite, but the intellectual appetite, that is, the will.

[1] TO THE FIRST ARGUMENT, THEREFORE, IT SHOULD BE SAID that the concupiscible power is part of the sensitive appetite, and not the intellectual appetite, as was shown in the *Prima Pars.*[5] To the divine good, which is intelligible, the concupiscible power cannot extend – only the will can. And so the concupiscible power cannot be the subject of charity.

[2] To the second it should be said that according to the Philosopher in *On the Soul* 3, "the will is also in reason."[6] And so charity's being in the will does not disconnect it from reason. Yet reason is not the rule of charity, as it is of the human virtues. Rather, charity is ruled by the wisdom of God, and surpasses the rule of human reason, according to Ephesians 3: "The charity of Christ, surpassing all knowledge."[7] So charity is not in reason – not as in its subject, as prudence is, nor as in its ruling part, as justice and temperance are – but only by a certain affinity of the will to reason.

[3] To the third it should be said that free decision is not a power other than the will, as was said in the *Prima Pars.*[8] Nevertheless charity is not in the will according to the aspect of free decision, whose act is to choose: "for choice is of the things that are for the sake of the end, whereas will is of the end itself," as is said in *Ethics* 3.[9] So that charity, whose object is the ultimate end, should be said to be in the will rather than in free decision.

4. *Summa* 1a q.80 a.2.
5. *Summa* 1a q.81 a.2.
6. Aristotle, *On the Soul* bk.3 chap.9 (432b5).
7. Ephesians 3.19.
8. *Summa* 1a q.83 a.4.
9. Aristotle, *Nicomachean Ethics* bk.3 chap.2 (1111b26).

Article 2. [Whether charity is caused in us by infusion.]

One proceeds in this way to the second query. IT SEEMS that charity is not caused in us by infusion.

[1] What is common to all creatures is naturally in human beings. As Dionysius says, *Divine Names,* chapter 4, "For everything, what is lovable and beloved is the divine good,"[10] which is the object of charity. Therefore charity is in us naturally, and not by infusion.

[2] Furthermore, the more lovable a thing is, the more easily it can be loved. But God is especially lovable, since he is good in the highest degree. Therefore it is easier to love him than other things. But we do not need some infused habit for loving other things. Nor, therefore, do we need it for loving God.

[3] Furthermore, the Apostle says, 1 Timothy 1, "The end of the precept is charity, out of a pure heart and a good conscience, and a faith unfeigned."[11] But these three things belong to human acts. Therefore charity is caused in us by preceding acts, and not by infusion.

BUT TO THE CONTRARY there is what the Apostle says, Romans 5: "The charity of God is poured forth into our hearts by the Holy Spirit, who is given to us."[12]

I ANSWER THAT IT SHOULD BE SAID that, as said above,[13] charity is a certain friendship of man with God, founded upon a sharing of eternal blessedness. Now this sharing is not according to natural goods, but rather according to gifts freely given, since "the grace of God is eternal life," as is said in Romans 6.[14] So charity itself surpasses the power of nature. What surpasses the power of nature can be neither natural nor acquired by natural powers, since a natural effect does not transcend its cause. So charity can be in us neither naturally, nor by natural powers that are acquired, but only by an infusion of the Holy Spirit, who is the love of the Father and the Son, whose participation in us is created by charity itself, as was said above.[15]

---

10. Ps-Dionysius, *Divine Names* chap.4 sect.10 (PG 3:708A; Chevallier 1:199).

11. 1 Timothy 1.5.

12. Romans 5.5.

13. In Question 23, Article 1.

14. Romans 6.23.

15. In Question 23, Article 2, Reply [1]. Compare Herbert McCabe: "God cannot, of course, love us as creatures, but 'in Christ' we are taken up into the exchange of love between the Father and the incarnate and human Son, we are filled with the

[1] TO THE FIRST ARGUMENT, THEREFORE, IT SHOULD BE SAID that Dionysius is speaking of the love of God that is founded upon a sharing of natural goods, and so is in us naturally. But charity is founded upon a certain supernatural sharing. So there is no similar reasoning [about the two].

[2] To the second it should be said that just as God in himself is most knowable, yet not to us because of a defect in our knowledge, which depends on sensible things, so too God in himself is most lovable, so far as he is the object of blessedness; but he is not in this way most lovable to us, because of the inclination of our affections to visible goods. So it is clear that for God to be loved most in this way, it is necessary that charity also be infused into our hearts.

[3] To the third it should be said that when charity is said to proceed in us "out of a pure heart and a good conscience, and a faith unfeigned," this should be referred to charity's act, which is aroused by the things mentioned. This is said also because such acts dispose a person to receive an infusion of charity. Likewise, what Augustine says about this should be mentioned – that "fear introduces charity,"[16] as well as what is said in the Gloss on Matthew 1: "Faith generates hope, and hope charity."[17]

Article 3. [Whether charity is infused according to the quantity of natural things.]

One proceeds in this way to the third query. IT SEEMS that charity is infused according to the quantity of natural things.[18]

[1] Matthew 25 says that "To each he gave . . . according to his own virtue."[19] But no virtue, except natural virtue, precedes charity in a person,

---

Holy Spirit, we become part of the divine life. We call this 'grace.' By grace we ourselves share in the divine and that is how God can love us" (*God Still Matters* [London: Continuum, 2002], 7). For the reader who wonders whether this exaggerates the place of deification in Thomas, compare the *Disputed Question on Charity* a.2 responsio 15: "Charity is not a virtue of a human being so far as he is human, but so far as he becomes God and a son of God, by the participation of grace, according to 1 John 3: 'See what manner of charity the Father has given us, that we are called and should be sons of God.'"

16. Augustine, *Tractatus in epistolam Ioannis ad Parthos* tr.9 on 1 John 4.18 (PL 35:2048).

17. *Glossa interlinearis,* on Matthew 1.2 (Strasbourg 5). Some versions read "faith generates hope and charity."

18. Some versions read "capacity of natural things."

19. Matthew 25.15.

since without charity there is no virtue, as was said.[20] Therefore charity is infused into man by God according to the capacity of natural things.

[2] Furthermore, for all things that are directed to one another, the second is proportioned to the first. Thus we see that in material things, the form is proportioned to the matter, and in freely given gifts, glory is proportioned to grace. But charity, since it is the completion of nature, is related to a natural capacity as a second to a first. Therefore it seems that charity is infused according to the capacity of natural things.

[3] Furthermore, human beings and angels participate in charity according to the same aspect,[21] since in both there is a similar aspect of blessedness, as attested by Matthew 22 and Luke 20.[22] But in angels charity and other free gifts are given according to the capacity of natural things, as the Master says in *Sentences,* Book 2.[23] Therefore it seems that the same also holds for human beings.

BUT TO THE CONTRARY there is what is said in John 3, "The Spirit breathes where he will," and 1 Corinthians 12, "All these things one and the same Spirit works, apportioning to everyone as he wills."[24] Therefore charity is given not according to the capacity of natural things, but according to the will of the Spirit distributing his gifts.

I ANSWER THAT IT SHOULD BE SAID that the quantity of anything whatever depends on the thing's cause, since a more universal cause produces a greater effect. Now charity, since it hyper-exceeds the proportion of human nature, as was said, does not depend on some natural virtue, but only on the grace of the Holy Spirit that infuses it. And so the quantity of charity does not depend on the condition of nature or the capacity of natural virtue, but only on the will of the Holy Spirit distributing his gifts as it wills. So the Apostle says at Ephesians 4: "To each of us grace is given according to the measure of the gift of Christ."[25]

[1] TO THE FIRST ARGUMENT, THEREFORE, IT SHOULD BE SAID that the virtue according to which God gives his gifts to each person

20. In Question 23, Article 7.
21. Some versions read "participate in blessedness according to the same aspect."
22. Matthew 22.30 and Luke 22.36.
23. Peter Lombard, *Sententiae* bk.2 d.3 chap.2 (Grottaferrata 1:342).
24. John 3.8; 1 Corinthians 12.11.
25. Ephesians 4.7.

is a preceding disposition or preparation, or a striving (*conatus*) of the one who receives grace. But the Holy Spirit comes before even this disposition or striving, moving the mind of a person either more or less according to its will. And so the Apostle says, Colossians 1: "[The Father] who has made us worthy to partake of the lot of saints in light."[26]

[2] To the second it should be said that a form does not exceed the proportion of the matter, but that both belong to the same genus. Likewise grace and glory are referred to the same genus, since grace is nothing other than a certain first beginning of glory in us. But charity and nature do not belong to the same genus. And so there is no similar reasoning [about the two].

[3] To the third it should be said that an angel is of an intellectual nature, and it belongs to an angel, according to his condition, that he receive entirely all that he receives, as was attested in the *Prima Pars*.[27] And so a greater striving was in the higher angels – both in persevering in good and in falling into evil. And so the higher angels who persisted became better than the others, and those who fell became worse than the others. But a human being is of rational nature, to which it belongs to be sometimes in potency and sometimes in act. And so it is not necessary that a person should be wholly borne to the thing toward which he is borne. Instead there can be less striving in what has better natural traits, and vice versa. Thus the cases are not alike.

Article 4. [Whether charity can be increased.]

One proceeds in this way to the fourth query. IT SEEMS that charity cannot be increased.

[1] Nothing is increased except by some amount. Now quantity is twofold – dimensive and virtual. The first of these is not appropriate to charity, since charity is a certain spiritual perfection. Virtual quantity applies to objects according to which charity does not grow, since the least bit of charity loves everything that should be loved out of charity. Therefore charity is not increased.

[2] Furthermore, that which comes to a limit does not undergo any increase. But charity comes to a limit, existing as it were as the greatest of the virtues and the highest love of the best good. Therefore charity cannot be increased.

26. Colossians 1.12.
27. *Summa* 1a q.62 a.6.

[3] Furthermore, increase is a certain motion. Therefore what is increased is moved. Therefore what is increased essentially is moved essentially. But nothing is moved essentially except as it is corrupted or generated. Therefore charity cannot be essentially increased, unless by chance it be generated or corrupted anew. But this is inappropriate.

BUT TO THE CONTRARY there is what Augustine says in his commentary on John, that "charity deserves to be increased, so that by increase it may merit and be completed."[28]

I ANSWER THAT IT SHOULD BE SAID that charity-of-the-way (*caritas viae*) can be increased. Thus we are called "wayfarers" (*viatores*) as we quest for God, who is the ultimate end of our blessedness. Now we proceed along this way (*via*) so far as we draw near to God, who is not approached by any of the body's steps, but by the mind's affections. Now charity brings about this nearness, since by it the mind is united to God. And so the very notion of charity-of-the-way suggests that it can be increased – for if it could not be increased, progress along this way would cease. And so the Apostle names the way "charity," saying in 1 Corinthians 12, "I show you a still more excellent way."[29]

[1] TO THE FIRST ARGUMENT, THEREFORE, IT SHOULD BE SAID that not dimensive quantity but only virtual quantity is appropriate to charity. Virtual quantity applies not only to the number of objects, so that more or fewer things are loved, but also to the intensity of an act, so that something is loved more or less. And in this way a virtual quantity of charity is increased.

[2] To the second it should be said that charity exists in the highest degree on the part of the object, so far as its object is the highest good. From this it follows that charity is more excellent than the other virtues. But not every charity exists in the highest degree as regards the intensity of an act.[30]

---

28. Augustine, *In Ioannis Evangelium tractatus* tr.74 sect.2, on John 14.16 (PL 35:1827; CCSL 36:513.53–56), strongly paraphrased. The maxim "caritas meretur augeri" appears in the *Summa Halensis* pt.2 sect.54 (Quaracchi 3:74) but not (as far as I can tell) in Augustine. See also Augustine, ep.186 to Paulinus chap.3 (PL 33:819).

29. 1 Corinthians 12.31.

30. Some versions read: "But charity does not exist in the highest degree as regards the intensity of an act."

[3] To the third it should be said that some have said that charity is not increased according to its essence, but only according to its taking-root (*radicatio*) in the subject, or according to its fervor. But those people did not know what they were talking about. Since charity is an accident, its being (*esse*) is being-in (*inesse*), so that to be increased according to its essence is nothing other than its being more in its subject – that is, being more deeply rooted in its subject. Likewise charity is essentially a virtue ordered to act. So that it is the same thing for charity to be increased according to its essence, and to have the efficacious power of producing an act of more fervent love. Therefore charity is increased essentially – not so that it begins to be or ceases to be in its subject, as the objection suggests, but so that it begins to be in its subject ever more deeply.

Article 5. [Whether charity is increased by addition.]

One proceeds in this way to the fifth query. IT SEEMS that charity is increased by addition.

[1] Just as an increase occurs according to bodily quantity, so it occurs according to virtual quantity. But an increase of bodily quantity happens by addition, as the Philosopher says in *On Generation and Corruption* 1: "An increase is an addition to a preexisting magnitude."[31] Therefore an increase of charity, which occurs according to virtual quantity, will occur by addition.

[2] Furthermore, charity in the soul is a certain spiritual light, according to 1 John 2: "He who loves his brother remains in light."[32] But light grows in the air by addition, as light in a house grows by other candles that are lit. Therefore charity too grows in the soul by addition.

[3] Furthermore, to increase charity belongs to God, just as to create it does, according to 2 Corinthians 9: "He will increase the growth of the fruits of your justice."[33] But by first infusing charity, God makes something in the soul that was not there before. Therefore by increasing charity he makes something that was not there before. Therefore charity is increased by addition.

31. Aristotle, *On Generation and Corruption* bk.1 chap.5 (320b30).
32. 1 John 2.10.
33. 2 Corinthians 9.10.

BUT TO THE CONTRARY charity is a simple form. Now a simple thing added to a simple thing does not make something greater, as was proved in *Physics* 6.[34] Therefore charity is not increased by addition.

I ANSWER THAT IT SHOULD BE SAID that any addition is of one thing to another. So that in any addition, when one thing is added to another, one must at least presume a distinction between the things, prior to the addition itself. If therefore charity is added to charity, one must presume the added charity to be distinct from the charity to which it is added – not from any necessity according to being, but simply according to the intellect. Now God could increase bodily quantity by adding some magnitude not previously existing, but then created. This magnitude, while not previously existing in the nature of things, is nonetheless such that its distinction from the quantity to which it is added can be understood. If, therefore, charity were added to charity, one must presuppose, at least according to the intellect, a distinction between one charity and another.

Now a distinction among forms is twofold. One is according to species, the other according to number. A distinction in habits according to species proceeds according to a difference of objects, whereas a distinction according to number proceeds according to a difference of subjects. It can happen, therefore, that some habit is increased by addition, when it is extended to a range of objects to which it was previously not extended; in this way the knowledge of geometry is increased in a person who begins de novo to understand some geometrical things of which he was previously ignorant. Now this cannot be said of charity, since the smallest charity extends to everything that should be loved from charity. Therefore such an addition to the increase of charity cannot be understood by a presumed distinction according to species between the added charity and the charity to which it is added.

It remains, then, that if an addition of charity to charity were to take place, it would do so by a presumed distinction according to number. This distinction occurs according to a difference of subjects – as whiteness is increased by the fact that one white thing is added to another white thing, although this increase does not make something more white. But this cannot be said about the case at hand. This is because the subject of charity is nothing except the rational mind, so that such an increase of charity could

34. Aristotle, *Physics* bk.6 chap.2 (232a23). See also Aristotle, *Metaphysics* bk.2 chap.4 (1001b8).

not occur except by adding one rational mind to another, which is impossible. Even if such an increase were possible, it would bring about a greater lover, but not one who is more loving. It remains, then, that charity can in no way be increased by an addition of charity to charity, as some have supposed.

Thus charity is increased only by this – that its subject participates in charity more and more – that is, so far as it is more led back to its act and more subjected to its act. For this mode of increase is proper to any form that is intensified (*intenditur*), since the being (*esse*) of such a form consists wholly in this – that it dwells in what receives it. And so, because a thing's magnitude follows upon its being,[35] to be a greater form is for the form to dwell more intensely in what receives it, and not for another form to arise. The latter would hold only if a form were to have some quantity from itself and not through its relation to a subject. In this way, therefore, charity is increased from this – that it is intensified in a subject. This means for it to be increased according to its essence, but not because charity is added to charity.

[1] TO THE FIRST ARGUMENT, THEREFORE, IT SHOULD BE SAID that bodily quantity has something so far as it is quantity, and also something so far as it is an accidental form. So far as it is quantity, it has what is distinguishable according to position or according to number. In this way one considers an increase of magnitude by addition, as is clear in animals. But so far as it is an accidental form, it is distinguishable only according to its subject. In this respect it has its own increase, just as other accidental forms do, by the measure of its intensity in its subject – as is clear in things that become less dense, as the Philosopher proves in *Physics* 4.[36] Likewise, knowledge (*scientia*), so far as it is a habit, has quantity on the part of its objects. And in this way it is increased by addition, to the extent that someone knows multiple things. It also has quantity as an accidental form, because it inheres in a subject. Accordingly, it is increased in a person who knows the same intelligible things more certainly now than he did before. Likewise charity also has quantity in two senses. But it is not increased on the part of its object, as was said. So it remains that it is increased only by intensity.

[2] To the second it should be said that an addition of light to light can be understood in the air on account of a difference in the illumination

---

35. Some versions read "follows upon the being of the form itself."
36. Aristotle, *Physics* bk.4 chap.9 (217a14).

causing the light. But such a distinction has no place in the matter at hand, since there is but one illumination flowing into (*influens*) the light of charity.

[3] To the third it should be said that an infusion of charity denotes a certain change according to whether something has or does not have charity. Thus it is proper that something should come to be which was not there before. But an increase of charity denotes a change according to having more or less. Thus it is not proper that something is present which had not been there before, but that something is more present which was less present before. And this is what God does by increasing charity – namely, he makes it more present, so that a more complete likeness of the Holy Spirit is participated in the soul.

Article 6. [Whether charity is increased by any particular act of charity.]

One proceeds in this way to the sixth query. IT SEEMS that charity is increased by any particular act of charity.

[1] What can be greater can also be smaller. But any act of charity merits eternal life, which is greater than a simple increase of charity, since eternal life includes the completion of charity. Much more, therefore, does any particular act of charity increase charity.

[2] Furthermore, just as a habit of the acquired virtues is generated from actions, so too an increase of charity is caused by an act of charity. But any virtuous act works toward the generation of virtue. Therefore so does any act of charity work toward the increase of charity.

[3] Furthermore, Gregory says that when one is on the way (*in via*) to God, to stand in place is to fall back.[37] But nothing falls back when it is moved by the act of charity. Therefore whoever is moved by an act of charity, proceeds *in via* to God. Therefore charity is increased by any particular act of charity.

BUT TO THE CONTRARY an effect does not surpass the power of a cause. But sometimes an act of charity is just thrown out there, in a tepid or

---

37. Compare Bernard of Clairvaux, *Sermones de sanctis: in purificatione beatae Mariae* serm.2 (PL 183:369C). Also see Gregory the Great, *Regula pastoralis* pt.3 chap.34 (PL 77:118C–D).

remiss way.[38] Such an act, therefore, does not lead one to a more excellent charity, but instead disposes one to a smaller version.

I ANSWER THAT IT SHOULD BE SAID that in a certain way, the spiritual increase of charity is like bodily increase. Now in animals and plants, bodily increase is not a continual motion, such that if a thing is increased by so much in some particular time, it is necessary for it to increase proportionally in some part of that time, as happens in local motion. Rather, for a certain time, nature works in a way that disposes a thing toward increase, without increasing the thing in act (*in actu*). After this time, it produces as an effect that toward which it had disposed the thing, increasing the animal or plant in act. So too, charity in act is not increased by any particular act of charity. Rather, a particular act of charity disposes one toward an increase of charity, so far as by one act of charity a person is restored more promptly to acting according to charity. As the aptitude grows, a person breaks out into an act of more fervent love, whereby[39] he strives toward progress in charity. And then charity is increased in act (*in actu*).

[1] TO THE FIRST ARGUMENT, THEREFORE, IT SHOULD BE SAID that any particular act of charity merits eternal life – not to be presented at once, but in its own time. Likewise any particular act of charity merits an increase of charity. Nevertheless, it is not increased at once, but when someone is striving toward such an increase.

[2] To the second it should be said that even in the generation of an acquired virtue, no single act completes the virtue's generation. Rather, a single act works as disposing toward the virtue. The final act, which is more complete, since it acts by the power of everything that came before it, brings the virtue into act. In the same way, a stone is hollowed out by many drops.[40]

[3] To the third it should be said that someone proceeds *in via* toward God not only when his charity is increased in act, but also when he is disposed toward an increase.

Article 7. [Whether charity is increased to infinity.]

One proceeds in this way to the seventh query. IT SEEMS that charity is not increased to infinity.

38. Some versions read "committed with some temporal interval or remission."
39. Some versions read "until" (*quosque*).
40. See Lucretius, *De rerum natura* I.313.

[1] Every motion is toward some end and limit, as is said in *Metaphysics* 2.[41] But an increase of charity is a certain motion. Therefore it tends toward some end and limit. Therefore it is not increased to infinity.

[2] Furthermore, no form exceeds the capacity of its subject. But the capacity of the rational creature, who is the subject of charity, is finite. Therefore charity cannot be increased to infinity.

[3] Furthermore, every finite thing can by continual increase reach the quantity of another finite thing, however much greater – unless perhaps whatever is added to the first thing becomes less and less. As the Philosopher says in *Physics* 3,[42] if what is added to one line is subtracted from another line that is divided infinitely, a line made by addition into infinite parts, we will never attain a certain determinate quantity that is composed of two lines – that is, the divided line and the line to which was added whatever was subtracted from the other line. But this does not happen in the case proposed, because it is not necessary that the second increase of charity be less than the first increase. Rather, it is more probable that it would be equal or greater. Therefore, since charity-of-the-homeland is a certain finite thing, if charity-of-the-way can be increased to infinity, it would follow that charity-of-the-way can be equated to charity-of-the-homeland, which is inappropriate. Therefore, charity-of-the-way cannot be increased to infinity.

BUT TO THE CONTRARY there is what the Apostle says in Philippians 3, "Not as though I had already attained, or were already complete, but I follow after, if I may by any manner comprehend."[43] On which the Gloss says: "Let none of the faithful say, even if he has made progress, 'Enough for me.' For he who says this departs from the way before the end."[44] Therefore charity *in via* can always be increased more and more.

I ANSWER THAT IT SHOULD BE SAID that the limit of some form's increase can be fixed in advance (*praefigi*) in three ways. In one way, from the character of the form itself, which has a limited measure so that, when one has reached it, one cannot go beyond it. But if one does proceed further, one attains another form, as is clear in the case of paleness, the limits of which a person transgresses by continual alteration, arriving at either

---

41. Aristotle, *Metaphysics* bk.2 chap.2 (994b13).
42. Aristotle, *Physics* bk.3 chap.6 (206b16).
43. Philippians 3.12.
44. *Glossa Lombardi* on Philippians 3.12 (PL 192:246C).

whiteness or blackness. In a second way, on the part of the agent, whose power does not extend to increasing any further the form in its subject. In a third way, on the part of the subject, which is not capable of greater completion.

Now in none of these ways is a limit placed on the increase of charity in the wayfaring state (*in statu viae*). For charity itself has no limit to its increase according to the notion of its proper species, since it is a certain participation in infinite charity, which is the Holy Spirit. Likewise the cause that increases charity,[45] namely God, is of infinite power. Likewise also on the part of the subject, a limit to this increase cannot be fixed in advance, since it is always the case that, when charity is growing, so also grows surpassingly (*superexcrescit*) the aptitude for a further increase. So it remains that in this life, no limit to the increase of charity can be fixed in advance.

[1] TO THE FIRST ARGUMENT, THEREFORE, IT SHOULD BE SAID that an increase of charity is for some end, but that end is not in this life, but in a future life.

[2] To the second it should be said that the capacity of a spiritual creature is increased by charity, since by it the heart is opened wide, according to 2 Corinthians, "Our heart is opened wide."[46] And so there still remains an aptitude for greater increase.

[3] To the third it should be said that this argument goes through for things that have quantity of the same type (*ratio*), but not for things that have a different type of quantity – just as a line, however much it grows, does not attain the quantity of a surface. The type of quantity belonging to charity-of-the-way, which follows the knowledge of faith, is not the same as the type of quantity belonging to charity-of-the-homeland, which follows clear vision. So the argument does not follow.

Article 8. [Whether charity can be completed in this life.]

One proceeds in this way to the eighth query. IT SEEMS that charity cannot be completed in this life.

[1] This completion would have most of all been in the apostles. But it was not in them, for the Apostle says in Philippians 3: "Not as though I

---

45. Some versions read "the cause that brings about charity."
46. 2 Corinthians 6.11.

had already comprehended, or were already complete."[47] Therefore charity cannot be completed in this life.

[2] Furthermore, Augustine says in the *Book of 83 Questions* that "the nourishment of charity is the diminishment of cupidity, and when charity is complete, no cupidity remains."[48] But this cannot be in this life, in which we are unable to live without sin, according to 1 John 1: "If we say that we have no sin, we deceive ourselves."[49] Now every sin proceeds from some inordinate cupidity. Therefore in this life charity cannot be completed.

[3] Furthermore, what is already complete has no further growth. But charity in this life can always be increased, as was said.[50] Therefore charity in this life cannot be completed.

BUT TO THE CONTRARY there is what Augustine says in his commentary on 1 John: "Charity is completed when it has been strengthened, and when it has been brought to completion, it says 'I want to be dissolved and to be with Christ.'"[51] But this is possible in this life, as it was in Paul. Therefore charity in this life can be completed.

I ANSWER THAT IT SHOULD BE SAID that the completion of charity can be understood in two ways: in one way, on the part of the lovable; in another way, on the part of the lover. On the part of the lovable, charity is complete if something is loved as much as it is lovable. Now God is as lovable as he is good. Moreover, his goodness is infinite. So that he is infinitely lovable. But no creature can love him infinitely, since any created power is finite. So that no creature's charity can be perfected in this way, but only God's charity, by which he loves himself.

But on the part of the lover, charity is said to be completed when someone loves according to all of his power. This happens in three ways. In one way, so that a person's whole heart is actually borne toward God. And this is the completion of charity of our homeland, which is not possible in this life, in which it is impossible, on account of the weakness of human life, always and actually to think about God and to be moved toward him by love. – In a second way, as when a person gives his own zeal to emptying

47. Philippians 3.12.

48. Augustine, *De diversis quaestionibus lxxxiii* q.36 sect.1 (PL 40:25; CCSL 44A:54.12–13), quoting Philippians 1.23.

49. 1 John 1.8.

50. In Articles 4 and 7 of this Question.

51. Augustine, *Tractatus in epistolam Ioannis ad Parthos* tr.5 on 1 John 3.9 (PL 35:2014).

himself for God and divine things, putting everything else aside except as far as the necessity of the present life requires. And this is the completion of charity that is possible *in via,* yet it is not common to all who have charity. – In a third way, so that a person habitually places his whole heart in God, so that he thinks of or wills nothing that is contrary to divine love. And this completion is common to all who have charity.

[1] TO THE FIRST ARGUMENT, THEREFORE, IT SHOULD BE SAID that the Apostle denies of himself the completion of our homeland. So the Gloss says that "he was a complete wayfarer, but had not yet attained the completion of the journey itself."[52]

[2] To the second it should be said that this is said on account of venial sins. These are not contrary to the habit of charity, but to its act – and so are repugnant not to the completion of the way, but to the completion of our homeland (*patria*).

[3] To the third it should be said that completion of a way is not completion simply (*simpliciter*). And so it always has that by which it increases.

Article 9. [Whether three steps of charity are appropriately distinguished.]

One proceeds in this way to the ninth query. IT SEEMS that three steps of charity are not appropriately distinguished – namely, charity beginning (*incipiens*), charity progressing (*proficiens*), and charity that is completed (*perfecta*).

[1] In between the origin of charity and its final perfection, there are many steps in the middle. Therefore, not only one middle step should be set down.

[2] Furthermore, when charity begins to be, at once it begins to progress. Therefore, charity progressing should not be distinguished from beginning charity.

[3] Furthermore, however much a person has complete charity in this world, his charity can still be increased, as was said.[53] But to say that charity is increased, is to say that it makes progress. Therefore complete charity must not be distinguished from charity progressing. Inappropriately, therefore, are the aforementioned three steps of charity assigned.

52. *Glossa Lombardi* on Philippians 3.12 (PL 192:247A).
53. In Article 7 of this Question.

BUT TO THE CONTRARY there is what Augustine says in his commentary on 1 John:[54] "When charity will have been born, it is nourished" – which belongs to beginners – "when it will have been nourished, it is strengthened" – which belongs to those in progress – "when it will have been strengthened, it is completed" – which belongs to those who are perfect. Therefore there is a threefold gradation of charity.

I ANSWER THAT IT SHOULD BE SAID that the spiritual increase of charity can be considered so far as it resembles the bodily increase of a human being. Although bodily increase can be distinguished into many parts, it nonetheless has some fixed distinctions, which follow fixed actions or pursuits toward which a person is led by increase. So a person is called an infant before he has the use of reason; afterwards, a different state of a person is distinguished, when he starts to speak and use reason. Again, a third state is puberty, when he starts to be able to procreate – and so on until he arrives at a complete state.

So too are different steps of charity distinguished, according to the different pursuits to which a person is led by charity's increase. At first, the main pursuit that presses upon a person is to keep away from sin and to resist his concupiscence, which move him away from charity. And this belongs to beginners, in whom charity should be nourished and fostered, lest it be corrupted. – Then follows the second pursuit, so that a person might principally tend toward what progresses in the good. And this pursuit belongs to those progressing (*proficientes*), who tend principally toward this, so that charity may be strengthened in them through growth. – The third pursuit is for a person principally to intend this – to adhere to God and to enjoy him. And this belongs to those who are complete, who "desire to be dissolved and to be with Christ."[55] –As we see in bodily motion, first comes movement away from one limit, then approach to another limit, and finally rest in the limit.

[1] TO THE FIRST ARGUMENT, THEREFORE, IT SHOULD BE SAID that any fixed distinction that one is able to grasp in the growth of charity is comprehended under the three things that have been stated. Just as any division of a continuum is comprehended under these three

54. Augustine, *Tractatus in epistolam Ioannis ad Parthos* tr.5 on 1 John 3.9 (PL 35:2014).
55. Philippians 1.23.

things – beginning, middle, and end, as the Philosopher says in *On the Heavens* 1.[56]

[2] To the second it should be said that for those in whom charity is beginning – though they are progressing – the main concern that hangs over them is to resist sins, by whose attack they are disturbed. But afterwards, feeling this attack less, they tend to make progress, now feeling somewhat more secure. From one perspective, they are doing a work; from another, they put their hand to the sword, as is said in 2 Esdras 4 about the builders of Jerusalem.[57]

[3] To the third it should be said that those who are complete also make progress in charity, but this is not their main concern. Rather, as regards charity, their zeal is turned so that most of all they might adhere to God. And while both those beginning and those progressing may also seek this, they feel solicitude more about other things – those beginning, about avoidance of sins; those progressing, about their progress in the virtues.

Article 10. [Whether charity can be decreased.]

One proceeds in this way to the tenth query. IT SEEMS that charity can be decreased.

[1] Contraries naturally happen about the same thing. But decrease and increase are contraries. So because charity is increased, as said above,[58] it seems that it is also decreased.

[2] Furthermore, Augustine says in *Confessions* 10, speaking to God: "He loves you less, he who loves something else along with you."[59] And in the *Book of 83 Questions,* he says that "the nourishment of charity is the decreasing of cupidity,"[60] from which it seems that, conversely, the increase of cupidity is the decrease of charity. But cupidity, by which something other than God is loved, can grow in human beings. Therefore charity can be decreased.

[3] Furthermore, Augustine says in *On Genesis to the Letter* 8, "God does not make a person by justifying him so that if the person turns away

---

56. Aristotle, *On the Heavens* bk.1 chap.1 (268a12).

57. 2 Ezra 4.17.

58. In Article 4 of this Question.

59. Augustine, *Confessiones* bk.10 chap.29 sect.40 (PL 32:796; CCSL 27: 176.6–7).

60. Augustine, *De diversis quaestionibus lxxxiii* q.36 sect.1 (PL 40:25; CCSL 44A:54.12–13).

from him, what he has done would remain in absentia."[61] From this one can grasp that God works his charity in a person by preserving it, in the same manner as he does when he first infuses it into him. But in the first infusion of charity, God infuses less charity into the person who prepares himself less. Therefore also in the preservation of charity, he preserves less charity in the person who prepares himself less. Therefore charity can be decreased.

BUT TO THE CONTRARY charity in Scripture is compared to fire, according to Song of Songs 8: "Its lamps," namely those of charity, are "lamps of fire and flames."[62] But fire, as long as it remains, always ascends. Therefore charity, as long as it remains, can ascend. But to descend, that is, to be decreased – this it cannot do.

I ANSWER THAT IT SHOULD BE SAID that the quantity of charity that bears comparison to its proper object cannot be decreased, just as it cannot be increased, as said above.[63] But since charity is increased according to a quantity that bears a comparison to its subject, one should consider whether it could be decreased on the subject's part. If charity were to be decreased, it must be that it would be decreased either by an act or by ceasing to act. By ceasing to act, the virtues acquired from acts are decreased and sometimes even corrupted, as said above, so that the Philosopher says in *Ethics* 8 about friendship that "a lack of address (*inappellatio*) has dissolved many friendships" – that is, not calling upon one's friend or speaking with him.[64] But this is because the preservation of anything whatever depends on its cause. Now the cause of an acquired virtue is a human act. So that, when human acts cease, the acquired virtue is lessened and in the end wholly corrupted. But this has no place in charity, since charity is not caused by human acts, but only by God, as said above.[65] So it remains that even in someone ceasing to act, charity is neither decreased nor corrupted on that account – provided there is no sin in the cessation itself.

It remains, therefore, that a decrease of charity cannot be caused except either by God or by some sin. Indeed, no defect in us is caused by God, except by way of penalty, according as he withdraws grace in the punish-

---

61. Augustine, *De Genesi ad litteram* bk.8 chap.12 sect.26 (PL 34:383; CSEL 28/1:249.27–250.1).

62. Song of Songs 8.6.

63. In Article 4 of this Question, Reply [2].

64. Aristotle, *Nicomachean Ethics* 8.5 (1157b13).

65. In Article 2 of this Question.

"Charity that can fail was never true."[74] Therefore it was never true charity. Therefore if charity is possessed once, it can never be lost.

[3] Furthermore, Gregory says in his homily on Pentecost that "the love of God works great things, if it exists; if it ceases to work, it is not charity."[75] But no one loses charity by doing great things. Therefore if charity is within, it cannot be lost.

[4] Furthermore, free decision is not inclined to sin except by some motive for sinning. But charity excludes all motives for sinning – love of self, cupidity, and anything else of this sort. Therefore charity cannot be lost.

BUT TO THE CONTRARY there is what is said in Revelation 2: "I have a few things against you, because you have abandoned the first charity."[76]

I ANSWER THAT IT SHOULD BE SAID that by charity the Holy Spirit dwells in us, as is clear from what was said above.[77] Therefore, we can consider charity in three ways. In the first way, on the part of the Holy Spirit moving the soul toward loving God. Here charity has sinlessness (*impeccabilitas*) by the power of the Holy Spirit, who infallibly works whatever he has willed. So it is impossible for these two things to be true at the same time – that the Holy Spirit should will to move someone to an act of charity, and that the person so moved should lose charity by sinning. For the gift of perseverance is reckoned among the "benefits of God by which those who are freed, are freed most certainly," as Augustine says in *On the Predestination of the Saints.*[78]

In a second way, charity can be considered according to its own aspect. And in this way charity cannot be anything except for what belongs to the aspect of charity. So that charity in no way can sin, just as heat cannot cool,

---

74. These words do not appear in Augustine's letters, but rather in Paulinus of Aquileia's *Liber exhortationis* chap.7 (PL 99:202A), as well as in three letters by his contemporary Alcuin of York. See Alcuin, *Epistolae,* ed. E. Dümmler (Berlin: Weidmann, 1895) ep.79 (Dümmler 120.20), ep.204 (Dümmler 337.34), ep.250 (Dümmler 404.25). The attribution to Augustine occurs in Peter Lombard, *Sententiae* bk.3 d.31 chap.1 (Grottaferrata 2:180).

75. Gregory the Great, *Homiliae in Evangelia* bk.2 hom.30 sect.2, on John 14.23–31 (PL 76:1221; CCSL 141:257.44–45).

76. Revelation 2.4.

77. In Article 2 of this Question and in Question 23, Article 2.

78. Augustine, *De dono perseverantiae* chap.14 sect.35 (PL 45:1014).

and injustice cannot do good, as Augustine says in *The Lord's Sermon on the Mount*.[79]

In a third way, charity can be considered on the part of the subject, which is changeable according to the freedom of decision. Now the relation of charity to this subject can be discerned both according to a universal aspect, by which form is compared to matter, and according to a special aspect, by which habit is compared to power. Now it belongs to the aspect of a form to be in its subject in such a way that it can be lost, when it does not fill the whole potentiality of the matter–as is clear in the forms of generable and corruptible things. Since the matter of these things thus receives one form, which remains in it as potency toward another form, the whole potentiality of the matter is not filled, as it were, by a single form. And so one form can be lost by the reception of another form. But the form of a heavenly body, which fills the whole potentiality of its matter, so that it does not remain in potency to another form, inheres in it in a way that cannot be lost (*inamissibiliter*). Therefore charity-of-the-homeland, since it fills the whole potentiality of the rational mind, so far as all of its actual motion is borne toward God, is possessed in a way that cannot be lost. But charity-of-the-way does not fill the potentiality of its subject in this manner, since it is not always actually borne toward God. So that when it is not actually borne toward God, something can occur by which charity might be lost.

In fact, it is proper to a habit that it incline the power toward action appropriate to the habit, so far as it makes what is appropriate to the habit seem good, and what is repugnant to the habit seem bad. Just as taste discerns flavors according to its own disposition, so the mind of man discerns something to be done according to its habitual disposition, so that the Philosopher says in *Ethics* 3 that "as a man is, so the end seems to him."[80] Hence, when charity is possessed in a way that cannot be lost, what is appropriate to charity cannot seem anything but good–namely in the homeland, where God is seen in his essence, which is the very essence of goodness. And so charity-of-the-homeland cannot be lost. But charity-of-the-way, in whose state the very essence of God–the essence of goodness–is not seen, can be lost.[81]

79. Augustine, *De sermone Domini in monte* bk.2 chap.24 (PL 34:1305; CCSL 35:178.1823–27).

80. Aristotle, *Nicomachean Ethics* bk.3 chap.5 (1114a32).

81. Some versions read "in whose state the very essence of God is not seen to be the essence of goodness."

[1] TO THE FIRST ARGUMENT, THEREFORE, IT SHOULD BE SAID that this authority is speaking according to the power of the Holy Spirit, whose preservation renders immune from sin those whom it moves so far as it wills.

[2] To the second it should be said that charity that can fail is, from the very notion of charity, not true charity. For this would be if charity's love were to contain within itself the act of loving for a time and then failing to love. But this would not belong to true love. But if charity were to be lost because of the subject's mutability, against the purpose of charity, a purpose included in its act – this is not repugnant to the truth of charity.

[3] To the third it should be said that the love of God always works great things for a purpose. This belongs to the notion of charity. It does not, however, always work great things in act, on account of the condition of the subject.

[4] To the fourth it should be said that charity, according to the reason of its own act, excludes every motive for sinning. But sometimes it happens that charity does not do something in act (*actu*). And then some motive for sinning can intervene. If one consents to this motive, charity is lost.

Article 12. [Whether charity is lost by a single act of mortal sin.]

One proceeds in this way to the twelfth query. IT SEEMS that charity is not lost by a single act of mortal sin.

[1] Origen says in *On First Principles,* chapter 3: "If satiety has taken hold in one of those who are in the highest degree of completion, I do not judge that he should suddenly be withdrawn or fall away – rather, it is necessary that he fall slowly and by stages."[82] But a human being who loses charity falls away. Therefore charity is not lost by only one act of mortal sin.

[2] Furthermore, Pope Leo I [Leo the Great] says in a sermon on the Passion, speaking of Peter: "The Lord saw in you not a conquered faith, not an averted love, but a constancy that had been shaken. Tears abounded, where the affection never failed, and the fount of charity washed away the words of terror."[83] And Bernard took this to mean that "in Peter charity had

---

82. Origen, *On First Principles* bk.1 chap.3 (PG 11:155B–C).
83. Leo the Great, *Sermones in praecupuis totius anni festivitatibus ad romanem plebem habiti* tr.60 chap.4 (PL 54:345; CCSL 138A:368.101–4).

not become extinct, but only sleepy."[84] But Peter, by denying Christ, sinned mortally. Therefore charity is not lost by one act of mortal sin.

[3] Furthermore, charity is stronger than an acquired virtue. But the habit of an acquired virtue is not destroyed by one act of an opposed sin. Therefore much less is charity destroyed by a single act of an opposed mortal sin.

[4] Furthermore, charity denotes the love of God and neighbor. But someone committing a mortal sin retains the love of God and neighbor, or so it seems, for the disorder of his affections regarding what is for the sake of the end does not destroy his love of the end, as was said above.[85] Therefore charity can remain toward God, despite the existence of mortal sin through disordered affection for some temporal good.

[5] Furthermore, the object of a theological virtue is the ultimate end. But the other theological virtues, namely faith and hope, are not removed by a single act of mortal sin—on the contrary, they remain, albeit unformed. Therefore charity can remain, albeit unformed, even if one mortal sin has been committed.

BUT TO THE CONTRARY by mortal sin a person becomes worthy of eternal death, according to Romans 6: "The wages of sin is death."[86] But anyone who has charity has the merit of eternal life, for John 14 says that "he who loves me, shall be loved by my Father, and I will love him, and will show myself to him."[87] Indeed, in that showing eternal life consists, according to John 17: "This is eternal life, that you may know me, true God, and the one whom you have sent, Jesus Christ."[88] Now no one can simultaneously be worthy of eternal life and eternal death. Therefore it is impossible that someone should have charity with mortal sin. Therefore, charity is destroyed by one act of mortal sin.

I ANSWER THAT IT SHOULD BE SAID that one contrary is destroyed by another supervening contrary. Now any act of mortal sin is opposed to charity according to its proper aspect (*ratio*), which consists in this—that God should be loved above everything, and that man should wholly subject himself to God, referring all things to him. Therefore it belongs to

84. Compare William of St. Thierry, *De natura et dignitate amoris* chap.6 sect.14 (PL 184:390).
85. In Article 10 of this Question.
86. Romans 6.23.
87. John 14.21.
88. John 17.3.

the aspect of charity that he love God in this way, so that in all things he wills to subject himself to God and to follow the rule of his precepts in everything. For whatever is contrary to his precepts is manifestly contrary to charity. So that [whatever is contrary to his precepts] has of itself this property – that it can shut out charity.

And if charity were an acquired habit, depending for its power on the subject, it would not be necessary for it to be destroyed at once by a single act of something contrary. For an act is not directly opposed to a habit, but rather to another action, whereas the preservation of a habit in its subject does not require continuous performance of the act. So that from an op-posed act that supervenes, the acquired habit is not shut out at once. But charity, since it is an infused habit, depends for its infusion on the action of God infusing it. God is to the infusion and preservation of charity as the sun is to the illumination of the air, as was said.[89] And so, just as light would at once cease to be in the air, were some obstacle to be set against the sun's illumination, so too charity at once fails to be in the soul when some obstacle is set against the inflowing of charity from God into the soul. For it is clear that by any mortal sin, which is opposed to divine precepts, an ob-stacle is set against the infusion that was mentioned. This is because from the very fact that a person by his own choice prefers sin over divine friend-ship – which requires that we follow God's will – it follows that at once, by a single act of mortal sin, the habit of charity is lost. So Augustine says, in *On Genesis to the Letter* 8, that "man is illumined when God is present, whereas when he is absent, man continues be darkened; he is withdrawn from God not by distance of place, but by a turning away of the will."[90]

[1] TO THE FIRST ARGUMENT, THEREFORE, IT SHOULD BE SAID that the word of Origen can be understood in such a way that a person who is in a state of perfection does not suddenly proceed to an act of mortal sin, but is disposed to this by some preceding negligence. So that venial sins are said to be a disposition to mortal sin, as was said above.[91] And yet by a single act of mortal sin, if a person has committed it, he falls away, and charity is lost. But since he adds, "If some small lapse should occur, and he recovers himself quickly, it seems that he is not ruined inwardly,"[92] it can be said that Origen understands a person who has become withdrawn and

---

89. *Summa* 2a2ae q.4 a.4 ad 3.

90. Augustine, *De Genesi ad litteram* bk.8 chap.12 (PL 34:383; CSEL 28/1:250.4–6).

91. *Summa* 1a2ae q.88 a.3.

92. Origen, *On First Principles* bk.1 chap.3 (PG 11:155C).

fallen away as a person who falls by sinning from malice. Which does not happen in a perfect human being at once from the beginning.

[2] To the second it should be said that charity is lost in two ways. In one way, directly, through actual contempt. In this way Peter did not lose charity. – In another way, indirectly, when something opposed to charity is committed on account of some passion of concupiscence or fear. And in this way Peter, acting against charity, lost charity, but he quickly recovered it.

[3] To the third it should be said that the response is clear from what was said.[93]

[4] To the fourth it should be said that not simply any disordered affection about what is for the sake of the end, that is, toward created goods, constitutes mortal sin, but only when such disorder is that which is repugnant to the divine will. And this is directly opposed to charity, as was said.[94]

[5] To the fifth it should be said that charity denotes a certain union with God, whereas neither faith nor hope denotes this union. Now any mortal sin[95] consists in a turning away from God, as was said above.[96] And so any mortal sin is opposed to charity. However, not every mortal sin is opposed to faith or hope, but only certain particular sins by which the habits of faith and hope are destroyed, whereas the habit of charity is destroyed by every mortal sin. So it is clear that charity cannot remain without form, since it is the ultimate form of the virtues. This is because it looks to God under the aspect of the ultimate end, as was said.[97]

93. In the Leonine edition, no reply appears to the third argument.
94. In the body of this Article.
95. Some versions omit "mortal."
96. *Summa* 2a2ae q.20 a.3.
97. In Question 23, Article 8.

[The Object of Charity]

One should next consider the object of charity. Regarding this, two points arise that should be considered. The first point concerns the things that should be loved out of charity; the second point concerns the order of the things that should be loved. About the first point, twelve queries are raised. (1) Whether only God should be loved out of charity, or also our neighbor. (2) Whether charity should be loved out of charity. (3) Whether irrational creatures should be loved out of charity. (4) Whether someone can love himself out of charity. (5) Whether one's own body can be loved out of charity. (6) Whether sinners should be loved out of charity. (7) Whether sinners love themselves. (8) Whether enemies should be loved out of charity. (9) Whether we should show them the signs of friendship. (10) Whether the angels should be loved out of charity. (11) Whether the demons should be loved out of charity. (12) On the enumeration of the things that should be loved out of charity.

Article 1. [Whether the love of charity stops at God, or also extends to our neighbor.]

One proceeds in this way to the first query. IT SEEMS that the love of charity stops at God and does not also extend to our neighbor.

[1] Just as we owe God love, so we also owe him fear, according to Deuteronomy 10: "And now, Israel, what does the Lord God ask, except that you fear and love him?"[1] But the fear by which a man is feared is one thing—it is called "human fear"—whereas the fear by which God is feared is another thing—it is either servile or filial fear, as is clear from what has been said above.[2] Therefore also the love of charity, by which God is loved, is one thing, and the love by which our neighbor is loved is another thing.

1. Deuteronomy 10.12.
2. *Summa* 2a2ae q.19 a.2.

[2] Furthermore, the Philosopher says in *Ethics* 8 that "to be loved is to be honored."[3] But the honor that is owed to God is one thing–it is the honor of adoration (*latria*)–and the honor that is owed to creatures is another thing–it is the honor of veneration (*dulia*). Therefore also the love by which God is loved is one thing, and that by which the neighbor is loved another.

[3] Furthermore, hope generates charity, as attested by the Gloss on Matthew 1.[4] But regarding God, hope is had in such a way that those who hope in man are reprehensible, according to Jeremiah 17: "Cursed is the man who trusts (*confidit*) in man."[5] Therefore charity is owed to God, but not so as to extend to our neighbor.

BUT TO THE CONTRARY there is what is said in 1 John 4: "We have from God this commandment–that he who loves God must also love his brother."[6]

I ANSWER THAT IT SHOULD BE SAID that, as was said above,[7] habits are not differentiated except by that which changes the act's kind (*species*), for all acts of a single kind belong to the same habit. Now when an act's kind is taken from its object according to its formal aspect (*formalis ratio*), it is necessary that an act directed to the object's aspect (*ratio*) and an act directed to the object [itself] under such an aspect are of the same kind–just as the vision by which light is seen and the vision by which color is seen according to the aspect of light are of the same kind. Now the aspect that belongs to loving our neighbor is God, since this we must love in our neighbor–that he is in God. So it is manifest that the act by which God is loved and that by which our neighbor is loved are of the same kind. And because of this, the habit of charity extends not only to the love of God, but also to the love of neighbor.

[1] TO THE FIRST ARGUMENT, THEREFORE, IT SHOULD BE SAID that the neighbor can be feared in two ways, just as he is loved [in two ways]. In one way, on account of what is proper to him, as when a person fears a tyrant on account of his cruelty, or when he loves the tyrant

---

3. Aristotle, *Nicomachean Ethics* bk.8 chap.8 (1159a16).
4. *Glossa interlinearis* on Matthew 1.2 (Strasbourg 5).
5. Jeremiah 17.5.
6. 1 John 4.21.
7. *Summa* 1a2ae q.54 a.3.

on account of his covetous desire (*cupiditas*) to acquire something from him. Such human fear is distinguished from the fear of God, and likewise love. In another way, a human being can be feared and loved on account of what in him is of God, as when the secular power is feared on account of its divine service in the punishment of wrongdoers and is loved on account of justice. Such fear of a human being is not distinguished from the fear of God, and nor is love.

[2] To the second it should be said that love looks to good in general, but honor looks to the good of the person honored, for it is given to someone as a testament of his own virtue. And so love is not differentiated by species on account of a diverse quantity of goodness of diverse persons, provided that it is referred to some single common good, but honor is differentiated according to goods proper to singular persons. So that by the same love of charity we love all of our neighbors, so far as they are referred to a single common good, which is God, but we confer different honors on different people according to the virtue of each singular person. And likewise we show God the singular honor of adoration (*latria*), on account of his singular virtue.

[3] To the third it should be said that those who hope in man as the principal author of their salvation are blameworthy, whereas those who hope in man as a ministering helper under God are not. And likewise it would be reprehensible if someone were to love the neighbor as a principal end, whereas it is not if someone loves the neighbor on account of God, which belongs to charity.

Article 2. [Whether charity should be loved out of charity.]

One proceeds in this way to the second query. IT SEEMS that charity should not be loved out of charity.

[1] The things that should be loved out of charity are included within the two precepts of charity, as is clear from Matthew 22.[8] But charity is contained under neither of these things, since charity is neither God nor the neighbor. Therefore charity should not be loved out of charity.

[2] Furthermore, charity is founded upon a sharing of blessedness, as was said above.[9] But charity cannot be a participator in blessedness. Therefore charity should not be loved out of charity.

8. Matthew 22.37–39.
9. In Question 23, Article 1.

[3] Furthermore, charity is a certain friendship, as was said above.[10] But no one can have friendship with charity, or with some accident, since things of this sort cannot love in return (*reamare*), which belongs to the notion of friendship, as is said in *Ethics* 8.[11] Therefore charity should not be loved out of charity.

BUT TO THE CONTRARY there is what Augustine says in *On the Trinity* 8: "He who loves his neighbor, must consequently also love love itself."[12] But our neighbor is loved out of charity. So consequently, charity is also loved out of charity.

I ANSWER THAT IT SHOULD BE SAID that charity is a certain love. Now love, from the nature of the power whose act it is, has this [feature]—that it can be turned back onto itself (*supra seipsum reflecti*). Since the will's object is universal good, whatever is contained under the aspect of good can fall under the will's act. Since willing is itself a certain good, one can will that one wills, just as the intellect, whose object is truth, understands that it understands, since this too is a particular truth. But love also, by reason of its own species, has [the feature] that it is turned back onto itself, since it is a spontaneous motion of the lover toward the beloved. So from the very fact that a person loves, he loves that he loves.

But charity is not simple love, but has the aspect of friendship, as said above.[13] Now something is loved by friendship in two ways. In one way, as the friend himself, with whom we have friendship and for whom we wish good things. In another way, as the good that we wish for a friend. And in this way, rather than the first, charity is loved by charity, since charity is the good that we desire for everyone whom we love out of charity. And the same reasoning holds for blessedness and for the other virtues.

[1] TO THE FIRST ARGUMENT, THEREFORE, IT SHOULD BE SAID that those with whom we have friendship are God and our neighbor. But in our love of them is included the love of charity. For we love our neighbor and God insofar as we love this—that we and our neighbor may love God. This is to love charity.[14]

10. In Question 23, Article 1.

11. Aristotle, *Nicomachean Ethics* bk.8 chap.2 (1155b29).

12. Augustine, *De trinitate* bk.8 chap.7 sect.10 (PL 42:957; CCSL 50: 285.31–32).

13. In Question 23, Article 1.

14. Some versions read "this is to have charity."

[2] To the second it should be said that charity is the very sharing of spiritual life, by which we arrive at blessedness. And so it is loved as the good desired for everyone whom we love out of charity.

[3] To the third it should be said that this reasoning proceeds according as those with whom we have friendship are loved by friendship.

Article 3. [Whether even irrational creatures should be loved out of charity.]

One proceeds in this way to the third query. IT SEEMS that even irrational creatures should be loved out of charity.

[1] By charity we are conformed to God most of all. But God loves irrational creatures out of charity, for he loves all things that are, as is attested by Wisdom 11[15] – and anything that he loves, he loves by himself, who is charity. And so we should love irrational creatures out of charity.

[2] Furthermore, charity is principally directed toward God, whereas it extends to others so far as they belong to God. But just as the rational creature belongs to God, so far as he has the likeness of an image, so also does the irrational creature, so far as it has the likeness of a vestige. Therefore charity also extends to irrational creatures.

[3] Furthermore, just as God is the object of charity, so too is he the object of faith. But faith extends to irrational creatures, so far as we believe that heaven and earth were created by God, that fish and birds were brought forth from the waters, and that animals able to walk and plants were brought forth from the earth. Therefore charity also extends to irrational creatures.

BUT TO THE CONTRARY the love of charity extends only to God and neighbor. But the name "neighbor" cannot be understood to apply to an irrational creature, since it does not share with man in the rational life. Therefore charity does not extend to irrational creatures.

I ANSWER THAT IT SHOULD BE SAID that according to what was said before,[16] charity is a certain friendship. Now by friendship something is loved in one way, as the friend with whom we have friendship; in another way, as the goods that are desired for the friend. By the first way, therefore, no irrational creature can be loved out of charity. This holds for three

15. Wisdom 11.25.
16. In Question 23, Article 1.

reasons. Two of these reasons belong generally to friendship, which cannot be had with irrational creatures. The first reason is that friendship is directed toward a person to whom we will a good. Now I cannot properly will a good to an irrational creature, since it is not proper to an irrational creature's nature to possess the good. This is proper only to the rational creature, who is the master of using the good that he possesses by free decision. And so in *Physics* 2 the Philosopher says that we do not call something that happens to irrational creatures "good" or "evil," except according to a likeness.[17] The second reason is that every friendship is founded upon some sharing of life, "for nothing is so proper to friendship as to live together," as is clear from the Philosopher in *Ethics* 8.[18] Now irrational creatures cannot have a share in human life, which is according to reason. So no friendship can be had with irrational creatures, except perhaps according to a metaphor. The third reason is proper to charity, since charity is founded upon a sharing of eternal blessedness, of which the irrational creature is not capable.

[But in the second way] irrational creatures can be loved out of charity, in the manner of goods that we can will to others, so far as out of charity we will them to be preserved for the honor of God and the advantage of human beings. And in this way God loves them out of charity.

[1] So the answer TO THE FIRST ARGUMENT is clear.

[2] To the second it should be said that the likeness of a vestige does not give the capacity for eternal life – only the likeness of an image does. So there is no similar reasoning.

[3] To the third it should be said that faith can extend to all things that are true in some way. But the friendship of charity extends only to the things that are born to have the good of eternal life. So the two are not similar.

Article 4. [Whether a person loves himself out of charity.]

One proceeds in this way to the fourth query. IT SEEMS that a person does not love himself out of charity.

[1] Gregory says in a homily that "charity between fewer than two people cannot be had."[19] Therefore no one has charity toward himself.

---

17. Aristotle, *Physics* bk.2 chap.6 (197b8).

18. Aristotle, *Nicomachean Ethics* bk.8 chap.5 (1157b19). For "live together" (*convivere*), some versions read the "goods of life"; still others the "good life."

19. Gregory the Great, *Homiliae in Evangelia* bk.1 hom.17 sect.1, on Luke 10.1–9 (PL 76:1139; CCSL 141.117:6–7).

[2] Furthermore, friendship by its own notion denotes a "loving in return" (*reamatio*) and an equality, which cannot be for a person toward himself, as is clear in *Ethics* 8.[20] But charity is a certain friendship, as was said.[21] Therefore a person cannot have charity toward himself.

[3] Furthermore, what belongs to charity cannot be blameworthy, since "charity deals not perversely" as is said in 1 Corinthians 13.[22] But to love oneself is blameworthy, for it says in 2 Timothy 3: "In the last days, dangerous times shall come, and men will be lovers of themselves."[23] Therefore a person cannot love himself out of charity.

BUT TO THE CONTRARY there is what is said in Leviticus 19, "Love your friend as yourself."[24] But we love our friend out of charity. Therefore we should also love ourselves out of charity.

I ANSWER THAT IT SHOULD BE SAID that, since charity is a certain friendship, as was said,[25] we can speak of charity in two ways. In one way, under the general aspect of friendship. And according to this it should be said that friendship is not properly had with oneself. Rather something greater than friendship is had with oneself, since friendship denotes a certain union. For Dionysius says that love is a unitive power.[26] Now anything whatever is unity in relation to itself, which is superior to union. So that just as unity is the principle of union, so the love by which one loves oneself is the form and root of friendship—for in this we have friendship with others, which we have with them as with ourselves. For it is said in *Ethics* 9 that "friendly sentiments for another arise from friendly sentiments for oneself."[27] Just as regarding starting points (*principia*), what is had is not knowledge (*scientia*), but something greater, namely understanding (*intellectus*).

In another way, we can speak of charity according to its own proper aspect, namely as the friendship of human beings with God principally, and consequently with the things that are of God. Among these things is man

20. Aristotle, *Nicomachean Ethics* bk.8 chap.2 (1155b28).
21. In Question 23, Article 1.
22. 1 Corinthians 13.4.
23. 2 Timothy 3.1–2.
24. Leviticus 19.18.
25. In Question 23, Article 1.
26. Ps-Dionysius, *Divine Names* chap.4 sect.12 (PG 3:709C–D; Chevallier 1:214).
27. Aristotle, *Nicomachean Ethics* bk.9 chap.4 (1166a1); bk.9 chap.8 (1168b5).

himself, who has charity. Thus among the other things that he loves out of charity, as belonging to God, he loves himself out of charity.

[1] TO THE FIRST ARGUMENT, THEREFORE, IT SHOULD BE SAID that Gregory is speaking of charity according to the general aspect of friendship.

[2] The second argument also proceeds from this [the general aspect of friendship].

[3] To the third it should be said that lovers of themselves are blamed so far as they love themselves according to sensitive nature, to which they submit. That is not truly to love oneself according to rational nature, so that one wills for oneself the good things that belong to the completion of reason. And in this way, it especially belongs to charity to love oneself.

Article 5. [Whether a person should love his own body out of charity.]

One proceeds in this way to the fifth query. IT SEEMS that a person should not love his own body out of charity.

[1] We do not love a person with whom we are not willing to associate. But human beings who have charity fly away from intimacy of the body, according to Romans 7: "Who will liberate me from the body of this death?"[28] And Philippians 1: "Having a desire to be dissolved and to be with Christ."[29] Therefore our body should not be loved out of charity.

[2] Furthermore, the friendship of charity is founded upon a sharing of divine enjoyment. But the body cannot be a participator in this enjoyment. Therefore the body should not be loved out of charity.

[3] Furthermore, charity – since it is a certain friendship – is had toward those who are able to love in return (*reamare*). But our body cannot love us out of charity. Therefore we should not love it out of charity.

BUT TO THE CONTRARY Augustine in *On Christian Doctrine*, Book 1, sets down four things that should be loved out of charity.[30] Among these things is one's own body.

---

28. Romans 7.24.

29. Philippians 1.23.

30. Augustine, *De doctrina christiana* bk.1 chap.23 sect.22 (PL 34:27; CCSL 32:18.6–9).

I ANSWER THAT IT SHOULD BE SAID that our body can be considered in two ways. In one way, in its nature; in another way, in the corruption of sin and its punishment. Now the nature of our body is not that it was created from an evil principle, as the Manicheans fabulized – rather, the body comes from God, so that we can use it for the service of God, according to Romans 6: "Present your members to God as instruments of justice."[31] And so from the love of charity by which we love God, we must also love our body. We must not, however, love the infection of sin and the corruption of its punishment in our body, but rather pant for its removal by a desire for charity.

[1] TO THE FIRST ARGUMENT, THEREFORE, IT SHOULD BE SAID that the Apostle did not fly away from sharing of the body as regards the body's nature – in fact, he did not want to be deprived of it, according to 2 Corinthians 5, "We wish not to be unclothed, but clothed over."[32] But he did want to be without the infection of concupiscence, which remains in the body, and without its corruption, which "oppresses the soul"[33] so that it cannot see God. So he expressly said "the body of this death."[34]

[2] To the second it should be said that although our body cannot enjoy God by knowing and loving him, we can nonetheless come to the complete enjoyment of God by means of works that we do through the body. So that a certain blessedness overflows from the soul's enjoyment to the body, namely "the vigor of cleanliness and incorruption," as Augustine says in a letter to Dioscorus.[35] And so, since the body is in some way a participator in blessedness, it can be loved by the love of charity.

[3] To the third it should be said that "loving in return" (*reamatio*) has its place in friendship that is directed to another, but not in the friendship that one has with oneself, whether according to the soul or according to the body.

Article 6. [Whether sinners should be loved out of charity.]

One proceeds in this way to the sixth query. IT SEEMS that sinners should not be loved out of charity.

31. Romans 6.13.
32. 2 Corinthians 5.4.
33. Wisdom 9.15.
34. Romans 7.24.
35. Augustine, *Epistulae* ep.118 to Dioscorus chap.3 sect.14 (PL 33:439; CCSL 31B:122.345–46).

[1] It says in the Psalm, "I have hated the unjust."[36] But David had charity. Therefore, out of charity sinners should be hated rather than loved.

[2] Furthermore, "the proof of love is the showing of a work," as Gregory says in a homily on Pentecost.[37] But the just do not show works of love before sinners, but works that seem to be of hatred, according to the Psalm: "In the morning I put to death all the sinners of the land."[38] And the Lord commanded, Exodus 22, "You shall not permit a sorceress to live."[39] Therefore sinners should not be loved out of charity.

[3] Furthermore, it belongs to friendship that we will and desire good things for friends. But the saints, out of charity, desire bad things for sinners, according to the Psalm: "Let sinners be turned toward hell."[40] Therefore sinners should not be loved out of charity.

[4] Furthermore, it is proper to friends to rejoice over the same things and to will the same. But charity does not make a person will what sinners will, nor does it make a person rejoice over that which sinners rejoice over; rather it makes them do the opposite. Therefore sinners should not be loved out of charity.

[5] Furthermore, "it is proper to friends to live together," as is said in *Ethics* 8.[41] But one should not live with sinners, according to 2 Corinthians 6: "Go out from their midst."[42] Therefore sinners should not be loved out of charity.

BUT TO THE CONTRARY Augustine says in *On Christian Doctrine*, Book 1, that when it says "Love your neighbor," then "it is clear that every person should be regarded as our neighbor."[43] But sinners do not stop being human, since sin does not destroy nature. Therefore sinners should be loved out of charity.

I ANSWER THAT IT SHOULD BE SAID that in sinners two things can be considered—namely, nature and fault (*culpa*). According to nature,

36. Psalm 118.113.
37. Gregory the Great, *Homiliae in Evangelia* bk.2 hom.30 sect.1, on John 14.23–31 (PL 76:1220; CCSL 141.256.14–15).
38. Psalm 100.8.
39. Exodus 22.18.
40. Psalm 9.18.
41. Aristotle, *Nicomachean Ethics* bk.8 chap.5 (1157b19).
42. 2 Corinthians 6.17.
43. Augustine, *De doctrina christiana* bk.1 chap.30 sect.32 (PL 34:31; CCSL 32:25.37–38).

which they have from God, they are capable of blessedness, upon whose sharing charity is founded, as said above.[44] And so according to their own nature they should be loved out of charity. But their fault sets them against God and is an obstacle to blessedness. So that according to fault, by which they are averse to God, all sinners whatever should be hated – even father and mother and near relations, as attested by Luke 14.[45] For in sinners we ought to hate that they are sinners, and to love that they are human beings, capable of blessedness. And this is truly to love them out of charity, on account of God.

[1] TO THE FIRST ARGUMENT, THEREFORE, IT SHOULD BE SAID that the prophet has hated the unjust so far as they are unjust, bearing hatred toward their injustice, which is their evil. And this is perfect hatred, of which he speaks: "I have hated them with a perfect hatred."[46] Now for the same reason, to hate a person's evil is to love that person's good. So that such perfect hatred also belongs to charity.

[2] To the second it should be said that when our friends sin, as the Philosopher says in *Ethics* 9,[47] the benefits of friendship should not be withdrawn from them, as long as hope remains for their healing. But more help should be given for recovering their virtue than for recovering their money, if they had lost it, since virtue is more akin to friendship than money. But when they fall into the greatest malice and become incurable, then the familiarity of friendship should not be shown to them. And so sinners of this sort, whose will to harm others is presumed over their amendment, are ordered by precept (*praecipiuntur*) to be killed, according to law divine and human. But this does not cause a judge to act out of hatred for them, but rather out of the love of charity, by which the public good is preferred to the life of an individual person. And yet death inflicted by a judge brings profit to a sinner – whether he is converted, for the expiation of fault (*culpa*), or whether he is not converted, for the ending of his fault, since by this his power of sinning more widely is destroyed.

[3] To the third it should be said that curses of this sort, which are found in sacred Scripture, can be understood in three ways. In the first way, by way of prediction[48] and not by way of wish, so that the sense is "sinners might be turned (*convertantur*) to hell" – that is, "shall be turned" (*convertentur*). In

44. In Article 3 of this Question and in Question 23, Articles 1 and 5.
45. Luke 14.26.
46. Psalm 138.22.
47. Aristotle, *Nicomachean Ethics* bk.9 chap.3 (1165b13).
48. Some versions read "by way of proclamation."

the second way, by way of wish, yet so that the desire of the one who wishes is not referred to the punishment of human beings, but to the justice of the one who punishes, according to the passage: "The just man shall be glad when he has seen vindication."[49] This is because God himself, when he punishes, is glad not for the ruin of the wicked, as is said in Wisdom 1,[50] but for his justice, "since the Lord is just and has loved justice."[51] Third, so that the desire is referred to the removal of fault, and not to the punishment itself–in order for sins to be destroyed and human beings to remain.

[4] To the fourth it should be said that we love sinners out of charity–not indeed so that we should will the things that they will, or rejoice over the things that they rejoice over–but so that we may cause them to will the things that we will, and to rejoice over the things that we rejoice over. So it is said in Jeremiah 15, "They shall be turned to you, and you shall not be turned to them."[52]

[5] To the fifth it should be said that for the weak, eating and drinking with sinners should be avoided, on account of the danger that threatens the weak, lest they be overturned by sinners. Now for the perfect, of whose corruption there is no fear, it is praiseworthy to converse with sinners, so as to convert them. Thus did the Lord lead sinners by the hand and drink with them, as attested by Matthew 9.[53] But intimacy with sinners, as regards partnership in sin, should be avoided by everyone. And so it is said in 2 Corinthians 6, "Go out from their midst, and do not touch what is unclean"[54] –that is, consent to sin.

Article 7. [Whether sinners love themselves.]

One proceeds in this way to the seventh query. IT SEEMS that sinners love themselves.

[1] That which is the principle of sin is found especially in sinners. But love of self (*amor sui*) is the principle of sin, for Augustine says, *City of God* 14, that it makes citizens of Babylon.[55] Therefore sinners love themselves most of all.

---

49. Psalm 57.11.
50. Wisdom 1.13.
51. Psalm 10.8.
52. Jeremiah 15.19
53. Matthew 9.10.
54. 2 Corinthians 6.17.
55. Augustine, *De civitate Dei* bk.14 chap.28 (PL 41:436; CCSL 48:451.1–3).

[2] Furthermore, sin does not destroy nature. But it is appropriate to any-one, out of his own nature, that he should love himself, so that even irrational creatures naturally desire their own good, such as the preservation of their own being and other things of this sort. Therefore sinners love themselves.

[3] Furthermore, "the good is lovable to all," as Dionysius says in *Divine Names*, chapter 4.[56] But many sinners regard themselves as good. Therefore many sinners love themselves.

BUT TO THE CONTRARY there is what is said in the Psalm, "He who loves iniquity, hates his own soul."[57]

I ANSWER THAT IT SHOULD BE SAID that to love oneself is in one way common to all; in another way, it is proper to good men; in a third way, it is proper to evil men. That someone should love that which he deems (*aestimat*) himself to be–this is common to all. Now man is said to be something in two ways. In one way, according to his substance and nature. According to this, all men deem the common good itself to be what they are–namely, composed of soul and body. And in this way all men, good and evil, love themselves, insofar as they love their own preservation. In the second way, a man is said to be something according to a preeminence, as the sovereign of a city is said to be the city. So that what sovereigns do is said to be what the city does. Now in this way not all men deem them-selves to be that which they are. For the primary thing in man is rational mind (*mens rationalis*), whereas sensitive and bodily nature is secondary. The Apostle names the first of these the "inner man," the second the "outer man," as is clear from 2 Corinthians 4.[58] Now good men esteem (*aestimant*) principally in themselves rational nature–that is, the inner man–so that according to this, they deem themselves to be what they are. But evil men esteem principally in themselves sensitive and bodily nature, namely the outer man. So that not rightly knowing themselves, they do not truly love themselves, but rather love that which they deem themselves to be. But good men, truly knowing themselves, truly love themselves.

And the Philosopher proves this in *Ethics* 9, by five things that are proper to friendship.[59] For any friend (1) wishes for his friend to exist and to live; (2) wishes good things for him; (3) does good things to him; (4) eats and

56. Ps-Dionysius, *Divine Names* chap.4 sect.10 (PG 3:708A; Chevallier 1:199).
57. Psalm 10.6.
58. 2 Corinthians 4.16.
59. Aristotle, *Nicomachean Ethics* bk.9 chap.4 (1166a3).

drinks pleasurably with him; and (5) harmonizes with him, as feeling pleasure and sorrow in virtually the same things. Accordingly, good men love themselves with respect to the inner man, since they wish him to be preserved in his wholeness; and they wish good things for him, which are spiritual goods; and they give themselves over to pursuing works; and they return pleasurably to their own heart, since they find in that place good thoughts in the present, and the memory of good things in the past, and hope for good things in the future—from all these things, pleasure is caused. Likewise they do not suffer dissension of the will in themselves, since their whole soul tends toward one thing. And conversely, evil men do not will that the wholeness of the inner man be preserved; nor do they desire his spiritual goods; nor do they work toward this; nor is it pleasurable for them to associate with themselves by returning to their heart, since they find in that place evil things in the present, past, and future, from which they shrink. Nor do they harmonize with themselves, on account of a gnawing conscience, according to the Psalm: "I will reprove you and set you against your face."[60] And by the same reason, it can be proved that evil men love themselves according to the corruption of the outer man. Whereas good men do not love themselves in this way.

[1] TO THE FIRST ARGUMENT, THEREFORE, IT SHOULD BE SAID that the love of self which is the principle of sin is that which is proper to evil men, reaching up to contempt of God, as is said in the passage from Augustine, since in this way evil men desire exterior goods and scorn spiritual goods.

[2] To the second it should be said that natural love, even if it should not be entirely destroyed by evil men, is nonetheless perverted in them, in the way already mentioned.[61]

[3] To the third it should be said that evil men, insofar as they deem themselves good, thus participate to some extent in love of themselves. Yet this is not true love of self, but apparent. Even this [apparent self-love] is not possible in those who are very evil.

Article 8. [Whether it is necessary for charity that enemies are loved.]

One proceeds in this way to the eighth query. IT SEEMS that it is not necessary for charity that enemies are loved.

60. Psalm 49.21.
61. In the body of this Article.

[1] Augustine says in the *Enchiridion* that so great a good, namely to love one's enemies, "is not possible for so great a multitude as we believe are heard when in prayer it is said, 'Forgive us our trespasses.'"[62] But no one is forgiven from sin without charity, since as is said in Proverbs 10, "Charity covers all sins."[63] Therefore it is not necessary for charity to love our enemies.

[2] Furthermore, charity does not destroy nature. But any thing whatever, even an irrational thing, naturally hates its contrary, as a sheep hates a wolf, and water hates fire. Therefore charity does not cause our enemies to be loved.

[3] Furthermore, "charity deals not perversely."[64] But it seems to be perverse that someone should love his enemies, just as that someone should hate his friends. So that Joab says to David in 2 Samuel, reproaching him: "You love those who hate you, and you hate those who love you."[65] Therefore charity does not bring it about that our enemies are loved.

BUT TO THE CONTRARY the Lord says, Matthew 5, "Love your enemies."[66]

I ANSWER THAT IT SHOULD BE SAID that love of enemies can be considered in three ways. In the first way, as enemies are loved so far as they are enemies. And this is perverse and repugnant to charity, since this is to love the evil of another. In a second way, love of enemies can be taken with respect to nature, but in a universal sense. And thus love of enemies is necessary for charity, as someone who by loving God and his neighbor does not exclude his enemies from the generality of love that he has for his neighbor. In a third way, love of enemies can be considered in a special sense, namely as someone is moved in a special way by the motion of love toward an enemy. And that is not absolutely necessary for charity, since it would then be necessary for charity to be moved by the motion of love in a special sense toward all men in particular–but this would be impossible. Nevertheless, it is necessary for charity according to the soul's preparation, that a person should have a soul ready for this–that he should love a particular enemy, if the necessity were to occur. But that, lacking a

---

62. Augustine, *Enchiridion ad Laurentium seu de fide, spe et caritate* chap.19 sect.73 (PL 40:266; CCSL 46:89.52–55).
63. Proverbs 10.12.
64. 1 Corinthians 13.4.
65. 2 Samuel 19.6. (Following the Vulgate, the Latin text refers to 2 Kings 19.)
66. Matthew 5.44.

crisis of necessity, a man should actually complete this preparation, so that he loves his enemy on account of God – this belongs to the completion of charity. For since a neighbor is loved out of charity on account of God, the more that a person loves God, the more he will show love to his neighbor, not being impeded by any hostility. Just as if someone were to love another person very much, he would also – owing to this love – love that person's children, even if they were hostile to him. And Augustine is speaking in this manner.

[1] The answer TO THE FIRST ARGUMENT is clear.

[2] To the second it should be said that anything whatever naturally bears hatred to what opposes it, so far as it opposes it. Now enemies are opposed to us, so far as they are enemies. So that we must hate them, since things hostile to us must be displeasing to us. But enemies are not opposed to us so far as they are human beings and capable of blessedness. And according to this, we must love them.

[3] To the third it should be said to love enemies so far as they are enemies – this is blameworthy. And this charity does not do, as was said.[67]

Article 9. [Whether it is necessary for charity that a person show the signs or effects of love to his enemy.]

One proceeds in this way to the ninth query. IT SEEMS necessary for charity that a person show the signs or effects of love to his enemy.

[1] It says in 1 John 3, "Let us love not in word or tongue, but in works and in truth."[68] But in works, someone loves a person by exhibiting to that person the signs and effects of love. Therefore, it is necessary for charity that a person show his enemies signs and effects of this sort.

[2] Furthermore, in Matthew 5 the Lord says at the same time, "Love your enemies and do good to those who hate you."[69] But to love our enemies is necessary for charity. Therefore it is also necessary to do good to our enemies.

[3] Furthermore, by charity not only God but also our neighbor is loved. But Gregory says in a homily on Pentecost that "the love of God cannot be idle, for it works great things, if it exists; if it ceases to work, it is not

67. In the body of this Article.
68. 1 John 3.18.
69. Matthew 5.44.

love."[70] Therefore the charity that is had toward the neighbor cannot exist without the effect of a work. But it is necessary for charity that every neighbor is loved, even the enemy. Therefore it is necessary for charity that we extend the signs and effects of love even to our enemies.

BUT TO THE CONTRARY there is Matthew 5, "Do good to those who hate you,"[71] on which the Gloss says: "To do good to enemies is the pinnacle of perfection."[72] But that which belongs to the completion of charity is not necessary for it. Therefore it is not necessary for charity that someone show the signs and effects of love to enemies.

I ANSWER THAT IT SHOULD BE SAID that effects and signs of charity proceed from inward love and are proportioned to it. Now inward love toward one's enemy in general necessarily belongs to the precept, in an absolute manner. In a specific case, however, it belongs not absolutely, but according to the soul's preparation, as was said above.[73] In this way, therefore, we should speak about showing an effect or sign[74] of outward love. For there are certain benefits or signs of love that are shown toward neighbors in general, as when someone prays for all the faithful or for the entire people, or when someone devotes himself to the whole community's benefit. To show these benefits or signs of love to enemies necessarily belongs to the precept, for if they were not shown to enemies, the motive would belong to the spite of revenge, against which it is said in Leviticus 19, "Do not seek revenge, and do not be mindful of the injury of your fellow citizens."[75] There are, however, other benefits or signs of love that one shows in a particular manner to certain persons. To show these benefits or signs of love to enemies does not belong to what is necessary for salvation, except according to the soul's preparation, for example, as when to help them in a crisis of necessity, according to Proverbs 25: "If your enemy is hungry, give him something to eat; if he is thirsty, give him

70. Gregory the Great, *Homiliae in Evangelia* bk.2 hom.30 sect.2, on John 14.23–31 (PL 76:1221; CCSL 141.257.43–45).

71. Matthew 5.44.

72. *Glossa ordinaria* on Matthew 5.44 (Strasbourg 5, "Perfecti," col.b), paraphrased. On the composition of the *Glossa,* see Margaret T. Gibson, "The Place of the *Glossa ordinaria* in Medieval Exegesis," in *"Ad litteram": Authoritative Texts and Their Medieval Readers,* ed. Mark D. Jordan and Kent Emery, Jr. (Notre Dame: University of Notre Dame Press, 1992), 5–27.

73. In Article 8 of this Question.

74. Some versions read "effect and sign."

75. Leviticus 19.18.

something to drink."[76] But benefits of this sort, which a person shows to enemies on account of a crisis of necessity, belong to the completion of charity. Through this completion a person not only takes precautions against being overcome by evil, out of necessity, but also wills to overcome evil in good, which also belongs to completion. For then a person not only takes precautions against being drawn into hatred on account of the injury done to him, but also intends, on account of the benefits he shows his enemy, to draw the enemy into his love.

[1]–[3] And from this the answer TO WHAT WAS OBJECTED is clear.

Article 10. [Whether we should love the angels out of charity.]

One proceeds in this way to the tenth query. IT SEEMS that we should not love the angels out of charity.

[1] As Augustine says in his book *On Christian Doctrine,* "The love of charity is a pair – namely, love of God and love of neighbor."[77] But love of angels is not contained under the love of God, since this love is of a created substance. Nor does it seem contained under the love of neighbor, since it would not share the same species as us. Therefore angels should not be loved out of charity.

[2] Furthermore, brute animals are more like us than angels are, for we and brute animals are in the same neighboring genus. But we do not have charity toward brute animals, as was said above.[78] Therefore nor do we have it toward angels.

[3] Furthermore, "Nothing is so proper to friends as to eat and drink together," as is said in *Ethics* 8.[79] But angels do not eat and drink with us, and we cannot even see them. Therefore we are unable to bear them the friendship of charity.

BUT TO THE CONTRARY Augustine says in *On Christian Doctrine,* Book 1: "Now either the person to whom one should render the kindness of mercy, or the person who renders the kindness of mercy to us, is rightly

76. Proverbs 25.21.
77. Augustine, *De doctrina christiana* bk.1 chap.26 sect.27 (PL 34:29; CCSL 32:21.10–11).
78. In Article 3 of this Question.
79. Aristotle, *Nicomachean Ethics* bk.8 chap.5 (1157b19).

called 'neighbor.' It is clear that in the precept by which we are ordered to love our neighbor are also included the holy angels, from whom we receive so many kindnesses of mercy."[80]

I ANSWER THAT IT SHOULD BE SAID that the friendship of charity, as was said above,[81] is founded upon a sharing of eternal blessedness, in whose participation men share with angels, for Matthew 22 says that "in the resurrection men will be like angels in heaven."[82] And so it is clear that the friendship of charity also extends to angels.

[1] TO THE FIRST ARGUMENT, THEREFORE, IT SHOULD BE SAID that the neighbor is called "neighbor" not only by a sharing of species, but also by a sharing of benefits that belong to eternal life. Upon this sharing the friendship of charity is founded.

[2] To the second it should be said that brute animals are like us in a neighboring genus by reason of their sensitive nature. We are not participants in eternal blessedness according to this, but according to rational mind, in which we share with angels.

[3] To the third it should be said that angels do not eat and drink with us by outward converse, which for us is according to sensitive nature. Yet we do eat and drink with angels according to mind – to be sure, incompletely in this life, but completely in the homeland, as was said above.[83]

Article 11. [Whether we should love the demons out of charity.]

One proceeds in this way to the eleventh query. IT SEEMS that we should love the demons out of charity.

[1] The angels are neighbors to us, so far as we share with them in rational mind. But demons also share with us in rational mind, since naturally bestowed gifts remain in them whole, namely being, living, and understanding, as is said in *Divine Names,* chapter 4.[84] Therefore we ought to love the demons out of charity.

---

80. Augustine, *De doctrina christiana* bk.1 chap.30 sect.33 (PL 34:31; CCSL 32:25.40–44).

81. In Articles 3 and 6 of this Question, and Question 23, Articles 1 and 5.

82. Matthew 22.30, condensed.

83. In Question 23, Article 1, Reply [1].

84. Ps-Dionysius, *Divine Names* chap.4 sect.23 (PG 3:725B; Chevallier 1:278).

[2] Furthermore, demons differ from the blessed angels by the distinguishing characteristic of sin, as human sinners differ from the just. But just men love sinners out of charity. Therefore they also ought to love demons out of charity.

[3] Furthermore, we should love out of charity, as our neighbor, those who confer benefits on us, as is clear from the authority of Augustine cited above.[85] But demons are useful to us in many things, for "in tempting us they fashion crowns for us," as Augustine says in *City of God*, Book 11.[86] Therefore demons should be loved out of charity.

BUT TO THE CONTRARY there is what is said in Isaiah 28, "Your covenant with death will be wiped out, and your pact with hell shall not stand."[87] But the completion of peace and covenant is by charity. Therefore we ought not to have charity toward demons, who are the inhabitants of hell and the bringers of death.

I ANSWER THAT IT SHOULD BE SAID that, as said above,[88] we ought to love out of charity what is natural in sinners, but hate their sin. Now the name "demon" signifies nature deformed by sin. And so demons should not be loved out of charity. If the point does not appear strongly enough in the name "demon," the question may be referred to the spirits who are called demons. The question "whether they should be loved out of charity" should be answered according to what has been established – that something is loved out of charity in two ways.[89] In one way, as there is friendship with it. We cannot thus have the friendship of charity with those spirits. For it belongs to the notion of friendship that we wish good to our friend. As for the good of eternal life that charity looks to, we cannot wish it for those spirits who are eternally damned by God, for this is repugnant to the charity of God, through which we confirm his justice. In another way, something is loved in that we wish it to endure as another's good. Thus do we love irrational creatures out of charity, so far as we wish that they endure for the glory of God and the advantage of men, as was said above.[90] In this manner, we can love out of charity even the nature of de-

85. In Article 10, *sed contra*.

86. Rather, Bernard of Clairvaux, *Sermones in Cantica Canticorum*, serm.17 (PL 183:858).

87. Isaiah 28.18.

88. In Article 6 of this Question.

89. See Articles 2 and 3 of this Question.

90. In Article 3 of this Question.

mons, so far as we wish that these spirits in their own natural powers are preserved for the glory of God.

[1] TO THE FIRST ARGUMENT, THEREFORE, IT SHOULD BE SAID that for the mind of angels, possessing eternal blessedness is not an impossibility, as it is for the mind of demons. And so the friendship of charity, which is founded upon a sharing of eternal life rather than upon a sharing of nature, is possessed by angels, but not by demons.

[2] To the second it should be said that in this life, human sinners have the possibility of arriving at eternal blessedness. This is not had by those who are damned to hell. Regarding those to whom this applies, the same account holds for them as for the demons.

[3] To the third it should be said that the advantage which comes to us from demons is not from their own intention, but from the ordering of divine providence. And so from this, we cannot be led toward having their friendship. But we can be led to this—that we are friends with God, who turns their perverse intention to our advantage.

Article 12. [Whether the four things that should be loved out of charity are inappropriately enumerated.]

One proceeds in this way to the twelfth query. IT SEEMS that the four things that should be loved out of charity are inappropriately enumerated, namely God, neighbor, our body, and ourselves.

[1] Augustine says, in his commentary on John: "He who does not love God, does not love himself."[91] Therefore love of self is included in the love of God. So it is not that love of self is one thing, and love of God another.

[2] Furthermore, a part ought not to be divided against the whole. But our body is a certain part of ourselves. Therefore our body ought not to be divided from ourselves, as though it were another lovable thing.

[3] Furthermore, just as we have a body, so does our neighbor. Therefore the love by which someone loves his neighbor, is distinguished from the love by which someone loves himself. And so the love by which someone loves his neighbor's body ought to be distinguished from the love by which someone loves his own body. Therefore, four things that should be loved out of charity are not appropriately distinguished.

91. Augustine, *In Ioannis Evangelium tractatus* tr.83 sect.3, on John 15.12 (PL 35:1846; CCSL 36:536.19–21), condensed.

BUT TO THE CONTRARY Augustine says in *On Christian Doctrine,* Book 1: "Four things should be loved. The first is what is above us," namely God. "The second is what we ourselves are; the third is what is close to us," namely our neighbor. "The fourth is what is below us," namely our own body.[92]

I ANSWER THAT IT SHOULD BE SAID that, as was said, the friendship of charity is founded upon a sharing of blessedness.[93] In this sharing, indeed, the first thing is what is considered as a source (*principium*) diffusing blessedness, namely God. The second is what directly participates in blessedness, namely man and angels. The third is that to which blessedness is given by a certain overflow, namely the human body. That which diffuses blessedness is for that very reason lovable, since it is the cause of blessedness. That which participates in blessedness, however, can be lovable for a twofold reason – either because it is one with us, or because it is associated with us in the participation in blessedness. And according to this [twofold reason], two things are taken as lovable out of charity – namely, so far as a person loves both himself and his neighbor.

[1] TO THE FIRST ARGUMENT, THEREFORE, IT SHOULD BE SAID that a different relation of the lover to different lovable things produces a different aspect of lovability. Accordingly, since the person who loves bears a different relation to God than he does to himself, two lovable things may therefore be set down, since love of the one is the cause of love of the other. So that if one is taken away, the other is also taken away.

[2] To the second it should be said that the subject of charity is the rational mind that can be capable of blessedness, to which the body does not attain directly, but only by a certain overflow. And so according to the rational mind, which is principal in man, a person loves himself according to charity in one way, and his own body in another way.

[3] To the third it should be said that man loves his neighbor both according to soul and according to body by reason of a certain association in blessedness. And so on the part of our neighbor, there is only one reason for love. So that our neighbor's body is not set down as a special lovable thing.

92. Augustine, *De doctrina christiana* bk.1 chap.23 sect.22 (PL 34:27; CCSL 32:18.6–9).

93. See Articles 3, 6, and 10 of this Question, and Question 23, Articles 1 and 5.

QUESTION 26

[The Order of Charity]

One should next consider the order of charity. Regarding this, thirteen queries are raised. (1) Whether there is an order in charity. (2) Whether a person should love God more than his neighbor. (3) Whether more than himself. (4) Whether himself more than his neighbor. (5) Whether a person should love his neighbor more than his own body. (6) Whether one neighbor more than another. (7) Whether a better neighbor more than one connected to himself. (8) Whether one connected to him by a relation of blood more than one connected by other bonds. (9) Whether out of charity a person should love his child more than his father. (10) Whether he should love his mother more than his father. (11) Whether a man should love his wife more than his father or mother. (12) Whether a person should love his benefactor more than his beneficiary. (13) Whether the order of charity remains in the homeland.

Article 1. [Whether there is an order in charity.]

One proceeds in this way to the first query. IT SEEMS that there is not an order in charity.

[1] Charity is a certain virtue. But no order is assigned in the other virtues. Therefore neither in charity should any order be assigned.

[2] Furthermore, just as the object of faith is the first truth, so the object of charity is the highest goodness. But no order is set down in faith; everything is believed equally. Therefore neither in charity should any order be set down.

[3] Furthermore, charity is in the will. Now ordering is not of the will, but of reason. Therefore order ought not to be attributed to charity.

BUT TO THE CONTRARY there is what is said in Songs of Songs 2: "The king brought me into the wine cellar; he has ordered charity in me."[1]

---

1. Song of Songs 2.4.

I ANSWER THAT IT SHOULD BE SAID that as the Philosopher says in *Metaphysics* 5, prior and posterior are said according to a relation to a first (*principium*).[2] Now order includes in itself some measure of what is prior and posterior. So it must be that wherever there is a first, there is also an order. Now it was said above[3] that the love of charity tends toward God as toward the origin (*principium*) of blessedness, in whose sharing the friendship of charity is founded. And so it must be that in the things that are loved out of charity, some order is observed, according to the relation of this love to the first principle, which is God.

[1] TO THE FIRST ARGUMENT, THEREFORE, IT SHOULD BE SAID that charity tends toward the ultimate end under the aspect of the ultimate end, which is not appropriate to any of the other virtues, as was said.[4] Now the end has the aspect of a principle in desirable things and in things to be done, as is clear from what was said above.[5] And so charity especially denotes a relation to the first principle. And so in charity especially an order is considered, according to a relation to the first principle.

[2] To the second it should be said that faith belongs to the knowing power, whose operation proceeds according to the way known things are in the knower. Now charity is in the affective power, whose operation consists in the fact that the soul tends toward things themselves. Now order is found more principally in things themselves, and from these things order is given to our knowing. And so an order is more appropriate in charity than in faith. — One may allow that there is an order in faith, according as it primarily concerns God and secondarily concerns other things that are referred to God.

[3] To the third it should be said that order belongs to reason as to what does the ordering, but it belongs to the appetitive power as to what is ordered. In this way an order in charity is set down.

Article 2. [Whether God should be loved more than one's neighbor.]

One proceeds in this way to the second query. IT SEEMS that God should not be loved more than one's neighbor.

---

2. Aristotle, *Metaphysics* bk.5 chap.11 (1018b9).
3. In Question 23, Article 1, and in Question 25, Article 2.
4. In Question 23, Article 6.
5. In Question 23, Article 7.

[1] In 1 John 4, it says "He who does not love his brother whom he sees—how can he love God, whom he cannot see?"[6] From this, it seems that what is more lovable is what is more visible, for vision is the principle of love, as is said in *Ethics* 9.[7] But God is less visible than the neighbor. Therefore he is less lovable out of charity.

[2] Furthermore, likeness is the cause of love, according to Sirach 13: "Every animal loves its like."[8] But the likeness of man to his neighbor is greater than his likeness to God. Therefore man loves his neighbor out of charity more than God.

[3] Furthermore, that which charity loves in the neighbor is God, as is clear from Augustine in *On Christian Doctrine*, Book 1.[9] But God is not greater in oneself than he is in one's neighbor. Therefore he should not be loved more in oneself than in one's neighbor. Therefore God ought not to be loved more than one's neighbor.

BUT TO THE CONTRARY a thing should be loved more, if other things must on its account be hated. But neighbors should be hated on account of God if they lead one away from God, according to Luke 14: "If someone comes to me and does not hate his father and mother and wife and brothers and sisters, he cannot be my disciple."[10] Therefore God should be loved out of charity more than one's neighbor.

I ANSWER THAT IT SHOULD BE SAID that any friendship looks principally to that in which is principally found the good upon whose sharing the friendship is founded. As political friendship more principally looks to the city's sovereign, on whom the city's entire common good depends, so that to him most of all is owed faith and obedience by the citizens. Now the friendship of charity is founded upon the sharing of blessedness, which consists essentially in God as in the first principle, from whom it flows to all who are capable of blessedness. And so God should principally and most of all be loved out of charity, for God is loved as the cause of blessedness, whereas our neighbor is loved as participating with us at the same time in blessedness.

6. 1 John 4.20.
7. Aristotle, *Nicomachean Ethics* bk.9 chap.5 (1167a4) and bk.9 chap.12 (1171b29).
8. Sirach 13.19.
9. Augustine, *De doctrina christiana* bk.1 chap.22 sect.21 (PL 34:27; CCSL 32: 18.38–42) and bk.1 chap.27 sect.28 (PL 34:29; CCSL 32:22.11–13).
10. Luke 14.26.

[1] TO THE FIRST ARGUMENT, THEREFORE, IT SHOULD BE SAID that any cause of love is twofold. In one way, as the reason for loving. In this way, good is the cause of loving, since anything whatever is loved so far as it has the aspect of good. In another way, since it is a certain road (*via*) to the acquisition of love. In this way, vision is the cause of love – not for the reason that if something is visible, it is lovable, but rather because we are led by vision to love. It is not that something which is more visible is more lovable, but rather that the visible is what first occurs to us to love. The Apostle argues in this way. For the neighbor, who is more visible to us, occurs to us to be loved first, "for from the things that it knows, the mind learns to love unknown things," as Gregory says in a homily.[11] So if someone does not love his neighbor, it can be argued that he does not love God, not because his neighbor is more lovable, but because it occurs to him first to love his neighbor. God, however, is more lovable on account of his greater goodness.

[2] To the second it should be said that the likeness that we have to God is prior to and the cause of the likeness that we have to our neighbor. For we are brought to resemble our neighbor by actively receiving from God (*participamus a Deo*) the same thing that our neighbor also has from him. And so by reason of likeness, we ought to love God more than our neighbor.

[3] To the third it should be said that God, considered according to his substance, is equal in whatever he might be, since he is not diminished by this – that he is in something. But our neighbor does not have God's goodness in the same way (*aequaliter*) as God has it, for God has goodness essentially (*essentialiter*), whereas our neighbor has it by participation (*participative*).

Article 3. [Whether a person should out of charity love God more than himself.]

One proceeds in this way to the third query. IT SEEMS that a person should not out of charity love God more than himself.

[1] The Philosopher says in *Ethics* 9 that "friendly sentiments for another arise from friendly sentiments for oneself."[12] But the cause is superior to the effect. Therefore the friendship of a person with himself is greater

11. Gregory the Great, *Homiliae in Evangelia* bk.1 hom.11 sect.1, on Matthew 13.44–52 (PL 76:1114–15; CCSL 141:74.1–5).

12. Aristotle, *Nicomachean Ethics* bk.9 chap.4 (1166a1).

than his friendship for anyone else. Therefore he should love himself more than God.

[2] Furthermore, anything is loved so far as it is one's own good. But that which is the reason for loving (*ratio diligendi*) is loved more than that which is loved on account of this reason—just as principles, which are the reason for knowing, are more known. Therefore a person loves himself more than any other loved good. Therefore he does not love God more than himself.

[3] Furthermore, a person loves God as much as he loves to enjoy him. But a person loves to enjoy God as much as he loves himself, since this is the highest good that someone can wish for himself. Therefore a human being should not, out of charity, love God more than himself.

BUT TO THE CONTRARY Augustine says in *On Christian Doctrine,* Book 1: "If you should love yourself not on account of yourself, but on account of him where the most correct end of your love is, do not let some other man take offense if you love him on account of God."[13] But that on account of which anything is, is greater. Therefore a man should love God more than himself.

I ANSWER THAT IT SHOULD BE SAID that from God we can receive a twofold good—namely, the good of nature and the good of grace. Upon the sharing of natural goods made for us by God is founded natural love, by which not only man in the wholeness (*integritas*) of his nature loves God above all things and more than himself, but also any creature in its own way, whether by intellectual love or rational love or animal love or at least natural love, as do stones and other things that lack knowledge, because any part naturally loves the common good of the whole more than its own particular good. Which is manifested by its work, for any part has a principal inclination to common action for the advantage of the whole. This also appears in political virtues, according to which citizens sometimes sustain losses to their property and persons for the common good. Much more is this verified in the friendship of charity, which is founded on a sharing of the gifts of grace. And so out of charity a man should love God, who is the common good of everything, more than himself, since blessedness is in God as in the common and original principle of everything that is able to participate in blessedness.

13. Augustine, *De doctrina christiana* bk.1 chap.22 sect.21 (PL 34:27; CCSL 32:17.26–28).

[1] TO THE FIRST ARGUMENT, THEREFORE, IT SHOULD BE SAID that the Philosopher is speaking of friendly sentiments for another in whom the good that is the object of friendship is found according to some particular manner, and not of friendly sentiments for another in which the good spoken of is found according to the aspect of the whole.

[2] To the second it should be said that a part does indeed love the good of the whole, according as it is appropriate to it – not so that it refers the good of the whole to itself, but rather so that it refers itself to the good of the whole.

[3] To the third it should be said that the fact that someone wishes to enjoy God belongs to the love by which God is loved with the love of concupiscence. But we love God with the love of friendship more than we love him with the love of concupiscence, since the good of God in itself is greater than we are able to participate in enjoying him. And so a person simply (*simpliciter*) loves God out of charity more than himself.

Article 4. [Whether a person should out of charity love himself more than his neighbor.]

One proceeds in this way to the fourth query. IT SEEMS that a man should not out of charity love himself more than his neighbor.

[1] The principal object of charity is God, as was said above.[14] But sometimes a man has a neighbor who is more closely connected to God than he himself is. Therefore he should love such a neighbor more than himself.

[2] Furthermore, the more we love a person, the more we avoid any harm to him. But a person sustains harm on behalf of his neighbor out of charity, according to Proverbs 12: "He who ignores a loss on account of his friend is just."[15] Therefore a person should, out of charity, love another more than himself.

[3] Furthermore, it is said in 1 Corinthians 13 that "charity does not seek things of its own."[16] But we especially love a thing whose good we especially seek. Therefore someone does not by charity love himself more than his neighbor.

---

14. In Article 2 of this Question and in Question 25, Articles 1 and 12.
15. Proverbs 12.26.
16. 1 Corinthians 13.5.

BUT TO THE CONTRARY there is what is said in Leviticus 19 and Matthew 22, "You shall love your neighbor as yourself,"[17] from which it seems that a person's love for himself stands as an exemplar of the love that is to be had for another. But the exemplar is superior to what is exemplified. Therefore a person should, out of charity, love himself more than his neighbor.

I ANSWER THAT IT SHOULD BE SAID that in a person are two things, namely spiritual nature and bodily nature. Through this a person is said to love himself, because he loves himself according to his spiritual nature, as was said above.[18] And according to this a person should love himself more, after God, than any other person. And this is clear from the very reason for loving. As was said above,[19] God is loved as the origin (*principium*) of good, upon which is founded the love of charity – whereas a person loves himself out of charity according to the reason by which he is a participator in the good spoken of, and the neighbor is loved according to the reason of his fellowship (*societas*) in that good.[20]

Now association is the reason of love according to a certain union, as ordered to God. Just as unity is superior to union, so the fact that a man himself participates in the divine good is a better reason for loving than the fact that he is associated with another in this participation. And so a person should, out of charity, love himself more than his neighbor. A sign of this is that a person should not lower himself to some evil that belongs to sin – which is opposed to his participation in blessedness – so that he may free his neighbor from sin.

[1] TO THE FIRST ARGUMENT, THEREFORE, IT SHOULD BE SAID that the love of charity has quantity not only on the part of its object, which is God, but also on the part of the one who loves – the person himself who has charity, just as the quantity of any particular action depends in a certain way on the subject himself. And so, though a better neighbor might be nearer to God, yet since he is not as near to the person who has charity as he is to himself, it does not follow that someone should love his neighbor more than himself.

17. Leviticus 19.18; Matthew 22.39.
18. In Question 25, Article 7.
19. In Question 25, Articles 1 and 12.
20. Some versions read "in the good itself."

[2] To the second it should be said that a person ought to sustain bodily harms on account of his friend. In this very act he loves himself more according to spiritual mind, since this belongs to the completion of virtue, which is the good of mind. But in spiritual things a person should not suffer harm by sinning, so that he might free his neighbor from sin, as was said.[21]

[3] To the third it should be said that, as Augustine says in his Rule, "the saying that 'Charity does not seek things of its own,' is understood in this way: things in common are set before those of one's own."[22] But the common good is always more lovable for anyone than his own good, just as even for a part itself, the good of the whole is more lovable than its own partial good, as was said.[23]

Article 5. [Whether a person should love his neighbor more than his own body.]

One proceeds in this way to the fifth query. IT SEEMS that a person should not love his neighbor more than his own body.

[1] Our neighbor's body is understood to be in the neighbor. If a person should love his neighbor more than his own body, it follows that he should love his neighbor's body more than he loves his own body.

[2] Furthermore, a person should love his own soul more than his neighbor,[24] as was said.[25] But our own body is closer to our soul than the neighbor is. Therefore we should love our own body more than our neighbor.

[3] Furthermore, any person abandons that which he loves less for that which he loves more. But not every person is bound to abandon his own body for the well-being of his neighbor, since this belongs to the perfect, according to John 15: "Greater charity has no man than this, that a man lay down his life for his friends."[26] Therefore a person is not bound out of charity to love his neighbor more than his own body.

---

21. In the body of this Article.

22. Augustine, *Epistulae* ep.211 chap.12 (PL 33:963; CSEL 57:366.16–19; Lawless 115, chap.5 sect.2). The "Rule" of which Thomas speaks derives principally from a letter of Augustine addressed to a community of nuns at the monastery in Hippo. See Lawless.

23. In Article 3 of this Question.

24. Some versions read "more than the soul of his neighbor."

25. In Article 4 of this Question.

26. John 15.13.

BUT TO THE CONTRARY Augustine says in *On Christian Doctrine,* Book 1, that "we should love our neighbor more than our own body."[27]

I ANSWER THAT IT SHOULD BE SAID that what should be loved more out of charity is what has a fuller aspect of the lovable out of charity, as was said.[28] Now association in the full participation of blessedness, which is the reason for loving the neighbor, is a greater reason for loving than participation in blessedness by an overflow, which is the reason for loving one's own body. And so we should love the neighbor, as regards the well-being of the soul, more than we should love our own body.

[1] TO THE FIRST ARGUMENT, THEREFORE, IT SHOULD BE SAID that according to the Philosopher in *Ethics* 9, "Anything seems to be that which is primary in it."[29] When it is said that one's neighbor should be loved more than one's own body, this may be understood with respect to the soul, which is one's better part.

[2] To the second it should be said that regarding the constitution of our own nature, our body is nearer to our soul than our neighbor is. But regarding participation in blessedness, the association of our neighbor's soul with our soul is greater than [the association of] even our own body.

[3] To the third it should be said that any person has the care of his own body, whereas not every person has the care of the well-being of his neighbor, except perhaps in a special case. And so it is not out of the necessity of charity that a person should abandon his own body for the well-being of his neighbor, except in the special case where he is bound to provide for his well-being. But that someone should offer himself to do this freely belongs to the completion of charity.

Article 6. [Whether one neighbor should be loved more than another.]

One proceeds in this way to the sixth query. IT SEEMS that one neighbor should not be loved more than another.

---

27. Augustine, *De doctrina christiana* bk.1 chap.27 sect.28 (PL 34:29; CCSL 32:22.11–12).

28. In Articles 2 and 4 of this Question.

29. Aristotle, *Nicomachean Ethics* bk.9 chap.8 (1169a2).

[1] Augustine says in *On Christian Doctrine,* Book 1: "All men should be loved equally. But since you cannot benefit everyone, you should especially consider those who by place or time, or by chance of other things like this, are joined more tightly to you by fate as it were."[30] Therefore one of your neighbors should not be loved more than another.

[2] Furthermore, where the reason for loving various people is one and the same, there should not be unequal love. But the reason for loving all of our neighbors is one, namely God, as is clear from Augustine in *On Christian Doctrine,* Book 1.[31] Therefore we should love all our neighbors equally.

[3] Furthermore, "to love is to wish someone a good," as is clear from the Philosopher in *Rhetoric* 2.[32] But we wish all our neighbors an equal good, namely eternal life. Therefore we should love all our neighbors equally.

BUT TO THE CONTRARY the more that a particular person should be loved, the more gravely he who works against this love sins. But he who acts against the love of some of his neighbors sins more gravely than he who acts against the love of other neighbors, so that Leviticus 20 teaches that "he who has cursed his mother or father, let him die,"[33] which is not taught about those who curse other men. Therefore we should love certain of our neighbors more than others.

I ANSWER THAT IT SHOULD BE SAID that about this matter, there was a twofold opinion. Certain people have said that all neighbors should be loved equally out of charity as regards affection, but not as regards the outward effect. These suppose that the order of love should be understood according to outward benefits, which we should give to our neighbors rather than to others – not, however, according to inward affection, which we should give equally to all, even our enemies. But this is said irrationally. For the affection of charity, which is the inclination of grace, is not less ordered than the natural appetite, which is the inclination of nature – for each inclination proceeds from the divine wisdom. Now we see in natural things that the inclination of nature is proportioned to the act or motion that is appropriate to the nature of each thing, just as earth has a greater

30. Augustine, *De doctrina christiana* bk.1 chap.28 sect.29 (PL 34:30; CCSL 32:22.1–4).

31. Augustine, *De doctrina christiana* bk.1 chap.22 sect.21 (PL 34:27; CCSL 32:18.38–42) and bk.1 chap.27 sect.28 (PL 34:29; CCSL 32:22.11–13).

32. Aristotle, *Rhetoric* bk.2 chap.4 (1380b35, 1381a19).

33. Leviticus 20.9.

inclination of heaviness than water, since it belongs to it to be under water. Therefore it is necessary that even the inclination of grace, which is the affection of charity, should be proportioned to those things that are to be done outwardly, so that we may bear the affection of charity more intensively toward those to whom it is appropriate for us to be more generous. And so it should be said that even according to affection it is right to love one of our neighbors more than another. The reason is that since the principle of love is God and the person who loves, it is necessary that according to the greater nearness of one or another of the principles, the affection of love is greater. For as was said above,[34] in all things in which some principle is found, an order is observed in relation to that principle.

[1] TO THE FIRST ARGUMENT, THEREFORE, IT SHOULD BE SAID that love can be unequal in two ways. In one way, on the part of the good that we desire for a friend. And regarding this, we should love all men equally out of charity, since we desire for all the same kind of good, namely eternal life. In another way, love is called greater on account of a more intensive act of love. And thus it is not necessary to love all equally. Alternatively, it should be said that love can be borne toward some people unequally in two ways. In one way, because some are loved and others are not loved. And it is necessary to preserve this inequality in benefits, since we cannot profit everybody, but in goodwill there should be no such inequality of love. There is another inequality of love caused by the fact that some people are loved more than others. Augustine does not intend to exclude this inequality, but only the first kind, as is clear from the things he says about doing good.

[2] To the second it should be said that not all neighbors are equally related to God, but some are nearer to him, on account of their greater goodness. These should be loved more out of charity than those who are less near to him.

[3] To the third it should be said that this reason proceeds from the quantity of love on the part of the good that we desire for our friends.

Article 7. [Whether we should love our better neighbors more than our closely connected ones.]

One proceeds in this way to the seventh query. IT SEEMS that we should love our better neighbors more than our closely connected ones.

34. In Article 1 of this Question.

[1] That which seems to be more loved is that which should for no reason be hated, rather than that which for some reason should be hated – just as something is whiter if it is less mixed with black. But persons close to us should be hated for some reason, according to Luke 14, "If someone comes to me and does not hate his father and mother,"[35] etc., whereas good men should not be hated for any reason. Therefore it seems that our better neighbors should be loved more than our closely connected ones.

[2] Furthermore, according to charity a human being is most of all conformed to God. But God loves our better neighbor more.[36] So too should a human being love his better neighbor through charity more than he should love someone connected to himself.

[3] Furthermore, according to any friendship, what should be loved more is what belongs more to that upon which the friendship is founded. For by natural friendship we love more those who are connected to us according to nature, such as parents or children. But the friendship of charity is founded upon a sharing of blessedness, to which our better neighbors belong more than those who are connected to us. Therefore out of charity we should love our better neighbors more than those connected to us.

BUT TO THE CONTRARY there is what is said in 1 Timothy 5, "If someone does not have care of his own, and especially those of his house, he has denied the faith and is worse than an infidel."[37] But the inward affection of charity should answer to the outward effect. Therefore charity should be had more toward those who are near to us than toward those who are better.

I ANSWER THAT IT SHOULD BE SAID that every act should be proportioned to the object and to the agent. Now an act has its species from its object, whereas it has the manner of its intention[38] from the power of the agent – just as any motion has its species from the term to which it tends, though it has the intensity of its velocity from the disposition of the thing moved and the power of the mover. Thus does love have its species from the object, but its intensity from the lover himself.

Now the object of charitable love is God; the lover is a human being. Therefore a difference of love that proceeds according to charity, with re-

35. Luke 14.26.
36. Some versions add "more than someone close to himself."
37. 1 Timothy 5.8.
38. Some versions read "the motion of its intention."

spect to the species that should be observed in our neighbors who must be loved, proceeds according to a relation to God—so that out of charity we wish a greater good for a person who is nearer to God. Though the good that charity wills to all, namely eternal blessedness, is one in itself, it nevertheless has different steps according to different participations in blessedness. This belongs to charity—that it wills to preserve God's justice, according to which our better neighbors participate more completely in blessedness. And this belongs to the species of love—that there are different species of love according to the different goods that we desire for those whom we love. But the intensity of love is observed by a relation to the very human being who loves. Accordingly, a person loves those who are nearer to him with a more intense affection regarding that good for the sake of which he loves them,[39] than he loves his better neighbors regarding a greater good.

There is another difference that we should attend to. For some neighbors are nearer to us according to natural origin, from which we cannot depart, since according to it they are what they are. But the goodness of virtue, according to which some approach more closely to God, can approach and withdraw, be increased or diminished, as is clear from what was said above.[40] And so I can will, out of charity, that a person who is connected to me be better than another, and that he can thus advance to a greater level of blessedness.

There is another way in which, out of charity, we love those connected to us more, since we love them in multiple ways. For we have no connection with those who are not close to us, except the friendship of charity. But we have other kinds of friendship with those who are connected to us, according to the manner of their connection to us. Now the good upon which any other noble friendship is founded is directed, as to an end, to the good upon which charity is founded. Consequently, charity commands the act of any other friendship, just as an art that is about an end commands an art that is about things which are directed toward the end. And thus the very act of loving someone because he is related by blood or because he is a connection, or a fellow citizen—or because of any other lawful thing of this sort that is referable to the end of charity—can be commanded by charity. And so out of charity eliciting or commanding, we love more, in multiple ways, those who are connected to us.

[1] TO THE FIRST ARGUMENT, THEREFORE, IT SHOULD BE SAID that in our relations we are not taught to hate that they are our

---

39. Some versions read "for the sake of which he loves everyone."
40. In Question 24, Articles 4, 10, and 11.

relations, but only that they hinder us from God. And in this they are not our relations, but our enemies, according to Matthew 10, "A man's enemies shall be of his own house."[41]

[2] To the second it should be said that charity causes a person to be conformed to God according to a proportion, as when a person bears himself toward what is his, just as God does toward what is his. For we can will certain things out of charity, because they are appropriate to us—which, however, God does not will, because it is not appropriate to him that he will them, as was attested above, when the will's goodness was treated.[42]

[3] To the third it should be said that charity elicits not only the act of love according to the aspect of the object, but also according to the aspect of the lover, as was said.[43] From this it happens that the person more connected [to us] is more loved.

Article 8. [Whether one who is connected to us by carnal origin should be loved most of all.]

One proceeds in this way to the eighth query. IT SEEMS that one who is connected to us by carnal origin should not be loved most of all.

[1] Proverbs 18 says: "A man lovable in society will be more friendly than a brother."[44] And Valerius Maximus says that "the bond of friendship is very strong, stronger than any lower powers based on blood. It is more certain and better known that the lot of being born produces a work of chance; but the will contracts the bond of friendship by a solid judgment."[45] Therefore those who are connected by blood should not be loved more than others.

[2] Furthermore, Ambrose says in *On Duties,* Book 1: "I do not love you less, you whom I have begotten in the Gospel, than if I had received you in marriage. For nature is not more vigorous in loving than grace. Certainly we should love those who we think will be with us forever more than those of this world only."[46] Therefore blood relatives should not be loved more than those who are otherwise connected to us.

41. Matthew 10.36. See also Micah 7.6.
42. *Summa* 1a q.19 a.10.
43. In the body of this Article and in Article 4, Reply to [1].
44. Proverbs 18.24.
45. Valerius Maximus, *Factorum et dictorum memorabilium* bk.4 chap.7.
46. Ambrose, *De officiis* bk.1 chap.7 (PL 16:34; CCSL 15:9.14–18).

[3] Furthermore, "the proof of love is the showing of a work," as Gregory says in a homily.[47] Now we ought to perform works of love for certain people more than for our blood relatives, just as in the army obedience must be given more to one's leader than to one's father. Therefore blood connections should not be loved most of all.

BUT TO THE CONTRARY there is what is specially commanded in the Decalogue's precepts regarding the honor due to one's parents, as is clear from Exodus 20.[48] Therefore we should love more specially those who are connected to us by fleshly origin.

I ANSWER THAT IT SHOULD BE SAID that, as said above,[49] those who are more connected to us should be loved more out of charity, both because they are loved more intensely and also because they are loved under multiple aspects. Now the intensity (*intensio*) stems from the connection of the beloved to the lover. And so the love of different things should be measured according to different aspects of connection – namely, so that a person is loved more in that which belongs to the connection according to which he is loved.

Furthermore, the comparison of one kind of love to another should follow a comparison of one kind of connection to another kind of connection. Thus we should say that friendship of blood relations is founded on a connection of natural origin, whereas friendship of fellow citizens is founded on a sharing of civil things, and friendship of brothers-in-arms is founded on a warlike sharing. So in the things that belong to nature, we should love blood relatives more, whereas in those that belong to civil fellowship, we should love our fellow citizens more; and in military matters, we should love our brothers-in-arms more. So the Philosopher says, in *Ethics* 9, that "what is proper and fitting to particular men should be given to them. Or so people seem to act. Indeed, we invite our relatives to weddings, and it seems right to give sustenance to our parents most of all, as well as paternal honor."[50] And likewise for the other cases.

Now if we compare one kind of connection to another kind of connection, we see that the connection of natural origin is prior and less easily

47. Gregory the Great, *Homiliae in Evangelia* bk.2 hom.30 sect.1, on John 14.23–31 (PL 76:1220; CCSL 141.256.14–15).
48. Exodus 20.12.
49. In Article 7 of this Question.
50. Aristotle, *Nicomachean Ethics* bk.9 chap.2 (1165a17).

moved, since it is according to that which belongs to substance, whereas the other kinds of connection follow upon this one, and can be removed. And so the friendship of blood relatives is more stable. But other friendships can be superior, according to that which is proper to each friendship.

[1] TO THE FIRST ARGUMENT, THEREFORE, IT SHOULD BE SAID that since a friendship of companions by choice is contracted in matters that fall under our choice, as in things to be done, this love is weightier than our love for blood relatives, so that we agree more with them in things to be done. The friendship of blood relatives, however, is more stable, to the degree that it exists more naturally and so prevails in those things that regard nature. So that in the provision of necessary things, we hold fast more to them.

[2] To the second it should be said that Ambrose is speaking of love regarding benefits that belong to the sharing of grace. This concerns instruction in moral matters. Here a man should help his spiritual children more, whom he generates spiritually, than he should his bodily children, to whom he is bound to give more regarding bodily benefits.

[3] To the third it should be said that from the fact that an army leader should be obeyed more in war than one's father, it is not proved that a father is to be loved less simply, but only that he is to be loved less in a certain respect, that is, according to a love of sharing warlike things.

Article 9. [Whether out of charity a person should love his child more than his father.]

One proceeds in this way to the ninth query. IT SEEMS that out of charity a person should love his child more than his father.

[1] The person on whom we should confer more benefits, we should love more. But we should confer more benefits on our children than on our parents, for the Apostle says, 2 Corinthians 12: "Children should not lay up treasures for their parents, but parents for their children."[51] Therefore our children should be loved more than our parents.

[2] Furthermore, grace perfects nature. But parents naturally love their children more than they are loved by them, as the Philosopher says in *Ethics* 8.[52] Therefore we should love our children more than we love our parents.

---

51. 2 Corinthians 12.14.
52. Aristotle, *Nicomachean Ethics* bk.8 chap.12 (1161b21).

[3] Furthermore, by charity man's affection is conformed to God. But God loves his children more than he is loved by them. Therefore we too should love our children more than we love our parents.

BUT TO THE CONTRARY Ambrose says, "First God should be loved, second our parents, then our children, and finally domestic servants."[53]

I ANSWER THAT IT SHOULD BE SAID that, as was said above,[54] the degrees of love can be thought of from two perspectives. In one way, from that of the object. According to this perspective, what has the greater aspect of good should be loved more, because it is more like God. Thus a father should be loved more than a child, namely because we love our father under the aspect of an origin (*principium*) – an aspect of a good more eminent and more like God.

From another perspective, the degrees of love are understood on the part of the lover himself. In this way, what is loved more is what is more connected to us. Accordingly, a child should be loved more than a father, as the Philosopher says in *Ethics* 8.[55] First, because parents love their children as something of their own being, whereas a father is not of his child's being – and so the love according to which a father loves his child is more like the love by which a person loves himself. Second, because parents know some people to be their children, more than the other way around. Third, because a child is nearer to a parent, as an existing part, than the father is to his child, to whom he bears the relation of an origin (*principium*). Fourth, because parents have loved longer – for a father begins to love his child at once, whereas a child begins to love his father with the passage of time. Now the longer love lasts, the stronger it is, according to Sirach 9: "Do not abandon an old friend, for the new will not be like him."[56]

[1] TO THE FIRST ARGUMENT, THEREFORE, IT SHOULD BE SAID that to an origin (*principium*) is owed the submission of reverence and honor, whereas it belongs to an effect to receive, in due proportion, the origin's influence and provision. On account of this, honor is owed by children to parents, whereas the care of provision is owed to the children.

53. In fact, Origen, *Homiliae in Canticum canticorum* hom.2 on Song of Songs 2.4 (PG 13:54A; see also PG 13:155–59).
54. In Article 4 of this Question, Reply [1], and in Article 7 of this Question, Reply [1].
55. Aristotle, *Nicomachean Ethics* bk.8 chap.12 (1161b19).
56. Sirach 9.14.

[2] To the second it should be said that a father naturally loves his child according to the aspect of connection to himself. But according to the aspect of a more eminent good, the child naturally loves his father more.

[3] To the third it should be said that, as Augustine says in *On Christian Doctrine*, Book 1: "God loves us to our advantage and to his honor."[57] And so because a father is related to us in the manner of an origin, as is God, it belongs properly to a father that his children should give him honor. Nonetheless, in a moment of necessity a child is obliged to provide for his parents, on account of the benefits that he has received.

Article 10. [Whether a person should love his mother more than his father.]

One proceeds in this way to the tenth query. IT SEEMS that a person should love his mother more than his father.

[1] As the Philosopher says in *On Generation,* Book 1: "In generation, woman provides the body."[58] But a person does not have his soul from his father, but by creation from God, as was said in the *Prima Pars*.[59] Therefore a person has more from his mother than from his father. Therefore he should love his mother more than his father.

[2] Furthermore, a person should give more love to someone who loves more. But a mother loves a child more than a father does, for the Philosopher says in *Ethics* 9 that "mothers are greater lovers of their children. For in generation, the mother suffers more, and she knows who are her children better than the father."[60] Therefore a mother should be more loved than a father.

[3] Furthermore, a greater affection of love is owed to a person who has suffered for us more greatly, according to the last chapter of Romans: "Salute Mary, who has labored much for you."[61] Now the mother labors more in generation and education than does the father, as it says in Sirach 7: "Do

---

57. Augustine, *De doctrina christiana* bk.1 chap.32 sect.35 (PL 34:32; CCSL 32:26.2–3). Here Thomas is paraphrasing or slightly misquoting. The Augustinian text speaks of God's *bonitas,* not his *honor.*

58. Aristotle, *On the Generation of Animals* bk.1 chap.20 (729a10); bk.2 chap.4 (738b23).

59. *Summa* 1a q.90 a.2 and q.118 a.2.

60. Aristotle, *Nicomachean Ethics* bk.9 chap.7 (1168a25).

61. Romans 16.6.

not forget the groaning of your mother."[62] Therefore a person should love his mother more than his father.

BUT TO THE CONTRARY Jerome says in *On Ezekiel* that after God, the father of all, one's father should be loved – and after that he adds "the mother."[63]

I ANSWER THAT IT SHOULD BE SAID that in these comparisons, what is said should be understood *per se,* so that the question should be understood as whether a father, so far as he is a father, should be loved more than a mother, so far as she is a mother. For in all things of this sort, the distance between virtue and malice is such that friendship can be dissolved or diminished, as the Philosopher says in *Ethics* 8.[64] And so, as Ambrose says, good domestic servants should be preferred to bad sons.[65] But speaking *per se,* the father should be more loved than the mother. For father and mother are loved as a certain principle of natural origin. Now the father has a more excellent aspect than the mother, since the father is the principle in the mode of an agent, whereas the mother is a principle in the mode of a patient and matter. And so, speaking *per se,* the father should be loved more.

[1] TO THE FIRST ARGUMENT, THEREFORE, IT SHOULD BE SAID that in the generation of a man the mother gives informing matter to the body, whereas the matter is formed by the formative power that is in the seed of the father. And although a power of this kind cannot create the rational soul, it nonetheless disposes the bodily matter to receive a form of this kind.

[2] To the second it should be said that this belongs to another aspect of love; for the species of friendship by which we love a lover is one thing, and that by which we love what procreates is another. We are now speaking of the friendship that is owed to father and mother under the aspect of procreator.

[3] To the third it should be said that the reply is clear.

62. Sirach 7.29.
63. Jerome, *On Ezekiel* bk.13, on Ezekiel 44.25 (PL 25:442; CCSL 75: 667.1821–24).
64. Aristotle, *Nicomachean Ethics* bk.8 chap.7 (1158b33).
65. Rather, Origen, *Homiliae in Canticum canticorum* hom.2 on Song of Songs 2.4 (PG 13:54A).

Article 11. [Whether a man should love his wife more than his father or mother.]

One proceeds in this way to the eleventh query. IT SEEMS that a man should love his wife more than his father or mother.

[1] For no man abandons something, except for another thing that is loved more. But Genesis 2 says that on account of his wife, "a man shall leave his father and mother."[66] Therefore a man should love his wife more than his father or mother.

[2] Furthermore, the Apostle says in Ephesians 5 that "men should love their wives as themselves."[67] But a man should love himself more than his parents. Therefore he should also love his wife more than his parents.

[3] Furthermore, where there are multiple reasons for love, there should be greater love. But in friendship with one's wife there are multiple reasons for love, since the Philosopher says in *Ethics* 8 that "in this friendship there seems to be the useful, the pleasurable, and what is for the sake of virtue, if the spouses are virtuous."[68] Therefore love for one's wife should be greater than for one's parents.

BUT TO THE CONTRARY "a man should love his wife as (*sicut*) he loves his own flesh," as is said in Ephesians 5.[69] But a man should love his own body less than he loves his neighbor, as was said above.[70] Now of our neighbors, we should love our parents more. Therefore we should love our parents more than our wives.

I ANSWER THAT IT SHOULD BE SAID that, as was said,[71] the degrees of love can be observed both according to the aspect of good and according to the connection to the lover. Therefore according to the aspect of good, which is the object of delight, parents should be loved more than wives, since they are loved under the aspect of an origin (*principium*) and a certain higher good. But according to the aspect of connection, a wife should be loved more, since a wife is united to a man as existing in one flesh, according to Matthew 19: "For you are now not two, but one flesh."[72]

66. Genesis 2.24.
67. Ephesians 5.28 and 5.33.
68. Aristotle, *Nicomachean Ethics* bk.8 ch.12 (1162a24).
69. Ephesians 5.28.
70. In Article 5 of this Question.
71. In Articles 7 and 9 of this Question.
72. Matthew 19.6.

And so a wife is loved more intensely, but greater reverence should be exhibited toward one's parents.

[1] TO THE FIRST ARGUMENT, THEREFORE, IT SHOULD BE SAID that a man does not leave his mother and father for the sake of his wife in respect of all things, for in certain things a man ought to assist his parents more than his wife. But in respect of the union of fleshly bond (*unio carnalis copulae*), and of living together, a man clings to his wife and leaves his parents.

[2] To the second it should be said that the Apostle's words should not be understood as claiming that a man should love his wife equally as he loves himself, because the love that a man has for himself is the reason for the love that he has for his wife, connected to himself.

[3] To the third it should be said that multiple reasons for love are also found in paternal friendship. And in one respect—that is, the aspect of good—these are weightier than the aspect under which a man loves his wife, although the other reasons are weightier according to the aspect of connection.

[4] To the fourth [to the argument TO THE CONTRARY] it should be said that the passage quoted should not be understood so that the word "as" denotes equality. Rather the word "as" (*ly sicut*)[73] denotes the aspect of love. For a man loves his wife principally under the aspect of fleshly connection.

Article 12. [Whether a person should love his benefactor more than his beneficiary.]

One proceeds in this way to the twelfth query. IT SEEMS that a person should love his benefactor more than his beneficiary.

[1] As Augustine says in his book *On the Catechizing of the Uninstructed:* "There is no greater invitation to love than to anticipate in loving: for quite hard is the spirit that does not want to give love and is also unwilling to return it."[74] But our benefactors precede us in the benefit of charity. Therefore we should love our benefactors most of all.

---

73. The definite article "*ly*" is introduced into medieval Latin just before Thomas begins to write. It appears with some frequency in the *Summa theologica* of Alexander of Hales (1185–1245).

74. Augustine, *De catechizandis rudibus* chap.4 sect.7 (PL 40:314; CCSL 46: 127.10–13).

[2] Furthermore, to the degree that a person should love more, he sins more gravely to the same degree should he cease giving this love, or act against it. But a person who does not love his benefactor sins more gravely, or acts against him, than if he cease loving the person whom he has benefited up to this point. Therefore benefactors should be loved more than those to whom we give benefits.

[3] Furthermore, of all the things that should be loved, God and after him one's father should be loved most of all, as Jerome says.[75] But these are most of all our benefactors. Therefore, a benefactor should be loved most of all.

BUT TO THE CONTRARY the Philosopher says, in *Ethics* 9: "Benefactors seem to love beneficiaries, more than the other way around."[76]

I ANSWER THAT IT SHOULD BE SAID that, as was said above,[77] something is loved more in two ways. In one way, since it has the aspect of a more excellent good. In another way, under the aspect of a greater connection. Now in the first way, a benefactor should be loved more, because he has a more excellent aspect of good, since he is the origin of the good in the beneficiary—as was said about one's father.[78] But in the second way, we love beneficiaries more, as the Philosopher proves in *Ethics* 9, giving four reasons.[79]

(1) The beneficiary is, as it were, a certain work of the benefactor, so that it is customary to say about someone, "that person was made by him." Now that a person should love his own work is natural for anyone, since we see that poets love their own poems. And so it is that anything loves its own being and its own living, which is manifested most of all in its own acting.

(2) Anyone naturally loves that in which he discerns his own good. Indeed the benefactor has something good in the beneficiary and vice versa—but the benefactor discerns in the beneficiary his own noble good, whereas the beneficiary discerns in the benefactor his own useful good. Now the noble good is considered more pleasant than the useful good, both because it lasts for a longer time—for the useful passes quickly, and the pleasure of memory is not like the pleasure of a thing present—and also because we

75. Jerome, *On Ezekiel* bk.13, on Ezekiel 44.25 (PL 25:442; CCSL 75: 667.1821–24).

76. Aristotle, *Nicomachean Ethics* bk.9 chap.7 (1167b17).

77. In Articles 7, 9, and 11 of this Question.

78. In Article 9 of this Question.

79. Aristotle, *Nicomachean Ethics* bk.9 chap.7 (1167b17).

recall noble goods with pleasure, rather than useful things that have come to us from others.

(3) It belongs to the lover to act, for he wills and does good to the beloved, whereas it belongs to the beloved to be acted upon. And so to love belongs to the person who is more excellent.[80] Because of this, it belongs to a benefactor that he should love more.

(4) It is more difficult to give benefits than to receive them. And truly, we love more the things on which we work hard, and in a way scorn the things that come easily to us.

[1] TO THE FIRST ARGUMENT, THEREFORE, IT SHOULD BE SAID that what stimulates the beneficiary to love the benefactor is in the benefactor. The benefactor, however, loves the beneficiary not as though the beneficiary stimulates him, but rather from his own motion. Now that which is from oneself is superior to that which is from one another.

[2] To the second it should be said that love of the beneficiary toward the benefactor is owed more, because it has an aspect of greater opposition to sin. But the benefactor's love of his beneficiary is more spontaneous, and so has a greater promptness.

[3] To the third it should be said that God also loves us more than we love him, and parents love their children more than they are loved by them. Nonetheless, it is not right that we should love just any of our beneficiaries more than our benefactors. For we prefer the benefactors from whom we receive the greatest benefits – namely God and our parents – over those to whom we give some lesser benefits.

Article 13. [Whether the order of charity remains in the homeland.]

One proceeds in this way to the thirteenth query. IT SEEMS that the order of charity does not remain in the homeland.

[1] Augustine says in his book *On True Religion*, "Complete charity exists when we love greater goods more, and lesser goods less."[81] But

---

80. Some versions read "to love is more excellent."

81. Augustine, *De vera religione* chap.48 sect.93 (PL 34:164; CCSL 32: 248.4–5). Here the objector misquotes the text, whose topic is not *perfecta caritas* but *perfecta justitia*.

there will be complete charity in the homeland. Therefore someone will love a person who is better more than he loves himself or someone connected to him.

[2] Furthermore, a person who is more loved is a person to whom we will a greater good. But someone existing in the homeland wills a greater good to a person who has more good; otherwise, his will would not be conformed by all things to the divine will. Now in the homeland, he is better who has more good. Therefore in the homeland, anyone will love a better person – another more than himself, and a foreigner more than someone near him.

[3] Furthermore, the whole reason for love in the homeland shall be God: for then will be fulfilled what is said in 1 Corinthians 15: "That God may be all in all."[82] Therefore he is loved more who is nearer to God. And so a person will love someone better more than himself, and a foreigner more than someone connected to him.

BUT TO THE CONTRARY nature is not destroyed by glory, but perfected. Now the order of charity, as set down above,[83] proceeds from nature itself. Now all things naturally love themselves more than others. Therefore this order of charity shall remain in the homeland.

I ANSWER THAT IT SHOULD BE SAID that with respect to the point that God should be loved above all things, it is necessary for the order of charity to remain in the homeland. That God will be loved above all things shall be the case simply (*simpliciter*) when man comes to enjoy him perfectly. But concerning the order of one person to another, it seems that we should make a distinction. This is because, as was said above,[84] the degrees of charity can be distinguished either according to a difference of the good that someone desires for another or according to the intensity (*intensio*) of love. In the first way, a person will love those who are better more than himself, and love less those who are less good. For any blessed person shall wish that anyone have what is owed to him according to divine justice, on account of the complete conformity of the human will to the divine. Nor later shall there be a time of progressing by means of merit to a greater reward, as it happens now, when a person can desire both virtue and reward

82. 1 Corinthians 15.28.
83. In Articles 3, 6, 7, and 8 of this Question.
84. In Article 7 of this Question.

for someone better. But later the will of each person shall halt below that which is divinely determined.

In the second way, someone will love himself more than his neighbor, even a better one. This is because the intensity of love's act arises on the part of the loving subject, as was said above.[85] And in relation to this, even the gift of charity to each person is conferred by God – first, in order to direct his mind toward God, which belongs to the love of a person for himself, and second so that regarding other things, he may wish for an order that is directed to God, and even work for that order according to his own measure. But regarding the order of his neighbors to one another simply, someone will love a better person more, according to the love of charity. For the whole blessed life consists in the ordering of the mind to God. So that the entire order of love among the blessed will be observed through relation to God, so that he who is loved more and considered nearer to himself will be nearer to God. For later the provision will come to an end – the provision that is necessary in the present life, whereby it is necessary that a person love more those who are connected to himself, out of the necessity that one provides more for one's own than for others. In the present life this is why, from the very inclination of charity, a man loves someone more who is connected to himself, a person to whom he should give more the effect of charity.

As it turns out, someone in the homeland will love another person connected to himself – and for multiple reasons,[86] since the causes of noble love will not cease to exist in the spirit of the blessed. But of all the reasons, the one to be preferred incomparably is the reason for love that is taken from nearness to God.

[1] TO THE FIRST ARGUMENT, THEREFORE, IT SHOULD BE SAID that this argument should be granted with respect to those connected to oneself. But with respect to oneself, it is necessary that a person should love himself more than others – the more so, as his charity is more complete – since the completion of charity directs man completely to God. This belongs to the love that a person has for himself, as was said.[87]

[2] To the second it should be said that this argument proceeds from the order of love according to the degree of good that someone wills to a beloved.

---

85. In Article 7 of this Question.
86. Some versions read "in multiple ways."
87. In the body of this Article.

[3] To the third it should be said that for anyone, God shall be the whole reason for loving, since God is man's whole good. For assuming *per impossibile* that God is not man's good, he would have no reason for loving. And so in the order of love, it is necessary that, after God, man should love himself most of all.

[The Principal Act of Charity, Which Is Love]

One should next consider the act of charity. And first, the principal act of charity, which is love; second, its other acts or subsequent effects. About the first point, eight queries are raised. (1) What is more proper to charity, loving or being loved. (2) Whether loving, so far as it is charity's act, is the same as goodwill. (3) Whether God should be loved on account of himself. (4) Whether he can be loved in this life without mediation. (5) Whether he can be loved wholly. (6) Whether love of him has a measure. (7) Which is better, to love a friend or to love an enemy. (8) Which is better, to love God or to love one's neighbor.

Article 1. [What is more proper to charity, being loved or loving.]

One proceeds in this way to the first query. IT SEEMS that being loved is more proper to charity than loving.

[1] Better charity is found in better people. But better people should be loved more. Therefore being loved is more proper to charity.

[2] Furthermore, that which is found in many things seems to be more appropriate to nature, and consequently better. But as the Philosopher says in *Ethics* 8, "most people wish to be loved rather than to love, which is why they are lovers of adulation."[1] Therefore being loved is better than loving, and consequently more appropriate to charity.

[3] Furthermore, that on account of which a thing is, is still more that thing. But human beings love in order to be loved. For Augustine says in his book *On the Catechizing of the Uninstructed* that "there is no greater invitation to love than to anticipate in loving."[2] Therefore charity consists in being loved rather than in loving.

---

1. Aristotle, *Nicomachean Ethics* bk.8 chap.8 (1159a12).
2. Augustine, *De catechizandis rudibus* chap.4 sect.7 (PL 40:314; CCSL 46: 127.10–11).

BUT TO THE CONTRARY the Philosopher says in *Ethics* 8 that "friendship exists in loving rather than in being loved."[3] But charity is a certain friendship. Therefore charity consists in loving rather than in being loved.

I ANSWER THAT IT SHOULD BE SAID that to love is appropriate to charity, so far as it is charity. For charity, since it is a certain virtue, has according to its essence an inclination to its proper act. Now being loved is not an act of charity that belongs to the person who is loved. Rather, the act of charity belongs to the person who loves. Now being loved suits a person according to the general aspect of good–namely as for his good another person is moved to an act of charity.[4] So it is clear that it is more appropriate to charity to love than to be loved.[5] For what is more appropriate to anything is what is appropriate for it through itself (*per se*) and substantially, rather than what is appropriate for it through another (*per aliud*). And the sign of this is twofold. First, since friends are praised more because they love than because they are loved; indeed if they are loved and do not themselves love, they are blamed. Second, since mothers–who love most of all–seek to love rather than to be loved, for as the Philosopher says in the same book, "they give nourishment to their children, and love them, whereas they do not seek to be loved in return, if this turns out not to be."[6]

[1] TO THE FIRST ARGUMENT, THEREFORE, IT SHOULD BE SAID that better people, because they are better, are more lovable. But because more complete charity is in them, they are more loving, though in proportion to what is loved. For a better person does not love what is below him any less than it is lovable–but he who is less good does not succeed in loving the better person as much as he is lovable.

[2] To the second it should be said that, as the Philosopher says in the same place,[7] human beings want to be loved inasmuch as they want to be honored. For honor is shown to someone as a certain testimony to the good for which he is honored. So from the fact that a person is loved, there is shown to be some good in him, since only good is lovable. In this way, then, men seek to be honored on account of something else, namely for the

3. Aristotle, *Nicomachean Ethics* bk.8 chap.8 (1159a27).

4. Some versions read "by an act of charity."

5. "Most people live *for* love and admiration. But it is *by* admiration and love that we should live" (Oscar Wilde, *De profundis*).

6. Aristotle, *Nicomachean Ethics* bk.8 chap.8 (1159a28).

7. Aristotle, *Nicomachean Ethics* bk.8 chap.8 (1159a16).

manifestation of a good existing in the person loved. Now those who have charity seek to love for its own sake, as though this itself were the good of charity, just as any act of a virtue is the good of that virtue. So that wishing to love, rather than wishing to be loved, belongs more to charity.

[3] To the third it should be said that some love on account of being loved, not so that being loved is the end of their loving, but because it is a kind of way leading to this—that a person may love.

Article 2. [Whether loving, so far as it is charity's act, is nothing other than goodwill.]

One proceeds in this way to the second query. IT SEEMS that loving, so far as it is charity's act, is nothing other than goodwill.

[1] The Philosopher, in *Rhetoric* 2, says that "to love is to wish someone good things."[8] But this is to will good. Therefore the act of charity is nothing other than goodwill.

[2] Furthermore, that to which a habit belongs is that to which an act belongs. But the habit of charity is a power of the will, as was said above.[9] Therefore an act of charity is also an act of the will. But the will's act is nothing except tending toward the good, which is goodwill. Therefore the act of charity is nothing other than goodwill.

[3] Furthermore, the Philosopher in *Ethics* 9 sets down five things that belong to friendship,[10] the first of which is that a man wishes a good to a friend; the second is that he wishes him to exist and to live; the third is that he eats and drinks (*convivere*) with him; the fourth is that he should choose the same things as him; the fifth is that he sorrows and rejoices with him. But the first two belong to goodwill. Therefore the first act of charity is goodwill.

BUT TO THE CONTRARY the Philosopher says in the same book that "goodwill is neither friendship nor loving, but is the origin (*principium*) of friendship."[11] But charity is friendship, as was said above.[12] Therefore goodwill is not the same as love, which is the act of charity.

8. Aristotle, *Rhetoric* bk.2 chap.4 (1380b35); bk.2 chap.7 (1381a19). Some versions read "good things."

9. In Question 24, Article 1.

10. Aristotle, *Nicomachean Ethics* bk.9 chap.4 (1166a3).

11. Aristotle, *Nicomachean Ethics* bk.9 chap.5 (1160b30, b32; 1167a3).

12. In Question 23, Article 1.

I ANSWER THAT IT SHOULD BE SAID that goodwill is properly called the act of the will by which we wish another good. Now in this way the will's act differs from actual love, whether it is in the sensitive appetite, or in the intellectual appetite, which is the will. For the love that is in the sensitive appetite is a certain passion. Now every passion inclines to its own object with a certain vigor. But the passion of love has this characteristic – that it does not arise all at once, but only through an incessant focus on the thing loved. And so the Philosopher in *Ethics* 9,[13] showing the difference between goodwill and the love that is a passion, says that "goodwill has no affective charge (*distensio*)[14] or push forward (*appetitus*)," that is, some vigor of inclination, but occurs when a man wishes another good only from a judgment of reason. Likewise the passion of love arises from a kind of being-accustomed, whereas goodwill occasionally arises from something unexpected – as happens to us when we are watching boxers who are fighting and want one of them to win.

But the love that is in the intellectual appetite also differs from goodwill. For it denotes a certain union, according to affection of the lover for the beloved, namely so far as the lover regards the beloved as one with himself in a certain way, or else belonging to him; in this way he is moved toward him. But goodwill is a simple act of the will by which we wish someone good, even if the aforementioned union of affection with that person is not assumed. In this way, then, goodwill is included in love (*dilectio*), so far as it is the act of charity – but *dilectio* or love (*amor*) adds the union of affection. On account of this, the Philosopher says in the same place that "goodwill is the origin of friendship."[15]

[1] TO THE FIRST ARGUMENT, THEREFORE, IT SHOULD BE SAID that the Philosopher there[16] defines loving not by setting forth its entire reason, but rather by something belonging to its reason, in which the act of love is especially displayed.

[2] To the second it should be said that love (*dilectio*) is the act of will tending toward the good, together with a certain union with the beloved, which indeed is not denoted by goodwill.

---

13. Aristotle, *Nicomachean Ethics* bk.9 chap.5 (1160b33).

14. Some versions read "distinction" (*distinctio*); still others read "dissension" (*dissensio*).

15. Aristotle, *Nicomachean Ethics* bk.9 chap.5 (1167a3).

16. Aristotle, *Nicomachean Ethics* bk.9 chap.4 (1166a3).

[3] To the third it should be said that to the extent that the things which the Philosopher there[17] sets down belong to friendship, they arise from the love that a person has for himself, as was said in the same place. Thus someone behaves toward his friend as he does toward himself. This belongs to the aforementioned union of affection.[18]

Article 3. [Whether God is loved out of charity on account of himself.]

One proceeds in this way to the third query. IT SEEMS that God is loved out of charity, not on account of himself, but on account of something other than himself.

[1] Gregory says in a certain homily: "From the things that it knows, the mind learns to love unknown things."[19] Now he calls unknown things "intelligible and divine," whereas he calls known things "sensible." Therefore God should be loved on account of other things.

[2] Furthermore, love follows knowledge. But God is known through another, according to Romans 1: "The invisible things of God are discerned, being understood by the things that are made."[20] Therefore he is also loved on account of something other, and not on account of himself.

[3] Furthermore, hope generates charity, as is said in a Gloss on Matthew 1.[21] Also, "fear introduces charity," as Augustine says in his commentary on 1 John.[22] But hope expects to obtain something from God, whereas fear turns back from something that can be inflicted by God. Therefore it seems that God should be loved on account of some hoped-for good, or on account of some evil that should be feared. Therefore he should not be loved on account of himself.

BUT TO THE CONTRARY Augustine says *On Christian Doctrine*, Book 1, "To enjoy is to adhere to something on account of itself."[23] But

---

17. Aristotle, *Rhetoric* bk.2 chap.4 (1380b35); bk.2 chap.7 (1381a19).

18. In the body of the Article.

19. Gregory the Great, *Homiliae in Evangelia* bk.1 hom.11 sect.1, on Matthew 13.44–52 (PL 76:1114–15; CCSL 141:74.1–5).

20. Romans 1.20.

21. *Glossa interlinearis,* on Matthew 1.2 (Strasbourg 5).

22. Augustine, *Tractatus in epistolam Ioannis ad Parthos* tr.9 on 1 John 4.18 (PL 35:2048).

23. Augustine, *De doctrina christiana* bk.1 chap.4 sect.4 (PL 34:20; CCSL 32:8.1–2).

God should be enjoyed, as is said in the same book.[24] Therefore God should be loved on account of himself.

I ANSWER THAT IT SHOULD BE SAID that the term "on account of" (*ly propter*) denotes a relation of some cause. Now the genus of cause is fourfold, namely final, formal, efficient, and material, to which "material disposition" is also traced back. Material disposition is not a cause simply (*simpliciter*), but only in a certain respect (*secundum quid*). And according to each of these four kinds of cause, we say that something should be loved on account of another thing. Indeed, according to the genus of final cause, as we love medicine on account of health. Or according to the genus of formal cause, as we love a man on account of his virtue, namely because by means of virtue he is formally good, and consequently lovable. Or according to the efficient cause, as we love some men so far as they are sons of such-and-such a father.

According to disposition, however–which is led back to the genus of the material cause–we speak of loving something on account of that which disposes us to love it, such as when we love something on account of some benefits that we have received. Though after we have already begun to love our friend, we love him not on account of these benefits, but on account of his virtue.

Therefore, among these first three ways we do not love God on account of something other, but on account of himself. For he is not directed to another as to an end, but is himself the ultimate end of all things. Nor is he informed by some other thing in order to be good, but rather his substance is his goodness, according to which as an exemplar (*exemplariter*) all good things are. Nor again does he have any goodness from another, but all other things have their goodness from him. But in a fourth way, he can be loved on account of another, namely since we are disposed by some other things to make progress in the love of God, for example, by benefits that we receive from him, or by rewards that are hoped for, or by punishments that through him we strive to avoid.

[1] TO THE FIRST ARGUMENT, THEREFORE, IT SHOULD BE SAID that the words "from the things that it knows, the mind learns to love unknown things" do not mean that the known things are the reason for

---

24. Augustine, *De doctrina christiana* bk.1 chap.5 sect.5 (PL 34:20; CCSL 32:9.1–4).

loving unknown things in the manner of a formal, efficient, or final cause. Rather, it is because through this a person is disposed to love unknown things.

[2] To the second it should be said that knowledge of God is indeed acquired through other things. But after he is already known, he is not known through other things, but through himself, according to John 4: "We now believe, but not on account of your discourse, since we ourselves have heard, and know that this is truly the Savior of the world."[25]

[3] To the third it should be said that hope and fear lead to charity by way of a certain disposition, as is clear from what was said above.[26]

Article 4. [Whether in this life God can be loved without mediation.]

One proceeds in this way to the fourth query. IT SEEMS that in this life God cannot be loved without mediation (*immediate*).[27]

[1] "Things unknown cannot be loved," as Augustine says in *On the Trinity* 10.[28] But we do not know God without mediation in this life, since "we see now through a looking glass, in a dark manner," as said in 1 Corinthians.[29] Neither, therefore, do we love him without mediation.

[2] Furthermore, he who cannot do what is lesser cannot do what is greater. But it is greater to love God than to know him, since "he who clings" to God by love becomes "one spirit with him," as said in 1 Corinthians.[30] But man cannot know God immediately. Therefore much less can he love him without mediation.

[3] Furthermore, man is severed from God by sin, according to Isaiah 59: "Your sins have brought about division between you and your God."[31] Now sin is more in the will than in the intellect. Therefore man is less able to love God without mediation than to know him without mediation.

---

25. John 4.42. Some versions read "since we ourselves have seen."

26. *Summa* 2a2ae q.17 a.8; q.19 aa.4, 7, 10.

27. Here, "*immediate*" takes the sense of "without mediation," as distinct from the sense of colloquial English, which uses the term as a synonym for "now."

28. Augustine, *De trinitate* bk.10 chap.1 sect.3 (PL 42:974; CCSL 50:315.122); bk.10 chap.2 sect.4 (PL 42:975; CCSL 50:316.28).

29. 1 Corinthians 13.12.

30. 1 Corinthians 6.17.

31. Isaiah 59.2.

BUT TO THE CONTRARY knowledge of God, because it is mediated, is called "enigmatic" and "falls away" in heaven, as is clear from I Corinthians 13.[32] But charity-of-the-way "does not fall away," as is said in the same place.[33] Therefore charity-of-the-way adheres to God without mediation.

I ANSWER THAT IT SHOULD BE SAID that, as was said above,[34] the act of a cognitive power is completed through this – that the thing known is in the knower – whereas the act of an appetitive power is completed through this – that the appetite is inclined to the thing itself. And so it is necessary that the motion of the appetitive power be in the thing according to the condition of things themselves,[35] whereas the act of a cognitive power proceeds according to the mode of the knower.

Now the very order of things, according to itself, is such that God is knowable and lovable on his own account, since he is essentially existing truth itself and goodness itself, through which other things are both known and loved. But for us, since our knowledge has its rise (*ortus*) from sense, the first knowable things are those that are nearer to our sense, and the last limit of our knowledge is that which is most of all remote from our sense.

Accordingly, it should be said that love, which is an act of the appetitive power, tends first to God, even in the wayfaring state (*in statu viae*), and from God is drawn to other things. According to this consideration, charity loves God without mediation, and other things by means of God. In knowledge, however, it is the other way around, because we know God through other things, either by effects as a cause or by the way of eminence or negation, as is clear from Dionysius in his book on the *Divine Names*.[36]

[I] TO THE FIRST ARGUMENT, THEREFORE, IT SHOULD BE SAID that although things unknown cannot be loved, it is nonetheless not correct that the order of knowledge and the order of love are the same. For love is the limit of knowledge. And so where knowledge comes to an end – namely, in the very thing that is known through another – there love can begin at once.

[2] To the second it should be said that since the love of God is something greater than knowledge of him – especially in the wayfaring state – it

32. I Corinthians 13.12.
33. Some versions read "charity 'does not fall away.'"
34. In Question 26, Article 1, Reply [2].
35. Some versions read "according to the cognition of things themselves."
36. Ps-Dionysius, *Divine Names* chap.1 sect.5 (PG 3:593C; Chevallier 1:39).

thereby presupposes knowledge. And since knowledge does not come to rest in created things, but through them tends toward another, love begins in this other, and from there is drawn to other things by way of a certain circular course. While knowledge begins from creatures and tends toward God, love begins from God as from an ultimate end and is drawn toward creatures.

[3] To the third it should be said that aversion from God, which occurs by sin, is destroyed by charity, but not by knowledge alone. And so charity is what, by loving, joins the soul to God without mediation, by a bond (*vinculum*) of spiritual union.

Article 5. [Whether God can be loved wholly.]

One proceeds in this way to the fifth query. IT SEEMS that God cannot be loved wholly.

[1] Love follows knowledge. But God cannot be wholly known by us, since this would be to comprehend him. Therefore he cannot be wholly loved by us.

[2] Furthermore, love is a kind of union, as is clear from Dionysius, *Divine Names,* chapter 4.[37] But the heart of man cannot be wholly united to God, since "God is greater than our heart," as said in 1 John 3.[38] Therefore God cannot be wholly loved.

[3] Furthermore, God loves himself wholly. If therefore he were loved wholly by another, that other one would love him as much as he loves himself. But this is inappropriate. Therefore God cannot be wholly loved by a creature.

BUT TO THE CONTRARY there is what Deuteronomy 6 says: "You shall love the Lord your God with your whole heart."[39]

I ANSWER THAT IT SHOULD BE SAID that since love may be understood as something between lover and beloved, when it is asked whether God can be wholly loved, the question may be understood in three ways. In the first way, so that the mode of wholeness is referred to the

---

37. Ps-Dionysius, *Divine Names* chap.4 sect.12 (PG 3:709C–D; Chevallier 1:214).

38. 1 John 3.20.

39. Deuteronomy 6.5.

thing loved. And thus God should be loved wholly, since man ought to love all that belongs to God. In a second way, the question can be understood so that wholeness is referred to the lover. And thus God also ought to be loved wholly, since man ought to love God with all his power, and to order anything he has to the love of God, according to Deuteronomy 6: "You shall love the Lord your God with your whole heart."[40] In a third way, the question can be understood according to a comparison of the lover with the thing loved, so that the mode of the lover is adequate to the mode of the thing loved. And this cannot be. Because anything is lovable to the degree that it is good, God – whose goodness is infinite – is infinitely lovable, whereas no creature can love God infinitely, since every power of a creature, whether natural or infused, is finite.

[1]–[3] and argument to the contrary. And from this the answer TO WHAT WAS OBJECTED is clear. For the first three objections proceed according to this third sense, whereas the last argument proceeds in the second sense.

Article 6. [Whether in divine love some measure should be observed.]

One proceeds in this way to the sixth query. IT SEEMS that in divine love some measure[41] should be observed.

[1] The aspect of good consists in "measure, species, and order," as is clear from Augustine in his book *On the Nature of the Good*.[42] But the love of God is greatest in man, according to Colossians 3: "Above all these things, put on charity (*super omnia caritatem habete*)."[43] Therefore the love of God should observe a measure (*modus*).

---

40. Deuteronomy 6.5.

41. Here, *modus* is translated as "measure" and *mensura* as "standard."

42. Augustine, *De natura boni contra Manicheos* chap.3 (PL 42:553; CSEL 25: 856.19).

43. Colossians 3.14. *Habere* as "to put on" may appropriately evoke the sense of *habitus* as monastic garment, for example, the Dominican "habit" that Thomas himself would have worn. See Katherine Breen, *Imagining an English Reading Public* (Cambridge: Cambridge University Press, 2010), 50–62; M. Michèle Mulchahey, *"First the Bow Is Bent in Study . . ." Dominican Education Before 1350* (Toronto: PIMS, 1998), 77–79.

[2] Furthermore, Augustine says in his book *On the Morals of the Catholic Church:* "Tell me, I ask you, what is the measure of loving. For I fear lest I burn more or less than is necessary with desire and love for my Lord."[44] It would, however, be in vain to seek the measure unless there were some measure of divine love. Therefore there is some measure of divine love.

[3] Furthermore, as Augustine says, *On Genesis to the Letter* 4: "A measure is that which assesses each thing according to its own standard."[45] Now the standard (*mensura*) of the human will, as also of external action, is reason. Therefore just as in the outward effect of charity it is right to have a measure observed by reason, according to Romans 12, "Your reasonable service,"[46] so also the interior love of God ought to have a measure.

BUT TO THE CONTRARY Bernard says in his book *On Loving God* that "the cause of our loving God, is God; the measure, to love without measure."[47]

I ANSWER THAT IT SHOULD BE SAID that, as is clear from the cited authority of Augustine, "measure" (*modus*) denotes a certain determinate standard (*mensura*). Now this determination is found both in the standard and in the thing assessed by the standard, but not in the same way. For it is found in the standard essentially, since the standard in itself is determinative and a measure of other things; whereas in the things assessed by the standard, the standard is found only in a certain respect, that is, so far as these things attain the standard. And so in the standard nothing can be taken as unmeasured, but the thing assessed by the standard is unmeasured unless it attains to the standard, whether it falls short or it exceeds it.

Now in all things desirable or actionable, the standard is the end, since in the things we desire and act, it is necessary to take the proper reason from the end, as is clear from the Philosopher in *Physics* 2.[48] And so the

44. Augustine, *De moribus ecclesiae catholicae* bk.1 chap.8 sect.13 (PL 32:1316; CSEL 90:15.10–12).

45. Augustine, *De Genesi ad litteram* bk.4 chap.3 (PL 34:299; CSEL 28/1:99.15–16).

46. Romans 12.1.

47. Bernard of Clairvaux, *De diligendo Deo* chap.1 (PL 182:974A).

48. Aristotle, *Physics* bk.2 chap.9 (200a32).

end, according to itself, has a measure, whereas things ordered to the end have a measure because they are proportioned to the end. And so, as the Philosopher says in *Politics* I, "in all the arts, desire for the end is without end or limit, whereas there is a limit to things ordered to the end."[49] For the physician does not impose any limit on health, but rather makes it as complete as he can – but he does impose a limit on medicine. For he does not give as much medicine as he can, but only according to a proportion to health. If the medicine were to exceed the proportion, or else be deficient, it would be immoderate.

Now the end of all human actions and affections is the love of God, by which we most of all attain the ultimate end, as was said above.[50] And so in the love of God, a measure cannot be grasped as though it were in the thing measured, so that we grasp "more" or "less" in the thing. Rather, the measure is found in the standard, in which there cannot be excess, but the more the rule is attained, the better it is. And so the more God is loved, the better the love is.

[1] TO THE FIRST ARGUMENT, THEREFORE, IT SHOULD BE SAID that that which exists through itself (*per se*) is better than that which exists through another (*per aliud*). And so the goodness of a standard, which has its measure through itself, is better than the goodness of something assessed by that standard, something that has its measure through another. Thus charity, which has a measure in the way appropriate to a standard, outranks the other virtues, which has a measure in the way appropriate to things assessed by a standard.

[2] To the second it should be said that as Augustine adds in the same passage, the measure of loving God is to love him with our whole heart, that is, to love him as much as he can be loved.[51] And this belongs to the measure that is appropriate to a standard.

[3] To the third it should be said that an affection, whose object is subject to the judgment of reason, should be measured by reason. But the object of divine love, which is God, surpasses the judgment of reason. And so it is not measured by reason, but surpasses reason. In this way the interior act of charity and exterior actions are not alike. For the interior act of

---

49. Aristotle, *Politics* bk.1 chap.3 (1257b26).
50. In Question 23, Article 6. See also *Summa* 2a2ae q.17 a.6.
51. See Augustine, *De moribus ecclesiae catholicae* bk.1 chap.8 sect.13 (PL 32:1316; CSEL 90:15.12–17).

charity has the aspect of an end, since the ultimate good of man consists in this – that his soul adhere to God, according to the Psalm: "It is good for me to adhere to God."[52] Whereas the exterior acts are as things ordered to the end. And so these should be measured both according to charity and according to reason.

Article 7. [Whether loving an enemy is more meritorious than loving a friend.]

One proceeds in this way to the seventh query. IT SEEMS that loving an enemy is more meritorious than loving a friend.

[1] Matthew 5 says: "If you love those who love you, what reward shall you have?"[53] Therefore loving one's friend does not merit a reward. But loving one's enemy does merit a reward, as is shown in the same place. Therefore loving enemies is more meritorious than loving friends.

[2] Furthermore, something is more meritorious to the degree that it proceeds from a greater charity. But loving an enemy belongs to "the complete children of God," as Augustine says in the *Enchiridion,* whereas to love a friend belongs still to incomplete charity.[54] Therefore loving an enemy is of greater merit than loving a friend.

[3] Furthermore, where there is a greater striving toward the good, there seems to be greater merit, since "every man shall receive his own reward according to his own labor," as said in 1 Corinthians 3.[55] Now a man is required to strive harder to love his enemy than to love his friend, because it is more difficult. Therefore it seems that loving an enemy is more meritorious than loving a friend.

BUT TO THE CONTRARY because something is better, it is more meritorious. But it is better to love a friend, since it is better to love a better person. Now the friend who loves is better than the enemy who hates. Therefore loving a friend is more meritorious than loving an enemy.

---

52. Psalm 72.28.
53. Matthew 5.46.
54. Augustine, *Enchiridion ad Laurentium seu de fide, spe et caritate* chap.19 sect.73 (PL 40:266; CCSL 46:88.41–45).
55. 1 Corinthians 3.8.

I ANSWER THAT IT SHOULD BE SAID that the reason for loving our neighbor out of charity is God, as said above.[56] When therefore it is asked what is better or more meritorious, to love a friend or an enemy, these two loves can be compared in two ways. In one way, on the part of our neighbor who is loved. In another way, on the part of the reason on account of which the neighbor is loved.

In the first way, the love of a friend outranks the love of an enemy. This is because a friend is both better and more connected to us, so that the matter for love is more appropriate. Because of this, the act of loving that passes over this matter is better. So that its opposite is less favorable, for it is worse to hate a friend than an enemy.

In the second way, however, the love of an enemy outranks [the love of a friend]. First, because there can be a reason other than God for loving a friend, but God alone is the reason for loving an enemy. Second, because assuming that both friend and enemy are loved on account of God, the love of God, which extends the spirit of man to things farther from him—namely, to the love of his enemies—is shown to be stronger. It is just as the power of fire is shown to be stronger, to the degree that it diffuses its heat to things farther away. In such a way, divine love is shown to be stronger, to the degree that we accomplish more difficult things on its account, just as the power of fire is stronger to the degree that it can reduce to ash some matter that is less combustible.

But just as the same fire acts more strongly on nearer things than it does on those farther away, so too charity loves more fervently those who are connected to us than those who are far removed. With respect to this point, the love of friends considered in itself is more fervent and better than the love of enemies.

[1] TO THE FIRST ARGUMENT, THEREFORE, IT SHOULD BE SAID that the words of the Lord should be understood through themselves (*per se*). For the love of our friends does not merit a reward when they are loved only because they are our friends. This seems to happen when our friends are loved in a way that our enemies are not loved. Nonetheless, the love of our friends is meritorious if they are loved on account of God, and not only because they are our friends.

[2]–[3] To the other arguments, the response is clear from the things that have been said. For the two reasonings that follow proceed on the part

56. In Question 25, Article 1.

of the reason for loving, while the last proceeds on the part of those who are loved.

Article 8. [Whether loving our neighbor is more meritorious than loving God.]

One proceeds in this way to the eighth query. IT SEEMS that loving our neighbor is more meritorious than loving God.

[1] What seems more meritorious is what the Apostle more chose. But the Apostle chose the love of neighbor over the love of God, according to Romans 9: "I desired to be anathema from Christ, for the sake of my brethren."[57] Therefore it is more meritorious to love our neighbor than to love God.

[2] Furthermore, in a certain way it seems to be less meritorious to love one's friend, as said above.[58] Now God is most of all our friend, since "he has first loved us," as said in 1 John 4.[59] Therefore loving him seems less meritorious.

[3] Furthermore, that which is more difficult seems to be more virtuous and meritorious, since a virtue is about the difficult and the good, as is said in *Ethics* 2.[60] But it is easier to love God than our neighbor, both because all things love God naturally and because in God nothing occurs that should not be loved, which is not the case concerning our neighbor. Therefore it is more meritorious to love our neighbor than to love God.

BUT TO THE CONTRARY, that on account of which a thing is such, is yet more so. Now the love of one's neighbor is not meritorious, except on account of this – that he is loved on account of God. Therefore the love of God is more meritorious than the love of our neighbor.

I ANSWER THAT IT SHOULD BE SAID that this comparison can be understood in two ways. In one way, by considering both loves separately. Then there is no doubt that the love of God is more meritorious. For a reward is due to this love on its own account, since the ultimate reward is to

57. Romans 9.3.
58. In Article 7 of this Question.
59. 1 John 4.10.
60. Aristotle, *Nicomachean Ethics* bk.2 chap.3 (1105a9).

enjoy God, toward whom the motion of divine love tends. So that a reward is promised to a lover of God: "He who loves me, shall be loved by my Father, and I shall manifest myself to him."[61]

In another way, the comparison can be made so that the love of God is understood according as only he is loved, whereas the love of neighbor is understood as our neighbor is loved on account of God. In this way love of our neighbor includes the love of God, but love of God does not include love of our neighbor. So that the comparison will be between the complete love of God, which extends also to the neighbor, and the insufficient and incomplete love of God, since "this commandment we have from God, that he who loves God should also love his brother."[62] And in this sense, the love of one's neighbor is preeminent.

[1] TO THE FIRST ARGUMENT, THEREFORE, IT SHOULD BE SAID that according to one exposition in the Gloss,[63] the Apostle did not desire this, namely that he should be separated from Christ for the sake of his brethren when he was in a state of grace. Rather, he had desired it when he was in a state of unfaithfulness. So we should not imitate him in this. Alternatively, it can be said, as Chrysostom says in his book *On Compunction*,64 that it is not shown from this passage that the Apostle loved his neighbor more than God. Rather, what is shown is that he loved God more than himself. For he wished to be deprived for a time of the divine enjoyment, which belongs to love of oneself, for this – that God's honor might be procured in his neighbors, which belongs to the love of God.

[2] To the second it should be said that love for a friend as such is sometimes less meritorious, because a friend is loved on his own account, and so falls short of the true reason for the friendship of charity, which is God. That God should be loved on his own account does not lessen the merit, but rather constitutes the entire reason for merit.

[3] To the third it should be said that the good does more than the difficult to bring about the reason for merit and virtue. So it is not necessary that everything that is more difficult is more meritorious, but only that what is more difficult in this way should also be better.

---

61. John 14.21.
62. 1 John 4.21.
63. See *Glossa Lombardi* on Romans 9.3 (PL 191:1454D).
64. John Chrysostom, *De Compunctione* bk.1 (PG 47:406); *On Romans* hom.16 (PG 60:599).

[On Joy]

One should next consider the subsequent effects of the principal act of charity, which is love. And first, the inward effects; second, the outward effects. About the first of these, three things should be considered: first, joy; second, peace; third, mercy. About the first point, four queries are raised. (1) Whether joy is an effect of charity. (2) Whether joy of this sort is compatible with sorrow. (3) Whether this joy can be full. (4) Whether it is a virtue.

Article 1. [Whether joy is an effect of charity in us.]

One proceeds in this way to the first query. IT SEEMS that joy is not an effect of charity in us.

[1] From the absence of something that is loved, sorrow follows more than joy. But God, whom we love by charity, is absent from us so long as we live in this life. "For so long as we are in the body, we are wandering away from the Lord," as it says in 2 Corinthians 5.[1] Therefore charity causes sorrow rather than joy in us.

[2] Furthermore, we merit blessedness most of all through charity. But set down among the things by which we merit blessedness is mourning, which belongs to sorrow, according to Matthew 5: "Blessed are they who mourn, for they shall be comforted."[2] Therefore sorrow rather than joy is an effect of charity.

[3] Furthermore, charity is a virtue distinct from hope, as is clear from what has been said above.[3] But joy is caused by hope, according to Romans 12: "Rejoicing in hope."[4] Therefore joy is not caused by charity.

---

1. 2 Corinthians 5.6.
2. Matthew 5.5.
3. *Summa* 2a2ae q.17 a.6.
4. Romans 12.12.

BUT TO THE CONTRARY is that, as said in Romans 5, "The charity of God is poured forth in our hearts by the Holy Spirit, who is given to us."[5] But joy is caused in us by the Holy Spirit, according to Romans 14: "The kingdom of God is not meat and drink, but justice and peace and joy in the Holy Spirit."[6] Therefore charity is a cause of joy.

I ANSWER THAT IT SHOULD BE SAID that, as was said above when we treated of the passions,[7] both joy and sorrow proceed from love, but in an opposite way. For joy is caused by love either on account of the presence [to the lover] of the good loved, or else because [the lover's] own good inheres and is preserved in the very good that is loved. This belongs especially to the love of benevolence (amor benevolentiae), by which a person rejoices over his friend's success, even if he is absent. But in an opposite way, sorrow follows from love, either on account of the beloved's absence, or because the beloved for whom we wish good is deprived of that good, or weighed down by some evil. Now charity is love of God, whose good is immutable, since he is his goodness. And from the very fact that God is loved, God is in the one who loves him by his noblest effect, according to 1 John 4: "He who abides in charity, abides in God, and God in him."[8] And so spiritual joy, which is had about God, is caused by charity.

[1] TO THE FIRST ARGUMENT, THEREFORE, IT SHOULD BE SAID that so long as we are in the body, we are said to be "wandering from the Lord," in comparison with that presence by which he is present to certain people by the vision of sight,[9] so that the Apostle adds in the same passage, "For we walk by faith (per fidem) and not by sight (per speciem)."[10] But he is also present to those who love him, even in this life, by the indwelling of grace.

[2] To the second it should be said that the mourning that merits blessedness is mourning over the things that are contrary to blessedness. So it belongs to the same reason that such mourning, as well as spiritual joy about God, is caused by charity. This is because it belongs to the same reason to rejoice about some good and to sorrow about the things that oppose it.

---

5. Romans 5.5.
6. Romans 14.17.
7. See Summa 1a2ae q.25 a.3, q.26 a.1 ad 2, q.28 a.5.
8. 1 John 4.16.
9. Some versions read "by the vision of hope."
10. 2 Corinthians 5.6.

[3] To the third it should be said that there can be spiritual joy about God in two ways. In one way, according as we rejoice about divine good considered in itself. In another way, according as we rejoice about divine good as it is participated in by us. Now the first joy is better, and this proceeds principally from charity. But the second joy proceeds also from hope, by which we anticipate (*expectamus*) the enjoyment of divine good. Even so, this enjoyment itself, whether complete or incomplete, is obtained according to the measure of charity.

Article 2. [Whether the spiritual joy that is caused by charity receives an admixture of sorrow.]

One proceeds in this way to the second query. IT SEEMS that the spiritual joy that is caused by charity receives an admixture of sorrow.

[1] To rejoice over the good of our neighbor belongs to charity, according to 1 Corinthians 13: "Charity does not rejoice over iniquity, but rejoices in truth."[11] But this joy receives a blending of sorrow, according to Romans 12: "Rejoice with those who rejoice, weep with those who weep."[12] Therefore the spiritual joy of charity suffers an admixture of sorrow.

[2] Furthermore, repentance is "weeping over past sins and not committing them again," as Gregory says.[13] But true repentance does not exist without charity. Therefore the joy of charity has an admixture of sorrow.

[3] Furthermore, from charity it happens that a person desires to be with Christ, according to Philippians 1: "Having a desire to be dissolved and to be with Christ."[14] Now this desire gives rise in a person to a certain sorrow, according to Psalm 119: "Woe to me, that my exile is prolonged!"[15] Therefore the joy of charity receives an admixture of sorrow.

BUT TO THE CONTRARY the joy of charity is joy about divine wisdom. But joy of this sort has no blending of sorrow, according to Wisdom 8: "Her converse has no bitterness."[16] Therefore the joy of charity does not undergo any blending with sorrow.

---

11. 1 Corinthians 13.6.
12. Romans 12.15.
13. Gregory the Great, *Homiliae in Evangelia* bk.2 hom.34 sect.15, on Luke 15.1–10 (PL 76:1256; CCSL 141:314.417–20). The quotation is far from exact.
14. Philippians 1.23.
15. Psalm 119.5.
16. Wisdom 8.16.

I ANSWER THAT IT SHOULD BE SAID that a twofold joy about God is caused by charity, as was said above.[17] The first and indeed principal joy, which is proper to charity, [is that] by which we rejoice about the divine good considered in itself. Such joy of charity does not suffer any blending with sorrow, as the good that is rejoiced about cannot have any admixture of evil. And so the Apostle says, Philippians 4: "Rejoice in the Lord always."[18] The other joy, however, is the joy of charity by which a person rejoices about the divine good according as it is participated in by us. Now this participation can be hindered by something contrary. And so from this side the joy of charity can have a blending of sorrow, namely so far as someone is sorrowful about that which is opposed to participation in the divine good, either in us or in our neighbor, whom we love as ourselves.

[1] TO THE FIRST ARGUMENT, THEREFORE, IT SHOULD BE SAID that our neighbor sheds no tears except over some evil. Now every evil denotes a lack of participation in the highest good. And so charity makes us suffer with our neighbor, to the extent that participation in the divine good is hindered in him.

[2] To the second it should be said that "sins bring about division between us and God," according to Isaiah 59.[19] This is the reason for grieving about our past sins, or about those of others, so far as we are hindered by them from participating in the divine good.

[3] To the third it should be said that although in the exile of this wretchedness we participate in the divine good in some fashion, by knowledge and love, the wretchedness of this life nevertheless hinders us from complete participation in the divine good—which is how it will be in the homeland. And so this sorrow, by which a person mourns the delay of glory, belongs to the hindrance of participation in the divine good.

Article 3. [Whether the spiritual joy that is caused by charity can be full in us.]

One proceeds in this way to the third query. IT SEEMS that the spiritual joy that is caused by charity cannot be full in us.

17. In Article 1, Reply [3] of this Question.
18. Philippians 4.4.
19. Isaiah 59.2.

[1] The more we have greater joy about God, the more his joy is full in us. But we can never rejoice about God as much as it is worthy to rejoice about him, because his goodness, which is infinite, always surpasses the creature's joy, which is finite. Therefore joy about God can never be full.

[2] Furthermore, that which is full cannot be greater. But even the joy of the blessed can be greater, since the joy of one is greater than the joy of another. Therefore joy about God cannot be full in a creature.

[3] Furthermore, comprehension seems to be nothing other than fullness of knowledge. But just as the cognitive power of a creature is finite, so too is its appetitive power. Since therefore God cannot be comprehended by a creature, it seems that a creature's joy about God cannot be full.

BUT TO THE CONTRARY the Lord said to his disciples, John 15: "That my joy may be in you, and your joy may be full."[20]

I ANSWER THAT IT SHOULD BE SAID that fullness of joy can be understood in two ways. In one way, on the part of the thing rejoiced about, so that it is rejoiced about as much as it is worthy of being rejoiced about. And thus only God's joy about himself is full, since his joy is infinite – and this is worthy of the infinite goodness of God, whereas the joy of any creature whatever must be finite.

In another way, the fullness of joy can be understood on the part of the one who rejoices. Now joy is compared to desire as rest is to motion, as was said above when we considered the passions.[21] Now rest is full when nothing of motion remains. So that joy is full when nothing remains to be desired. But so long as we are in this world, the motion of desire does not come to rest in us, because it still remains that we draw nearer to God by grace, as is clear from what was said above.[22] But when one has already arrived at complete blessedness, nothing shall remain to be desired, since then the enjoyment of God shall be full. In this enjoyment, a person shall obtain whatever he has desired, even regarding other goods, according to the Psalm: "Who fills your desire with good things."[23] And thus does desire come to rest – not only the desire by which we desire God, but there will also be rest for all desires. So that the joy of the blessed is completely full, and even overfull, since they shall obtain more than suffices for their

20. John 15.11.
21. See *Summa* 1a2ae q.25 aa.1–2.
22. In Question 24, Articles 4 and 7.
23. Psalm 102.5.

desire: for "nor has it entered into the heart of man, the things that God has prepared for those who love him," as said in 1 Corinthians 2.[24] And this is what is said in Luke 6: "They shall give good measure and running over in your bosom."[25] But since no creature is capable of any joy about God that is worthy of God, it follows that such full joy is not entirely captured by a person, but rather that he enters into it, according to Matthew 25: "Enter into the joy of your Lord."[26]

[1] TO THE FIRST ARGUMENT, THEREFORE, IT SHOULD BE SAID that this reason proceeds from the fullness of joy on the part of the thing that is rejoiced about.

[2] To the second it should be said that when he will have arrived at blessedness, each person will have attained the limit affixed to him by divine predestination, and nothing further will remain to which he may tend – though within that limit, one person may arrive at a greater nearness to God, and another at a lesser nearness. And so the joy of each person will be full on the part of the one who rejoices, since the desire of each person will be fully brought to rest. Nonetheless, the joy of one will be greater than the joy of another, on account of a fuller participation in divine blessedness.

[3] To the third it should be said that comprehension denotes a fullness of knowledge on the side of the thing known, so that the thing is known as much as it can be known. Nonetheless, knowledge also has some fullness on the side of the knower, as was said about joy.[27] So the Apostle says, Colossians 1: "That you may be filled with the knowledge of his will, in all wisdom and spiritual understanding."[28]

Article 4. [Whether joy is a virtue.]

One proceeds in this way to the fourth query. IT SEEMS that joy is a virtue.

[1] Vice is contrary to virtue. But sorrow is set down as a vice, as is clear from acedia and envy. Therefore joy should also be set down as a virtue.

---

24. 1 Corinthians 2.9.
25. Luke 6.38.
26. Matthew 25.21.
27. In the body of the Article and in the Reply to [2].
28. Colossians 1.9.

[2] Furthermore, as love and hope are certain passions whose object is good, so too is joy. But love and hope are set down as virtues. Therefore joy should also be set down as a virtue.

[3] Furthermore, precepts of the law are given about acts of the virtues. But we are taught by precept that we should rejoice about God, according to Philippians 4: "Rejoice in the Lord always."[29] Therefore joy is a virtue.

BUT TO THE CONTRARY it is not numbered among the theological virtues, nor among the moral virtues, nor among the intellectual virtues, as is clear from what was said above.[30]

I ANSWER THAT IT SHOULD BE SAID that virtue, as attested above,[31] is a certain operative habit – and so has an inclination to some act, according to its own proper nature (*ratio*). Now it happens that from a single habit, there proceed several ordered acts of the same nature; of these acts, one follows from another. And since subsequent acts do not proceed from a habit of virtue except by some prior act, so it is that the virtue is not defined or named except from the prior act, although the other acts also follow from the virtue. Now from what has been said above about the passions,[32] it is clear that the first affection of the appetitive power is love, from which both desire and joy follow. Hence what inclines [a person] toward loving some good, toward desiring the good so loved, and toward rejoicing over it[33] is the same habit of virtue. But since among these acts love is prior, the virtue is named not from joy or desire, but from love, and is called "charity." In this way, then, joy is not some virtue distinct from charity, but is a certain act or effect of charity. On account of this, it is numbered among the fruits, as is clear from Galatians 5.[34]

[1] TO THE FIRST ARGUMENT, THEREFORE, IT SHOULD BE SAID that the sorrow which is a vice is caused by inordinate self-love, which is not a special vice, but rather a certain general root of the vices, as was said above.[35] Hence it was necessary to set down certain special

29. Philippians 4.4.
30. See *Summa* Ia2ae q.57 a.2, q.60 a.3, q.62 a.3.
31. *Summa* Ia2ae q.55 a.2.
32. *Summa* Ia2ae q.25 aa.1–3, q.27 a.4.
33. Some versions read "over God."
34. Galatians 5.22.
35. *Summa* Ia2ae q.77 a.4.

sorrows as special vices, since they are not derived from some special vice, but from the general vice. But the love of God is set down as a special virtue, which is charity – to which joy is traced back as its proper act, as was said.[36]

[2] To the second it should be said that hope follows from love, as joy also does, but hope adds on the part of the object a certain special aspect – namely, the difficult but possible to obtain. Hence it is set down as a special virtue. But on the part of its object, joy adds no special aspect beyond love that would bring about a special virtue.

[3] To the third it should be said that a precept of the law is given about joy, so far as it is an act of charity, though joy is not its first act.

36. In the body of this Article.

[On Peace]

One should next consider peace. About this point, four queries are raised. (1) Whether peace is the same as concord. (2) Whether all things desire peace. (3) Whether peace is an effect of charity. (4) Whether peace is a virtue.

Article 1. [Whether peace is the same as concord.]

One proceeds in this way to the first query. IT SEEMS that peace is the same as concord.

[1] Augustine says, *City of God,* Book 19: "The peace of human beings is well ordered concord."[1] But we are not speaking now of anything except the peace of human beings. Therefore peace is the same as concord.

[2] Furthermore, concord is a certain union of wills. But the nature (*ratio*) of peace consists in such union, for Dionysius says, *Divine Names,* chapter 11, that "peace is unitive of all things and brings about consensus."[2] Therefore peace is the same as concord.

[3] Furthermore, things whose opposites are the same are themselves the same. But the same thing is opposed to concord and peace, namely dissension; so that it is said in 1 Corinthians 14: "God is not the God of dissension but of peace."[3] Therefore peace is the same as concord.

BUT TO THE CONTRARY concord in evil can exist among wicked men. But "there is no peace for the wicked," as is said in Isaiah 48.[4] Therefore peace is not the same as concord.

1. Augustine, *De civitate Dei* bk.19 chap.13 (PL 41:640; CCSL 48:679.6).
2. Ps-Dionysius, *Divine Names* chap.11 sect.1 (PG 3:948D; Chevallier 1: 495–96).
3. 1 Corinthians 14.33.
4. Isaiah 48.22.

I ANSWER THAT IT SHOULD BE SAID that peace includes concord and adds something to it. So wherever peace is, there is concord – yet it is not that wherever there is concord, there is peace, if the name "peace" be taken properly. For concord, taken properly, is directed toward another, so far as the wills of diverse hearts come together in a single accord. It can also happen that the heart of a single man tends to diverse things, and this in two ways. In one way, according to diverse appetitive powers, as the sensitive appetite often tends to the contrary of rational appetite, according to Galatians 5: "The flesh desires (*concupiscit*) against the spirit."[5] In another way, so far as one and the same appetitive power tends toward diverse desirable things, which it cannot obtain at the same time. So that there must be a conflict between the motions of appetite. Now the union of these motions does indeed regard the aspect of peace, for a person cannot have a peaceful heart, as long as he does not have what he wants – or if he has something that he wants, but there remains something else that he wants, which he cannot have at the same time. Now this union does not belong to the nature of concord. So that concord denotes a union of the desires among various people who desire, whereas peace – over and above this union – denotes a union of desires within a single person who desires.

[1] TO THE FIRST ARGUMENT, THEREFORE, IT SHOULD BE SAID that Augustine is speaking there of the peace that is between one person and another. And he says that this peace is concord – not just any kind of concord, but concord well ordered in that one person agrees (*concordat*) with another, according to what is appropriate for both. For if one person were to agree with another not out of a spontaneous will, but by being forced, as it were, by the fear of some threatening evil to himself, such concord is not true peace. This is because the order of both parties who agree is not preserved but is disturbed by something that brings fear with it. On account of this, he premises that "peace is the tranquility of order."[6] Which tranquility consists in this – that all the appetitive motions in one person come to rest.

[2] To the second it should be said that if one person should consent with another person to the same thing, his consent is nevertheless not entirely united, unless all of his appetitive motions are also in agreement with themselves.

---

5. Galatians 5.17.
6. Augustine, *De civitate Dei* bk.19 chap.13 (PL 41:640; CCSL 48:679.10–11). Thomas condenses the sentence, abbreviating "*pax omnium rerum*" to "*pax*."

[3] To the third it should be said that a twofold dissension is opposed to peace, namely dissension of a person with himself, and dissension between one person and another. Now only this second [type of] dissension is opposed to concord.

Article 2. [Whether all things desire peace.]

One proceeds in this way to the second query. IT SEEMS that not all things desire peace.

[1] According to Dionysius, peace is a "unitive consensus."[7] But in things that lack knowledge, consensus cannot be united. Therefore things of this sort cannot desire peace.

[2] Furthermore, appetite is not borne at the same time to contraries. But there are many who desire war and dissension. Therefore not everyone desires peace.

[3] Furthermore, only good is desirable. But a certain kind of peace seems to be evil; otherwise the Lord would not have said, Matthew 10: "I have not come to bring peace."[8] Therefore not all things desire peace.

[4] Furthermore, that which all things desire seems to be the highest good, which is the ultimate end. But peace is not a thing of this sort, since it is also had in the wayfaring state. Otherwise the Lord would in vain have commanded, Mark 9, "Have peace among you."[9] Therefore not all things desire peace.

BUT TO THE CONTRARY Augustine says, *City of God,* Book 19, that all things desire peace.[10] And Dionysius also says the same, *Divine Names,* chapter 11.[11]

I ANSWER THAT IT SHOULD BE SAID that from the very fact that a man desires something, it follows that his desire itself is that he desires to secure that thing, and consequently he also desires the removal of the things that can hinder his securing it. Now a man can be hindered from securing the desired good by a contrary appetite either of his own or of

7. Ps-Dionysius, *Divine Names* chap.11 sect.1 (PG 3:948D; Chevallier 1: 495–96).

8. Matthew 10.34.

9. Mark 9.49.

10. Augustine, *De civitate Dei* bk.19 chap.12 (PL 41:638; CCSL 48:676.35).

11. Ps-Dionysius, *Divine Names* chap.11 sect.1 (PG 3:948D; Chevallier 1:496).

another – and so peace is taken away from both, as was said above.[12] And so it is necessary that every seeker should desire peace, so far as every seeker seeks to arrive, tranquilly and without hindrance, at that which he desires. In this consists the nature of peace, which Augustine defines as the "tranquility of order."[13]

[1] TO THE FIRST ARGUMENT, THEREFORE, IT SHOULD BE SAID that peace denotes a union not only of the intellective or rational appetite, or of the animal appetite, to both of which consent can belong, but also of the natural appetite. And so Dionysius says that "peace brings about both agreement and natural affinity,"[14] so that "agreement" (*consensus*) denotes the union of appetites proceeding from knowledge, whereas "natural affinity" (*connaturalitas*) denotes the union of natural appetites.

[2] To the second it should be said that even those who seek war and dissension do not desire anything except peace, which they take themselves not to have. For as was said above,[15] there is no peace if one person should enter into concord with another, but contrary to the thing that he wants more. And so men seek to break this concord by warring, as though having a lack of peace, so that they may arrive at a peace in which nothing is opposed to their will. On account of this, all warring men seek through war to arrive at some peace that is more complete than what they previously had.

[3] To the third it should be said that peace consists in the bringing-to-rest and the union of appetite. Now just as appetite can be either for what is good simply or for the apparent good, so too peace can be either true or apparent. Indeed, true peace cannot exist unless it regard the appetite for true good. This is because every evil, though it may appear good in some respect, so that it brings appetite to rest in some respect, nonetheless has many defects, from which the appetite remains restless and disturbed. So that true peace cannot exist except in good men and about good things. Now the peace that is of evil things is apparent peace and not true peace. So it is said in Wisdom 14: "Living in a great war of ignorance, they call so many and so great evils peace."[16]

---

12. In Article 1 of this Question.

13. Augustine, *De civitate Dei* bk.19 chap.13 (PL 41:640; CCSL 48:679. 10–11).

14. Ps-Dionysius, *Divine Names* chap.11 sect.1 (PG 3:948D; Chevallier 1: 495–96).

15. In Article 1, Reply [1] of this Question.

16. Wisdom 14.22.

[4] To the fourth it should be said that since true peace regards nothing but the good, it follows that just as the true good is had in two ways – namely, completely and incompletely – so true peace is twofold. The first is a kind of complete peace, which consists in the complete enjoyment of the highest good, through which every appetite is united by means of rest in one object. And this is the ultimate end of the rational creature, according to Psalm 147: "Who has placed peace in your borders."[17] The other is incomplete peace, which is had in this world. For even if the principal motion of the soul should find rest in God, there are nevertheless certain repugnant things, both within and without, which disturb this peace.

Article 3. [Whether peace is a proper effect of charity.]

One proceeds in this way to the third query. IT SEEMS that peace is not a proper effect of charity.

[1] Charity cannot be had without the grace that makes one pleasing. But peace is had by some who do not have the grace that makes one pleasing, just as the pagans sometimes have peace. Therefore peace is not an effect of charity.

[2] Furthermore, something whose contrary can exist with charity is not the effect of charity. But dissension, which is contrary to peace, can exist with charity; for we see that even holy doctors, such as Jerome and Augustine, dissented in some of their opinions. We also read that Paul and Barnabas dissented from one another, Acts 15.[18] Therefore it seems that peace is not an effect of charity.

[3] Furthermore, the same thing is not the proper effect of diverse things. But peace is the effect of justice, according to Isaiah 32: "And the work of justice is peace."[19] Therefore it is not an effect of charity.

BUT TO THE CONTRARY it is said in Psalm 118: "Much peace have they, who love your law."[20]

I ANSWER THAT IT SHOULD BE SAID that a twofold union belongs to the nature of peace, as was said.[21] The first of these is according to a

17. Psalm 147.3
18. Acts 15.37.
19. Isaiah 32.17.
20. Psalm 118.165.
21. In Article 1 of this Question.

directedness of one's own appetites to a single thing. The second is according to a union of one's own appetite with the appetite of another. And charity brings about both of these unions. It brings about the first union, according as God is loved with one's whole heart, so that we refer all things to him – and in this way every appetite of ours is referred to a single thing. In the second way, so far as we love our neighbor as ourselves, from which it happens that we wish to fulfill our neighbor's will as though it were ours. On account of this, an identity of choice is set down among friendly relations, as is said in *Ethics* 9.[22] And Cicero says in his book *On Friendship* that it belongs to friends to wish for and not to wish for the same things.[23]

[1] TO THE FIRST ARGUMENT, THEREFORE, IT SHOULD BE SAID that no one lacks the grace that makes one pleasing except on account of sin, from which it happens that a person is turned away from his due end, erecting the end in something undue. And according to this, his appetite does not adhere principally to the true final good, but to apparent good. And on account of this, without the grace that makes one pleasing, there cannot be true peace, but only apparent peace.

[2] To the second it should be said that, as the Philosopher says in *Ethics* 9,[24] what belongs to friendship is not concord in opinions, but rather concord in the goods conducing to life, and chiefly in great things. This is because dissenting in some small things seems almost not to be dissension. And on account of this, nothing prevents some who have charity from dissenting in opinions. Nor is this opposed to peace, since opinions belong to the intellect, which precedes appetite, which is united by peace. Likewise, when there is concord regarding the principal goods, dissent in some small things is not against charity. For such dissension proceeds from a difference of opinions, because one person deems the particular good, which is the object of dissension, to belong to the good in which he and another person agree, while the other deems it not to belong. Accordingly, such dissension about small things and about opinions is indeed repugnant to complete peace, in which truth shall be fully known and every appetite fulfilled. This is not, however, repugnant to incomplete peace, which is had on the way (*in via*).

[3] To the third it should be said that peace is the work of justice indirectly, namely so far as justice removes things prohibiting peace. But peace

22. Aristotle, *Nicomachean Ethics* bk.9 chap.4 (1166a7).
23. See Cicero, *De amicitia* sect.20 and sect.61.
24. Aristotle, *Nicomachean Ethics* bk.9 chap.6 (1167a22).

is the work of charity directly, since according to its own nature, charity causes peace. For love is a "unitive power," as Dionysius says, *Divine Names*, chapter 4,[25] whereas peace is the union of the inclinations belonging to appetites.

Article 4. [Whether peace is a virtue.]

One proceeds in this way to the fourth query. IT SEEMS that peace is a virtue.

[1] Precepts are not given, except about acts of virtue. But precepts are given about keeping peace, as is clear from Mark 9: "Have peace among you."[26] Therefore peace is a virtue.

[2] Furthermore, we do not merit except by acts of virtue. But to make peace is meritorious, according to Matthew 5: "Blessed are the peacemakers, for they shall be called the children of God."[27] Therefore peace is a virtue.

[3] Furthermore, vices are opposed to virtues. But dissensions, which are opposed to peace, are numbered among the vices, as is clear from Galatians 5.[28] Therefore peace is a virtue.

BUT TO THE CONTRARY a virtue is not the ultimate end, but a way (*via*) to the end. But in a certain way, peace is the ultimate end, as Augustine says, *City of God*, Book 19.[29] Therefore peace is not a virtue.

I ANSWER THAT IT SHOULD BE SAID that, as was said above,[30] when all acts [of a certain kind] follow from one another, proceeding from an agent according to the same aspect, then all acts of this sort proceed from one virtue, since singular acts do not have singular virtues from which they proceed. This is clear in bodily things, for since fire melts and rarefies by heating, there is not in fire one liquefying power and another rarefying power; rather, fire produces all of these acts by its one power of heating.

25. Ps-Dionysius, *Divine Names* chap.4 sect.12 (PG 3:709C–D; Chevallier 1:214).

26. Mark 9.49.

27. Matthew 5.9.

28. Galatians 5.20.

29. Augustine, *De civitate Dei* bk.19 chap.11 (PL 41:637; CCSL 48:674.1–2, 675.24–26).

30. In Question 28, Article 4.

Since, therefore, peace is caused by charity according to the very aspect of love of God and neighbor, as was shown,[31] there is no other virtue of which peace is the proper act except charity, as was also said about joy.[32]

[1] TO THE FIRST ARGUMENT, THEREFORE, IT SHOULD BE SAID that a precept is given about keeping peace because it is an act of charity. Because of this, it is also a meritorious act. And so it is set down among the beatitudes, which are acts of complete virtue, as was said above.[33] It is also set down among the fruits, so far as it is a certain final good having a spiritual sweetness.

[2] And from this the solution TO THE SECOND ARGUMENT is clear.

[3] To the third it should be said that many vices are opposed to one virtue, according to its diverse acts. Accordingly, not only hatred is opposed to charity, by reason [of its opposition to] the act of love (*actus dilectionis*), but so are acedia and envy, by reason [of their opposition to] joy. And so is dissension [opposed to charity], by reason [of its opposition to] peace.

---

31. In Article 3 of this Question.
32. In Question 28, Article 4.
33. *Summa* 1a2ae q.69 a.1 and a.3.

[On Mercy]

One should next consider mercy (*misericordia*). Regarding this, four queries are raised. (1) Whether an evil is the cause of mercy on the part of the person to whom mercy is shown. (2) To whom it belongs to be merciful. (3) Whether mercy is a virtue. (4) Whether it is the greatest of the virtues.

Article 1. [Whether an evil is properly the motive of mercy.]

One proceeds in this way to the first query. IT SEEMS that an evil is not properly the motive for mercy.

[1] As was shown above,[1] fault (*culpa*) is an evil rather than a penalty. But fault provokes one to indignation rather than mercy. Therefore an evil does not provoke one to mercy.

[2] Furthermore, the things that are cruel or horrible seem to have a certain excess of evil. But the Philosopher says, in *Rhetoric* 2, that "the horrible is different from the wretched, and drives away the wretched."[2] Therefore some evil thing, so far as it is of this type, is not a motive for mercy.

[3] Furthermore, signs of evils are not true evils. But signs of evils provoke one to mercy, as is clear from the Philosopher in *Rhetoric* 2.[3] Therefore an evil does not properly provoke mercy.

BUT TO THE CONTRARY there is what the Damascene says, that "mercy is a kind of sorrow."[4] But the motive for sorrow is an evil. Therefore the motive for mercy is an evil.

1. *Summa* 2a2ae q.19 a.1; *Summa* 1a2ae q.48 a.6.
2. Aristotle, *Rhetoric* bk.2 chap.8 (1386a22).
3. Aristotle, *Rhetoric* bk.2 chap.8 (1386b2).
4. John Damascene, *On the Orthodox Faith* bk.2 chap.14 (PG 94:932B; Buytaert chap.28, 121.3–4).

I ANSWER THAT IT SHOULD BE SAID that, as Augustine says in *City of God,* Book 9, "mercy is compassion in our heart for the wretchedness of another, by which we are certainly compelled to help him, if we are able to do so."[5] For mercy (*misericordia*) is named from the fact that someone has a wretched heart (*miserum cor*) over the wretchedness of another. Now wretchedness is opposed to happiness (*felicitas*). It belongs to the nature of blessedness or happiness that someone should acquire what he wants, for as Augustine says, *On the Trinity* 13: "Blessed is he who has all things that he wants, and wants nothing evil."[6] And so on the other hand, it belongs to wretchedness that a man should suffer that which he does not want. Now a person wants a thing in three ways. In the first way, by natural appetite, and so all men want to exist (*esse*) and to live (*vivere*). In a second way, a man wants something through his own choice, by some premeditation. In a third way, a man wants something not in itself, but in its cause – as when someone wants to eat what is harmful, we say in a certain way that he wants to be ill. Thus the motive of mercy, belonging as it were to wretchedness, is in the first way something that is opposed to the natural appetite of the person who wills, namely corruptive and sorrowful evils, whose contraries men naturally desire. So that the Philosopher says, in *Rhetoric* 2, that "mercy is a kind of sorrow about apparent corruptive or sorrowful evils."[7] In the second way, evils of this type are more effective provocations to mercy if they are against the will that belongs to choice.[8] So the Philosopher says in the same place that evil things "of which fortune is cause" are wretched, as when "something turns out evil when we were hoping for good."[9] In the third way, they are still more wretched if they are against the whole will – for example, a person who has always pursued good things, but then evil things happen to him. And so the Philosopher says, in the same book, that "mercy most of all concerns the evils of a person who has suffered undeservedly."[10]

[1] TO THE FIRST ARGUMENT, THEREFORE, IT SHOULD BE SAID that it belongs to the nature of fault that it should be voluntary. And

---

5. Augustine, *De civitate Dei* bk.9 chap.5 (PL 41:261; CCSL 47:254.17–19).

6. Augustine, *De trinitate* bk.13 chap.5 sect.8 (PL 42:1020; CCSL 50A: 393.37–38).

7. Aristotle, *Rhetoric* bk.2 chap.8 (1385b13).

8. "Voluntas electionis" is a strange construction: literally, "the will of choice." Perhaps it is shorthand for the act of will that Aquinas calls *electio* (see *Summa* 1a2ae q.13).

9. Aristotle, *Rhetoric* bk.2 chap.8 (1386a5, a11).

10. Aristotle, *Rhetoric* bk.2 chap.8 (1386b6).

in this respect, it does not have the aspect of mercy, but instead the aspect of punishing. But since fault can in some way be a penalty, so far as it has something joined to it that is against the will of the sinner, then it can accordingly have the aspect of mercy. And so we are merciful to and suffer with sinners. As Gregory says in a certain homily, "true justice does not have disdain"—namely, toward sinners—"but rather compassion."[11] And Matthew 9 says, "Jesus, seeing the multitudes, had mercy on them: because they were distressed, and lying down like sheep that have no shepherd."[12]

[2] To the second it should be said that since mercy is compassion for another's wretchedness, mercy is properly shown to another, and not to oneself, except according to a certain likeness—in the same way that justice is, according as diverse parts are considered in a man, as is said in *Ethics* 5.[13] Accordingly, it is said in Sirach 30, "Have mercy on your own soul, pleasing God."[14] Therefore just as mercy is not properly shown to oneself, but rather sorrow is—as when we suffer something cruel in ourselves—so too for some persons who are so connected to us as if they were some part of ourselves, for example, our children or our parents, we are not merciful about their evils but rather grieve for our own wounds. Accordingly, the Philosopher says that "what is horrible drives out mercy."[15]

[3] To the third it should be said that just as pleasure follows upon hope and the memory of good things, so does sorrow follow upon hope and the memory of evil things, but not so violently as when these evil things are present to the senses. And so the signs of evil, so far as they represent evil and wretched things as though they were present to us, jolt us to mercy.

Article 2. [Whether a defect on the part of the one who is merciful is the reason for being merciful.]

One proceeds in this way to the second query. IT SEEMS that a defect on the part of the one who is merciful is not the reason for being merciful.

[1] It is proper to God to be merciful, so that it says in the Psalm: "His tender mercies are over all his works."[16] But in God, nothing is a defect. Therefore a defect cannot be the reason for being merciful.

11. Gregory the Great, *Homiliae in Evangelia* bk.2 hom.34 sect.2, on Luke 15.1–10 (PL 76:1246; CCSL 141:300.16–17).

12. Matthew 9.36.

13. Aristotle, *Nicomachean Ethics* bk.5 chap.11 (1138b8).

14. Sirach 30.24.

15. Aristotle, *Rhetoric* bk.2 chap.8 (1386a22).

16. Psalm 144.9.

[2] Furthermore, if a defect is the reason for being merciful, it is necessary that those who are especially defective would be especially merciful. But this is false, for the Philosopher says in *Rhetoric* 2 that "those who are ruined entirely are not merciful."[17] Therefore it seems that a defect is not the reason for being merciful on the part of the person who is merciful.

[3] Furthermore, to put up with contumely belongs to a defect. But the Philosopher says that "those who are disposed to contumely are not merciful."[18] Therefore a defect on the part of the person who is merciful is not the reason for being merciful.

BUT TO THE CONTRARY mercy is a kind of sorrow. But a defect is a reason for sorrow. So that those who are weak yield to sorrow more easily, as was said above.[19] Therefore the reason for being merciful is a defect in the one who is merciful.

I ANSWER THAT IT SHOULD BE SAID that since mercy is compassion for another's distress, as said above,[20] it happens therefore that a person is merciful when it happens that he grieves for another's wretchedness. Now since sorrow or pain regards one's own evil, a person sorrows or grieves for another's wretchedness to the extent that he apprehends another's wretchedness as his own. Now this happens in two ways. In one way, according to the union of affection, which arises by love. For since the lover regards his friend as himself, he regards the friend's evil as his own evil. And so he grieves over the evil of his friend as his own. Thus the Philosopher in *Ethics* 9 declares that "to sorrow with a friend" belongs among the things to do with friendship.[21] And the Apostle says, Romans 12: "Rejoice with those who rejoice, weep with those who weep."[22] In another way [we apprehend another's wretchedness as our own] according to real union, inasmuch as when the evil of others draws near, it crosses over from them to us. And so the Philosopher says in *Rhetoric* 2[23] that men are merciful toward those who are connected to and like them, because the judgment thus occurs to them that they can also suffer like things. So it is that the old and the wise, who consider themselves able to

17. Aristotle, *Rhetoric* bk.2 chap.8 (1385b19).
18. Aristotle, *Rhetoric* bk.2 chap.8 (1385b31).
19. *Summa* Ia2ae q.47 a.3.
20. In Article I of this Question.
21. Aristotle, *Nicomachean Ethics* bk.9 chap.4 (1166a7).
22. Romans 12.15.
23. Aristotle, *Rhetoric* bk.2 chap.8 (1385b16).

fall upon evil things, are more merciful – as are the weak and the fearful. On the other hand, those who regard themselves as happy and so powerful that they suppose themselves able to suffer nothing evil, are not so merciful. – In this way, therefore, a defect is always the reason for being merciful, either so far as someone regards the defect of another as his own on account of the union of love, or else on account of the possibility of suffering similar evils.

[1] TO THE FIRST ARGUMENT, THEREFORE, IT SHOULD BE SAID that God is not merciful except on account of love, so far as he loves us as something that belongs to him.

[2] To the second it should be said that those who are already amidst terrible evils do not fear to suffer further, and so are not merciful. This is likewise true of those who fear greatly. Since they are so focused on their own passion, they do not focus on the wretchedness of another.

[3] To the third it should be said that those who are disposed to contumely, whether because they have suffered from contumely or because they wish to inflict contumely, are provoked to anger and daring, which are certain passions of manliness that raise the spirit of a man to what is arduous. So they make a man judge that he will suffer something in the future. So such men, while they are in this disposition, are not merciful, according to Proverbs 27: "Anger has no mercy when it erupts, and neither does fury."[24] For a similar reason, the proud are not merciful, because they despise others and think them evil. So that they think that the others deservedly suffer whatever they suffer. So Gregory says that "false righteousness, namely that of the proud, has no compassion, but rather disdain."[25]

Article 3. [Whether mercy is a virtue.]

One proceeds in this way to the third query. IT SEEMS that mercy is not a virtue.

[1] The principal thing in virtue is choice, as is clear from the Philosopher in *Ethics* 2.[26] "Now choice is the desire for what has been already

24. Proverbs 27.4.
25. Gregory the Great, *Homiliae in Evangelia* bk.2 hom.34 sect.2, on Luke 15.1–10 (PL 76:1246; CCSL 141:300.16–17).
26. Aristotle, *Nicomachean Ethics* bk.2 chap.5 (1106a3); see also bk.3 chap.2 (1111b5).

deliberated upon," as is said in the same book.[27] That which hinders choice, therefore, cannot be called a virtue. But mercy hinders counsel, according to a passage from Sallust: "All men who take counsel about matters of doubt should be free from . . . anger and mercy, for the mind does not easily see what is true, when these things stand in the way."[28] Therefore mercy is not a virtue.

[2] Furthermore, nothing that is contrary to virtue is praiseworthy. But "nemesis is contrary to mercy," as the Philosopher says in *Rhetoric* 2.[29] Now nemesis is a praiseworthy passion, as is said in *Ethics* 2.[30] Therefore mercy is not a virtue.

[3] Furthermore, joy and peace are not special virtues, since they follow from charity, as said above.[31] But mercy also follows from charity, for out of charity do we "weep with those who weep," just as we "rejoice with those who rejoice."[32] Therefore mercy is not a special virtue.

[4] Furthermore, since mercy belongs to the appetitive power, it is not an intellectual virtue. Nor is it a theological virtue, since it does not have God for its object. Likewise, it is not a moral virtue, since neither is it about operations, for this belongs to justice; nor is it about the passions, for it is not traced back to any of the twelve means that the Philosopher sets down in *Ethics* 2.[33] Therefore mercy is not a virtue.

BUT TO THE CONTRARY Augustine says in *City of God,* Book 9: "Much better—that is, both more humanely and more in line with a sense of piety—does Cicero speak in praise of Caesar when he says: 'Of all your virtues, none is more admirable or more graceful than your mercy.'"[34] Therefore mercy is a virtue.

I ANSWER THAT IT SHOULD BE SAID that mercy signifies pain at another's wretchedness. Now this pain can name, in one way, a motion of the sensitive appetite. According to this, mercy is a passion and not a

27. Aristotle, *Nicomachean Ethics* bk.3 chap.2 (1112a14); see also bk.6 chap.2 (1139a23).

28. Sallust, *De coniuratione Catilinae* chap.51.

29. Aristotle, *Rhetoric* bk.2 chap.9 (1386b9).

30. Aristotle, *Nicomachean Ethics* bk.2 chap.7 (1108a35).

31. In Question 28, Article 4, and in Question 29, Article 4.

32. Romans 12.15.

33. Aristotle, *Nicomachean Ethics* bk.2 chap.7 (1107a28).

34. Augustine, *De civitate Dei* bk.9 chap.5 (PL 41:260; CCSL 47:254).

virtue. – In another way, it can name a motion of the intellective appetite, according as one person's evil displeases another. In this way the motion can be ruled according to reason, and according to this motion ruled by reason, the motion of the lower appetite can be ruled. So Augustine says in *City of God,* Book 9, that "this motion of the mind," namely mercy, "obeys reason, when mercy is shown in such a way that justice is preserved, whether we give to the needy or forgive the repentant."[35] And since the nature (*ratio*) of human virtue consists in this – that the motion of the mind is ruled by reason, as is clear from what was said above[36] – it follows that mercy is a virtue.

[1] TO THE FIRST ARGUMENT, THEREFORE, IT SHOULD BE SAID that this passage (*auctoritas*) from Sallust is understood to regard mercy according as it is a passion not ruled by reason. For thus does it hinder the counsel of reason, as long as it makes it withdraw from justice.

[2] To the second it should be said that the Philosopher is speaking there of mercy and nemesis according as each is a passion. They have a certain contrariety on the part of a judgment regarding another's evils, over which mercy grieves, so far as it judges that someone is suffering undeservedly, whereas nemesis rejoices, so far as it judges someone to suffer deservedly, and grieves if things go well for the undeserving. And "each passion is praiseworthy, coming from the same character," as is said in the same place.[37] But properly, envy is opposed to mercy, as will be said below.[38]

[3] To the third it should be said that joy and peace add nothing over and above the aspect of good that is the object of charity. And so they do not require any virtues other than charity. But mercy looks to a certain special aspect, namely the wretchedness of the person shown mercy.

[4] To the fourth it should be said that mercy, according as it is a virtue, is a moral virtue about existing passions, and it is traced back to the mean that is called "nemesis," because "they proceed from the same character," as is said in *Rhetoric* 2.[39] Now the Philosopher does not set down these means as virtues, but rather as passions, since even according as they are passions, they are praiseworthy. Yet nothing in fact prevents them from arising from some elective habit. And according to this, they take on the aspect of a virtue.

35. Augustine, *De civitate Dei* bk.9 chap.5 (PL 41:261; CCSL 47:14–17).
36. *Summa* 1a2ae q.56 a.4, q.59 a.4, q.60 a.5, q.66 a.4.
37. Aristotle, *Rhetoric* bk.2 chap.9 (1386b11).
38. In Question 36, Article 3, Reply [3].
39. Aristotle, *Rhetoric* bk.2 chap.9 (1386b11).

Article 4. [Whether mercy is the greatest of the virtues.]

One proceeds in this way to the fourth query. IT SEEMS that mercy is the greatest of the virtues.

[1] Divine worship seems most of all to belong to virtue. But mercy is preferred over divine worship, according to Hosea 6 and Matthew 12: "I want mercy and not sacrifice."[40] Therefore mercy is the greatest virtue.

[2] Furthermore, on the passage of 1 Timothy 4, "Piety is useful to all things,"[41] the Gloss of Ambrose says: "The highest point (*summa*) of every Christian discipline is in mercy and piety."[42] But Christian discipline contains every virtue. Therefore the highest point of every virtue consists in mercy.

[3] Furthermore, virtue is that which makes good the person who has it. Therefore the more that some virtue is better, the more it makes a person more similar to God, since a man is better through this – that he is more like God. But mercy especially brings this about, since in the Psalm it says about God that "his tender mercies are over all his works."[43] So that the Lord says, Luke 6: "Be merciful, just as your Father is merciful."[44] Mercy, therefore, is the greatest of the virtues.

BUT TO THE CONTRARY the Apostle, Colossians 3, after he had said "Put on, as the chosen ones of God, the bowels of mercy," etc., adds afterwards, "Above all else, have charity."[45] Therefore mercy is not the greatest of virtues.

I ANSWER THAT IT SHOULD BE SAID that a virtue can be the greatest in two ways. In one way, in itself; in another way, in relation to the possessor of the virtue. In itself, mercy is indeed the greatest. For it belongs to mercy that it overflows to others, and, what is more, that it alleviates the defects of others. And this belongs most of all to the higher. So to be merciful is set down as proper to God, and in this most of all his omnipotence is said to be manifested. But in relation to the virtue's possessor, mercy is not

---

40. Hosea 6.6 and Matthew 12.7.

41. 1 Timothy 4.8.

42. The quotation comes not from Ambrose, but from the author known since Erasmus as "Ambrosiaster." See Ambrosiaster, *In epistolam 1 ad Timotheum,* on 1 Timothy 4.8 (PL 17:500C) and *Glossa Lombardi* (PL 192:348D).

43. Psalm 144.9.

44. Luke 6.36.

45. Colossians 3.12.

the greatest, unless he who has it is the greatest – that is, he who has nothing above himself, but rather has everyone under him. This is because it is greater and better for a person who has someone above himself to be joined to the higher, than to supply the defect of the lower. And so regarding man, who has God above him, charity – by which he is united to God – is preferable to mercy, by which he supplies the defects of his neighbors. But among all the virtues that pertain to one's neighbor, mercy is the most preferable, even as its act is preferable. For to supply the defect of another, so far as the other has a defect, belongs to the higher and better.

[1] TO THE FIRST ARGUMENT, THEREFORE, IT SHOULD BE SAID that we do not worship God with external sacrifices and gifts on God's account, but rather on account of ourselves and our neighbors. For he does not need our sacrifices, but wishes them to be offered to himself on account of our devotion and for the advantage of our neighbors. And so mercy, by which we remedy the defects of others, is a sacrifice more pleasing to him, so far as it leads more directly to the advantage of our neighbors, according to the last chapter of Hebrews: "Do not be forgetful of doing good and communion, for by such sacrifices God is merited."[46]

[2] To the second it should be said that the highest point of the Christian religion consists in mercy, as regards outward works. But the inward affection of charity, by which we are joined to God, is of greater weight than both love (*dilectio*) and mercy toward our neighbors.

[3] To the third it should be said that by charity we are made like God, as united to him by affection. And so it is better than mercy, by which we are made like God according to a likeness of activity (*secundum similitudinem operationis*).

---

46. Hebrews 13.16.

[On Doing Good]

One should next consider the outward acts or effects of charity. And first, doing good (*beneficentia*); second, works of mercy (*eleemosynae*), which are a certain part of doing good; third, fraternal correction, which is a particular work of mercy. About the first point, four queries are raised. (1) Whether doing good is an act of charity. (2) Whether good should be done to everyone. (3) Whether more good should be done to those more connected [to us]. (4) Whether doing good is a special virtue.

Article 1. [Whether doing good is an act of charity.]

One proceeds in this way to the first query. IT SEEMS that doing good is not an act of charity.

[1] Charity is had most of all toward God. But we cannot do good to him, according to Job 35: "What shall you give to him? Or what shall he receive from your hand?"[1] Therefore doing good is not an act of charity.

[2] Furthermore, doing good consists most of all in the conferring of gifts. But this belongs to generosity. Therefore doing good is not an act of charity, but of generosity.

[3] Furthermore, anything that a person gives, he gives either as something obligatory or as something not obligatory. But a benefit conferred as something obligatory belongs to justice, whereas something conferred as not obligatory is given freely, and accordingly belongs to mercy. Therefore all doing good is either an act of justice or an act of mercy. It is not, therefore, an act of charity.

BUT TO THE CONTRARY charity is a certain friendship, as was said.[2] But the Philosopher, in *Ethics* 9, sets down among the other acts of friend-

---

1. Job 35.7.
2. In Question 23, Article 1.

ship this one – "to work good (*operari*) for friends,"[3] which is to do good to friends. Therefore doing good is an act of charity.

I ANSWER THAT IT SHOULD BE SAID that doing good (*beneficentia*) denotes nothing other than to bring about a good for someone (*facere bonum alicui*). Now this good can be considered in two ways. In one way, according to the general aspect of good. And this belongs to the general aspect of doing good. And this is an act of friendship, and consequently of charity. For goodwill is included in the act of love, by which someone wishes good for his friend, as was attested above.[4] Now the will is effective of the things it wills, if the power to effect them is present. Consequently, to do good to a friend follows upon an act of love. Thus doing good, according to its general aspect, is an act of friendship or charity. But if the good that someone does to another is received under some special aspect of good, then doing good receives a special aspect and will belong to some special virtue.

[1] TO THE FIRST ARGUMENT, THEREFORE, IT SHOULD BE SAID that according to Dionysius, *Divine Names,* chapter 4: "Love moves those whom it directs to a mutual blessedness and turns lower things toward higher things, so that they might be completed by them; and it moves the higher things to provide for the lower things."[5] With respect to this, doing good is an effect of love. And so it is not ours to do good to God, but to honor him by subjecting ourselves to him. It does, however, belong to God to do good to us, out of his love.

[2] To the second it should be said that two things should be observed in the conferring of gifts. One of these is the thing given outwardly; the other is the inward passion that a person has regarding the wealth in which he takes pleasure. Now it belongs to generosity to moderate the inward passion, so that someone does not go beyond the wealth that should be desired and loved – and this causes a person to give away his wealth more easily. So that if a person should give some great gift, but still with some desire for keeping it, his giving is not free. But on the part of the outward gift, the conferring of benefits belongs in general to friendship or charity. So it does not detract from friendship if a person gives something that he desires to

3. Aristotle, *Nicomachean Ethics* bk.9 chap.4 (1166a3).

4. In Question 23, Article 1, and in Question 27, Article 2.

5. Ps-Dionysius, *Divine Names* chap.4 sect.12 (PG 3:709C–D; Chevallier 1:214).

keep to another person, on account of love. Rather, from this is shown the completion of friendship.

[3] To the third it should be said that just as friendship or charity looks to the general aspect of good in conferring a benefit, so justice looks to the aspect of the obligatory. Mercy looks to the aspect of alleviating[6] wretchedness or defect.

Article 2. [Whether good should be done to everyone.]

One proceeds in this way to the second query. IT SEEMS that good should not be done to everyone.

[1] Augustine says in *On Christian Doctrine,* Book 1, that "we cannot profit everyone."[7] But virtue does not incline one to the impossible. Therefore it is not necessary to do good to everyone.

[2] Furthermore, Sirach 12 says: "Give to the good, and do not receive a sinner."[8] But many men are sinners. Therefore one should not do good to everyone.

[3] Furthermore, "charity deals not perversely," as is said in 1 Corinthians 13.[9] But to do good to some people is to deal perversely – for example, if someone were to do good to enemies of the commonwealth, or if someone were to do good to an excommunicated person, since by this action he shares something (*communicat*) with him. Therefore, since doing good is an act of charity, one should not do good to all.

BUT TO THE CONTRARY there is what the Apostle says in the last chapter of Galatians: "While we have time, let us do good to all."[10]

I ANSWER THAT IT SHOULD BE SAID that, as was said above,[11] doing good follows upon love with respect to that which moves higher things to provide for lower things. Now degrees in human beings are not unchangeable, as they are in angels, because human beings can suffer many defects, so that he who is higher according to one consideration (*secundum*

6. Some versions read "revealing wretchedness or defect."

7. Augustine, *De doctrina christiana* bk.1 chap.28 sect.29 (PL 34:30; CCSL 32: 22.1–2).

8. Sirach 12.5.

9. 1 Corinthians 13.4.

10. Galatians 6.10.

11. In Article 1, Reply [1] of this Question.

quid) either is or can be lower according to another (*secundum aliud*). And so, since the love of charity extends to all, doing good must also extend to all, but as time and place require. For every act of the virtues must be limited according to due circumstances.

[1] TO THE FIRST ARGUMENT, THEREFORE, IT SHOULD BE SAID that, simply speaking, we cannot do good to everyone in particular. Nonetheless, nobody is such that a case cannot arise in which he must do good to someone in particular. And so charity requires that a person, even if he does not actually do good to someone, bear it in mind by way of preparation, so that he may do any such person good, were the time to arise. – Nonetheless, there is some benefit that we can confer on everyone, if not in particular, then at least in general. This is when we pray for everybody, the faithful and the unfaithful.

[2] To the second it should be said that in a sinner there are two things, namely fault (*culpa*) and nature. Therefore, with respect to the sustenance of nature, assistance should be given to the sinner. But assistance should not be given to him that enables his fault, for this would not be to do good, but rather to do evil.

[3] To the third it should be said that benefits should be withdrawn from the excommunicated and the enemies of the commonwealth, so far as by this they are warded off from sin. If, however, necessity were to hang over them, so that their nature would be lacking in something, then we should give them assistance – but in a due manner. For example, if they were dying from hunger or thirst, or suffering some other loss of this sort, then we should help them, unless their suffering is according to the order of justice.

Article 3. [Whether more good should be done to those who are more connected to us.]

One proceeds in this way to the third query. IT SEEMS that more good should not be done to those who are more connected to us.

[1] It says in Luke 14: "When you make a dinner or a supper, do not invite your friends or your brothers or your kinsmen."[12] But these are the ones more connected to us. Therefore we should not do more good to those connected to us, but rather to strangers and those in need, for as the text

12. Luke 14.12.

proceeds to say, "But when you give a feast (*convivium*), invite the poor, the maimed," etc.

[2] Furthermore, the greatest benefit is that a man should give aid to another man in war. But a soldier in war should give more help to a fellow soldier who is a stranger, than to an enemy blood relative. Therefore benefits should not be shown more to those who are more closely connected to us.

[3] Furthermore, things owed should be returned before gratuitous benefits are conferred. But one person owes a benefit to another person from whom he has received a benefit. Therefore more good should be done to our benefactors than to those who are near us.

[4] Furthermore, one's parents should be loved more than one's children, as was said above.[13] Yet more good should be done to one's children, since "children should not lay up treasures for their parents," but rather the other way around,[14] as is said in 2 Corinthians 12.[15] Therefore more good should not be done to those more connected to us.

BUT TO THE CONTRARY Augustine says in *On Christian Doctrine,* Book 1: "Since you cannot profit everyone, those to whom the most preference should be shown are those who are connected to you by reason of place or time, or united to you by any other occurrence of things, as by a kind of chance."[16]

I ANSWER THAT IT SHOULD BE SAID that grace and virtue imitate the order of nature, which is set up out of divine wisdom. Now the order of nature is such that any natural agent first diffuses its action more toward the things that are nearer to it, just as fire gives more heat to a thing that is nearer to it. Likewise, God diffuses the gifts of his goodness first and most copiously into the substances that are nearer to himself, as is clear from Dionysius, *Celestial Hierarchy,* chapter 4.[17] Now the showing of benefits is a certain action of charity toward others. And so it is necessary that the nearer we are to others, the more good we should do them.

But the nearness of one man to another can be observed according to the different things in which human beings share among themselves – as

13. In Question 26, Article 9.

14. Some versions omit "but rather the other way around."

15. 2 Corinthians 12.14.

16. Augustine, *De doctrina christiana* bk.1 chap.28 sect.29 (PL 34:30; CCSL 32: 22.1–4).

17. Ps-Dionysius, *On the Celestial Hierarchy* chap.4 sect.3 (PG 3:209A; Chevallier 2:853).

in the sharing of blood relatives in natural things, fellow citizens in civic things, the faithful in spiritual things, and so forth. And according to different connections, different benefits should be distributed in different ways. For any person, simply speaking, should be given a benefit that belongs to the thing according to which he is most closely connected to us. This can, however, vary according to a difference of times and places and business activities. For in a particular case, a stranger should be given more help, if he be in extreme need, than one's father, at least when one's father is not experiencing such need.

[1] TO THE FIRST ARGUMENT, THEREFORE, IT SHOULD BE SAID that the Lord did not simply prohibit us to invite our friends and blood relatives to a feast, but rather prohibited us to invite them with the intention "so they might invite you back."[18] For this would not be charity but cupidity. It can happen, nonetheless, that in some particular case strangers should be more invited, on account of their greater need. For it should be understood that, other things being equal, one should do more good to those more connected to us. And if there are two people, one of whom is more connected to us and the other is more in need, the person to whom more help should be given cannot be determined by a universal rule, since there are different levels of both need and closeness. Rather, this requires the judgment of the prudent person.

[2] To the second it should be said that the common good of many is more divine than the good of one. So that for the good of the commonwealth, whether spiritual or temporal, it is virtuous for a person to expose his own life to danger. And so, since sharing in warlike actions is directed to the preservation of the commonwealth, a soldier who gives help to his fellow soldier does not, in this act, help him as a private person, but rather aids the entire commonwealth. And so it is not surprising if in this act, a stranger is preferred over someone connected to us by blood.

[3] To the third it should be said that a thing is owed in two ways. The first is when a thing should not be counted among the goods of the person who owes, but rather among the goods of the person to whom the thing is owed. For example, if someone has money or something else that belongs to another—whether because it was stolen from him, or because it was taken on loan or as a deposit, or in some other like way—with respect

18. For another provocative reading of this passage, see Søren Kierkegaard, *Works of Love,* trans. Howard and Edna Hong (New York: Harper Torchbooks), 90–92.

to this, a man should first return what is owed, rather than use it to benefit his connections. Unless, by chance, there were to be a case of such need in which it would also be allowable for him to take another's things in order to bring assistance to the need of the person suffering. But it may be that the person to whom the thing is owed stands in a similar need. In this case, the condition of each person should be weighed according to other conditions, with the judgment of the prudent person. This is because a universal rule cannot be given in such matters, on account of the variety of singular cases, as the Philosopher says in *Ethics* 9.[19]

The other way in which a thing is due is that it is counted among the goods of the person who owes,[20] and not among those of the person to whom something is owed. For example, when something is owed not out of any necessity of justice, but out of a kind of moral equity, as happens in benefits freely received. Now a benefit from any benefactor is not so great as that which comes from one's parents, and so parents should be preferred to all others in paying back benefits, unless need in some other respect should be given more weight, or some other condition—for example, the common advantage of the Church or commonwealth. In other matters, however, we should have a judgment of both the connection and the benefit received. These things likewise cannot be determined by a general rule.

[4] To the fourth it should be said that parents are like one's superiors, and so the love of parents is directed to doing good, whereas the love of children is directed toward giving honor to one's parents. Nevertheless, in a case of extreme need, it would be more allowable to abandon one's children than to abandon one's parents, whom in no way is it allowable to abandon, on account of the obligation stemming from the benefits received from them, as is clear from the Philosopher in *Ethics* 8.[21]

Article 4. [Whether doing good is a special virtue.]

One proceeds in this way to the fourth query. IT SEEMS that doing good is a special virtue.

[1] Precepts are directed to virtue, since "legislators intend to make human beings virtuous," as is said in *Ethics* 2.[22] But the precepts about doing

---

19. Aristotle, *Nicomachean Ethics* bk.9 chap.2 (1164b27).

20. Some versions read "the goods of the person who has it."

21. Aristotle, *Nicomachean Ethics* bk.8 chap.14 (1163b18).

22. Aristotle, *Nicomachean Ethics* bk.2 chap.1 (1103b3); also see bk.1 chap.13 (1102a9).

good and about love are given separately, for Matthew 5 says: "Love your enemies, and do good to those who hate you."[23] Therefore doing good is a virtue distinct from charity.

[2] Furthermore, vices are opposed to virtues. But against doing good are opposed some special vices, by which harm is inflicted on a neighbor, such as robbery, theft, and other things of this sort. Therefore doing good is a special virtue.

[3] Furthermore, charity is not distinguished into multiple species. But doing good seems to be distinguished into several species, according to the different species of benefits. Therefore doing good is a virtue other than charity.

BUT TO THE CONTRARY the inward act and the outward act do not require different virtues. But doing good and goodwill do not differ except as the outward act and the inward act differ, since doing good is the execution of goodwill. Therefore just as goodwill is not a virtue other than charity, so neither is doing good.

I ANSWER THAT IT SHOULD BE SAID that virtues are diversified according to the different aspects of the object. The same aspect, however, is the formal object of charity and doing good, for both look to the common aspect of good, as is clear from what was said before.[24] So that doing good is not a virtue other than charity, but names a certain act of charity.

[1] TO THE FIRST ARGUMENT, THEREFORE, IT SHOULD BE SAID that precepts are given in relation not to the habits of the virtues, but to their acts. And so a difference of precepts does not signify different habits of the virtues, but rather different acts.

[2] To the second it should be said that just as all benefits given to a neighbor, as far as they are considered under the common aspect of good, are traced back to love, so all harms, as far as they are considered under the common aspect of evil, are traced back to hatred. But to the extent that they are considered according to some special aspects of good or evil, they are traced back to some special virtues or vices. Accordingly, there are also different species of benefits.

[3] So the response to the third argument is clear.

23. Matthew 5.44.
24. In Article 1 of this Question.

[On Hatred]

One should next consider the vices opposed to charity. And first, hatred, which is opposed to love itself; second, acedia and envy, which are opposed to the joy of charity; third, discord and schism, which are opposed to peace; fourth, offense and scandal, which are opposed to doing good and fraternal correction.

About the first point, six queries are raised. (1) Whether God can be hated. (2) Whether hatred of God is the greatest of sins. (3) Whether hatred of one's neighbor is always a sin. (4) Whether it is the greatest among the sins that are against one's neighbor. (5) Whether it is a capital sin. (6) From which capital sin does hatred arise?

Article 1. [Whether anyone can hate God.]

One proceeds in this way to the first query. IT SEEMS that nobody can hate God.

[1] Dionysius, *Divine Names,* chapter 4, says that "the beautiful and the good itself are lovable and choiceworthy to all."[1] But God is beauty and goodness itself. Therefore he is hated by nobody.

[2] Furthermore, in the Apocrypha of 3 Esdras, it is said that "all things call upon truth, and do well in her works."[2] But God is truth itself, as is said in John 14.[3] Therefore all human beings love God, and nobody can hate him.

[3] Furthermore, hatred is a kind of aversion. But as Dionysius says, in *Divine Names,* chapter 4, God turns all things to himself.[4] Therefore nobody can hate him.

1. Ps-Dionysius, *Divine Names* chap.4 sect.10 (PG 3:708A; Chevallier 1:199).
2. 3 Esdras 4.36, 39.
3. John 14.6.
4. Ps-Dionysius, *Divine Names* chap.4 sect.4 (PG 3:700A; Chevallier 1:167).

BUT TO THE CONTRARY there is what is said in the Psalm, "The pride of those who hate you mounts always."[5] And John 15: "But now they have both seen and hated both me and my Father."[6]

I ANSWER THAT IT SHOULD BE SAID that, as was said above,[7] hatred is a certain motion of the appetitive power, which is not moved except by something apprehended. Now God can be apprehended by a person in two ways. In one way, according to himself, as when he is seen in his essence. In another way, by his effects, since "the invisible things of God are clearly seen, being understood by the things that are made."[8] Now God in his essence is goodness itself, which nobody can hate, since to be loved belongs to the aspect of good. And so it is impossible that a person, seeing God in his essence, should hate him. But some of God's effects can in no manner be contrary to the human will, since to be, to live, and to understand – which are certain effects of God – are desirable and lovable for everyone. So that according as God is apprehended as the author of these effects, he cannot be hated.

But there are certain effects of God that are repugnant to the disordered will, for example, the infliction of punishment, or the restriction of sins by the divine law, which is repugnant to the will depraved by sin. As far as the consideration of such effects goes, God can be hated by some, to the extent that he is apprehended as the prohibitor of sins and the inflictor of punishments.

[1] TO THE FIRST ARGUMENT, THEREFORE, IT SHOULD BE SAID that this reasoning applies to those who see the essence of God, which is the very essence of goodness.

[2] To the second it should be said that this reasoning goes through to the extent that God is apprehended as the cause of the effects that are naturally loved by human beings. Among these effects are the works of truth, who makes her knowledge available to human beings.

[3] To the third it should be said that God turns all things to himself, so far he is the first principle of beings, since all things, so far as they are, tend toward the likeness of God, who is being itself (*ipsum esse*).

---

5. Psalm 73.23.
6. John 15.24.
7. *Summa* 1a2ae q.29 a.1.
8. Romans 1.20.

Article 2. [Whether hatred of God is the greatest of sins.]

One proceeds in this way to the second query. IT SEEMS that hatred of God is not the greatest of sins.

[1] The gravest sin is the sin against the Holy Spirit, which is unforgivable, as Matthew 12 says.[9] But hatred of God is not counted among the kinds of sin against the Holy Spirit, as is clear from what was said above.[10] Therefore hatred of God does not belong to the gravest sins.

[2] Furthermore, sin consists in estrangement from God. But an unfaithful person, who has no knowledge of God, seems to be more estranged from God than a faithful person, who even if he should hate God, at least knows him. Therefore, it seems that the sin of unfaithfulness is graver than the sin of hating God.

[3] Furthermore, God is hated only by reason of his effects that are repugnant to the will, among which is chiefly punishment. But to hate punishment is not the greatest of sins. Therefore hatred of God is not the greatest of sins.

BUT TO THE CONTRARY the "worst is opposed to the best," as is clear from the Philosopher in *Ethics* 8.[11] Therefore hatred of God is opposed to the love of God (*dilectio Dei*), in which consists the best thing of man. Therefore hatred of God is the worst of man's sins.

I ANSWER THAT IT SHOULD BE SAID that the defect of sin consists in turning away from God, as was said above.[12] Now such turning away does not have the aspect of fault (*culpa*) unless it is voluntary. So the aspect of fault consists in a voluntary turning away from God. Now this voluntary turning away from God is indeed denoted *per se* in hatred of God, whereas in other sins it is, as it were, participated and according to something else. For just as the will adheres *per se* to that which it loves, so it flees by its own nature whatever it hates. Thus when someone hates God, his will by its own nature turns away from God. But in other sins, for example, when someone fornicates, he does not by his own nature turn away from God, but according to something else, so far as he desires an inordinate pleasure, which has joined to it a turning away from God. Now whatever exists *per*

---

9. Matthew 12.32.
10. *Summa* 2a2ae q.14 a.2.
11. Aristotle, *Nicomachean Ethics* bk.8 chap.10 (1160b9).
12. *Summa* 2a2ae q.10 a.3.

se is always weightier than whatever exists according to another. So hatred of God is graver than other sins.

[1] TO THE FIRST ARGUMENT, THEREFORE, IT SHOULD BE SAID that, as Gregory says, *Moralia* 25, "It is one thing not to do good, and another thing to hate the giver of good things, even as it is one thing to sin out of carelessness, and another thing to sin out of deliberation"[13] –from which one is given to understand that to hate God, the giver of all goods, is to sin out of deliberation, which is a sin against the Holy Spirit. So it is clear that hatred of God is especially a sin against the Holy Spirit, according as "sin against the Holy Spirit" names some particular genus of sin. Nonetheless, it is not counted among the species of sin against the Holy Spirit, since it is generally found in every species of sin against the Holy Spirit.

[2] To the second it should be said that unfaithfulness itself does not have the aspect of guilt, except to the extent that it is voluntary. And so it is graver, to the extent that it is more voluntary. That something is voluntary arises from this–that a person hates the truth which is proposed. So it is clear that the aspect of sin in unfaithfulness arises from hatred of God, whereas faith is about his truth. And so, just as a cause is superior to an effect, so hatred of God is a greater sin than unfaithfulness.

[3] To the third it should be said that not just anyone who hates punishments hates God, the author of punishments–for many who hate punishments nevertheless bear them patiently, out of reverence for divine justice. So Augustine says, *Confessions* 10, that God orders us to "tolerate penal evils, not to love them."[14] But to erupt into hatred of the punishing God–this is to hate the very justice of God, which is a most grave sin. So Gregory says, *Moralia* 25, "Just as it is sometimes graver to love a sin than to perpetrate it, so it is more wicked to have hated justice than not to have done it."[15]

Article 3. [Whether all hatred of one's neighbor is a sin.]

One proceeds in this way to the third query. IT SEEMS that not all hatred of neighbor is a sin.

13. Gregory the Great, *Moralia* bk.25 chap.11 sect.28 (PL 76:339; CCSL 143B: 1254.18–20). Gregory's text says "*odisse doctorum*"; Thomas (or his source) misquotes the words as "*odisse datorem.*"

14. Augustine, *Confessiones* bk.10 chap.28 sect.39 (PL 32:795; CCSL 27: 175.10–11).

15. Gregory the Great, *Moralia* bk.25 chap.11 sect.28 (PL 76:339; CCSL 143B: 1254.24–26).

[1] No sin is found in the precepts or the counsels of divine law, according to Proverbs 8: "All my words are just; there is nothing in them that is depraved or perverse."[16] But Luke 14 says, "If someone comes to me and does not hate his father and mother, he cannot be my disciple."[17] Therefore not all hatred of neighbor is a sin.

[2] Furthermore, nothing can be a sin so far as we imitate God. But in imitating God, we hate certain people, for Romans 1 says: "Detractors, hateful to God."[18] Therefore, without sin, we can hate some people.

[3] Furthermore, nothing belonging to natural things is a sin, since sin is a withdrawal from that which is according to nature, as the Damascene says, in Book 2.[19] But it is natural to anything whatever that it should hate what is contrary to itself and what strives for its corruption. Therefore it does not seem to be a sin for a person to hate his enemy.

BUT TO THE CONTRARY there is what 1 John 2 says, "He who hates his brother is in darkness."[20] But spiritual darknesses are sins. Therefore hatred of one's neighbor cannot be without sin.

I ANSWER THAT IT SHOULD BE SAID that hatred is opposed to love, as was said above.[21] So that such hatred has the aspect of evil, insofar as love has the aspect of good. Now love is owed to one's neighbor, according to that which he has from God, that is, according to nature and grace, whereas it is not owed to him, according to that which he has from himself and the devil, namely according to sin and a defect of justice. And so it is allowable to hate the sin in one's brother and everything that belongs to a defect of divine justice, but a person cannot, without sin, hate the very nature and grace of one's brother. Whereas the very fact that we hate sin and a defect of good in our brother belongs to the love of our brother – since it belongs to the same reason that we wish another good and that we hate his evil. So, taking hatred of one's brother simply (*simpliciter*), it is always with sin.

16. Proverbs 8.8.
17. Luke 14.26.
18. Romans 1.30.
19. John Damascene, *On the Orthodox Faith* bk.2 chap.4 (PG 94:876A; Buytaert chap.18 sect.1, 75.11–12) and bk.2 chap.30 (PG 94:976A; Buytaert chap.44 sect.2, 161.16–18).
20. 1 John 2.9.
21. *Summa* 1a2ae q.29 a.2.

[1] TO THE FIRST ARGUMENT, THEREFORE, IT SHOULD BE SAID that parents, with respect to the nature and affinity by which we are joined to them, should be honored according to the precept of God, as is clear from Exodus 20.[22] Whereas they should be hated so far as they stand before us as a hindrance to our approaching the perfection of divine justice.

[2] To the second it should be said that God hates the fault in his detractors, not their nature. And in this way, without fault, we can hate detractors.

[3] To the third it should be said that human beings are not set against us according to the good things that they have from God – so that with regard to this, they should be loved. Whereas they are set against us, according as they practice hostile things against us, which belongs to their sin – and with regard to this, they should be hated. For we should hate this in them – that they are enemies to us.

Article 4. [Whether hatred of one's neighbor is the gravest of the sins that are committed against one's neighbor.]

One proceeds in this way to the fourth query. IT SEEMS that hatred of one's neighbor is the gravest of the sins that are committed against one's neighbor.

[1] It is said in 1 John 3: "Everyone who hates his brother is a killer."[23] But killing is the gravest of the sins that are committed against one's neighbor. Therefore so is hate.

[2] Furthermore, the worst is opposed to the best. But of the things we show our neighbor, the best is love, since all other things are referred to love. Therefore the worst thing is hatred.

BUT TO THE CONTRARY "what does harm" is called evil, according to Augustine in the *Enchiridion*.[24] But someone does more harm to his neighbor by other sins than by hatred – for example, theft and killing and adultery. Therefore hatred is not the gravest sin.

22. See Exodus 20.12.
23. 1 John 3.15.
24. Augustine, *Enchiridion ad Laurentium seu de fide, spe et caritate* chap.4 sect.12 (PL 40:237; CCSL 46:54.11–12).

Furthermore, Chrysostom, expounding the passage in Matthew that reads "He who has broken anything of these smallest commandments"[25] says "The commandments of Moses 'Thou shalt not kill,' 'Thou shalt not commit adultery' are small in reward, but great in sin, whereas the commandments of Christ – that is, 'Thou shalt not be angry,' 'Thou shalt not indulge concupiscence' – are great in reward, but small in sin."[26] Now hatred belongs to inward motion, just like anger and concupiscence do. Therefore it is less a sin to hate one's neighbor than to kill him.

I ANSWER THAT IT SHOULD BE SAID that a sin which is committed against one's neighbor has the aspect of evil from two things. In one way, from the disordering of the person who sins; in another way, from the harm inflicted on the person sinned against. In the first way, hatred is a greater sin than outward acts that are harmful to one's neighbor, since by hatred a person's will – which is the foremost thing in a person – is disordered, and from this is the root of sin. So that if disordered outward acts occur separately from a disordered will, they are not sins – as for example when someone ignorantly kills a person owing to his zeal for justice. And if something of fault does exist in the outward sins that are committed against one's neighbor, then the whole [act] arises from inward hatred. But with respect to the harm that is inflicted on one's neighbor, outward sins are worse than inward hatred.

[1]–[2] And from this the answer TO WHAT WAS OBJECTED is clear.

Article 5. [Whether hatred is a capital vice.]

One proceeds in this way to the fifth query. IT SEEMS that hatred is a capital vice.

[1] Hatred is directly opposed to charity. But charity is the most principal of the virtues and the mother of the others. Therefore hatred is especially a capital vice, and the principle of all the other vices.

[2] Furthermore, sins arise in us according to the inclination of the passions, according to Romans 7: "The passions of sins worked in our mem-

25. Matthew 5.19.

26. Ps-Chrysostom, *Opus imperfectum in Matthaeum* hom.10, on Matthew 5.19 (PG 56:688).

bers, so as to bring the fruit of death."[27] But in the passions of the soul, all of the other passions seem to follow from love and hatred, as is clear from what was said above.[28] Therefore hatred should be set among the capital vices.

[3] Furthermore, vice is moral evil. But hatred principally looks to evil, more than any other passion does. Therefore it seems that hatred should be set down as a capital vice.

BUT TO THE CONTRARY is that Gregory, *Moralia* 31, does not enumerate hatred among the seven capital vices.[29]

I ANSWER THAT IT SHOULD BE SAID that, as was said above,[30] a capital vice is that from which other vices arise more frequently. Now a vice is against man's nature, so far as he is a rational animal. In things that happen against nature, what is natural in them is corrupted little by little. So necessarily, a thing withdraws first from what is least according to nature, and last from what is most according to nature, since what is first in construction (*in constructione*) is last in resolution (*in resolutione*). Now what is especially and chiefly natural to man is that he loves the good, and primarily the divine good and the good of his neighbor. And so hatred, which is opposed to this love, is not first in the destruction of the virtues,[31] which happens through the vices, but last. And so hatred is not a capital sin.

[1] TO THE FIRST ARGUMENT, THEREFORE, IT SHOULD BE SAID that, as is said in *Physics* 7, "the virtue of anything consists in this – that it be well disposed according to its nature."[32] And so there must be in the virtues something first and principal, which is first and principal in the natural order. Because of this, charity is set down as the most principal of the virtues. And by the same reason, hatred cannot be first among the vices, as was said.[33]

[2] To the second it should be said that hatred of an evil that is contrary to a natural good is first among the passions of the soul, just as love of a

27. Romans 7.5.
28. *Summa* 1a2ae q.27 a.4, q.28 a.6 ad 2, q.41 a.2 ad 1.
29. Gregory the Great, *Moralia* bk.31 chap.45 sect.87 (PL 76:621; CCSL 143B: 1610.17–18).
30. *Summa* 1a2ae q.84 aa.3–4.
31. Some versions read "in the love (*dilectio*) of the virtues."
32. Aristotle, *Physics* bk.7 chap.3 (246a13).
33. In the body of the Article.

natural good is first. But hatred of a connatural good cannot be first, but has the aspect of something last, since such hatred attests a corruption of nature already accomplished, along with love for an unsuitable good.

[3] To the third it should be said that evil is twofold. First, it may denote a true evil – namely, a thing repugnant to a natural good. Hatred of such an evil can have the aspect of priority among the passions. But another kind of evil is not a true evil, but an apparent evil – namely, something that is a true good and connatural, but deemed to be evil because of nature's corruption. Necessarily, the hatred of such an evil would come last. Now this kind of hatred is vicious, whereas the first is not.

Article 6. [Whether hatred arises from envy.]

One proceeds in this way to the sixth query. IT SEEMS that hatred does not arise from envy.

[1] Envy is a certain sorrow about the goods of another. Now hatred cannot arise from sorrow, but rather the converse, since we sorrow about the presence of evils that we hate. Therefore hatred does not arise from envy.

[2] Furthermore, hatred is opposed to love. But love of neighbor is referred to the love of God, as was attested above.[34] Therefore hatred of neighbor is also referred to hatred of God. But hatred of God is not caused by envy, since we do not envy the things that stand farthest from us, but rather those that seem nearest, as is clear from the Philosopher in *Rhetoric* 2.[35] Therefore hatred is not caused by envy.

[3] Furthermore, for one effect there is one cause. But hatred is caused by anger, for Augustine says in his Rule that "anger grows into hatred."[36] Hatred, therefore, is not caused by envy.

BUT TO THE CONTRARY Gregory says, *Moralia* 31, that "from envy, hatred arises."[37]

I ANSWER THAT IT SHOULD BE SAID that, as was said,[38] the hatred of neighbor comes last in the progress of sin, because it is opposed to the

34. In Question 25, Article 1, and in Question 26, Article 2.
35. Aristotle, *Rhetoric* bk.2 chap.10 (1387b22, 1388a5).
36. Augustine, *Epistulae* ep.211 chap.14 (PL 33:964; CSEL 57:368.11–12; Lawless 116, chap.6 sect.1).
37. Gregory the Great, *Moralia* bk.31 chap.45 sect.88 (PL 76:621; CCSL 143B: 1610.25).
38. In Article 5 of this Question.

love by which our neighbor is naturally loved. That a person withdraws from what is natural happens because he intends to avoid something that should naturally be fled. Now every animal naturally flees sorrow, just as every animal seeks pleasure, as is clear from the Philosopher in *Ethics* 7 and 10.[39] And just as love is caused by pleasure, so hatred is caused by sorrow. For we are moved toward loving the things that bring us pleasure, inasmuch as by that very fact, they are taken under the aspect of good. Thus we are moved toward hating the things that bring us sorrow, inasmuch as by that very fact, they are taken under the aspect of evil. So because envy is sorrow about our neighbor's good, it follows that our neighbor's good is made hateful to us. And so it is that hatred arises from envy.

[1] TO THE FIRST ARGUMENT, THEREFORE, IT SHOULD BE SAID that because the appetitive power, like the apprehensive, is reflected in its own acts, it follows that in the motions of the appetitive power there is a certain circular course. Therefore according to the first process of appetitive motion, desire follows from love and from desire follows pleasure, when someone has obtained what he desired. And since the very thing experienced as pleasurable in the loved good has a certain aspect of good, it follows that pleasure causes love. And according to the same reason, it follows that sorrow causes hatred.

[2] To the second it should be said that different reasoning applies to love and to hatred. For the object of love is good, which in creatures is derived from God, and so love is first in God, and second in neighbor. But hatred is of evil, which has no place in God himself, but [only] in his effects. So it was said above[40] that God cannot be hated, except so far as he is apprehended according to his effects. Hence hatred of neighbor is prior to hatred of God. So because envy of our neighbor is the mother of the hatred that is directed toward him, it consequently becomes the cause of hatred that is directed toward God.

[3] To the third it should be said that nothing hinders something from arising from different causes, according to different reasons. Accordingly, hatred can arise both from anger and from envy. Yet it arises more directly from envy, by which the very good of our neighbor becomes sorrowful and consequently hateful. But hatred arises from anger according to a certain increase. For through anger we first desire our neighbor's evil according to a

---

39. Aristotle, *Nicomachean Ethics* bk.7 chap.13 (1153b1); bk.7 chap.12 (1153a28); bk.10 chap.2 (1172b9).
40. In Article 1 of this Question.

certain measure – namely, so far as it has the aspect of vindication. Whereas afterwards, through the continuation of anger, a man reaches the point that he desires his neighbor's evil absolutely, which belongs to the aspect of hatred. So it is clear that hatred is caused by envy formally, according to the aspect of its object, whereas [it is caused] by anger dispositively.

QUESTION 35

[On Acedia]

One should next consider the vices opposed to the joy of charity. This joy is about both divine good, to which is opposed acedia, and about our neighbor's good, to which is opposed envy. So first one should consider acedia,[1] and second envy.[2] About the first point, four queries are raised. (1) Whether acedia is a sin. (2) Whether it is a special vice. (3) Whether it is a mortal sin. (4) Whether it is a capital vice.

Article 1. [Whether acedia is a sin.]

One proceeds in this way to the first query. IT SEEMS that acedia is not a sin.

[1] "We are neither praised nor blamed for our passions," according to the Philosopher in *Ethics* 2.[3] But acedia is a certain passion, for it is a species of sorrow, as the Damascene says,[4] and as was attested above.[5] Therefore acedia is not a sin.

[2] Furthermore, no bodily defect that occurs at set times has the aspect of sin. But acedia is of this sort, for Cassian says in *On the Institutes of the Coenobia,* Book 10, "Acedia especially troubles a monk in the sixth hour [i.e., noon], as a kind of fever that flares up in a certain time, inflicting the souls of the afflicted with sultry fires at stable and fixed times."[6] Therefore acedia is not a sin.

---

1. *Acedia,* sometimes also spelled *accidia,* names a sin that English readers sometimes encounter under the name of "sloth." For reasons not to translate *acedia* with "sloth," see "Note on the Translation and Texts" in the Introduction.

2. See Question 36.

3. Aristotle, *Nicomachean Ethics* bk.2 chap.4 (1105b31–1106a2).

4. John Damascene, *On the Orthodox Faith* bk.2 chap.14 (PG 94:932B; Buytaert chap.28, 121.3–4).

5. *Summa* 1a2ae q.35 a.8.

6. John Cassian, *De institutis coenobiorum* bk.10 chap.1 (PL 49:363).

[3] Furthermore, whatever proceeds from a good root does not seem to be a sin. But acedia proceeds from a good root, for Cassian says in the same book that acedia arises from this – that a person "sighs over not having spiritual fruit and has reckoned other monasteries that are far away as something great"[7] – which seems to belong to humility. Therefore acedia is not a sin.

[4] Furthermore, every sin should be fled, according to Sirach 21: "Flee from sin, as from the face of a snake."[8] But Cassian says, in the same book, "Experience proves that acedia should not be fled from, by swerving from it – instead it should be conquered, by making a stand."[9] Therefore acedia is not a sin.

BUT TO THE CONTRARY whatever is forbidden in sacred Scripture is a sin. But acedia is of this sort, for Sirach 6 says, "Put your shoulder to the yoke and bear it" – that is, spiritual wisdom – "and do not be weary (*acedieris*) in her chains."[10] Therefore acedia is a sin.

I ANSWER THAT IT SHOULD BE SAID that according to the Damascene,[11] acedia is a "certain oppressive sorrow" – namely, one that so depresses a person's spirit that there is nothing pleasing for him to do, just as things that are acidic are also cold. And so acedia denotes a certain tedium of acting, as is clear from what is said in the Gloss about the Psalm, "Their soul abominated every kind of meat,"[12] as well as from those who say that acedia is "a torpor of the mind, neglecting to initiate good things."[13] Now sorrow of this sort is always evil – but at some times according to itself, and at other times according to its effect. Sorrow is evil according to itself when it is sorrow about something that appears evil but is really good – just as conversely, pleasure is evil when it is pleasure about something that appears good but is really evil. Therefore, since the spiritual

---

7. John Cassian, *De institutis coenobiorum* bk.10 chap.25 (PL 49:398).

8. Sirach 21.2.

9. John Cassian, *De institutis coenobiorum* bk.10 chap.25 (PL 49:398).

10. Sirach 6.26.

11. John Damascene, *On the Orthodox Faith* bk.2 chap.14 (PG 94:932B; Buytaert chap.28, 121.4).

12. *Glossa Lombardi* on Psalm 106.18 (PL 191:977A). The psalm continues: "And they drew nigh even to the gates of death." That Thomas chooses not to quote this part is striking.

13. See Rabanus Maurus, *De ecclesiastica disciplina* bk.3 "De acedia" (PL 112:1260).

good is really good, any sorrow about spiritual good is evil in itself. But even sorrow about what is really evil is itself evil, according to its effect, if it weighs down a person so that he withdraws entirely from acting out of good. So the Apostle, 2 Corinthians 2, does not wish the penitent "to be greatly absorbed by sorrow" over sin.[14] Since, therefore, acedia – in the sense that it is taken here – names a sorrow over spiritual good, it is evil in two ways, both according to itself and according to its effect. And so acedia is a sin: for we say that evil in appetitive motions is a sin, as is clear from what was said above.[15]

[1] TO THE FIRST ARGUMENT, THEREFORE, IT SHOULD BE SAID that the passions in themselves are not sins, but are blamed according as they are applied to something evil – just as they are praised when they are applied to something good. So that sorrow in itself names nothing worthy of either praise or blame. But moderate sorrow about evil names something praiseworthy, whereas sorrow about good, as well as immoderate sorrow, names something blameworthy. Accordingly, acedia is set down as a sin.

[2] To the second it should be said both that the passions of the sensitive appetite can in themselves be venial sins, and that they incline the soul to mortal sin. And since the sensitive appetite has a bodily organ, it follows that through some bodily change a man becomes more accustomed to some particular sin. And so it can happen that according to particular bodily changes, arising in certain times, some sins assail us more. Now any bodily defect of itself disposes us to sorrow. And so those fasting at midday, when they already begin to feel the lack of food, and are beaten down by the fiery sun, are more attacked by acedia.

[3] To the third it should be said that it belongs to humility for a person, considering his own defects, not to extol himself. But for a person to scorn the goods that he has from God belongs not to humility, but rather to ingratitude. And from such scorn, acedia follows – for we sorrow over the things that we regard as evil or vile. In this way, then, it is necessary for a person to extol the goods of others, yet without scorning the goods divinely provided for himself, since they would thus bring him sorrow.

[4] To the fourth it should be said that sin should always be avoided, but that the attack of a sin should sometimes be overcome by fleeing, and sometimes by making a stand. One should flee when continual thought

14. 2 Corinthians 2.7.
15. *Summa* 2a2ae q.10 a.2; *Summa* 1a2ae q.71 a.6 and q.74 a.3.

increases the enticement of sin, as happens in lust, so that 1 Corinthians 6 says "Flee fornication."[16] But one should make a stand when persistent thought destroys the enticement of sin, which arises from some trifling apprehension. And this happens in acedia, since the more we think about spiritual goods, the more this brings us pleasure. From this thinking, acedia ceases.

Article 2. [Whether acedia is a special vice.]

One proceeds in this way to the second query. IT SEEMS that acedia is not a special vice.

[1] That which is appropriate to every vice does not constitute a special aspect of vice. But any vice causes a person to sorrow over the opposed spiritual good, for the lustful sorrow over the good of continence, and the gluttonous over the good of abstinence. Since, therefore, acedia is sorrow about spiritual good, as was said,[17] it seems that acedia is not a special sin.

[2] Furthermore, acedia is opposed to joy, since it is a certain sorrow. But joy is not set down as a special virtue. Nor therefore should acedia be set down as a special vice.

[3] Furthermore, spiritual good – since it is a kind of common object that virtue desires and vice flees – does not constitute a special aspect of virtue or vice, unless it is narrowed by something added to it. But nothing would seem to narrow a vice to acedia, if it be a special vice, except work – since some flee spiritual goods because they are laborious, so that acedia is a certain tedium. But fleeing labors and seeking bodily rest seem to belong to the same thing, namely sloth (*pigritia*). Therefore acedia would be nothing other than sloth. But this seems to be false, since sloth is opposed to solicitude, whereas acedia is opposed to joy. Acedia is not, therefore, a special vice.

BUT TO THE CONTRARY is that Gregory, *Moralia* 31, distinguishes acedia from the other vices.[18] Therefore it is a special sin.

---

16. 1 Corinthians 6.18.
17. In Article 1 of this Question.
18. Gregory the Great, *Moralia* bk.31 chap.45 sect.88 (PL 76:621; CCSL 143B: 1610.27–30). Gregory never mentions "acedia" by name.

I ANSWER THAT IT SHOULD BE SAID that, since acedia is sorrow over spiritual good, if "spiritual good" is taken generally, then acedia will not have a special aspect of vice – because every vice, as was said,[19] flees from the spiritual good of the opposed virtue. – Likewise acedia cannot be called a special vice, so far as it flees from spiritual good to the extent that it is laborious or troublesome to the body, or a hindrance to its pleasure, since this would not even separate acedia from the fleshly vices, by which a person seeks the rest and pleasure of the body.

And so it should be said that in spiritual goods, there is a certain order – for all the spiritual goods that are present in the acts of the particular virtues are directed to one spiritual good. This is the divine good, about which there is a special virtue – charity. So it belongs to any virtue to rejoice over one's own spiritual good, which consists in its own act. But the spiritual joy by which a person rejoices over divine good belongs specially to charity. And likewise, the sorrow by which a person sorrows over spiritual good, which is present in the acts of the specific virtues, does not belong to some special vice, but to all the vices. But to sorrow over the divine good, over which charity rejoices, belongs to a special vice, which is called "acedia."

[1]–[3] And from this the answer TO WHAT WAS OBJECTED is clear.

Article 3. [Whether acedia is a mortal sin.]

One proceeds in this way to the third query. IT SEEMS that acedia is not a mortal sin.

[1] Every mortal sin is contrary to the precept of God's law. But acedia seems contrary to no precept, as is clear when one runs through the particular precepts of the Decalogue. Therefore acedia is not a mortal sin.

[2] Furthermore, a sin of action is not lesser than a sin of the heart in the same genus. But to withdraw in action from some spiritual good that leads one to God is not a mortal sin. Otherwise a person would sin mortally whenever he does not observe the counsels. But to withdraw in one's heart through sorrow from spiritual actions of this type is not a mortal sin. Acedia, therefore, is not a mortal sin.

---

19. *Summa* 1a2ae q.71 a.1.

[3] Furthermore, no mortal sin is found in perfect men. But acedia is found in perfect men, for Cassian says, in Book 10 of *On the Institutes of the Coenobia,* that "acedia is better known to solitaries, and for those lingering in the desert, it is a very dangerous and constant enemy."[20] Therefore acedia is not a mortal sin.

BUT TO THE CONTRARY there is what is said in 2 Corinthians 7, "The sorrow of the world brings about death."[21] But acedia is of this sort, for it is not "sorrow according to God," which is distinguished from sorrow of the world, a sorrow that brings about death. Therefore it is a mortal sin.

I ANSWER THAT IT SHOULD BE SAID that, as was said above,[22] something is called a mortal sin that destroys spiritual life, which comes through charity, according to which God lives in us. So that a sin, by its own genus, is a mortal sin, when of itself and according to its own aspect it is contrary to charity. Now acedia is a sin of this sort. For the proper effect of charity is joy about God, as was said above,[23] whereas acedia is sorrow about spiritual good, so far as this is divine good. So that according to its own kind, acedia is a mortal sin.

But one should consider that in all sins that are mortal according to their own genus, they are not mortal except when they arrive at their completion. Now the consummation of sin lies in the consent of reason, for we are now speaking of human sin, which consists in the human act, whose principle is reason. So that if the beginning of sin is in sensuality alone and does not reach the point of reason's consent, then it is a venial sin, on account of the act's incompleteness. Thus in the genus of adultery, the concupiscence that consists in sensuality alone is a venial sin. If, however, it reaches the point of reason's consent, then it is a mortal sin. So too the motion of acedia sometimes lies in sensuality alone, on account of the flesh's repugnance toward the spirit, and is then a venial sin. But sometimes it reaches the point of reason, which consents in fleeing and dreading and detesting divine good – the flesh prevailing altogether against the spirit. And then it is clear that acedia is a mortal sin.

[1] TO THE FIRST ARGUMENT, THEREFORE, IT SHOULD BE SAID that acedia is contrary to the precept about keeping the Sabbath holy.

20. John Cassian, *De institutis coenobiorum* bk.10 chap.2 (PL 49:363).
21. 2 Corinthians 7.10.
22. *Summa* 1a2ae q.72 a.5 and q.88 aa.1–2.
23. In Question 28, Article 1.

So far as this is a moral precept, it prescribes the mind's rest in God, to which is opposed the mind's sorrow about divine good.

[2] To the second it should be said that acedia is not a mental withdrawal from any spiritual good whatever, but from the divine good, to which the mind must adhere out of necessity. So if a person sorrows because someone forces him to perform works of virtue that he is not bound to do, there is no sin of acedia. But [there is a sin of acedia] when he sorrows about things that hang over his head, things that should be done for the sake of God (*propter Deum*).

[3] To the third it should be said that some incomplete motions of acedia are found in holy men, which nonetheless do not reach the point of reason's consent.

Article 4. [Whether acedia should be set down as a capital vice.]

One proceeds in this way to the fourth query. IT SEEMS that acedia should not be set down as a capital vice.

[1] What moves a person toward acts belonging to sins is called a capital vice, as was attested above.[24] But acedia does not move a person toward acting, but rather draws him away from acting. Therefore it should not be set down as a capital sin.

[2] Furthermore, a capital sin has daughters assigned to it. Now Gregory, *Moralia* 31, assigns six daughters to acedia: *malice, rancor, smallness of soul, despair, torpor about the precepts, wandering of the mind among illicit things.*"[25] These do not seem appropriately to arise out of acedia. For rancor seems to be the same as hatred, which arises out of envy, as was said above.[26] Malice is the genus of every vice, and likewise wandering of the mind among illicit things is also found in all the vices. Torpor about the precepts seems to be the same as acedia. Smallness of soul and despair can arise from any of the sins. Therefore, acedia is not appropriately set down as a capital vice.

[3] Furthermore, Isidore, in his book *On the Highest Good,* distinguishes the vice of acedia from the vice of sorrow, calling sorrow the vice of

24. In Question 34, Article 5.
25. Gregory the Great, *Moralia* bk.31 chap.45 sect.88 (PL 76:621; CCSL 143B: 1610.28–30).
26. In Question 34, Article 6.

withdrawing from grave and laborious tasks to which one is bound, and calling acedia the vice of treating oneself to undeserved rest.[27] And he says that from sorrow arise *"rancor, smallness of soul, bitterness,* and *despair."* From acedia, he says, arise seven things, which are *"idleness, sleepiness, insolence of the mind, unrest of the body, instability, verbosity,* and *curiosity."*[28] Therefore it seems that acedia has been wrongly assigned – either by Gregory or by Isidore – as a capital vice, along with its daughters.

BUT TO THE CONTRARY Gregory says, *Moralia* 31, that acedia is a capital vice and has the daughters mentioned above.[29]

I ANSWER THAT IT SHOULD BE SAID that, as was said above,[30] a vice is called "capital" because something is brought forth from it, as the other vices arise from it, according to the aspect of final cause. Now just as many men act on account of pleasure, so that they both may attain it and are moved by its impulse to do something else, so too many things are done on account of sorrow – either to avoid it, or by its weight to be pushed to do something else. So that since acedia is a certain sorrow, as was said above,[31] it is appropriately set down as a capital vice.

[1] TO THE FIRST ARGUMENT, THEREFORE, IT SHOULD BE SAID that acedia, by weighing down the spirit, hinders a person from the actions[32] that cause sorrow. It does, however, lead the spirit to do some things that are either consonant with sorrow, such as weeping, or else to do some things by which sorrow is avoided.

[2] To the second it should be said that Gregory does appropriately assign the daughters of acedia. Since as the Philosopher says, in *Ethics* 8, "no

27. Isidore of Seville, *Sententiae libri tres,* bk.2 chap.37 sect.2 (PL 83:638; CCSL 111:).

28. Isidore of Seville, *Questions on the Old Testament,* on Deuteronomy, chap.16, sect.3–4 (PL 83:366). The list of acedia's effects in Isidore's text actually contains eight things: the seven named by Thomas, plus *"pervagatio."*

29. Gregory the Great, *Moralia* bk.31 chap.45 sect.88 (PL 76:621; CCSL 143B: 1610.28–30). In fact, Gregory assigns these to *trisitia,* and not to *acedia.* Acedia itself does not appear by name on Gregory's list of the seven capital vices: "inanis gloria, invidia, ira, tristitia, avaritia, ventris ingluvies, luxuria." Nor does it appear anywhere else in the *Moralia.*

30. *Summa* 1a2ae q.84 a.3 and q.84 a.4.

31. In Article 1 of this Question.

32. Some versions read "other actions."

one can remain for a long time with sorrow and what is unpleasant,"[33] it is necessary that something can arise from sorrow in two ways. In one way, as a person withdraws from sorrowful things. In another way, as he passes to other things in which he takes pleasure – as those who are unable to rejoice in spiritual pleasures give themselves over to bodily pleasures, according to the Philosopher in *Ethics* 10.[34] In the flight that belongs to this sorrow, one notices a process. First, a person flees sorrowful things. Second, he fights against the things that bring sorrow. Now spiritual goods, over which acedia sorrows, are both the end and that which is directed to the end. Flight from the end happens by *despair*. But flight from goods that are directed to the end – so far as they are directed to arduous things, which fall under deliberation – occurs by *smallness of soul*. Now so far as these things belong to common justice, there arises a *torpor about the precepts*. – Fighting against the things that bring sorrow about spiritual goods is sometimes about human beings who are led toward spiritual goods[35] – and this is *rancor*. Sometimes it extends to spiritual goods themselves, which a person is led to detest – and this, properly, is *malice*. Now so far as a person, on account of his sorrow about spiritual things, gives himself over to pleasurable outward goods, the daughter of acedia that is set down is *wandering among illicit things*.

From this, the response to the things that were objected about the particular daughters is clear. For malice is not taken here as a genus of the vices, but rather as was said. Rancor too is not taken here for hatred in general, but for a certain indignation, as was said. And the same should be said about the other daughters.

[3] To the third it should be said that Cassian, in his book *On the Institutes of the Coenobia,* also distinguishes sorrow from acedia,[36] but that Gregory more appropriately names acedia sorrow. Since as was said above,[37] sorrow is not a vice distinct from the others, according as a person withdraws from a grave and laborious task, or as he might sorrow from certain other causes, but only according as he sorrows over the divine good.

---

33. Aristotle, *Nicomachean Ethics* bk.8 chap.5 (1157b15); bk.8 chap.6 (1158a23).

34. Aristotle, *Nicomachean Ethics* bk.10 chap.6 (1176b19); bk.7 chap.14 (1154b2).

35. Some versions read "against human beings who lead [others] toward spiritual goods."

36. John Cassian, *De institutis coenobiorum* bk.10 chap.1 (PL 49:359).

37. In Article 2 of this Question.

This belongs to the aspect of acedia,[38] which insofar as it turns to undeserved rest, spurns the divine good.

Now the things that Isidore sets down as arising from sorrow and acedia can be traced back to the things that Gregory sets down.[39] For *bitterness,* which Isidore sets down as arising from sorrow, is a certain effect of rancor. *Idleness* and *sleepiness* may be traced back to torpor about the precepts, about which one person is idle, overlooking them altogether,[40] and another person is sleepy, fulfilling them negligently. Each of the other five daughters that Isidore sets down as arising from acedia belong to the "wandering of the mind among illicit things." According as it resides in the very stronghold of the mind, wishing to spread itself out over various things in an insolent way, it is called *insolence of the mind.* But as it belongs to thought, it is called *curiosity.* So far as it belongs to speech, it is called *verbosity.* So far as it belongs to a body that does not remain in the same place, it is called *unrest of the body*–namely, when a person indicates the wandering of his mind by the inordinate motion of his members. When the motion is to different places, it is called *instability.* Or one can take instability as a fluctuation of purpose.

38. Some versions read "to the aspect of envy."

39. Gregory the Great, *Moralia* bk.31 chap.45 sect.88 (PL 76:621; CCSL 143B: 1610.28–30).

40. Some versions read "overlooking them all."

[On Envy]

One should next consider envy. Regarding this, four queries are raised. (1) What is envy. (2) Whether it is a sin. (3) Whether it is a mortal sin. (4) Whether it is a capital vice – and about its daughters.

Article 1. [Whether envy is sorrow.]

One proceeds in this way to the first query. IT SEEMS that envy is not sorrow.

[1] The object of sorrow is evil. But the object of envy is good, for Gregory says in *Moralia* 5, speaking of the envious person: "By his own punishment he wounds his dwindling spirit, which is tortured by the happiness of another."[1] Therefore envy is not sorrow.

[2] Furthermore, likeness is not a cause of sorrow, but rather of pleasure. But likeness is a cause of envy. For the Philosopher says in *Rhetoric* 2: "They envy those who are like them in either birth (*genus*), or relationship (*cognatio*), or stature (*statura*), or clothes (*habitus*), or reputation (*opinio*)."[2] Therefore envy is not sorrow.

[3] Furthermore, sorrow is caused by some lack, so that those who are lacking in something great are prone to sorrow, as was said above, when we treated of the passions.[3] But those "in whom only a little is lacking, and who are lovers of honor, and who are reputed to be wise men" are envious, as is clear from the Philosopher in *Rhetoric* 2.[4] Therefore envy is not sorrow.

[4] Furthermore, sorrow is opposed to pleasure. Now opposed things do not have the same cause. Therefore, since the memory of goods once possessed

1. Gregory the Great, *Moralia* bk.5 chap.46 sect.85 (PL 75:728; CCSL 143: 282.32–33).
2. Aristotle, *Rhetoric* bk.2 chap.10 (1387b22, b25).
3. *Summa* 1a2ae q.32 a.3.
4. Aristotle, *Rhetoric* bk.2 chap.10 (1387b27, b31).

is the cause of pleasure, as was said above,[5] it would not be the cause of sorrow. It is, however, the cause of envy, for the Philosopher says in *Rhetoric* 2 that some envy those "who have or have had the things that were suitable to ourselves, or which we once possessed."[6] Therefore envy is not sorrow.

BUT TO THE CONTRARY the Damascene, in Book 2, sets down envy as a species of sorrow, and says that envy is sorrow "over the goods of others."[7]

I ANSWER THAT IT SHOULD BE SAID that the object of sorrow is one's own evil. Now it can happen that what is another's good is apprehended as one's own evil. Accordingly, there can be sorrow about another's good. But this happens in two ways. In one way, when a person sorrows over the good of another, to the extent that it threatens him by the danger of some harm—just as when a person sorrows over the rise of his enemy, lest this wound him. And such sorrow is not envy, but is rather an effect of fear, as the Philosopher says in *Rhetoric* 2.[8] In another way, the good of another is judged as one's own evil, so far as it lessens one's own glory or excellence. And in this way, envy sorrows over the good of another. Thus men are primarily envious "of the things in which there is glory, and in the things in which men love to be honored, and in which reputation exists," as the Philosopher says.[9]

[1] TO THE FIRST ARGUMENT, THEREFORE, IT SHOULD BE SAID that nothing prevents what is good for one from being apprehended as evil for another. Accordingly, there can be a sorrow about good, as was said.[10]

[2] To the second it should be said that since envy concerns the glory of another, so far as it lessens the glory that a person seeks, it follows that he envies only those whom he wants to equal or surpass in glory. But this is not in respect of those who are very much distant from him: for no one, unless he is insane, seeks to equal or surpass in glory those who are greater than him by much, for example, a common man vis-à-vis a king, or even

5. *Summa 1a2ae* q.32 a.3.

6. Aristotle *Rhetoric* bk.2 chap.10 (1388a20).

7. John Damascene, *On the Orthodox Faith* bk.2 chap.4 (PG 94:932B; Buytaert chap.28, 121.5).

8. Aristotle, *Rhetoric* bk.2 chap.9 (1386b22).

9. Aristotle, *Rhetoric* bk.2 chap.10 (1387b35).

10. In the body of this Article.

a king vis-à-vis a common man, whom he surpasses by much. Hence a person does not envy those who are far removed from him by time or place or condition. But he does envy those who are close to him, whom he strives to equal or surpass. For when they surpass him in glory, this occurs against his advantage, and thereby sorrow is caused. Likeness, however, causes pleasure, so far as it agrees with the will.

[3] To the third it should be said that no one strives for the things in which he is greatly lacking. And so when someone surpasses him in such a thing, he is not envious. But if he is lacking only a little, then it seems that he can reach up to this point, and thus does he strive for it. So that if his attempt is in vain, on account of an excess of glory of another, he sorrows. And so it is that lovers of honor are more envious. Likewise, those who are small in soul are also envious, since they regard everything as great, and take anything good that happens to another as having overcome them in something great. So also Job 5 says, "Envy kills the little ones."[11] And Gregory says in *Moralia* 5 that "we cannot envy others, unless we think them better than ourselves in something."[12]

[4] To the fourth it should be said that the memory of past goods, so far as they were once possessed, causes pleasure – but such goods, so far as they have been lost, cause sorrow. To the extent they are possessed by others, they cause envy, since this especially seems to subtract from our own glory. And so the Philosopher says, in *Rhetoric* 2, that "the old envy the young, and those who have spent much to obtain something envy those who have acquired the same thing at a small expense,"[13] for they grieve over the loss of their goods, and over this – that others have acquired the goods.

Article 2. [Whether envy is a sin.]

One proceeds in this way to the second query. IT SEEMS that envy is not a sin.

[1] Jerome says, in *To Laeta: On the Education of a Girl:* "Let her have companions with whom she learns, whom she may envy, and by whom she is stung when they are praised."[14] But no one should be encouraged to sin. Therefore envy is not a sin.

11. Job 5.2.
12. Gregory the Great, *Moralia* bk.5 chap.46 sect.84 (PL 75:727; CCSL 143: 281.1–3).
13. Aristotle, *Rhetoric* bk.2 chap.10 (1388a22).
14. Jerome, *Epistulae* ep.107 (PL 22:871; CSEL 55:294.14–15).

[2] Furthermore, envy is "sorrow about the goods of others," as the Damascene says.[15] But this sometimes happens in a praiseworthy manner, for Proverbs 29 says, "When the wicked will have assumed control, the people will lament."[16] Therefore envy is not always a sin.

[3] Furthermore, envy names a certain zeal. But a certain zeal is good, according to the Psalm, "Zeal for your house has consumed me."[17] Therefore envy is not always a sin.

[4] Furthermore, punishment is distinct from sin. But envy is a certain punishment, for Gregory says, *Moralia* 5: "When the rottenness of envy (*livor*) has corrupted the defeated heart, the very exterior also indicates how heavily the spirit has been instigated by frenzy. The complexion, as you see, grows pale, the eyes are weighed down, the mind is inflamed, the members grow cold – and from this arises madness in thought and gnashing of teeth."[18] Therefore envy is not a sin.

BUT TO THE CONTRARY there is what is said in Galatians 5, "Let us not be made desirous of vainglory, provoking one another, envying one another."[19]

I ANSWER THAT IT SHOULD BE SAID that envy is a certain sorrow "over the goods of others," as was said.[20] But this sorrow can happen in four ways. In the first way, when a person grieves over another's good, to the extent that he fears harm from that good, whether to himself or to the goods of others. Such sorrow is not envy, as was said, and it can exist without sin. So Gregory says, *Moralia* 22: "Often it comes to pass that, without any loss of charity, the ruin of an enemy brings us joy, and in turn his glory causes us to sorrow, without any fault of envy, since we believe that when he falls, some others are well raised up, and we fear that when he makes progress, many others will be unjustly oppressed."[21]

---

15. John Damascene, *On the Orthodox Faith* bk.2 chap.14 (PG 94:932B; Buytaert chap.28, 121.4).
16. Proverbs 29.2.
17. Psalm 68.10.
18. Gregory the Great, *Moralia* bk.5 chap.46 sect.85 (PL 75:728; CCSL 143: 282.26–30).
19. Galatians 5.26.
20. In Argument [2] of this Article.
21. Gregory the Great, *Moralia* bk.22 chap.11 sect.23 (PL 76:226; CCSL 143A: 1109.21–25).

In the second way, someone can sorrow over another's good, not because the other has the good, but because the good that we do not have is the good that he has. And this, properly speaking, is zeal, as the Philosopher says in *Rhetoric* 2.[22] If this zeal is about noble goods (*bona honesta*), then it is praiseworthy, according to 1 Corinthians 14: "May you be zealous for spiritual things."[23] But if the zeal is about temporal goods, then it can be either with sin or without sin.

In the third way, a person sorrows over another's good so far as he to whom that good falls is unworthy of it. This sorrow cannot arise from noble goods, from which a person is made just. But as the Philosopher says, in *Rhetoric* 2,[24] this sorrow arises from riches and other such things, which can favor the worthy and the unworthy. In itself, this sorrow is called "nemesis," and it belongs to good customs. He says this because he considered temporal goods themselves, according to their own nature, as they may appear great to those who do not look to eternal things. But according to the teaching of faith, the temporal goods that favor the unworthy are, from the just direction of God, disposed either to their correction or to their damnation – and goods of this type are as nothing in comparison to future goods, which are reserved for the good. Hence sorrow of this type is prohibited in sacred Scripture, according to the Psalm: "Do not wish to emulate evildoers, nor be envious of those who work iniquity."[25] And in another place: "My steps had just about slipped, since I was envious of the iniquitous, seeing the peace of sinners."[26]

In the fourth way, a person sorrows over the goods of another, so far as another surpasses him in good things. And this is envy proper. It is always depraved, as the Philosopher says in *Rhetoric* 2,[27] since it grieves over that in which one should rejoice – namely, our neighbor's good.

[1] TO THE FIRST ARGUMENT, THEREFORE, IT SHOULD BE SAID that "envy" is there taken to mean the zeal by which a person should be inspired to make progress in relation to his betters.

[2] To the second it should be said that this argument proceeds from sorrow over the goods of others, according to the first way [mentioned above].

22. Aristotle, *Rhetoric* bk.2 chap.11 (1388a30).
23. 1 Corinthians 14.1.
24. Aristotle, *Rhetoric* bk.2 chap.9 (1387a11).
25. Psalm 36.1.
26. Psalm 72.2.
27. Aristotle, *Rhetoric* bk.2 chap.11 (1388a34).

[3] To the third it should be said that envy differs from zeal, as was said.[28] So that some instances of zeal can be good, but envy is always evil.

[4] To the fourth it should be said that nothing prevents a sin from being penal by reason of something else connected to it – as was said above, when we considered the sins.[29]

Article 3. [Whether envy is a mortal sin.]

One proceeds in this way to the third query. IT SEEMS that envy is not a mortal sin.

[1] Since envy is sorrow, it is a passion of the sensitive appetite. But mortal sin does not lie in sensuality, but only in reason, as is clear from Augustine, *On the Trinity* 12.[30] Therefore envy is not a mortal sin.

[2] Furthermore, there cannot be mortal sin in infants. But there can be envy in them, for Augustine says in *Confessions* 1: "I have myself seen and experienced an envious baby, still not speaking, who turned pale as he was looking bitterly on his foster-brother."[31] Therefore envy is not a mortal sin.

[3] Furthermore, every mortal sin is opposed to a virtue. But envy is opposed not to a virtue, but to nemesis, which is a certain passion, as is clear from the Philosopher in *Rhetoric* 2.[32] Therefore envy is not a mortal sin.

BUT TO THE CONTRARY there is what is said in Job 5, "Envy kills the little ones."[33] Now nothing kills spiritually, except mortal sin. Therefore envy is a mortal sin.

I ANSWER THAT IT SHOULD BE SAID that envy, by its very genus, is a mortal sin. For the genus of sin is considered according to the object. Now envy, according to the aspect of its object, is contrary to charity, by which the spiritual life of the soul exists, according to 1 John 3: "We know

28. In the body of this Article.

29. See *Summa* 1a2ae q.87 a.2.

30. Augustine, *De trinitate* bk.12 chap.12 sect.17 (PL 42:1007; CCSL 50: 371.10–12).

31. Augustine, *Confessiones* bk.1 chap.7 sect.11 (PL 32:665–66; CCSL 27: 6.20–22).

32. Aristotle, *Rhetoric* bk.2 chap.10 (1387b31).

33. Job 5.2.

that we have passed from death to life, because we love the brethren."[34] For the object of each – of both charity and envy – is our neighbor's good, but according to contrary motions. For charity rejoices over our neighbor's good, whereas envy sorrows over the same good, as is clear from what has been said.[35] So it is clear that envy is, by its very genus, a mortal sin. But as was said above,[36] in any genus of mortal sin, some incomplete motions are found existing in sensuality, motions that are venial sins – such as the first motions of concupiscence in the genus of adultery, or the first motions of anger in the genus of homicide. So also in the genus of envy, some first motions are found at times, even in perfect men – and these are venial sins.

[1] TO THE FIRST ARGUMENT, THEREFORE, IT SHOULD BE SAID that the motion of envy, according as it is a passion of sensuality, is a certain imperfection in the genus of human acts, whose principle is reason. Such envy is not mortal sin.[37] Similar reasoning applies to the envy of little children, in whom there is no use of reason.

[2] So the response to the second argument is clear.

[3] To the third it should be said that envy, according to the Philosopher in *Rhetoric* 2,[38] is opposed to both nemesis and mercy, but according to diverse aspects. For it is directly opposed to mercy, according to the contrariety of its principal object, since envy sorrows over our neighbor's good, whereas mercy sorrows over our neighbor's evil. So the envious are not merciful, as is said in the same place, and the merciful are not envious. But on the part of the person whose good the envious person sorrows over, envy is opposed to nemesis, for nemesis sorrows over the good of those who act in an undeserving manner, according to the Psalm, "I was jealous of the wicked, seeing the peace of sinners," whereas the envious person sorrows over the good of those who are deserving.[39] So it is clear that the first contrariety is more directly opposed than the second. Now mercy is a certain virtue, and a proper effect of charity. So that envy is opposed to mercy and to charity.

---

34. 1 John 3.14.
35. In Articles 1 and 2 of this Question.
36. In Question 35, Article 3.
37. Some versions read "is mortal sin."
38. Aristotle, *Rhetoric* bk.2 chap.9 (1387a3).
39. Psalm 72.3.

Article 4. [Whether envy is a capital vice.]

One proceeds in this way to the fourth query. IT SEEMS that envy is not a capital vice.

[1] The capital vices are distinguished from the daughters of the capital vices. But envy is the daughter of vainglory, for the Philosopher says in *Rhetoric* 2 that "lovers of honor and glory are more envious."[40] Therefore envy is not a capital vice.

[2] Furthermore, the capital vices seem to be lighter than the other vices that arise from them. For Gregory says, *Moralia* 31, "The first vices work their way into the deceived mind, as though under a certain reason, but the ones that follow drag the mind into every insanity, and confound the mind with a bestial clamor."[41] But envy seems to be the gravest sin, for Gregory says, *Moralia* 5: "Although the venom of our old enemy is poured into the human heart by every vice that is perpetrated, yet in this particular wickedness the serpent reaches deep into his guts and vomits a plague of malice to be sealed within."[42] Therefore envy is not a capital vice.

[3] Furthermore, it seems that the daughters of envy are inappropriately assigned by Gregory, *Moralia* 31, where he says that "from envy arises hatred, whispering campaigns, exultation over the setbacks of our neighbor, and affliction at his prospering."[43] For exultation over the setbacks of our neighbor and affliction at his prospering seem to be the same as envy, as is clear from what was premised above.[44] Therefore these should not be set down as daughters of envy.

BUT TO THE CONTRARY is the authority of Gregory, *Moralia* 31, who sets down envy as a capital vice and assigns to her the daughters mentioned above.[45]

---

40. Aristotle, *Rhetoric* bk.2 chap.10 (1387b31).

41. Gregory the Great, *Moralia* bk.31 chap.45 sect.90 (PL 76:622; CCSL 143B: 1611.64–67).

42. Gregory the Great, *Moralia* bk.5 chap.46 sect.85 (PL 75:728; CCSL 143: 281–82.21–24).

43. Gregory the Great, *Moralia* bk.31 chap.45 sect.88 (PL 76:621; CCSL 143B: 1610.25–26).

44. In Article 3 of this Question.

45. Gregory the Great, *Moralia* bk.31 chap.45 sect.88 (PL 76:621; CCSL 143B: 1610.25–26).

I ANSWER THAT IT SHOULD BE SAID that just as acedia is sorrow about divine spiritual good, so envy is sorrow about our neighbor's good. Now it was said above[46] that acedia is a capital sin, for the reason that from acedia a person is impelled to do certain things – either to flee from sorrow or to satisfy it. So for the same reason, envy is set down as a capital vice.

[1] TO THE FIRST ARGUMENT, THEREFORE, IT SHOULD BE SAID that, as Gregory says in *Moralia* 31: "The capital vices are joined together with one another, so that there is not a single one that does not produce another one. For the first offspring of pride is vainglory, which when it corrupts the oppressed mind, soon generates envy, since when it seeks the power of an empty name, it dwindles away, lest someone else should prevail and gain power."[47] It is not, therefore, contrary to the aspect of a capital vice that it should arise from another vice. What is contrary to this aspect is only that it should not have some principal aspect for producing many genera of sins out of itself. Perhaps, however, because envy is clearly born out of vainglory, it was not set down as a capital vice – neither by Isidore in *On the Highest Good*,[48] nor by Cassian in *On the Institutes of the Coenobia.*[49]

[2] To the second it should be said that one should not gather from these words that envy is the greatest of the sins. Rather, one should gather that when the devil suggests envy, he leads a person to this – that he should have it principally in his heart, since as is introduced there in the following passage, "By the devil's envy, death has entered into the world."[50] A certain kind of envy, nonetheless, is reckoned among the gravest sins – namely, envying the grace of one's brother, according as a person grieves over the very increase of God's grace, and not only over his neighbor's good. So it is set down as a sin against the Holy Spirit, since by this envy a person envies in a certain way the Holy Spirit, which is glorified in its works.

46. In Question 35, Article 4.
47. Gregory the Great, *Moralia* bk.31 chap.45 sect.89 (PL 76:621; CCSL 143B: 1611.41–46).
48. Isidore of Seville, *Sententiae libri tres,* bk.2 chap.37 (PL 83:638). Compare Isidore of Seville, *Questions on the Old Testament,* on Deuteronomy, chap.16, sect.4 (PL 83:366).
49. John Cassian, *De institutis coenobiorum* bk.5 chap.1 (PL 49:201).
50. Wisdom 2.24. And see Gregory the Great, *Moralia* bk.5 chap.46 sect.85 (PL 75:728; CCSL 143:282.25–26).

[3] To the third it should be said that the number of the daughters of envy can be taken in this way, since in envy's striving there is a sort of beginning, a sort of middle,[51] and a sort of terminus. The beginning is that a person lessens the glory of another – either in hiding, and so there is a whispering campaign, or clearly, and so there is detraction. There is a middle, since a person who intends to diminish the glory of another is either able to do so, and so there is exultation over his setbacks, or is unable to do so, and so there is affliction over his triumphs. Now the terminus is in hatred itself, since just as a good that gives pleasure causes love, so does sorrow cause hatred, as was said above.[52] Now affliction over the triumphs of one's neighbor is envy itself, so far as a person sorrows over the triumphs of another according as they have a certain glory. In another way, it is the daughter of envy, according as the triumphs of one's neighbor occur despite the effort of the envious person, who strives to hinder them. Now exultation over setbacks is not directly the same as envy, but it does follow from it. For out of sorrow over our neighbor's good, which is envy, there follows exultation over the same person's evil.

51. Some versions omit "a sort of middle."
52. In Question 34, Article 6.

QUESTION 37

[On Discord]

One should next consider the sins that are opposed to peace. First, discord, which is in the heart; second, contention, which is on the lips; third, the things that belong to the deed – namely, schism, quarreling, and war. About the first point, two queries are raised. (1) Whether discord is a sin. (2) Whether it is the daughter of vainglory.

Article 1. [Whether discord is a sin.]

One proceeds in this way to the first query. IT SEEMS that discord is not a sin.

[1] To be discordant from something is to draw back from the will of another. But this does not seem to be a sin, since the rule of our will is not our neighbor's will, but only the divine will. Therefore discord is not a sin.

[2] Furthermore, whoever leads a person into sin, himself sins. But to induce discord among some people does not seem to be a sin, for it is said in Acts 23 that "Paul, knowing that one part was of the Sadducees and the other part of the Pharisees, exclaimed in the council: 'Men, brethren, I am a Pharisee, the son of Pharisees; regarding the hope and resurrection of the dead, I am judged.' And when he had said this, there arose dissension between the Pharisees and Sadducees."[1] Therefore discord is not a sin.

[3] Furthermore, sin – and chiefly mortal sin – is not found in holy men. But discord is found in holy men, for it is said in Acts 15: "There arose dissension between Paul and Barnabas, so that they departed one from the other."[2] Therefore discord is not a sin, and especially not a mortal sin.

BUT TO THE CONTRARY there is Galatians 5: "dissensions," that is, discords, are set down among works of the flesh, about which is added,

1. Acts 23.6.
2. Acts 15.39.

"They who do such things shall not attain the kingdom of God."[3] Nothing, however, shuts one out from the kingdom of God except mortal sin. Therefore discord is a mortal sin.

I ANSWER THAT IT SHOULD BE SAID that discord is opposed to concord. Now concord, as was said above,[4] is caused by charity—namely, so far as charity joins the hearts of many into one thing, which indeed is principally the divine good, and secondarily the good of our neighbor. Therefore discord is for this reason[5] a sin, so far as it is opposed to concord of this sort. But one should know that this concord is destroyed by discord in two ways—in one way, *per se;* in another way, *per accidens*. In human acts and motions, that which is said to be *per se* is that which is according to intention. So that someone is discordant from his neighbor *per se* when, knowingly and intentionally, he dissents from the divine good and from his neighbor's good, in which he should consent. And this is a mortal sin by its kind, on account of its contrariety to charity—even though the first motions of this discord are venial sins, on account of the act's incompleteness.

What is *per accidens* in human acts, however, is considered from this—that it lies outside the intention (*praeter intentionem*). So when the intention of a group of people is directed to a good that belongs to the honor of God or the advantage of our neighbor, but one person judges this to be good, whereas another person has a contrary opinion—then discord is against the divine good or the neighbor's good *per accidens*. And such discord is neither a sin nor repugnant to charity, unless discord of this sort comes with an error about things that are necessary for salvation, or else administered with an undue doggedness—since it has also been said above[6] that the concord which is an effect of charity is a union of wills, not a union of opinions.

From this it is clear that discord sometimes arises from the sin of only one person, as when one person wills the good and another knowingly resists. Sometimes, however, it arises from the sin of both, as when each dissents from the good of the other, and each loves only his own good.

[1] TO THE FIRST ARGUMENT, THEREFORE, IT SHOULD BE SAID that one person's will, considered in itself, is not the rule of another

---

3. Galatians 5.20.
4. In Question 29, Article 3.
5. Some versions read "for the same reason."
6. In Question 29, Article 1, and Question 29, Article 3, Reply to [2].

person's will. But so far as our neighbor's will adheres to the will of God, the result is that his rule is ruled according to its proper rule. And so to be discordant from such a will is a sin, since one is discordant by this means from the divine rule.

[2] To the second it should be said that just as a man's will adhering to God is a certain right rule, to be discordant from which is a sin, so too a man's will contrary to God is a certain perverse rule, to be discordant from which is good. Therefore it is a grave sin to cause the discord by which the good concord that charity brings about is destroyed. So Proverbs 6 says, "There are six things that the Lord hates, and a seventh that his soul detests"[7] – and Proverbs sets down this seventh thing as "the person who sows the seeds of discord among the brethren."[8] But to cause the discord by which evil concord – namely, concord in an evil will – is destroyed is praiseworthy. In this way, it was praiseworthy that Paul generated dissension among those who were concordant in evil. Moreover, the Lord said about himself, Matthew 10: "I have not come to bring peace, but a sword."[9]

[3] To the third it should be said that the discord between Paul and Barnabas was discord *per accidens* and not *per se*. For both were intending the good, but what seemed to be good to one, seemed otherwise to the other. This belonged to human defect. For that particular controversy was not about things necessary to salvation, however much it had been ordained by divine providence on account of the advantage that followed therefrom.

Article 2. [Whether discord is the daughter of vainglory.]

One proceeds in this way to the second query. IT SEEMS that discord is not the daughter of vainglory.

[1] Anger is another vice [that arises] from vainglory. But discord seems to be the daughter of anger, according to Proverbs 15: "The angry man provokes quarreling."[10] Therefore it is not the daughter of vainglory.

[2] Furthermore, expounding what is attested in John 7, "The spirit was not yet given," Augustine says in his commentary on John: "Spite separates, charity joins together."[11] But discord is nothing other than a certain

7. Proverbs 6.16.
8. Proverbs 6.19.
9. Matthew 10.34.
10. Proverbs 15.18.
11. Augustine, *In Ioannis Evangelium tractatus* tr.32 sect.8, on John 7.39 (PL 35:1646; CCSL 36:304.14–15).

separation of wills. Therefore discord proceeds from spite, that is, envy, rather than from vainglory.

[3] Furthermore, something from which many evils arise seems to be a capital vice. But discord is of this sort, because on the passage in Matthew 12, "Every kingdom divided against itself will be forsaken," Jerome says: "In this way small things grow by concord, and so the greatest things fall apart by discord."[12] Therefore discord itself should be set down as a capital vice, rather than as a daughter of vainglory.

BUT TO THE CONTRARY is the authority of Gregory, *Moralia* 31.[13]

I ANSWER THAT IT SHOULD BE SAID that discord denotes a certain coming-apart (*disgregatio*) of wills, namely so far as the will of one person sticks to one thing, and the will of another person sticks to another thing. But that a person's will should halt at his own object arises from this – that he prefers the things that are his own to the things that are of another. When this occurs inordinately, it belongs to pride and to vainglory. And so discord, by which anyone follows that which is his own and withdraws from that which is of another, is set down as a daughter of vainglory.

[1] TO THE FIRST ARGUMENT, THEREFORE, IT SHOULD BE SAID that quarreling is not the same as discord. For quarreling consists in the outward deed, so that it is appropriately caused by anger, which moves the spirit to harm one's neighbor. But discord consists in the disjunction of the will's motion, which brings about pride and vainglory, for the reason already said.[14]

[2] To the second it should be said that in discord, something may be considered as a starting point (*terminus a quo*): the will of another, from which we withdraw. In relation to this, discord is caused by envy. [Something may also be considered] as an ending point (*terminus ad quem*): what belongs to oneself, toward which we approach. In relation to this, discord is caused by vainglory. Since in any motion the ending point is better than the starting point – for the end is better than the beginning – it is better to set down discord as a daughter of vainglory rather than envy. Even so, it can arise from both, according to different aspects, as was said.

12. Jerome, *On Matthew* bk.2, on Matthew 12.26 (PL 26:82; CCSL 77: 92.425–26).

13. Gregory the Great, *Moralia* bk.31 chap.45 sect.88 (PL 76:621; CCSL 143B: 1610.23–24).

14. In the body of the Article.

[3] To the third it should be said that small things increase by concord and great things fall apart by discord, because the more a power (*virtus*) is united, the stronger it is, while it is weakened by separation, as is said in the *Book of Causes*.[15] So it is clear that this belongs to the proper effect of discord, which is a division of wills, whereas it does not belong to the origin of different vices from discord, through which it would have the aspect of a capital vice.

15. *Liber de causis* chap.16 sect.141. (Compare *The Book of Causes,* trans. Dennis Brand [Milwaukee: Marquette University Press, 1984], 34.)

QUESTION 38

[On Contention]

One should next consider contention. About this, two queries are raised. (1) Whether contention is a mortal sin. (2) Whether it is the daughter of vainglory.

Article 1. [Whether contention is a mortal sin.]

One proceeds in this way to the first query. IT SEEMS that contention is not a mortal sin.

[1] Mortal sin is not found in spiritual men. Yet contention is found in them, according to Luke 22: "Contention was generated among the disciples of Jesus, as to which of them would be greater."[1] Therefore contention is not a mortal sin.

[2] Furthermore, mortal sin in our neighbor should not be pleasing to anyone of good disposition. But the Apostle says, Philippians 1, "Some make Christ known out of contention" and adds, "In this also I rejoice, and shall rejoice."[2] Therefore contention is not a mortal sin.

[3] Furthermore, it happens that some contend either in court or in disputation, not with any spirit of maligning, but rather intending the good – just as those do who contend in disputing with heretics. So on 1 Kings 14, "It came to pass one day,"[3] the Gloss says: "Catholics do not agitate for contentions against heretics, unless they are first summoned to the dispute."[4] Therefore contention is not a mortal sin.

[4] Furthermore, Job seems to have contended with God, according to Job 39: "Can it be that he who contends with God is so easily silenced?"[5]

1. Luke 22.24.
2. Philippians 1.17.
3. 1 Samuel 14.1. (Following the Vulgate, the Latin text refers to 1 Kings 14.)
4. *Glossa ordinaria* on 1 Samuel 14.1 (Strasbourg 2, "Et accidit quadam die," col.a).
5. Job 39.32.

Yet Job did not sin mortally, since about this matter the Lord said, "You have not spoken rightly before me, as my servant Job has," as attested by the last chapter of Job.[6] Therefore contention is not always a mortal sin.

BUT TO THE CONTRARY there is what is opposed by the precept of the Apostle, who says, 2 Timothy 2: "Do not contend by words."[7] And in Galatians 5, contention is numbered among the works of the flesh: "Those who do such things shall not inherit the kingdom of God," as is said in the same place.[8] But everything that excludes one from the kingdom of God and that is opposed by a precept is a mortal sin. Therefore contention is a mortal sin.

I ANSWER THAT IT SHOULD BE SAID that to contend is to tend against someone. So just as discord denotes a certain opposition (*contrarietas*) in the will, so contention denotes a certain opposition in speech. And because of this, when a person's speech pours itself out by means of contrary things, this is called "contention," which is set down as one of the shades of rhetoric by Cicero, who says: "Contention is caused when a speech is made out of contrary things, in this way: 'He who receives flattery–that is, adulation from a pleasing source–brings about by the same thing the most bitter end.'"[9]

Now opposition in speech can be observed in two ways. In one way, regarding the intention (*intentio*) of the person contending; in another way, regarding the manner (*modus*) of contention. In the intention, one should consider whether someone is opposing truth, which is blameworthy, or whether he is opposing falsehood, which is praiseworthy. In the manner (*modus*), however, one should consider whether such a manner of opposing is appropriate both to the persons (*personae*) and to the business at hand (*negotii*). If it is, then it is praiseworthy, so that Cicero says in *Rhetoric* 3 that "contention is brisk speech (*oratio acris*), adapted to edifying and refuting."[10] Alternatively, the speech may go beyond what is appropriate to the persons or business at hand. In this way, contention is blameworthy.

6. Job 42.7.
7. 2 Timothy 2.14.
8. Galatians 5.20.
9. Rather, the anonymous *Rhetorica ad Herennium* bk.4 chap.15. This text, so prominent in the teaching of rhetoric, was frequently attributed to Cicero by medieval authors.
10. *Rhetorica ad Herennium* bk.4 chap.13.

If, therefore, contention be taken as denoting an attack on truth or an inordinate manner, it is thus a mortal sin. Ambrose defines contention in this way, saying: "Contention is an attack on truth with all the confidence of loud noise."[11] If, however, contention is said to be an attack on falsehood with a due measure of briskness (*acrimonia*), then contention is praiseworthy. If, however, contention be taken according as it denotes an attack on falsehood, accompanied by an inordinate manner, it can thus be a venial sin – unless perhaps so much inordinateness arises in contending that a stumbling block (*scandalum*) is generated for others. So the Apostle, after he said in 2 Timothy 2, "Do not contend in words," adds, "For it is useful for nothing, except for destroying those who hear it."[12]

[1] TO THE FIRST ARGUMENT, THEREFORE, IT SHOULD BE SAID that in the disciples of Christ, there was not contention accompanied by the intention of attacking truth, since each of them was defending what seemed true to him. There was, however, inordinateness in their contention, since they were contending over what should not have been a matter of contention – namely, over the primacy of honor. For they were not yet spiritual men, as a Gloss says on the same passage.[13] So as a result, the Lord checked them.

[2] To the second it should be said that those who used to preach Christ out of contention were reprehensible, since while they were not attacking the truth of faith (rather, they were preaching it), they did nonetheless attack the truth in this respect – that they thought to "put pressure"[14] on the Apostle who was preaching the truth of faith. So the Apostle did not rejoice over their contention, but over the fruit that came forth from it, namely "that Christ would be made known,"[15] since even from evils as occasions, good things follow.

[3] To the third it should be said that according to the full definition (*completa ratio*) of contention, as a mortal sin, the person who contends in court is he who attacks the truth of justice, and the person who contends in disputation is he who intends to attack the truth of doctrine. And in this sense Catholics do not contend against heretics, but rather vice versa. If,

11. Ambrose, in *Glossa Lombardi* on Romans 1.29 (PL 191:1335C).
12. 2 Timothy 2.14.
13. *Glossa ordinaria* on Luke 22.24 (Strasbourg 5, "Facta est autem contentio," col.a).
14. Luke 22.17.
15. Luke 22.18.

however, contention in court or in a disputation is taken according to an incomplete aspect, namely so far as it denotes a certain briskness of speech, then it is not always a mortal sin.

[4] To the fourth it should be said that contention here is taken generally for "disputation." For Job had said, in chapter 13, "I speak to the Almighty, and I desire to dispute with God"[16] – not, however, intending to attack, nor actually attacking, the truth, but rather to inquire. Nor did this inquiry make use of any inordinateness, whether in spirit (*animus*) or in tone (*vox*).

Article 2. [Whether contention is the daughter of vainglory.]

One proceeds in this way to the second query. IT SEEMS that contention is not the daughter of vainglory.

[1] Contention bears an affinity to zeal, so that 1 Corinthians 3 says: "When there is zeal and contention among you, are you not carnal, and do you not walk around in the manner of men?"[17] Now zeal belongs to envy. Therefore contention arises more out of envy.

[2] Furthermore, contention is accompanied by a certain loud noise (*clamor*). But "loud noise arises from anger," as is clear from Gregory, *Moralia* 31.[18] Therefore contention also arises from anger.

[3] Furthermore, among other things, knowledge seems to be the matter of pride and vainglory, according to 1 Corinthians 8: "Knowledge puffs up."[19] But contention often comes out of a lack of the knowledge by which the truth is known, not attacked. Therefore contention is not the daughter of vainglory.

BUT TO THE CONTRARY is the authority of Gregory, *Moralia* 31.[20]

I ANSWER THAT IT SHOULD BE SAID that, as was said above,[21] discord is a daughter of vainglory, because each of the discordants sticks to

---

16. Job 13.3.

17. 1 Corinthians 3.3.

18. Gregory the Great, *Moralia* bk.31 chap.45 sect.88 (PL 76:621; CCSL 143B: 1610.26–28).

19. 1 Corinthians 8.1.

20. Gregory the Great, *Moralia* bk.31 chap.45 sect.88 (PL 76:621; CCSL 143B: 1610:23–25).

21. In Question 37, Article 2.

his own sense of things[22] and neither yields to the other. Now it is proper to pride and vainglory to seek one's own excellence. Now just as some are discordant from this – that they stick in their hearts to their own notions (*stant corde in propriis*) – so some are contentious from this – that each one defends in word (*verbo*) that which appears to him. And so, for the same reason, contention is set down as a daughter of vainglory, as discord was.[23]

[1] TO THE FIRST ARGUMENT, THEREFORE, IT SHOULD BE SAID that contention, like discord, bears an affinity to envy, with respect to the drawing back (*recessus*) by which a person is discordant, or by which he contends. But with respect to that in which the contending person clings, it bears a fitting relation to pride and vainglory, so far as he is stuck in his own sense of things, as was said above.[24]

[2] To the second it should be said that loud noise (*clamor*) is taken up into the contention of which we are speaking, whose end is attacking truth. So that it is not the principal thing in contention. Hence there is no need for contention to be derived from the same thing as that from which clamor is derived.

[3] To the third it should be said that pride and vainglory take their enabling occasion (*occasio*) chiefly from goods, even from goods contrary to them, as when someone is proud of his humility. For a derivation of this sort is not *per se* but *per accidens*. According to this measure, nothing prevents one contrary's arising from another contrary. And so nothing prevents the things that arise *per se* and directly out of pride and vainglory from being caused by the contraries of the things out of which pride arises, as from an occasion.

22. Following Piana, "discordantium uterque in sensu proprio stat." A similar phrase occurs below, at the end of the Reply to the first argument: "in proprio sensu statur."

23. Some versions read "contention is set down as a daughter of vainglory, as it is of discord."

24. In the body of this Article.

[On Schism]

One should next consider the vices opposed to peace, vices that belong to action. These are schism, quarreling, sedition, and war. First, then, four queries are raised about schism. (1) Whether schism is a special sin. (2) Whether it is graver than faithlessness. (3) On the power of schismatics. (4) On their punishment.

Article 1. [Whether schism is a special sin.]

One proceeds in this way to the first query. IT SEEMS that schism is not a special sin.

[1] As Pope Pelagius says, "*Schisma* [schism] sounds like *scissura* [fissure]."[1] But every sin brings about a certain kind of fissure, according to Isaiah 59: "Your sins have brought about division between you and your God."[2] Therefore schism is not a special sin.

[2] Furthermore, those who do not obey the Church seem to be schismatic. But a person becomes disobedient against the teachings of the Church by every sin, because sin, according to Ambrose, is "disobedience against heavenly commandments."[3] Therefore every sin is a schism.

[3] Furthermore, heresy also divides a person from the unity of faith. If, therefore, the name "schism" denotes division, it seems that it does not differ from the sin of faithlessness as a special sin.

BUT TO THE CONTRARY Augustine, *Against Faustus,* distinguishes between schism and heresy, saying that "schism is opining the same thing or worshipping by the same rite as the rest, but only delighting in the dis-

---

1. Pope Pelagius I, fragment of a letter to Victor and Pancratius (Mansi 9.731), abbreviated. (The full version runs: "Schisma si quidem ipsum, quod Graecum nomen est, scissuram sonat.")
2. Isaiah 59.2.
3. Ambrose, *De paradiso* chap.8 (PL 14:309).

sension of the congregation; but heresy opines things different from those that the Catholic Church believes."[4] Therefore schism is not a general sin.

I ANSWER THAT IT SHOULD BE SAID that, as Isidore says in the *Etymologies,* the name *schism* "is called from the fissure of spirits (*scissura animorum*)."[5] Now division (*scissio*) is opposed to unity. So the sin attributed to the schismatic is opposed directly and *per se* to unity. Just as in natural things, that which is *per accidens* does not constitute the species, so too in moral things. In these things, what is intended is *per se,* whereas what falls outside the intention (*praeter intentionem*) is, as it were, *per accidens.* And so the sin of the schismatic is a proper and special sin,[6] because it intends to separate itself from the unity that charity brings about. Charity unites not only one person to another in a bond of spiritual love, but also the whole Church into a unity of spirit. And so those who are properly called schismatics have, voluntarily and by their own intention, separated themselves from the unity of the Church, which is unity principally. For the unity of particular individuals among themselves is ordered to a united Church, just as the composition of individual members in a natural body is ordered to the unity of the whole body.

Now unity of the Church is observed in two things: in the connection of the members of the Church to one another, that is, in communion; and in the ordering of all the members of the Church to one head, according to Colossians 2: "Puffed up by the sense of his flesh, and not holding the head, from which the whole body, by joints and bands, being nourished and built up, grows into the increase of God."[7] Now this head is Christ himself, whose vicar in the Church is the Sovereign Pontiff. And so they are called schismatics who decline to be under the Sovereign Pontiff and who refuse communion (*communicare*) with the members of the Church who are subject to him.

---

4. Augustine, *Contra Faustum Manichaeum* bk.20 chap.3 (PL 42:369; CSEL 25:537.4–8). Here Thomas appears to be reproducing the version of the text (mis) quoted by Alexander of Hales; see *Summa Halensis* pt.2 sect.764 (Quaracchi 3:754). Contrary to the quotation, Augustine speaks of the "sect" (*secta*) as "opining things quite different from the others." His text does not explicitly draw a contrast between "heresy" and "the things that the Catholic Church believes."

5. Isidore of Seville, *Etymologiae* bk.8 chap.3 sect.5 (PL 82:297; Lindsay sect.5, line 23).

6. Some versions omit the words "of the schismatic is a proper and special sin."

7. Colossians 2.18–19.

[1] TO THE FIRST ARGUMENT, THEREFORE, IT SHOULD BE SAID that the division of man from God by sin is not intended by the sinner, but falls outside his intention from his inordinate turning toward the changeable good. And so this is not schism, speaking *per se.*

[2] To the second it should be said that not to obey the precepts, along with a certain rebellion, constitutes the aspect (*ratio*) of schism. Now I say "along with rebellion," since he both obstinately scorns the precepts of the Church and refuses to submit to her judgment. But not every sinner does this. So not every sin is schism.

[3] To the third it should be said that heresy and schism are distinguished according to that in which each is opposed, directly and *per se.* For heresy is opposed *per se* to faith, whereas schism is opposed *per se* to the ecclesiastical unity of charity. And so just as faith and charity are different virtues – though he who lacks faith lacks charity – so too schism and heresy are different vices, though anyone who is a heretic is also a schismatic, but not vice versa. This is what Jerome says, *On the Letter to Galatians:* "I judge this to be the difference between schism and heresy: that heresy holds a perverse dogma, whereas schism separates from the Church."[8] – And so just as the loss of charity is a way to losing faith, according to 1 Timothy – "From which things," that is, charity and other things of this sort, "some going astray, being turned toward empty speech"[9] – so too schism is a way to heresy. Thus Jerome adds in the same place that "at first, one can understand some difference between schism and heresy, but there is no schism that does not fabricate some heresy for itself, so that it seems rightly to have slipped away from the Church."[10]

Article 2. [Whether schism is a graver sin than faithlessness.]

One proceeds in this way to the second query. IT SEEMS that schism is a graver sin than faithlessness.

[1] The greater the sin, the graver the penalty administered, according to Deuteronomy: "According to the measure of the sin, will also be the

8. In fact, Jerome, *On Paul's Letter to Titus,* on Titus 3.10 (PL 26:633; CCSL 77C:70.322–24).

9. 1 Timothy 1.6.

10. In fact, Jerome, *On Paul's Letter to Titus,* on Titus 3.10 (PL 26:633; CCSL 77C:70.324–27).

measure of the stripes."[11] But the sin of schism is found to be more gravely punished than even the sin of unfaithfulness or idolatry. For we read in Exodus 32 that on account of idolatry, some were slain by hand with the sword of their fellow men.[12] Whereas regarding the sin of schism, we read in Numbers 16: "If the Lord were to do a new thing, and the earth opening her mouth were to swallow them and all things that belong to them, and they descend, while still living, into hell, you shall know that they have blasphemed the Lord God."[13] Also, the ten tribes who by the vice of schism had slipped away from the rule of David were punished most gravely, as attested by 2 Kings 17.[14] Therefore the sin of schism is a graver sin than faithlessness.

[2] Furthermore, "The good of many is greater and more divine than the good of one," as is clear from the Philosopher in *Ethics* 1.[15] But schism is against the good of many, that is, against the united Church, whereas faithlessness is against the particular good of one, which is the faith of one single person. Therefore it seems that schism is a graver sin than faithlessness.

[3] Furthermore, a greater good is opposed to a greater evil, as is clear from the Philosopher in *Ethics* 8.[16] But schism is opposed to charity, which is a greater virtue than faith, to which faithlessness is opposed, as is clear from what was premised above.[17] Therefore schism is a graver sin than faithlessness.

BUT TO THE CONTRARY what comes out of an addition to another is superior, either in good or in evil. But heresy comes by an addition to schism, for it adds a perverse dogma, as is clear from the authority of Jerome cited above.[18] Therefore schism is less a sin than faithlessness.

I ANSWER THAT IT SHOULD BE SAID that the gravity of a sin can be taken in two ways. In one way, according to its species. In another way, according to circumstances. Since particular circumstances are infinite, and can be varied in infinite ways, when it is inquired generally about two

11. Deuteronomy 25.2.
12. Exodus 32.27.
13. Numbers 16.30.
14. 2 Kings 17.20. (Following the Vulgate, the Latin text refers to 4 Kings 17.)
15. Aristotle, *Nicomachean Ethics* bk.1 chap.2 (1094b10).
16. Aristotle, *Nicomachean Ethics* bk.8 chap.10 (1160b9).
17. See Question 23, Article 6.
18. In fact, Jerome, *On Paul's Letter to Titus,* on Titus 3.10 (PL 26:633; CCSL 77C:70.322–23).

sins, "which is more grave?" the question about gravity should be understood as a question regarding the sin's genus. Now the genus or the species of sin is observed from the object, as is clear from what was said above.[19] And so the sin that is contrary to a greater good in its kind is more grave, as a sin against God is more grave than a sin against our neighbor. Now it is clear that faithlessness is a sin against God himself, according as he is in himself the first truth, to which faith strives. Schism is against ecclesiastical unity, which is a certain participated good and is less than God himself. So it is clear that the sin of faithlessness is in its kind graver than the sin of schism. But it can happen that a particular schismatic sins more gravely than a particular faithless person – either on account of greater scorn, or on account of the greater danger that he leads others toward, or on account of something else of this sort.

[1] TO THE FIRST ARGUMENT, THEREFORE, IT SHOULD BE SAID that it had already been made clear to these people, by the law they accepted, that there was one God and that they should not worship any other gods – and this had been confirmed among them by multiple signs. And so it was not necessary that sinners against this faith, who sinned by idolatry, would be punished in some unaccustomed way; the common way was enough. But it was not known in this way among them that Moses should always be their prince. And so it was necessary for those rebelling against his supremacy to be punished by penalties miraculous and unaccustomed. – Or it can be said that the sin of schism was sometimes punished more gravely in this people, since they were disposed to seditions and schisms. For it says in I Esdras 4: "This city from the days of old rebelled against the kings, and both seditions and wars were inflamed in it."[20] Now sometimes a greater punishment is inflicted against a sin more accustomed, as was attested above[21] – for punishments are a kind of medicine for protecting people against sin. So that where there is a greater proneness to sinning, a more severe punishment should be administered. – The ten tribes were punished not only for the sin of schism but also for the sin of idolatry, as is said in the same place.[22]

[2] To the second it should be said that just as the good of a multitude is greater than the good of one person who comes from a multitude, so also it is less than the extrinsic good to which the multitude is ordered – just as the

19. *Summa* 1a2ae q.72 a.1, q.73 a.3.
20. 1 Ezra 4.19.
21. *Summa* 1a2ae q.105 a.2 ad 9.
22. 4 Kings 17.21; compare 3 Kings 12.28.

good of order in an army is less than the good of its leader. Likewise, the good of the unity of the Church, to which schism is opposed, is less than the good of divine truth, to which faithlessness is opposed.

[3] To the third it should be said that charity has two objects. One is principal, namely, divine goodness. The other is secondary, namely, our neighbor's good. Now schism and other sins that arise against our neighbor are opposed to charity with respect to the secondary good, which is less than the object of faith, which is God himself. And so these sins are lesser than faithlessness. But the hatred of God, which is opposed to charity with respect to its principal object, is not lesser. – Nevertheless, among the sins that are against our neighbor, the sin of schism seems to be greatest, since it is against the spiritual good of the many.

Article 3. [Whether schismatics have any power.]

One proceeds in this way to the third query. IT SEEMS that schismatics have some power.

[1] Augustine says, in his book *On Baptism, Against the Donatists:* "As those returning to the Church after they first received baptism are not re-baptized, so those returning after receiving holy orders are not ordained again."[23] But orders are a kind of power. Therefore schismatics have some power, since they retain orders.

[2] Furthermore, Augustine says, in his book *On the Unity of Baptism,* "One who is separated can give a sacrament, just as he can have it."[24] But the power of giving the sacrament is power to the highest degree. Therefore schismatics, who are separated from the Church, have spiritual power.

[3] Furthermore, Pope Urban says that "we order that those who were consecrated by bishops who themselves were ordained as Catholics, but who have separated themselves in schism from the Roman Church, should be received mercifully and their orders be preserved, when they return to the unity of the Church, if their life and knowledge recommend them."[25]

23. Augustine, *De baptismo contra Donatistas* bk.1 chap.1 sect.2 (PL 43:109).

24. Though Thomas cites another title, the reference is to Augustine, *De baptismo contra Donatistas* bk.6 chap.5 sect.7 (PL 43:200).

25. Pope Urban II, Council of Piacenza, chap.10 (Mansi 20.806). Both the Leonine edition and the document printed in Mansi's text speak of "life and knowledge" (*vita et scientia*), but some versions of the *Summa* have "life and conscience" (*vita et conscientia*).

But this would not be the case, unless spiritual power were to remain among schismatics. Therefore schismatics have spiritual power.

BUT TO THE CONTRARY Cyprian says in a certain letter: "He who observes neither unity of spirit nor the peace of concord, and severs himself from the bonds of the Church and from the collegiality of her priests, can have neither episcopal power nor honor."[26]

I ANSWER THAT IT SHOULD BE SAID that spiritual power is two-fold: the first sacramental, the second juridical. Sacramental power is in-deed conferred by some consecration. Now all consecrations of the Church are immovable, as long as the thing that is consecrated remains – as is clear even in things inanimate. For an altar, once consecrated, is not consecrated again unless it has been dissipated. And so such power, according to its essence, remains in a person who has received it by a consecration as long as the person receives it, whether he falls into schism or into heresy. The matter is clear from this – that those returning to the Church are not conse-crated again. But since a lower power ought not to exercise its act, except according as it is moved by a higher power, as is clear even in natural things, it happens that such people lose the use of their power – and so it is not allowed for them to use their power. Were it to be used nevertheless, the power would have its effect in the sacraments, since in these things a person does not work except as the instrument of God. So sacramental effects are not excluded on account of any fault on the part of the person conferring the sacrament.

Juridical power, however, is that which is conferred by the simple in-junction of a person. And such power does not inhere unchangeably. So it does not remain in schismatics and heretics. So that they can neither absolve nor excommunicate nor grant indulgences, or any thing of this sort – which if they were to do it, the act would be null. Since, therefore, such people are said not to have spiritual power, either this claim should be understood to apply to the second kind of power or, if it is referred to the first kind of power, it should not be referred to this power's very essence, but to its legitimate use.

[1]–[3] And from this the answer TO WHAT WAS OBJECTED is clear.

26. Cyprian, *Epistolae ad Antonianum pars altera* sect.24 (PL 3:791A).

Article 4. [Whether it is appropriate to punish schismatics by excommunication.]

One proceeds in this way to the fourth query. IT SEEMS that it is not appropriate to punish schismatics by excommunication.

[1] Excommunication especially separates a person from communion with the sacraments. But Augustine says in his book *On Baptism, Against the Donatists* that baptism can be received from a schismatic.[27] Therefore it seems that excommunication is not an appropriate punishment for schism.

[2] Furthermore, it belongs to those with faith in Christ to bring back those who have scattered, against those who are spoken about in Ezekiel 34: "That which was cast away you have not brought back, nor have you sought that which was lost."[28] But schismatics are most appropriately brought back by those who communicate with them. Therefore it seems that they should not be excommunicated.

[3] Furthermore, two punishments are not inflicted for the same sin, according to Nahum 1: "God will not judge the same twice."[29] But for the sin of schism, a temporal punishment is inflicted, as attested in Gratian, *Book of Decrees,* Causa 23, Article 5, where it is said: "Both divine and earthly laws have decreed that those who are cut off from the unity of the Church, and disturb her peace, must be crushed (*comprimantur*) by the secular powers."[30] They should not, therefore, be punished by excommunication.

BUT TO THE CONTRARY there is what Numbers 16 says, "Leave the tents of these impious men" – namely, those who have brought about schism, "and touch none of the things that belong to them, lest you become involved in their sins."[31]

I ANSWER THAT IT SHOULD BE SAID that by the things though which a person sins, a person should be punished, as is said in Wisdom 11.[32] Now a schismatic, as was said above,[33] sins in two things. The first is that he separates himself from communion with the members of the Church.

---

27. Augustine, *De baptismo contra Donatistas* bk.6 chap.5 sect.8 (PL 43:200).
28. Ezekiel 34.4.
29. Nahum 1.9.
30. Gratian, *Decretum,* pt.2 causa 23, q.5, can.44 Quali nos (Richter-Friedberg 1:943).
31. Numbers 16.26.
32. Wisdom 11.17.
33. In Article 1 of this Question.

With respect to this, it is an appropriate punishment for schismatics to be excommunicated. The second is that he refuses to place himself under the head of the Church. And so, because they do not want to be forcibly punished (*coerceri*) by the spiritual power of the Church, it is just for them to be forcibly punished (*coerceantur*) by the temporal power.

[1] TO THE FIRST ARGUMENT, THEREFORE, IT SHOULD BE SAID that it is not allowed to receive baptism from a schismatic, except in a crisis of necessity, since it is better to exit this life with the sign of Christ, given by whomever, even if this be a Jew or a pagan, than without this sign, which is conferred by baptism.

[2] To the second it should be said that the kind of communication by which a person, issuing salubrious warnings, leads those cut off back to the unity of the Church, is not prohibited. Moreover, the very separation brings them back in a certain way when, confused about their separation, they are sometimes led to penance.

[3] To the third it should be said that the punishments of the present life are medicinal. And so when a single penalty does not suffice for a person to be forcibly punished, another is added. Just as physicians give several bodily medicines when the first is not efficacious, so the Church administers the forcible punishment of the secular arm when a person is not sufficiently repressed by excommunication. But if a single punishment does suffice, then a second should not be administered.

[On War]

One should next consider war. Regarding this point, four queries are raised. (1) Whether any war is lawful. (2) Whether it is lawful for clerics to make war. (3) Whether it is lawful for war-makers to lay ambushes. (4) Whether it is lawful to make war on feast days.

Article 1. [Whether to make war is always a sin.]

One proceeds in this way to the first query. IT SEEMS that to make war is always a sin.

[1] A punishment is not inflicted, except for sin. But punishment is declared by the Lord for war-makers, according to Matthew 26: "All who take up the sword will die by the sword."[1] Therefore every war is illicit.

[2] Furthermore, anything that is contrary to divine teaching is a sin. But to make war is contrary to divine teaching, for Matthew 5 says: "I tell you not to resist evil."[2] And Romans 12 says: "Not defending yourselves, my dearest beloved, but give place to your anger."[3] Therefore to make war is always a sin.

[3] Furthermore, nothing is contrary to the act of a virtue except a sin. But war is contrary to peace. Therefore war is always a sin.

[4] Furthermore, every practice of something lawful is itself lawful, as is clear in the practices of the sciences. But the practices related to wars that occur in tournaments are prohibited by the Church, since those who die in trials (*tyrocinia*) of this sort are deprived of a church-approved burial. Therefore war absolutely seems to be a sin.

BUT TO THE CONTRARY Augustine says, in a sermon on the son of the centurion: "If Christian discipline were to condemn war alto-

---

1. Matthew 26.52.
2. Matthew 5.39.
3. Romans 12.19.

gether, then those who sought healthy advice in the Gospel would rather have been advised to lay down their arms, and to take themselves out of military service altogether. But it was said to them: 'Do not violently rob anyone . . . and be content with your pay.' Since he taught them that their pay would be enough, he did not prohibit them from serving as a soldier."[4]

I ANSWER THAT IT SHOULD BE SAID that for any war to be just, three things are required. First, the authority of the prince, by whose command war is to be waged. For it does not belong to a private person to instigate war, since he can seek his own right (*ius*) in the judgment of a higher court. Likewise, to call together the masses – which must happen in wars – does not belong to a private person. Rather, care for the public good is given to princes, to whom belongs the public good of the city, or the kingdom or the province, which is placed under them to protect. And just as it is lawful for them to defend the public good by the relevant sword against internal agitators, when they punish such malefactors, according to the Apostle in Romans 13: "Not without cause does he bear the sword, for he is a minister of God, a protector (*vindex*) to bring wrath upon him who does evil"[5] – so too it belongs to them to use the sword of war to protect the public good from external enemies. So it is said to princes in the Psalm: "Rescue the poor, and liberate those in need from the sinner's hand."[6] So Augustine says, in *Against Faustus,* "The natural order, adapted to peace for mortal men, demands this – that the authority to wage war and to counsel it lies in the hands of princes."[7]

Second, a just cause is required – namely, that those who are attacked should deserve the attack on account of some offense (*culpa*). So Augustine says, in his *Seven Questions Concerning the Heptateuch:* "Just wars are customarily defined as those which avenge injuries, if a nation or city should be beaten down for neglecting to make right the wrongs committed by its people, or to give back what it unjustly taken away."[8]

---

4. Rather, Augustine, *Epistulae* ep.138 to Marcellinus chap.2 sect.15 (PL 33:531; CCSL 31B:285.287–92). Augustine is quoting a truncated version of Luke 3.14.

5. Romans 13.4.

6. Psalm 81.4.

7. Augustine, *Contra Faustum Manichaeum* bk.22 chap.75 (PL 42:448; CSEL 25:673.11–13).

8. Augustine, *Quaestiones in Heptateuchum libri septem* bk.6 q.10 on Joshua 8.2 (PL 34:781; CCSL 33:319.259–62).

Third, a right intention is required on the part of those making war— namely, that by which it is intended that either a good be advanced or an evil be avoided. So Augustine, in his book *On the Words of the Lord:* "Among true worshippers of God, those wars are peaceful which are waged not out of covetous desire (*cupiditas*) or cruelty, but out of a zeal for peace, so that the evil are forcibly punished and the good are raised up."[9] Now it can happen that even if there is a legitimate authority declaring war, as well as a just cause, the war nevertheless is waged unlawfully on account of a corrupt intention. For Augustine says, in *Against Faustus,* "The covetous desire to inflict harm, the cruelty of seeking vengeance, the unplacated and unplacatable spirit, the savageness of rebelling, the lust for dominating, and other like things—these things in wars are condemned by right (*ius*)."[10]

[1] TO THE FIRST ARGUMENT, THEREFORE, IT SHOULD BE SAID that as Augustine says, "He takes up his sword, who is out for the blood of anyone, with no command or consent from a higher or lawful power."[11] But he who uses the sword, acting from the authority of a prince or judge, if he should be a private person, or else from zeal for justice, as though from God's authority, if he is a public person, does not take up the sword himself, but uses it, having been commissioned by another. So he ought not to be punished. Nonetheless, those who sinfully use the sword are not always killed. But they will always die by their own sword, since for their sin by the sword they will be punished eternally, unless they repent.

[2] To the second it should be said that precepts of this sort, as Augustine says in his book *The Lord's Sermon on the Mount,* should always be observed in the preparation of the spirit, so that a person is always prepared not to resist, or not to defend himself, if need be.[12] At times, however, one should act otherwise on account of the common good, or for [the good] of those with whom he is fighting. So Augustine says, in his letter to Marcellinus: "Many things must be done against their will in punishing those who must be punished by a certain benign harshness . . . For he who is stripped

9. See Gratian, *Decretum* pt.2 causa 23, q.1 can.6 Apud veros (Richter-Friedberg 1:893). See also Augustine, *De civitate Dei* bk.19 chap.12 sect.1 (PL 41:637; CCSL 48:675.7–8).

10. Augustine, *Contra Faustum Manichaeum* bk.22 chap.74 (PL 42:447; CSEL 25:672.8–10).

11. Augustine, *Contra Faustum Manichaeum* bk.22 chap.70 (PL 42:444; CSEL 25:667.22–24).

12. Augustine, *De sermone Domini in monte* bk.1 chap.19 (PL 34:1260; CCSL 35:69.1491–92).

of the license of iniquity is overcome advantageously, since nothing is un-happier than the happiness of sinners, by which a penal impunity is fed, and an evil will is strengthened, just like an internal enemy."[13]

[3] To the third it should be said that even those who wage just wars are intending peace. And so they are not against peace, unless this be the evil peace, which the Lord "did not come into the world to send," as is said in Matthew 10.[14] So Augustine says to Boniface: "Peace is not sought, in order that war may be practiced – but war is waged so that peace might be acquired. Therefore, in warring be peaceful, so that you bring those whom you outfight and conquer to the advantage of peace."[15]

[4] To the fourth it should be said that warlike practices of men are not universally prohibited – but only the disordered and dangerous practices from which arise killings and plunderings. Among the ancients, however, practices geared toward wars were without dangers of this sort. And so they were called "meditations of arms" or "wars without blood," as is clear from Jerome in a certain letter.[16]

Article 2. [Whether it is lawful for clerics and bishops to fight.]

One proceeds in this way to the second query. IT SEEMS that it is lawful for clerics and bishops to fight.

[1] Wars are lawful and just, as was said,[17] to the extent that they protect poor people and the whole public good from the harms of enemies. But this seems to belong especially to prelates, for Gregory says in a certain homily: "The wolf comes upon the sheep, when anyone who is unjust and rapacious oppresses those who are faithful and humble. But he who seems to be a shep-herd, but is not, abandons the sheep and flees, since when he fears danger to himself from the wolf, he does not take it upon himself to make a stand against its injustice."[18] Therefore it is lawful for prelates and clerics to fight.

13. Augustine, *Epistulae* ep.138 to Marcellinus chap.2 sect.14 (PL 33:531; CCSL 31B:284.259–62, 268–71).

14. Matthew 10.34.

15. Augustine, *Epistulae* ep.189 to Boniface sect.6 (PL 33:856; CSEL 57: 135.9–12).

16. See Vegetius, *Epitoma rei militaris* bk.1 chap.9.

17. In Article 1 of this Question.

18. Gregory the Great, *Homiliae in Evangelia* bk.1 hom.14 sect.2, on John 10.11–16 (PL 76:1128; CCSL 141:98.36–40).

[2] Furthermore, Pope Leo IV writes, Book 23, Question 8: "Since bad news had often come from the Saracen side, certain people said that the Saracens were about to come to the Roman port secretly and in hiding. For this reason, we commanded our people to gather, and ordered them to go down to the seashore."[19] Therefore it is lawful for bishops to make an appearance in wars.

[3] Furthermore, it seems to be for the same reason that a man should do something, and that he should consent to its doing, according to Romans 1: "Not only those who do such things are worthy of death, but also those who consent to their being done."[20] But he especially consents to a thing who leads other people to do it. Now it is lawful for bishops and clerics to lead others to make war, for it is said in Book 23, Question 28, that "at the urging and with the prayers of Adrian, bishop of Rome, Charles took up war against the Lombards."[21] Therefore it is also lawful for them to fight.

[4] Furthermore, that which is noble and meritorious of itself is not unlawful for prelates and clerics. But to make war is sometimes noble and meritorious, for it is said in Cause 23, Question 8, that "if a person dies for the true faith, or the salvation of his homeland, or the defense of Christians, a heavenly reward from God will follow."[22] Therefore it is lawful for bishops and clerics to make war.

BUT TO THE CONTRARY Matthew 26 says to Peter, bearing the person of bishops and clerics: "Drive your sword back into its sheath."[23] Therefore it is not lawful for them to fight.

I ANSWER THAT IT SHOULD BE SAID that many things are necessary for the good of human society. Now different things are done better and more expediently by different persons than by one person—as is clear from the Philosopher in the *Politics*.[24] And certain jobs are so mutually incompatible that they cannot appropriately be done at the same time. And so those who are assigned great things are prohibited from doing small things,

19. See Gratian, *Decretum,* pt.2 causa 23 q.8 can.7 Igitur (Richter-Friedberg 1:954).

20. Romans 1.32.

21. Gratian, *Decretum,* pt.2 causa 23 q.8 can.10 Hortatu (Richter-Friedberg 1:955).

22. Gratian, *Decretum,* pt.2 causa 23 q.8 can.9 Omni timore (Richter-Friedberg 1:955).

23. Matthew 26.52.

24. Aristotle, *Politics* bk.1 chap.1 (1252b3).

just as according to human laws, soldiers who are assigned to the practices of war are forbidden from conducting negotiations. Now the practices of war are most of all repugnant to those who are assigned episcopal and clerical duties, on account of two things. First, for the general reason that the practices of war contain the most unrest, and so hinder the spirit from the contemplation of divine things and from the praise of God and prayer for the people, which belong to the duty of clerics. And so just as business endeavors, because they very much entangle the spirit, are forbidden to clerics, so too are the practices of war, according to 2 Timothy 2: "No man who is a soldier of God entangles himself in secular business."[25] Second, for a special reason. All the orders of clerics are directed to the ministry of the altar, in which the passion of Christ is represented under the sacrament, according to 1 Corinthians 11: "As often as you shall eat this bread, and drink the chalice, you shall make known the death of the Lord, until he comes."[26] And so it does not belong to them to kill or to shed blood–rather, they are ready to shed their own blood for Christ, so as to imitate by the deed what they do in the ministry. On account of this, it is instituted that [clerics] who spill their blood, even without sin, are irregular. Now for any person who has been assigned to some office (*officium*), that by which he is made unfit for his office is not lawful. So it is altogether unlawful for clerics to wage wars, which are directed to the spilling of blood.

[1] TO THE FIRST ARGUMENT, THEREFORE, IT SHOULD BE SAID that prelates should make a stand not only against the wolves who spiritually kill their flock, but also against robbers and tyrants who harm them in a bodily manner–using in their own person not bodily arms, but spiritual, according to the Apostle, 2 Corinthians 10: "The arms of our warfare are not fleshly, but spiritual."[27] These are healthy warnings, devout prayers, and–against the obstinate–the sentence of excommunication.

[2] To the second it should be said that prelates and clerics can, by a higher authority, enter into wars–not in order to fight by their own hand, but in order to give help spiritually by fighting justly, through their exhortations and absolutions and other such spiritual helps. So in the Old Law, it is commanded, Joshua 6,[28] that in wars priests would blow the sacred trumpets. Because of this, it was first granted that bishops and clerics

25. 2 Timothy 2.4.
26. 1 Corinthians 11.26.
27. 2 Corinthians 10.4.
28. Joshua 6.4.

should make an appearance in wars. But that some would fight by their own hand – this is an abuse.

[3] To the third it should be said that, as was attested above,[29] every power or art or virtue to which an end belongs has to dispose the things that are directed to the end. Now fleshly wars in a faithful people should be referred, as to an end, to the divine spiritual good, to which clerics are assigned. And so it belongs to clerics to dispose and lead others to the making of just wars. For making war is prohibited to them not because it is a sin, but because such a practice is not befitting to their role (*persona*).

[4] To the fourth it should be said that, while it is meritorious to practice just wars, it is nonetheless rendered unlawful for clerics to do so, on account of this – that they are assigned to things that are more meritorious. In the same way, the act of marriage can be meritorious but is nonetheless rendered damnable for those who have vowed their virginity, on account of their obligation to a greater good.

Article 3. [Whether in wars it is lawful to lay ambushes.]

One proceeds in this way to the third query. IT SEEMS that in wars it is not lawful to lay ambushes.

[1] Deuteronomy 16 says: "You will strive justly for that which is just."[30] But ambushes, since they are a kind of fraud, seem to belong to injustice. Therefore one should not lay ambushes, even in just wars.

[2] Furthermore, ambushes and frauds seem opposed to faithfulness, as are lies. But since we ought to keep faith with everyone, we should not lie to any person, as is clear from Augustine in his book *Against Lying*.[31] Therefore since faith with enemies should be kept – as Augustine says, *To Boniface*[32] – it seems that ambushes should not be laid against enemies.

[3] Furthermore, Matthew 7 says: "Whatever you wish that men should do to you, do you also to them."[33] And this should be observed toward all our neighbors. Now our enemies are our neighbors. Since therefore no one wishes ambushes or frauds to be prepared against himself, it seems that no one should wage wars by ambushes.

29. In Question 23, Article 4, Reply [2].
30. Deuteronomy 16.20.
31. Augustine, *Contra mendacium* chap.15 sect.31 (PL 40:539).
32. Augustine, *Epistulae* ep.189 to Boniface sect.6 (PL 33:856; CSEL 57: 135.5–7).
33. Matthew 7.12.

BUT TO THE CONTRARY Augustine says, in his *Seven Questions Concerning the Heptateuch:* "When a just war is undertaken, whether someone fights openly or by ambushes makes no difference to justice."[34] And he shows this by the authority of the Lord, who commanded Joshua to lay ambushes against the inhabitants of the city of Ai, as is attested in Joshua 8.[35]

I ANSWER THAT IT SHOULD BE SAID that ambushes are directed to deceiving one's enemies. In two ways, a person can be deceived by the deed or word of another person. In one way, because something false is said to him, or a promise is not kept. And this is always unlawful. No one ought to deceive his enemies in this way, for there are certain rights and compacts of war that should be kept even among enemies, as Ambrose says in his book *On Duties.*[36] In another way, someone can be deceived by our word or deed, since we do not openly disclose to him our purpose or meaning. Now this we are not always bound to do, since in holy teaching (*sacra doctrina*) many things should be hidden, particularly from the unfaithful, lest they laugh at these things, according to Matthew 7: "Do not give what is holy to dogs."[37] Much more, then, should we hide from our enemies the things that we plan for our attack. So among the other things for a soldier to learn, the lesson on concealing his plans should be set down as primary, lest his enemies discover them—as is clear from the *Stratagems* of Frontinus.[38] Such hiding belongs to the notion of ambushes, the laying of which is lawful in just wars. Nor are ambushes of this type properly called frauds. They are repugnant neither to justice nor to an ordinate will. For there would be an inordinate will, if a person were to will that nothing should be hidden from him by others.

[1]–[3] And from this the answer TO WHAT WAS OBJECTED is clear.

Article 4. [Whether it is lawful to make war on feast days.]

One proceeds in this way to the fourth query. IT SEEMS that it is not lawful to make war on feast days.

---

34. Augustine, *Quaestiones in Heptateuchum libri septem* bk.6 q.10 on Joshua 8.2 (PL 34:781; CCSL 33:319.257–59).

35. See Joshua 8.2.

36. Ambrose, *De officiis* bk.1 chap.29 (PL 16:68; CCSL 15:50.34–36).

37. Matthew 7.6.

38. See Frontinus, *Stratagems* bk.1 chap.1.

[1] Feasts are directed to being unoccupied, for divine things, so that they are included in keeping the Sabbath, which is taught by Exodus 20, for there "sabbath" is interpreted as "rest."[39] But wars especially contain unrest. Therefore in no manner should one fight on feast days.

[2] Furthermore, in Isaiah 58 certain people are blamed, since on days of fasting, "they demanded things owed to them and instigated quarrels, striking up a fight."[40] Much more, then, it is unlawful to make war on feast days.

[3] Furthermore, nothing should be done inordinately for the sake of avoiding temporal inconvenience. But to make war on a feast day–this seems to be inordinate in itself. Therefore, on behalf of no necessity should anyone make war on a feast day, in order to avoid temporal inconvenience.

BUT TO THE CONTRARY there is what 1 Maccabees 2 says: "The Jews discerned in a manner worthy of praise, saying 'Any man whoever that shall come against us in war on the day of the Sabbath, we will fight against him.'"[41]

I ANSWER THAT IT SHOULD BE SAID that the observation of feasts does not hinder the things that are directed to a person's bodily health. So the Lord censures the Jews, saying in John 7: "Are you indignant with me because I have healed the whole man on the Sabbath?"[42] So it is that physicians can lawfully treat people on a feast day. Now much more than the bodily health of a single person, one ought to preserve the health of the public good, through which the killings of many, as well as innumerable evils both temporal and spiritual, are prevented. And so on behalf of protecting the public good of the faithful, it is lawful to practice just wars on feast days, at least if necessity demands this. For it would be testing God, if in the face of such threatening necessity, a person were to will to abstain from war. But when such necessity ceases, it is not lawful to make war on feast days, on account of the arguments cited.

[1]–[3] And from this the answer TO WHAT WAS OBJECTED is clear.

39. See Exodus 20.8.
40. Isaiah 58.3.
41. 1 Maccabees 2.41.
42. John 7.23.

[On Quarreling]

One should next consider quarreling. Regarding this point, two queries are raised. (1) Whether quarreling is a sin. (2) Whether it is the daughter of anger.

Article 1. [Whether quarreling is always a sin.]

One proceeds in this way to the first query. IT SEEMS that quarreling is not always a sin.

[1] Quarreling seems to be a kind of contention, for Isidore in his book of *Etymologies* says that "'rixosus' [the quarrelsome person] is said from 'rictus caninus' [canine snarling], for the quarrelsome person is always ready to contradict, and takes pleasure in disputing, and provokes contention."[1] But contention is not always a sin. Nor therefore is quarreling.

[2] Furthermore, Genesis 26 says that "the servants of Isaac dug another well, and also quarreled over it."[2] But it should not be believed that the family of Isaac quarreled publicly, without his contradicting them, if quarreling were a sin. Therefore quarreling is not a sin.

[3] Furthermore, quarreling seems to be a certain particular war. But war is not always a sin. Therefore quarreling is not always a sin.

BUT TO THE CONTRARY quarrels are set down in Galatians 5 among works of the flesh: "Those who engage in them shall not attain the kingdom of God."[3] Therefore quarrels are not only sins, but even mortal sins.

I ANSWER THAT IT SHOULD BE SAID that just as contention denotes a kind of contradiction in words, so too quarreling denotes a contra-

---

1. Isidore of Seville, *Etymologiae* bk.10 letter "R" sect.239 (PL 82:392; Lindsay lines 2–3).
2. Genesis 26.21.
3. Galatians 5.21.

diction in deeds, so that the Gloss on Galatians 5 says that "quarrels are when, out of anger, people strike one another."[4] And so quarreling seems to be a kind of private war, which occurs between private persons – not by some public authority, but rather by an inordinate will. And so quarreling seems to denote a sin. In a person who unjustly attacks another, there is mortal sin, for to inflict a harm on one's neighbor, even by the work of one's hand, is not without mortal sin. As for a person who defends himself, he can be without sin – or sometimes in venial sin and sometimes in mortal sin, according to a different motion of his spirit, or a different manner of defending himself. For if he acts only in the spirit of warding off the harm attempted against him, and defends himself with due moderation, there is no sin – nor can it properly said to be quarreling on his part. But if he defends himself with a spirit of revenge or hatred, or with an excess beyond due moderation, there is always sin. When some light motion of hatred or revenge mixes itself into the act, or when the act does not exceed a moderate defense by much, the sin is venial. It is mortal, however, when the motion of hatred or revenge rises up with a determined spirit in the attacker, for the sake of killing or gravely wounding another.

[1] TO THE FIRST ARGUMENT, THEREFORE, IT SHOULD BE SAID that quarreling is not named contention simply. Three things are set down in the above words of Isidore – three things that reveal quarreling to be inordinate. The first is readiness of the spirit for contention, which the passage signifies when it says "always ready to contradict" – namely whether the other person speaks or acts, either well or badly. Second, when a person takes pleasure in contradiction itself – and so follow the words "takes pleasure in disputing." Third, when a person provokes others to contradictions – and so follow the words "and provokes contention."

[2] To the second it should be said that in this passage, one should not understand that the servants of Isaac quarreled, but that the residents of the country had quarreled against them. So that they had sins, and not the servants of Isaac, who suffered the calumny.

[3] To the third it should be said that if a war is to be just, it is required that it arise by the authority of the governing power, as was said above.[5] Quarrelling, however, arises out of the private emotion of anger or hatred. For if the minister of a prince or judge attacks, by the authority of the public power, a certain group of people who defend themselves, the party said

4. *Glossa Lombardi* on Galatians 5.21 (PL 192:159B).
5. In Question 40, Article 1.

to have quarreled is not the minister, but those who take a stand against the public power. And thus those who attack neither quarrel nor sin – rather, those who defend themselves inordinately do so.

Article 2. [Whether quarreling is the daughter of anger.]

One proceeds in this way to the second query. IT SEEMS that quarreling is not the daughter of anger.

[1] James 4 says: "From where are wars and contentions among you? Are they not from the desires (*concupiscientiae*) that war in your members?"[6] But anger does not belong to the concupiscible power. Therefore quarreling is not the daughter of anger, but rather of concupiscence.

[2] Furthermore, Proverbs 28 says, "He who boasts and puffs himself up causes brawls."[7] But it seems that brawling is the same as quarreling. Therefore it seems that quarreling is the daughter of pride or vainglory, to which belong boasting and puffing oneself up.

[3] Furthermore, Proverbs 18 says, "A fool's lips mix themselves with quarreling."[8] But folly differs from anger, for folly is opposed not to meekness, but to wisdom or prudence. Therefore quarreling is not the daughter of anger.

[4] Furthermore, Proverbs 10 says, "Hatred arouses quarrels."[9] But "hatred is born from envy," as Gregory says, *Moralia* 31.[10] Therefore quarreling is not the daughter of anger, but of envy.

[5] Furthermore, Proverbs 17 says, "He who ponders discords, sows quarrels."[11] But discord is the daughter of vainglory, as was said above. Therefore, quarreling is too.

BUT TO THE CONTRARY Gregory says, *Moralia* 31, that "from anger, quarreling is born."[12] And Proverbs 15 and 29 say: "The angry man provokes quarrels."[13]

6. James 4.1.

7. Proverbs 28.25.

8. Proverbs 18.6.

9. Proverbs 10.12.

10. Gregory the Great, *Moralia* bk.31 chap.45 sect.88 (PL 76:621; CCSL 143B: 1610.25–26).

11. Proverbs 17.19.

12. Gregory the Great, *Moralia* bk.31 chap.45 sect.88 (PL 76:621; CCSL 143B: 1610.26–28).

13. Proverbs 15.18 and 29.22.

I ANSWER THAT IT SHOULD BE SAID that, as said above,[14] quarreling denotes a kind of contradiction that extends up to the point of deeds, when one person undertakes to wound another. Now one person intends to wound another in two ways. In one way, by intending absolute evil, as it were, to another. And such a wound belongs to hatred, whose intention is the wounding of an enemy, whether in the open or in secret. In another way, someone intends to wound another whom he knows and disagrees with—and this is denoted by the name "quarreling." This properly belongs to anger, which is the desire for revenge. It is not enough for the angry person to harm in secret the one against whom he is angry. Rather, the angry person wants him to know that he has done something in revenge, and that he suffer something against his will—as is clear from what has been said above about the passion of anger.[15] And so quarreling properly arises from anger.

[1] TO THE FIRST ARGUMENT, THEREFORE, IT SHOULD BE SAID that, as was said above,[16] all the irascible passions arise from the concupiscible passions. Accordingly, anything that arises proximately from anger, arises also from concupiscence, as from its first root.

[2] To the second it should be said that boasting and puffing oneself up, which arise from pride and vainglory, do not directly cause brawling or quarreling, but they do so as occasions. When a person takes himself to be harmed because another is preferred over himself, anger is aroused. In this way, brawling and quarreling follow from anger.

[3] To the third it should be said that, as was said above,[17] anger hinders the judgment of reason, and so has a likeness to folly. From this, it follows that they have a common effect, for from a lack of reason, it happens that a person undertakes to wound another inordinately.

[4] To the fourth it should be said that quarreling, though sometimes born out of hatred, is not the proper effect of hatred. This is because wounding the enemy in a quarrelsome manner, and doing so openly, lies outside the intention (*praeter intentionem*) of the person who hates—for sometimes he seeks to wound him in secret. But when he sees himself as prevailing, he does intend to inflict a wound in a quarrelsome and brawling manner. And

---

14. In Article 1 of this Question.
15. See *Summa* 1a2ae q.46 a.6 ad 2.
16. *Summa* 1a2ae q.25 a.1.
17. *Summa* 1a2ae q.48 a.3.

to wound someone in a quarrelsome manner is a proper effect of anger, for the reason stated.[18]

[5] To the fifth it should be said that from quarrels, hatred and discord follow in the hearts of the quarrelsome. And so he who ponders discords – that is, he who intends to sow discords among others – brings it about that they quarrel among themselves – just as any sin is able to command the act of another sin, by directing it to its own end. But it does not follow from this that quarreling is the daughter of vainglory, properly and directly.

18. In the body of the Article.

QUESTION 42

[On Sedition]

One must next consider sedition. Regarding this point, two queries are raised. (1) Whether it is a special sin. (2) Whether it is a mortal sin.

Article 1. [Whether sedition is a special sin, distinct from other sins.]

One proceeds in this way to the first query. IT SEEMS that sedition is not a special sin, distinct from other sins.

[1] As Isidore says, in the *Etymologies,* "the seditious person is one who causes dissension of spirits and generates discords."[1] But in bringing about some sin, he does not sin by any other kind of sin, except by the one that he brings about. Therefore it seems that sedition is not a special sin, distinct from discord.

[2] Furthermore, sedition denotes a kind of division. But the name "schism" is taken from "cutting" (*scissura*), as was said above.[2] Therefore the sin of sedition does not seem to be distinct from the sin of schism.

[3] Furthermore, every special sin that is distinct from others is either a capital sin or else arises from some capital vice. But sedition is counted neither among the capital vices nor among the vices that arise from the capital vices, as is clear from *Moralia* 31, where both kinds of vice are numbered.[3] Therefore sedition is not a special sin, distinct from other sins.

BUT TO THE CONTRARY in 2 Corinthians 12, seditions are distinguished from other sins.[4]

---

1. Isidore of Seville, *Etymologiae* bk.10 letter "S" sect.250 (PL 82:394; Lindsay lines 17–18).

2. In Question 39, Article 1.

3. Gregory the Great, *Moralia* bk.31 chap.45 sect.87–88 (PL 76:621; CCSL 143B:1610.15–37).

4. 2 Corinthians 12.20.

I ANSWER THAT IT SHOULD BE SAID that sedition is a certain special sin, which converges in one respect with war and quarreling, while diverging from them in another respect. It converges with them in this – that it denotes a certain contradiction. But it diverges from them in two ways. First, since war and quarreling denote mutual attack in actuality, but sedition can be said to occur either when there is an actual attack of this sort or when there is preparation for such an attack. So the Gloss on 2 Corinthians 12 says that seditions are "uproars for the sake of an attack," since people prepare themselves and intend to fight.[5] Second, seditions differ from war and quarreling, since war proper is against foreigners and enemies – a multitude against a multitude, as it were – whereas quarreling is one person against one person, or a few against a few. But sedition, properly speaking, is between parts of a single multitude, dissenting among themselves – as when one part of the city is aroused in an uproar against another part. Thus sedition, since it has a particular good to which it is opposed, namely the unity and peace of the multitude, is a special sin.

[1] TO THE FIRST ARGUMENT, THEREFORE, IT SHOULD BE SAID that the seditious person is said to be the person who arouses sedition. And because sedition denotes a kind of discord, the seditious person is one who brings about discord not simply of any kind, but rather between parts of some multitude. Now the sin of sedition is not only in the person who sows discord, but also in those who dissent among themselves inordinately.

[2] To the second it should be said that sedition differs from schism in two things. First, schism is opposed to the spiritual unity of the multitude, namely to the unity of the Church, whereas sedition is opposed to the temporal or secular unity of the multitude, for example, the unity of a city or a kingdom. Second, schism does not denote any preparation for bodily combat, but only denotes spiritual dissension, whereas sedition denotes preparation for bodily combat.

[3] To the third it should be said that sedition is contained under discord, as is schism. For both are a certain discord – not of one person against another, but of one part of a multitude against another part.

Article 2. [Whether sedition is always a mortal sin.]

One proceeds in this way to the second query. IT SEEMS that sedition is not always a mortal sin.

5. *Glossa Lombardi* on 2 Corinthians 12.20 (PL 192:89B).

[1] Sedition implies "uproar and fighting," as is clear from the Gloss cited above.[6] But fighting is not always a mortal sin – as when it is just and lawful, as was attested above.[7] Much more, therefore, can sedition be without mortal sin.

[2] Furthermore, sedition is a certain discord, as was said above.[8] But discord can be without mortal sin, and sometimes even without any sin at all. Therefore, so can sedition.

[3] Furthermore, those who free the multitude from tyrannical power are praised. But this does not easily happen without some dissension of a multitude, as when one part of a multitude strives to keep a tyrant, and another strives to overthrow him. Therefore sedition can arise without sin.

BUT TO THE CONTRARY the Apostle, 2 Corinthians 12, prohibits seditions among the things that are mortal sins.[9] Therefore sedition is a mortal sin.

I ANSWER THAT IT SHOULD BE SAID that, as was said above,[10] sedition is opposed to the unity of the multitude – that is, to the unity of the people of a city or a kingdom. Now Augustine says, *City of God,* Book 2, that wise men define "the people" as "not any multitudinous assembly, but as an assembly allied by the consensus of law and by common advantage."[11] So it is clear that the unity to which sedition is opposed is the unity of law and common advantage. It is clear, therefore, that sedition is opposed to justice and to the common good. And so by its very kind, sedition is a mortal sin. It is more serious than quarreling by as much as the common good attacked by sedition is greater than the private good, which is attacked by quarrelling. – Now the sin of sedition belongs first and principally to those who arouse sedition. These sin most gravely. Second, it belongs to people who follow those who are disturbing the common good. But those who defend the common good, resisting them who disturb it, should not be called seditious – just as those who defend themselves should not be called quarrelsome, as was said above.[12]

6. *Glossa Lombardi* on 2 Corinthians 12.20 (PL 192:89B).

7. In Question 40, Article 1, and Question 41, Article 1.

8. In Article 1, Reply [3] of this Question.

9. 2 Corinthians 12.20.

10. In Article 1, Reply to [3].

11. Augustine, *De civitate Dei* bk.2 chap.21 (PL 41:67; CCSL 47:53.50–51).

12. In Question 41, Article 1.

[1] TO THE FIRST ARGUMENT, THEREFORE, IT SHOULD BE SAID that fighting which is lawful occurs on behalf of the common advantage, as was said above.[13] But sedition occurs against the common good of the multitude. So it is always a mortal sin.

[2] To the second it should be said that discord against what is not manifestly good can be without sin. But discord against what is manifestly good cannot be without sin. And such discord is sedition, which is opposed to the advantage of the multitude, which is manifestly good.

[3] To the third it should be said that a tyrannical regime is not just, since it is not directed to the common good, but to the private good of the ruler, as is clear from the Philosopher in *Politics* 3 and *Ethics* 8.[14] And so disturbing such a regime does not have the aspect of sedition, except perhaps when a tyrant's regime is disturbed inordinately, so that the subjected multitude suffers greater harm from the disturbance that follows than from the tyrant's rule. Now it is rather the tyrant who is seditious – he who nourishes discords and seditions in the people subjected to himself, so that they can be ruled more securely. For this is tyrannical – that rule is directed to the private good of the one ruling, along with the multitude's harm.

13. In Question 40, Article 1.
14. Aristotle, *Politics* bk.3 chap.5 (1279b6) and *Nicomachean Ethics* bk.8 chap.10 (1160b8).

QUESTION 43

[On Scandal]

It remains for us to consider the vices that are opposed to doing good. Among these, some belong to the aspect of justice, namely the vices by which a person unjustly wounds his neighbor. But scandal seems particularly to be against charity. Therefore, we should treat scandal in this place. About scandal, eight queries are raised. (1) What is scandal. (2) Whether scandal is a sin. (3) Whether it is a special sin. (4) Whether it is a mortal sin. (5) Whether it belongs to the perfect to be scandalized. (6) Whether it belongs to them to scandalize. (7) Whether spiritual goods should be given up on account of scandal. (8) Whether on account of scandal, temporal goods should be given up.

Article 1. [Whether scandal is inappropriately defined as "something said or done less rightly, bringing an occasion of ruin."]

One proceeds in this way to the first query. IT SEEMS that scandal is inappropriately defined as "something said or done less rightly, bringing an occasion of ruin."[1]

[1] Scandal is a sin, as will be said later.[2] But according to Augustine, *Against Faustus,* Book 22, "sin is something said or done or desired against the law of God."[3] Therefore the aforementioned definition is insufficient, since it overlooks something thought or desired.

1. *Glossa interlinearis* on Matthew 18.5 (Strasbourg 5).
2. In Article 2 of this Question.
3. Augustine, *Contra Faustum Manichaeum* bk.22 chap.27 (PL 42:418; CSEL 25:621.12–13). Here Thomas appears not to be reading Augustine's text directly, but a modified version by Alexander of Hales; see *Summa Halensis* pt.2 sect.266 (Quaracchi 4:390). Augustine's text reads "contra aeternam legem"; the version quoted by Alexander and Thomas reads "contra legem Dei."

[2] Furthermore, since among virtuous or right acts, one is more virtuous or more right than another, it seems that only one of them is not less right – namely, the one that is most right. If therefore scandal is something said or done less rightly, it would follow that every virtuous act except for the best one is a scandal.

[3] Furthermore, "occasion" names a cause *per accidens*. But that which is *per accidens* should not be placed in the definition, since it does not give the species. Therefore "occasion" is inappropriately placed in the definition of scandal.

[4] Furthermore, from any deed whatever of another, a person can take the occasion of his ruin, since causes *per accidens* are indeterminate. If therefore scandal is that which brings the occasion of ruin to another, anything done or said could be a scandal. This seems inappropriate.

[5] Furthermore, the occasion of ruin is given to our neighbor when he is offended or weakened. But scandal is distinguished from offense or weakness, for the Apostle says, Romans 14, "It is good not to eat flesh, and not to drink wine, nor do anything in which your brother is offended or scandalized or weakened."[4] Therefore the aforementioned definition of scandal is not appropriate.

BUT TO THE CONTRARY there is Jerome, expounding Matthew 15, "You know that the Pharisees, having heard this word,"[5] etc., says "When we read 'whoever shall scandalize,' we should understand this – 'he who has brought an occasion of ruin to someone, by a thing said or a thing done.'"[6]

I ANSWER THAT IT SHOULD BE SAID that, as Jerome says in the same place, "in Greek something is called a 'scandalon' when we can say that something is an offense or ruin, or a stumbling of the foot."[7] For it sometimes happens that some obstacle is placed in the bodily way of someone, disposing the person stumbling against it to ruin – and such an obstacle is called a "scandal." Likewise in the progress of the spiritual way, it happens that a person is disposed to spiritual ruin through something said or

4. Romans 14.21.

5. Matthew 15.12.

6. Jerome, On Matthew bk.2, on Matthew 15.12 (PL 26:111; CCSL 77: 129.1469–71). Jerome's exact words are "qui dicto factove occasionem ruinae cuiquam dederit."

7. Jerome, On Matthew bk.2, on Matthew 15.12 (PL 26:11; CCSL 77: 129.1468–69).

done on the part of another—namely, so far as someone by his warning or leading or example drags another toward sinning. And this is properly called scandal. Now, nothing according to its own nature disposes one to spiritual ruin, except that which has some lack of rightness, since that which is perfectly right strengthens a man against a fall, rather than leading him to his ruin. And so scandal is appropriately said to be "something said or done less rightly, bringing an occasion of ruin."

[1] TO THE FIRST ARGUMENT, THEREFORE, IT SHOULD BE SAID that thought or the desire for an evil lies hidden in the heart, so that it is not proposed to another as an obstacle disposing him to ruin. Because of this, it cannot have the aspect of scandal.

[2] To the second it should be said that "less rightly" here does not mean that the thing is surpassed in rightness by something else, but that it has some lack of rightness, whether because it is evil in itself, as sins are, or because it has a look (*species*) of evil, as when a person eats at the temple of an idol (*recumbit in idolio*).⁸ This is not in itself a sin, if someone were to do it with an intention that is not corrupt. Nevertheless, since it has a kind of appearance or likeness to the veneration of an idol, it can bring about the occasion of ruin of another. And so the Apostle warns, 1 Thessalonians 5, "Abstain from every evil appearance."⁹ And so "less rightly" is appropriately said, so as to comprehend both the things that are sins in themselves and the things that have the look of evil.

[3] To the third it should be said that, as attested above,¹⁰ nothing can be for a person the sufficient cause of sin—which is his spiritual ruin—except for his own will. And so things said or done by another person can be only the incomplete cause, somehow leading to his ruin. Accordingly, "giving the cause of ruin" is not said, but rather "giving the occasion," which signifies an incomplete cause, and not always a cause *per accidens*. Nevertheless, nothing prevents one from placing in the same definitions "that which is *per accidens*," since that which happens by accident to one, can agree with another *per se*—as "cause *per accidens*" is placed in the definition of "chance" (*fortuna*) in *Physics* 2.¹¹

[4] To the fourth it should be said that "something said or done by another" can be the cause of another's sinning in two ways. In one way,

8. See 1 Corinthians 8.10.
9. 1 Thessalonians 5.22.
10. *Summa* 1a2ae q.75 aa.2–3; *Summa* 1a2ae q.80 a.1.
11. Aristotle, *Physics* bk.2 chap.5 (197a5).

per se. In another way, *per accidens. Per se,* when someone by his own evil word or deed intends to lead another person toward sinning; or, even if he himself does not intend this, the very deed is such that by its own nature it leads toward sinning, as when a person publicly commits a sin or does what has the likeness of sin. And then he who does an act of this sort properly gives the occasion of ruin, so that it is called "active scandal." *Per accidens,* when something said or done by an agent is the cause of another person's sinning. This happens when the thing said or done lies outside the intention of the agent, as well as outside the condition of the act, and yet the person who is badly disposed by an act of this sort is led toward sinning, for example, when a person envies the goods of others. And then he who does a right act of this type does not give the occasion, so far as it is in him. Rather, another takes the occasion, according to Romans 7: "having taken the occasion," etc.[12] And so this is passive scandal without active scandal, since he who acts rightly, so far as the matter concerns himself, does not give the occasion of ruin that the other person suffers. Sometimes, therefore, it happens that at the same time, there is both active scandal in one person and passive scandal in another person – for example, when by the leading of one person, another person sins. Sometimes, however, there is active scandal without passive scandal – for example, when someone by his word or deed leads another person toward sinning, but the person does not consent. And sometimes there is passive scandal without active scandal, as was just said.

[5] To the fifth it should be said that weakness names a proneness for scandal, whereas offense names the indignation of one person against another who sins, which can sometimes be without ruin. Scandal, however, denotes the very stumbling that leads to ruin.

Article 2. [Whether scandal is a sin.]

One proceeds in this way to the second query. IT SEEMS that scandal is not a sin.

[1] Sins do not happen out of necessity, since any sin is voluntary, as was attested above.[13] But Matthew 18 says, "It is necessary that scandals should come."[14] Therefore scandal is not a sin.

---

12. Romans 7.8.
13. *Summa* 1a2ae q.74 aa.1–2.
14. Matthew 18.7.

[2] Furthermore, no sin proceeds from the affect of piety, since "a good tree cannot bear evil fruits," as Matthew 7 says.[15] But some scandal is from the affect of piety, for the Lord says to Peter, Matthew 16, "You are a scandal to me,"[16] whereupon Jerome says that "the error of the Apostle, coming from the affect of piety, never seems to be playing the tune of the devil."[17] Therefore not every scandal is a sin.

[3] Furthermore, scandal denotes a kind of stumbling. But not everyone who stumbles, falls. Therefore scandal can be without sin, which is a spiritual fall.[18]

BUT TO THE CONTRARY scandal is something said or done less rightly. Anything that is lacking in rightness has some aspect of sin. Therefore scandal is always accompanied by sin.

I ANSWER THAT IT SHOULD BE SAID that, as was just said above,[19] scandal is twofold. There is passive scandal, in the person who is scandalized, and active scandal, in the person who scandalizes, giving the occasion of ruin. Passive scandal, therefore, is always a sin in the person who is being scandalized, for he is not scandalized except to the extent that in some way he rushes headlong into the abyss (ruit) toward his spiritual ruin, which is sin. Nevertheless, there can be passive scandal without sin in a person whose deed has been scandalizing, as when someone is scandalized over the things that another does well. Likewise, active scandal is always a sin in the person who scandalizes. Because the thing itself that the scandalizer does is a sin, or at least has the look of sin, it should be given up for the sake of charity toward one's neighbor – charity from which a person strives to make provision for the well-being of his neighbor. Thus he who does not give up such a deed acts against charity. Nevertheless, there can be active scandal without sin on the part of another who is scandalized, as was said above.[20]

[1] TO THE FIRST ARGUMENT, THEREFORE, IT SHOULD BE SAID that regarding the passage quoted, "It is necessary that scandals

15. Matthew 7.18.
16. Matthew 16.23.
17. Jerome, *On Matthew* bk.3, on Matthew 16.23 (PL 26:124; CCSL 77: 144.150–52).
18. Some versions read, "Therefore the scandal that is a spiritual fall can be without sin."
19. In Article 1, Reply [4] of this Question.
20. In Article 1, Reply [4] of this Question.

should come," it should not be understood to speak of absolute necessity, but rather of conditional necessity, by which it is necessary for things foreknown or foretold by God to happen, if the scandals to come are taken to be connected to foreknowledge, as was said in the *Prima Pars*.[21] Alternatively, it is necessary for scandals to happen according to a necessity of the end, since they are advantageous for this—that those who are approved may become manifest.[22] Another alternative: it is necessary for scandals to happen according to the condition of men, who fail to protect themselves from sins. Just as a doctor, seeing certain people adopting an unsuitable diet, would say that it is necessary for such people to be infirm—a necessity that should be understood to obtain on the condition that they do not change their diet. And likewise it is necessary for scandals to happen if men do not change their evil way of life.

[2] To the second it should be said that here scandal is being spoken of in a wide sense, as meaning any hindrance. For Peter was wanting to hinder the suffering of Christ, by a certain affect of piety toward Christ.

[3] To the third it should be said that nobody stumbles spiritually unless he is in some way slowed from advancing in the way of God, which occurs at least by a venial sin.

Article 3. [Whether scandal is a special sin.]

One proceeds in this way to the third query. IT SEEMS that scandal is not a special sin.

[1] Scandal is a "thing said or done less rightly." But every sin is of this type. Therefore every sin is a scandal. Not every scandal, therefore, is a special sin.

[2] Furthermore, every special sin, or every special injustice, is discovered separately from the others, as is said in *Ethics* 5.[23] But scandal is not discovered separately from the other sins. Therefore scandal is not a special sin.

[3] Furthermore, every special sin is constituted according to the thing that gives it the species of its moral act. But the aspect of scandal is constituted by this—that it is sinning publicly in the presence of others. Now to sin in the open, though it is an aggravating circumstance, does not seem to constitute a species of sin. Therefore scandal is not a special sin.

21. *Summa* 1a q.14 a.13 ad 3, q.23 a.6 ad 2.
22. See 1 Corinthians 11.19.
23. Aristotle, *Nicomachean Ethics* bk.5 chap.2 (1130a19).

BUT TO THE CONTRARY a special virtue is opposed to a special sin. But scandal is opposed to a special virtue, namely to charity, for Romans 14 says: "If, on account of your meat-eating, your brother is sorrowful, you are not walking according to charity."[24] Therefore scandal is a special sin.

I ANSWER THAT IT SHOULD BE SAID that, as was said above,[25] scandal is twofold – namely active and passive. Passive scandal cannot be a special sin, since from a thing said or a thing done by another, a person rushes headlong into the abyss, following upon any kind of sin. Nor does the fact that a person takes an occasion of sinning from another's word or deed constitute any special aspect of sin, since this does not denote a special deformity that is opposed to a special virtue. Now active scandal can be taken in two ways – *per se* and *per accidens*. Active scandal is *per accidens* when it is outside the intention of the agent – as when a person by his inordinate deed or word does not intend to give an occasion of ruin to another, but only to satisfy his own will. In this way, active scandal too is not a special sin, since that which is *per accidens* does not constitute a species. But active scandal is *per se* when someone intends by his inordinate word or deed to drag another into sin. And in this way, from the intention of a special end, it takes on a special aspect of sin, for the end gives the species in morals, as was said above.[26] So just as theft is a special sin, or homicide, on account of the special harm to neighbor that it intends, so too scandal is a special sin, because it intends a special harm to one's neighbor. And it is directly opposed to fraternal correction, in which the removal of a particular harm is sought.

[1] TO THE FIRST ARGUMENT, THEREFORE, IT SHOULD BE SAID that every sin can be materially related to active scandal. But it can have the formal aspect of a special sin from the intention of an end, as was said.[27]

[2] To the second it should be said that active scandal can be discovered separately from the other sins, as for example when a person scandalizes his neighbor by a deed that of itself is not a sin, but has the look of evil.

---

24. Romans 14.15.
25. In Article 2 of this Question.
26. *Summa* 1a2ae q.1 a.3 and q.18 aa.4–6.
27. In the body of this Article.

[3] To the third it should be said that scandal does not have the aspect of a special sin from the aforementioned circumstances, but from the intention of an end, as was said.[28]

Article 4. [Whether scandal is a mortal sin.]

One proceeds in this way to the fourth query. IT SEEMS that scandal is a mortal sin.

[1] Every sin that is opposed to charity is a mortal sin, as was said above.[29] But scandal is opposed to charity, as was said.[30] Therefore scandal is a mortal sin.

[2] Furthermore, no sin deserves the punishment of eternal damnation except for mortal sin. But scandal deserves the punishment of eternal damnation, according to Matthew 18: "He who shall scandalize one of these little ones who believe in me – it would be better for him that a millstone should be hanged around his neck and that he should be drowned in the depth of the sea."[31] Because, as Jerome says, "much better is it to receive a small punishment for sin than to be preserved in tortures eternal."[32] Therefore scandal is a mortal sin.

[3] Furthermore, every sin that is committed against God is a mortal sin, since only a mortal sin turns a man away from God. But scandal is a sin against God, for the Apostle says, 1 Corinthians 8, "Striking the weak conscience of the brethren, you sin against Christ."[33] Therefore scandal is always a mortal sin.

BUT TO THE CONTRARY to lead a person toward sinning venially can be a venial sin. But this belongs to the aspect of scandal. Therefore scandal can be a venial sin.

I ANSWER THAT IT SHOULD BE SAID that, as was said above,[34] scandal denotes a kind of stumbling, through which a person is disposed

28. In the body of this Article.
29. In Question 35, Article 3, and *Summa* 1a2ae q.88 a.2.
30. In the Prologue of this Question.
31. Matthew 18.6.
32. Jerome, *On Matthew* bk.3, on Matthew 18.6 (PL 26:133; CCSL 77: 158.530–32).
33. 1 Corinthians 8.12.
34. In Article 1 of this Question.

to ruin. And so passive scandal can sometimes be a venial sin, as when the person stumbling does so in such a way that by another's inordinate word or deed, he is agitated by a motion of venial sin. But sometimes it is a mortal sin, as when a person stumbles to his ruin. This happens as when by another's inordinate word or deed a person proceeds to the point of mortal sin.

Now active scandal, if it is indeed *per accidens,* can sometimes be a venial sin, as when a person commits an act of venial sin, or else an act that is not in itself a sin but has some appearance of evil, along with some trifling indiscretion. But sometimes active scandal is a mortal sin, either because a person commits an act of mortal sin or because he scorns the well-being of his neighbor, so that he does whatever is pleasing to himself, with no regard for preserving his neighbor's well-being. But if there is active scandal *per se,* as when someone intends to lead another into sinning, it is a mortal sin. Likewise, if he intends to lead another to sinning venially by an act of mortal sin. But if he intends to lead his neighbor to sinning venially by an act of venial sin, then it is a venial sin.

[1]–[3] And from this the answer TO WHAT WAS OBJECTED is clear.

Article 5. [Whether passive scandal can fall upon even those who are perfect.]

One proceeds in this way to the fifth query. IT SEEMS that passive scandal can fall upon even those who are perfect.

[1] Christ was most of all perfect. But he said to Peter, "You are a scandal to me."[35] Much more, then, can others who are perfect undergo scandal.

[2] Furthermore, scandal denotes a hindrance that is opposed to someone in the spiritual life. But even perfect men can be hindered in the processes of the spiritual life, according to 1 Thessalonians 2: "We would have come to you, indeed I, Paul, would have, but Satan has hindered us."[36] Therefore even perfect men can undergo scandal.

[3] Furthermore, venial sins can be found even in perfect men, according to 1 John 1, "If we say that we have no sin, we deceive ourselves."[37] But

---

35. Matthew 16.23.
36. 1 Thessalonians 2.18.
37. 1 John 1.8.

passive scandal is not always a mortal sin; sometimes it is venial, as was said.[38] Therefore passive scandal can be found in perfect men.

BUT TO THE CONTRARY there is what Jerome says on Matthew 18, "He who shall scandalize one of these little ones":[39] "Note that it is the little one who is scandalized, for the elders do not undertake scandals."[40]

I ANSWER THAT IT SHOULD BE SAID that passive scandal denotes a certain agitation of the spirit, in the person who undergoes scandal, away from the good. No one, however, who adheres firmly to the unmovable good is agitated. Now the elders – or rather the perfect who adhere to God alone, whose goodness is unchangeable – though they adhere to their prelates, they do not adhere to them except to the extent that they adhere to Christ, according to 1 Corinthians 4: "Be imitators of me, as I am of Christ."[41] So however much it may appear that they are related to others by inordinate words or deeds, they themselves do not withdraw from their own rightness, according to the Psalm: "Those who trust in the Lord are as Mount Zion; he who dwells in Jerusalem will not be moved in eternity."[42] And so in those who perfectly adhere to God by love, scandal is not found, according to the Psalm: "Much peace have they, who love your law, and in them there is no scandal."[43]

[1] TO THE FIRST ARGUMENT, THEREFORE, IT SHOULD BE SAID that, as was said above,[44] "scandal" there is taken in a wide sense, for any hindrance whatever. So the Lord tells Peter, "You are a scandal to me," since Peter was striving to hinder his purpose of suffering the Passion.

[2] To the second it should be said that perfect men can be hindered in outward acts. But in the inward will, they are not hindered by the words or deeds of others, so that they fail to tend toward God, according to Romans 8: "Neither death nor life will be able to separate us from the charity of God."[45]

---

38. In Article 4 of this Question.
39. Matthew 18.6.
40. Jerome, *On Matthew* bk.3, on Matthew 18.6 (PL 26:133; CCSL 77: 157:516–17).
41. 1 Corinthians 4.16.
42. Psalm 124.1.
43. Psalm 118.165.
44. In Article 2, Reply to [2], of this Question.
45. Romans 8.38.

[3] To the third it should be said that perfect men, out of the weakness of the flesh, sometimes fall into venial sins, whereas they are not scandalized by the words or deeds of others according to the true aspect of scandal. But there can be in them a kind of nearness to scandal, according to the Psalm: "My feet were almost moved."[46]

Article 6. [Whether active scandal can be found in perfect men.]

One proceeds in this way to the sixth query. IT SEEMS that active scandal can be found in perfect men (*in viris perfectis*).

[1] Passion is an effect of action. But by the words and deeds of the perfect, some are passively scandalized, according to Matthew 15: "Do you know that the Pharisees, when they heard this word, were scandalized?"[47] Therefore active scandal can be found in perfect men.

[2] Furthermore, after having accepted the Holy Spirit, Peter was in the state of the perfect. But the Gentiles were scandalized afterwards, as is said in Galatians 2: "When I saw that they did not walk uprightly, toward the truth of the Gospel, I said to Cephas," that is, Peter, "before all: if you, being a Jew, live as the Gentiles live and not as do the Jews, how do you compel the Gentiles to live in the Jewish manner (*iudaizare*)?"[48] Therefore active scandal can be in perfect men.

[3] Furthermore, active scandal is sometimes a venial sin. But venial sins can be found even in perfect human beings. Therefore active scandal can be in perfect men.

BUT TO THE CONTRARY active scandal is more repugnant than passive scandal to a perfect human being. But passive scandal cannot be in perfect men. Much less, therefore, can active scandal.

I ANSWER THAT IT SHOULD BE SAID that active scandal is properly when a person says or does a thing which of itself is such that another is naturally led to his ruin – which indeed is only when something is done or said inordinately. Now it belongs to the perfect to direct the things they

---

46. Psalm 72.2. Here the Latin differs slightly from what Thomas quotes at 36.2 corp.

47. Matthew 15.12.

48. Galatians 2.14.

do according to the rule of reason, according to 1 Corinthians 14: "Let everything in you be done nobly and according to order."⁴⁹ And they take this precaution chiefly in matters in which they might not only do offensive things, but also produce offense in others. And should something in their open words or deeds fall short of this moderation, this arises from human weakness, according as they fall short of perfection. Nevertheless, they do not fall short so greatly as to withdraw by much from the order of reason, but only a little and in a trifling manner—which is not so great that another can reasonably take from it an occasion for sinning.

[1] TO THE FIRST ARGUMENT, THEREFORE, IT SHOULD BE SAID that passive scandal is always caused by some active scandal, but not always by the active scandal of another, since the person who causes scandal may be the same as the person who is scandalized—because, that is, he scandalizes himself.

[2] To the second it should be said that in withdrawing himself from the Gentiles, so that he might avoid scandalizing the Jews, Peter sinned, and was worthy of blame, according to the opinion of Augustine⁵⁰ and of Paul himself. This is because he did this somewhat incautiously, so that from this withdrawal, Gentiles who had been turned to the faith were scandalized. Nevertheless, the deed of Peter was not such a grave sin that others were deservedly able to be scandalized. So they underwent passive scandal, whereas there was not active scandal in Peter.

[3] To the third it should be said that the venial sins of the perfect consist chiefly in sudden motions which, since they are hidden, are not able to scandalize. If in fact they also commit venial sins in their outward words and deeds, they are so trifling as not to have of themselves any power of scandalizing.

Article 7. [Whether spiritual goods should be given up on account of scandal.]

One proceeds in this way to the seventh query. IT SEEMS that spiritual goods should be given up on account of scandal.

---

49. 1 Corinthians 14.40.
50. See Augustine, *Epistulae* ep.28 to Jerome chap.3 sect.4 (PL 33:113; CCSL 31:94.66–76); ep.40 to Jerome chap.3 sect.5 (PL 33:156; CCSL 31:162.71–84); ep.82 to Jerome chap.2 sect.7 (PL 33:277; CCSL 31A:101.109–29).

[1] Augustine, in his book *Against a Letter of Parmenian,* teaches that where the danger of schism is feared, one should cease punishing sins.[51] But the punishment of sins is a certain spiritual thing, since it is an act of justice. Therefore a spiritual good should be given up on account of scandal.

[2] Furthermore, holy teaching (*sacra doctrina*) especially seems to be spiritual. But one should cease from this on account of scandal, according to Matthew 7: "Do not give what is holy to dogs, and do not cast your pearls before swine, lest turning upon you, they tear you."[52] Therefore a spiritual good should on account of scandal be given up.

[3] Furthermore, fraternal correction, since it is an act of charity, is a certain spiritual good. But sometimes it should be given up out of charity, for the sake of avoiding scandal on the part of others, as Augustine says in *City of God,* Book 1.[53] Therefore a spiritual good should be given up on account of scandal.

[4] Furthermore, Jerome[54] says that one should give up on account of scandal anything that can be omitted while preserving the threefold truth, namely that of life, of justice, and of teaching. But the fulfillment of deliberations, and an abundance of works of mercy, can be omitted many times while preserving the aforementioned threefold truth; otherwise, those who omit them would always sin. And these are the greatest among spiritual works. Therefore spiritual works should be omitted on account of scandal.

[5] Furthermore, the avoidance of any sin is a certain spiritual good, since any sin whatever brings some spiritual harm to the sinner. But it seems that for the sake of avoiding scandal to one's neighbors, a person should sometimes avoid sinning venially, as when sinning venially hinders the mortal sin of another, for a man should hinder the damnation of his neighbor, so far as he can without harm to his own salvation, which is not destroyed by venial sin. Therefore a man should omit a spiritual good on account of avoiding scandal.

BUT TO THE CONTRARY Gregory says, *On Ezekiel,* "If scandal is taken from the truth, it is more advantageous to allow scandal to be born

---

51. Augustine, *Contra epistolam Parmeniani* bk.3 chap.2 sect.13 (PL 43:92; CSEL 51/1:114–15).

52. Matthew 7.6.

53. Augustine, *De civitate Dei* bk.1 chap.9 (PL 41:22; CCSL 47:9.31–33).

54. Rather, Alexander of Hales; see *Summa Halensis* pt.2 sect.862 (Quaracchi 3:821). See also William of Auxerre, *Summa aurea* pt.3 tr.24 q.4.

than for truth to be left behind."[55] But spiritual goods most of all belong to truth. Therefore spiritual goods should not be given up on account of scandal.

I ANSWER THAT IT SHOULD BE SAID that since scandal is two-fold, namely active and passive, this question has no place with respect to active scandal, since when active scandal is a word or deed [spoken or done] nothing is done with active scandal. One should consider, therefore, what one gives up, lest another be scandalized. Now one should make a distinction among spiritual goods. For certain of these are necessary for salvation, which cannot be omitted without mortal sin. Now it is clear that no one should mortally sin, so that he might hinder the sin of another, since according to the order of charity, a man should love his own spiritual well-being more than that of another. And so the things that are necessary for salvation should not be omitted for the sake of avoiding scandal. But in the spiritual goods that are not necessary for salvation, it seems that one should distinguish. Since the scandal that is born from such goods some-times proceeds from malice, namely when some people wish to hinder spiritual goods of this sort by arousing scandal. And this is the scandal of the Pharisees, who were scandalized concerning the teaching of the Lord. That this should be scorned, the Lord teaches, Matthew 15.[56] Sometimes, however, scandal proceeds from weakness or ignorance. And the scandal of the little ones is of this sort. On account of this, spiritual works should be hidden or sometimes even delayed, where danger does not threaten, until an account is given and any scandal of this type ceases. But should scandal of this type endure, after an account has been given, the scandal would now seem to proceed from malice. Thus on its account, spiritual works of this type should not be given up.

[1] TO THE FIRST ARGUMENT, THEREFORE, IT SHOULD BE SAID that the infliction of punishments is not sought for its own sake; rather, penalties are inflicted as a kind of medicine for the repression of sins. And so, as far as they have the aspect of justice, sins are to that extent repressed through them. If, however, it is clear that more and greater sins will follow from the infliction of punishments, then the infliction of pun-ishments will not be contained under justice. Augustine is speaking of this

55. Gregory, *Homiliae in Ezechielem prophetam* bk.1 hom.7 sect.5 (PL 76:842; CCSL 142:85.89–90).
56. See Matthew 15.14.

case—namely when from the excommunication of some people, the danger of schism looms large—for in this case to impose excommunication would not belong to the truth of justice.

[2] To the second it should be said that regarding teaching, two things should be considered—namely, the truth that is taught and the act of teaching itself. Of these the first is necessary for salvation, so that he to whom the duty of teaching is given should not teach the contrary of truth, but rather put the truth forward according to the fittingness of time and persons. And so on account of no scandal that might seem to follow should a person teach falsehood while omitting the truth. But the act of teaching itself is reckoned among spiritual works of mercy, as was said above.[57] And so for the same reason, it belongs to teaching (*doctrina*) and to the other works of mercy, which will be addressed later.[58]

[3] To the third it should be said that fraternal correction is directed to the correction of a brother, as was said above.[59] And so just as far as it is reckoned among the spiritual goods, to that extent it can follow. But this does not occur if a brother should be scandalized by correction. And so if correction is given up on account of scandal, the spiritual good is not given up.

[4] To the fourth it should be said that the truth of life, of teaching, and of justice embraces not only that which is necessary for salvation, but also that by which one is more completely brought to salvation, according to 1 Corinthians 12: "Be zealous for the better gifts."[60] So that neither counsels nor even the works of mercy should simply be omitted on account of scandal—but sometimes they should be hidden or delayed on account of the scandal of little ones, as was said.[61] Yet sometimes the observation of counsels and the fulfillment of works of mercy are necessary for salvation. This is clear in those who have vowed to keep the counsels, and in those for whom it threatens out of duty to alleviate the defects of others—either in temporal things, as by feeding the hungry, or in spiritual things, as teaching the ignorant. This holds whether duties of this type arise on account of the enjoined duty, as is clear with prelates, or else on account of the necessity of those in want. And then the same reason belongs to things of this type, as it does to others that are necessary for salvation.

57. In Question 32, Article 2.
58. In this Article, Reply [4].
59. In Question 33, Article 1.
60. 1 Corinthians 12.31.
61. In the body of the Article.

[5] To the fifth it should be said that some people have said that venial sin should be committed for the sake of avoiding scandal. But this implies contrary things, for if this ought to be done, then there is neither evil nor sin, for sin would not be able to be chosen. Yet it can happen on account of some circumstance that something is not a venial sin that, if these circumstances were removed, would be a venial sin – just as a buffoonish word is sometimes a venial sin when it is said without any usefulness, whereas if a reasonable cause is brought forward, it is neither buffoonish nor a sin. Now although the grace by which a person is saved is not destroyed by a venial sin, it remains that insofar as venial sin disposes a person to mortal sin, it inclines to harming his salvation.

Article 8. [Whether temporal things should be given up on account of scandal.]

One proceeds in this way to the eighth query. IT SEEMS that temporal things should be given up on account of scandal.

[1] We ought to love the spiritual well-being of our neighbor, which is hindered by scandal, more than any temporal goods. But that which we love less, we give up on account of that which we love more. Therefore we ought to give up temporal things for the sake of avoiding scandal on the part of our neighbor.

[2] Furthermore, according to the rule of Jerome, everything can be omitted for the sake of giving up scandal, so long as the threefold truth is preserved. But temporal goods can be omitted while preserving the threefold truth. Therefore they should be given up on account of scandal.

[3] Furthermore, in temporal goods, nothing is more necessary than food. But food should be omitted on account of scandal, according to Romans 14: "Do not wish to destroy with your food a person for whom Christ died."[62] Much more, therefore, should all other temporal things be given up on account of scandal.

[4] Furthermore, we can preserve or recover temporal things in no way that is more appropriate than by the law courts. But to use the law courts is not allowed, and especially with scandal, for Matthew 5 says: "If someone wants to contend with you in the law courts and take your shirt, give him your cloak as well."[63] And 1 Corinthians 6: "It is already bad enough that

62. Romans 14.15.
63. Matthew 5.40.

you have lawsuits among yourselves. Why not let yourselves be wronged? Why not allow yourselves to be defrauded?"[64] Therefore it seems that temporal things should be given up on account of scandal.

[5] Furthermore, among temporal things, those that it seems should be given up least are the ones which are joined to spiritual things. But on account of scandal, these should be given up, for the Apostle says that while sowing spiritual things, he does not accept temporal wages, lest he give a stumbling block to the Gospel of Christ, as is clear from 1 Corinthians 9.[65] And from a like cause, the Church in some lands does not demand tithes, for the sake of avoiding scandal. Much more, therefore, should other temporal things be given up on account of scandal.

BUT TO THE CONTRARY the blessed Thomas of Canterbury demanded the return of things belonging to the Church, to the scandal of the king.

I ANSWER THAT IT SHOULD BE SAID that regarding temporal goods, one should make a distinction. For either they are ours or they are entrusted to us for the sake of preserving them for others – just as the goods of the Church are entrusted to prelates, and communal goods to the republic's rulers. The preservation of such goods, as of deposits, hangs on those to whom they are entrusted out of necessity. And so they should not be given up on account of scandal, as neither should other things that are necessary for salvation. But temporal things of which we are the master – they should be given up if we have them in our hands, or not demanded back if they are in the hands of others – sometimes we should give them up on account of scandal, and sometimes not. For if a scandal arises from this on account of ignorance or weakness of others – which we said above[66] is the scandal of the little ones – then we should give up temporal things entirely, or otherwise settle the scandal by some kind of warning. So Augustine says, in his book *The Lord's Sermon on the Mount:* "You should give as much as you can lend, so that harm comes neither to yourself nor to another. And if you refuse what he asks, justice must be shown to him – and you will give him something better, if you correct the person who asks unjustly."[67]

64. 1 Corinthians 6.7.
65. 1 Corinthians 9.13.
66. In Article 7 of this Question.
67. Augustine, *De sermone Domini in monte* bk.1 chap.20 (PL 34:1264; CCSL 35:76–77.1675–80), condensed.

But sometimes scandal is born out of malice; this is the scandal of the Pharisees. On account of those who cause scandals in this way, temporal things should not be given up, since this would both harm the common good – for it would give an occasion to evil men for plundering – and harm the plunderers themselves, who would remain in sin by keeping things that belong to others. So Gregory says, in the *Moralia:* "Those who steal our temporal things from us should sometimes be endured, and sometimes be restrained, while still observing equity. This is out of concern not only lest our things be taken away, but also lest those who plunder what is not theirs should lose themselves."[68]

[1] And from this is clear the solution TO THE FIRST THING THAT WAS OBJECTED.

[2] To the second it should be said that if evil men were permitted here and there to rob others, this would incline to the harm of truth, life, and justice. And so it is not right that temporal things should be given up on account of just any scandal.

[3] To the third it should be said that to warn that food should be given up entirely on account of scandal did not belong to the intention of the Apostle, since to eat food is necessary for health. But some particular food should be given up on account of scandal, according to 1 Corinthians 8: "I shall never eat flesh, lest I scandalize my brother."[69]

[4] To the fourth it should be said that according to Augustine, in his book *The Lord's Sermon on the Mount,* this precept of the Lord should be understood "according to preparation of the spirit," so that a man should be ready first to suffer harm or fraud, before he goes to court, if this should be liberating.[70] Yet sometimes this is not liberating, as said above.[71] The word of the Apostle should be understood in a similar way.

[5] To the fifth it should be said that the scandal which the Apostle avoided proceeded out of ignorance on the part of the Gentiles, who were not familiar with this practice. And so for a time he was to abstain from it, so that they might first be taught that this was due. And for a similar cause, the Church abstains from demanding titles in lands in which it is not customary to pay tithes.

68. Gregory the Great, *Moralia* bk.31 chap.13 sect.22 (PL 76:586; CCSL 143B: 1566–67.43–48), paraphrased.

69. 1 Corinthians 8.13.

70. Augustine, *De sermone Domini in monte* bk.1 chap.19 (PL 34:1260; CCSL 35:69.1491–92).

71. In the body and the Reply to [2] of this Article.

[The Precepts of Charity]

One should next consider the precepts of charity. Regarding this, eight queries are raised. (1) Whether precepts should be given about charity. (2) Whether only one, or two. (3) Whether two suffice. (4) Whether it is appropriately taught by precept that God should be loved "with one's whole heart." (5) Whether it is appropriately added "with one's whole mind," etc. (6) Whether this precept can be fulfilled in this life. (7) On this precept: "Love your neighbor as you love yourself." (8) Whether the order of charity falls under a precept.

Article 1. [Whether a precept should be given about charity.]

One proceeds in this way to the first query. IT SEEMS that a precept should not be given about charity.

[1] Charity imposes a measure within the acts of all the virtues, about which precepts are given, since it is the form of the virtues, as was said above.[1] But a measure is not in a precept, as is generally said. Therefore precepts should not be given about charity.

[2] Furthermore, charity, which "is infused into our hearts by the Holy Spirit," makes us free, since "where the Spirit of God is, there is freedom," as is said in 2 Corinthians 3.[2] But obligation, which is born out of precepts, is opposed to freedom, since it imposes necessity. Therefore precepts should not be given about charity.

[3] Furthermore, charity is chief among all the virtues to which precepts are directed, as is clear from what was said above.[3] If, therefore, some pre-

---

1. In Question 23, Article 8.
2. 2 Corinthians 3.17.
3. *Summa* 1a2ae q.100 a.9 ad 2.

cepts are given about charity, they should be placed among the chief precepts, which are the precepts of the Decalogue. But they are not so placed. Therefore no precepts should be given about charity.

BUT TO THE CONTRARY that which God requires from us falls under a precept. Now God requires from man "that he love him," as is said in Deuteronomy 10.[4] Therefore precepts should be given about the love of charity, which is the love of God.

I ANSWER THAT IT SHOULD BE SAID that, as was said above,[5] a precept denotes the aspect of "the due." Therefore so far as something falls under a precept, it has to that extent the aspect of "the due." Now something is due in two ways: in one way, by itself (*per se*); in another way, because of something else (*propter aliud*). What is due *per se* in any activity (*negotio*) is that which is its end, since the end has the aspect of good *per se*. But what is due because of something else is what is directed to the end—just as it is due *per se* for a physician to heal, and due because of something else that medicine should be given for the sake of healing. Now the end of spiritual life is for a human being to be united to God, which occurs by charity. And all things that belong to the spiritual life are directed to this, as to an end. So the Apostle says, 1 Timothy 1: "The end of the precept is charity, out of a pure heart and a good conscience, and a faith unfeigned."[6] For all the virtues, about whose acts precepts are given, are directed either to cleansing the heart from the whirlwind (*turbines*) of the passions, as with the virtues that are about the passions; or at least to having a good conscience, as with the virtues that are about actions; or to having right faith, as with the virtues that belong to divine worship. And these three things are required for loving God. For an impure heart is dragged away from the love of God on account of passion inclining it toward earthly things; a bad conscience makes a person dread divine justice because of fear of punishment; whereas a feigned faith draws the affection toward that which is feigned about God, separating a person from divinity and from God's truth. Now in any genus, that which is *per se* is better than that which is because of something else. And so the "greatest precept" is about charity, as is said in Matthew 22.[7]

4. Deuteronomy 10.12.
5. *Summa* 1a2ae q.99 a.1 and a.5, q.100 a.5 ad 1.
6. 1 Timothy 1.5.
7. Matthew 22.38.

[1] TO THE FIRST ARGUMENT, THEREFORE, IT SHOULD BE SAID that, as was said above when the rest of the precepts were treated,[8] the measure of love does not fall under the precepts that are given about the other acts of the virtues – as, for example, that which arises from charity does not fall under the precept "Honor your father and your mother." Yet the act of love does fall under particular precepts.

[2] To the second it should be said that a precept's obligation does not oppose freedom, except in a person whose mind is set against whatever is taught by the precept – as is clear in those who observe precepts only out of fear. But the precept of love cannot be fulfilled except by one's own will. And so it is not repugnant to freedom.

[3] To the third it should be said that all the precepts of the Decalogue are directed to the love of God and neighbor. And so the precepts of charity were not enumerated among the precepts of the Decalogue, but were included in all of them.

Article 2. [Whether two precepts should have been given.]

One proceeds in this way to the second query. IT SEEMS that two precepts about charity should not have been given.

[1] The precepts of law are directed to a virtue, as was said above.[9] But charity is one virtue, as is clear from what was said above.[10] Therefore only one precept should have been given about charity.

[2] Furthermore, as Augustine says in *On Christian Doctrine*, Book 1, charity loves nothing in our neighbor except God.[11] But we are sufficiently directed to loving God by this precept: "Love the Lord your God."[12] Therefore it was not necessary to add another precept about love of our neighbor.

[3] Furthermore, different sins are opposed to different precepts. But a person does not sin in overlooking the love of his neighbor, if he does not overlook the love of God – indeed Luke 14 says: "If someone comes to me

8. *Summa* 1a2ae q.100 a.10.
9. In Article 1, Argument [3] of this Question.
10. In Question 23, Article 5.
11. Augustine, *De doctrina christiana* bk.1 chap.22 sect.21 (PL 34:27; CCSL 32:18.38–42) and bk.1 chap.27 sect.28 (PL 34:29; CCSL 32:22.11–13).
12. Deuteronomy 6.5.

and does not hate his father and his mother, he cannot be my disciple."[13] Therefore the precept about the love of God is not other than that about the love of neighbor.

[4] Furthermore, the Apostle says, Romans 13: "He who loves his neighbor fulfills the law."[14] But the law is not fulfilled except by the observance of all the precepts. Therefore all the precepts are included in the love of one's neighbor. It suffices, therefore, to have one precept about the love of neighbor. About this matter, therefore, there should not be two precepts of charity.

BUT TO THE CONTRARY there is what is said in 1 John 4: "This commandment we have from God, that he who loves God love his brother also."[15]

I ANSWER THAT IT SHOULD BE SAID that precepts bear the same relation to the law as propositions bear to the speculative sciences, as was said above when we treated the precepts.[16] In the speculative sciences, the conclusions are virtually contained in the first principles. So that he who completely knows the principles according to their whole power (*secundum tota suam virtutem*) would have no need for the conclusions to be put before him separately. But since not all who know principles are up to the task of considering everything that is virtually contained in the principles, it is necessary for their sake that in the sciences, conclusions should be drawn out from the principles. Now in matters of action, in which precepts of the law guide us, the end has the aspect of a principle, as was said above.[17] Now the love of God is the end to which the love of our neighbor is directed. And so there needs to be given not only a precept about the love of God, but also one about the love of our neighbor, on account of those who are less capable of easily considering one of these precepts as being contained under the other.

[1] TO THE FIRST ARGUMENT, THEREFORE, IT SHOULD BE SAID that while charity is one virtue, it nonetheless has two acts, one of which is directed to the other, as to an end. Now precepts are given about

13. Luke 14.26.
14. Romans 13.8.
15. 1 John 4.21.
16. *Summa* 1a2ae q.91 a.3, q.100 a.1.
17. In Question 23, Article 7, Reply [2], and Question 26, Article 1, Reply [1].

the acts of the virtues. And so it was necessary to have multiple precepts of charity.

[2] To the second it should be said that God is loved in our neighbor, just as an end [is loved] in that which is directed to the end. And yet it was necessary that precepts were explicitly given about both, for the reason already mentioned.[18]

[3] To the third it should be said that what is directed to the end has the aspect of good from its ordering to the end. Accordingly, to withdraw from the end has the aspect of evil, and not otherwise.

[4] To the fourth it should be said that the love of God is included in the love of our neighbor, just as an end is included in that which is directed to the end, and vice versa. And yet it was necessary for each precept to be given explicitly, for the reason already mentioned.[19]

Article 3. [Whether two precepts of charity suffice.]

One proceeds in this way to the third query. IT SEEMS that two precepts of charity do not suffice.

[1] Precepts are given about the acts of the virtues. Now the acts are distinguished according to their objects. Since, therefore, man should love four things out of charity – namely God, himself, his neighbor, and his own body, as is clear from what was said above[20] – it seems that there should be four precepts of charity. Thus two do not suffice.

[2] Furthermore, the act of charity is not only love, but also joy, peace, and doing good. But precepts should be given about the acts of the virtues. Therefore two precepts about charity do not suffice.

[3] Furthermore, just as doing good belongs to virtue, so too does turning away from evil. But we are led to do good by affirmative precepts, and to turn away from evil by negative precepts. Therefore not only affirmative, but also negative precepts should have been given about charity. And thus the two precepts of charity mentioned above do not suffice.

BUT TO THE CONTRARY the Lord says, Matthew 22: "On these two commandments hang the whole Law and the Prophets."[21]

---

18. In the body of the Article.
19. In the body of the Article.
20. In Question 25, Article 12.
21. Matthew 22.40.

I ANSWER THAT IT SHOULD BE SAID that charity is a certain friendship, as was said above.[22] Now friendship is borne toward another. So Gregory says in a certain homily that "charity cannot be had between fewer than two people."[23] But in a certain way, a person loves himself out of charity, as was said above.[24] Since, however, *dilectio* and *amor* are love of the good, whereas the good is either the end or that which is directed to the end, it is appropriate that two precepts about charity should suffice. The first is that by which we are led to love God, as the end. The second is that by which we are led to love our neighbor on account of God, as on account of the end.

[1] TO THE FIRST ARGUMENT, THEREFORE, IT SHOULD BE SAID that, as Augustine says in *On Christian Doctrine,* Book 1, "though there are four things that should be loved out of charity, about the second and the fourth"—that is, self-love and love of our own body—"no precepts were given, for however much a man should fall away from truth, the love of himself and of his own body always stays with him."[25] But the way of loving was taught to man by precept, so that he would love himself and his own body in an ordinate manner. Indeed, such ordinate love occurs by this—that a person loves God and his neighbor.

[2] To the second it should be said that the other acts of charity follow from the act of love, as an effect follows from a cause, as is clear from the things said above.[26] So the precepts of the other acts are virtually included in the precepts of love.—And yet for the sake of the slower (*propter tardiores*), there are precepts explicitly handed down about particular things. On joy, Philippians 4: "Rejoice in the Lord always."[27] On peace, Hebrews 12: "Follow peace with all."[28] On doing good, the last chapter of Galatians: "While we have time, let us do good to all."[29] On the particular parts of doing good, precepts handed down in sacred Scripture can be discovered, as is clear to one who considers the matter diligently.

22. In Question 23, Article 1.
23. Gregory the Great, *Homiliae in Evangelia* bk.1 hom.17 sect.1, on Luke 10.1–9 (PL 76:1139; CCSL 141:117.6–7).
24. In Question 25, Article 4.
25. Augustine, *De doctrina christiana* bk.1 chap.23 sect.22 (PL 34:27; CCSL 32:18.6–11).
26. In Question 28, Articles 1 and 4; Question 29, Article 3; Question 31, Article 1.
27. Philippians 4.4.
28. Hebrews 12.14.
29. Galatians 6.10.

[3] To the third it should be said that doing good is greater than avoiding evil. And so the negative precepts are virtually included within the affirmative precepts. –Yet there are precepts given explicitly against the vices opposed to charity. For against hatred, Leviticus 19 says: "May you not hate your brother in your heart."[30] Against acedia, Sirach 6: "May you not be weary in her chains."[31] Against envy, Galatians 5: "May we not become lustful for vainglory, provoking one another, envying one another."[32] Against discord, 1 Corinthians 1: "May you all say the same thing, and may there not be schisms among you."[33] Against scandal, Romans 14: "May you not put an obstacle or a stumbling block (*scandalum*) before your brother."[34]

Article 4. [Whether it is appropriately commanded that God should be loved with one's whole heart.]

One proceeds in this way to the fourth query. IT SEEMS to be inappropriately commanded that God should be loved with one's whole heart.

[1] The measure of virtuous acts is not in a precept, as is clear from what was said above.[35] But that which is said to be "with one's whole heart" denotes the mode of divine love. Therefore it is inappropriately taught by precept that God should be loved with one's whole heart.

[2] Furthermore, "the whole and complete is that to which nothing is lacking," as is said in *Physics* 3.[36] If therefore it falls under a precept that God should be loved with one's whole heart, anyone who does something that does not belong to the love of God acts against the precept, and consequently sins mortally. But venial sin does not belong to the love of God. Therefore venial sin would be mortal. This is inappropriate.

[3] Furthermore, to love God with one's whole heart belongs to perfection, since according to the Philosopher, "the whole and the perfect are the same."[37] But the things that belong to perfection do not fall under a precept,

---

30. Leviticus 19.17.
31. Sirach 6.26. "Her chains" refers to the chains of wisdom. Compare Question 35, Article 1, *sed contra*.
32. Galatians 5.26.
33. 1 Corinthians 1.10.
34. Romans 14.13.
35. *Summa* 1a2ae q.100 a.9.
36. Aristotle, *Physics* bk.3 chap.6 (207a9).
37. Aristotle, *Physics* bk.3 chap.6 (207a13).

but under counsel. Therefore it should not be taught by precept that God should be loved with one's whole heart.

BUT TO THE CONTRARY there is what is said in Deuteronomy 6, "You shall love the Lord your God with your whole heart."[38]

I ANSWER THAT IT SHOULD BE SAID that, since precepts are given about the acts of the virtues, an act does in this way fall under a precept, according as it is an act of virtue. Now for an act of virtue, it is required not only that it fall under its due matter, but also that it be vested (*vestiatur*) in the due circumstances, by which the act is proportioned to that matter. Now God should be loved as an ultimate end, to which all things should be referred. And so about the precept concerning God's love, a certain wholeness had to be marked out.

[1] TO THE FIRST ARGUMENT, THEREFORE, IT SHOULD BE SAID that the measure that an act possesses from some higher virtue does not fall under the precept that is given about the act of the virtue [proper to it]. Yet the measure that belongs to the aspect of its proper virtue does fall under a precept. And such a measure is signified when it is said, "with one's whole heart."

[2] To the second it should be said that loving God with one's whole heart happens in two ways. In one way, in act – that is, as a man's whole heart is always and actually borne toward God. And this way is the perfection of the homeland (*perfectio patriae*). – In another way, as a man's whole heart is habitually borne toward God: namely, so that a man's whole heart receives nothing that goes against the love of God. And this is perfection of the way (*perfectio viae*). To this, venial sin is not opposed, since it does not destroy the habit of charity. This is because it does not tend to the opposed object, but only hinders the use of charity.

[3] To the third it should be said that the perfection of charity to which counsel is directed is a midpoint between the two perfections already mentioned[39] – namely so that a man, so far as it is possible, should draw himself away from temporal things, even those that are lawful but which, occupying the spirit, hinder the actual motion of the heart toward God.

38. Deuteronomy 6.5.
39. In Reply [2] of this Article.

Article 5. [Whether it is appropriately added "and with your whole soul and with your whole strength," etc.]

One proceeds in this way to the fifth query. IT SEEMS that it is inappropriate to add to the passage quoted above ("You shall love the Lord your God with your whole heart") the words "and with your whole soul and with your whole strength."[40]

[1] "Heart" is not here taken as a bodily member, since to love God is not the act of the body. Therefore it is necessary that "heart" be taken spiritually. But "heart" taken spiritually is either the soul itself or something pertaining to the soul. It was superfluous, therefore, to set down both.

[2] Furthermore, a person's strength depends chiefly on the heart, whether this is taken spiritually or bodily. Therefore after it had been said "You shall love the Lord your God with your whole heart," it was superfluous to add "and with your whole strength."

[3] Furthermore, Matthew 22 says "with your whole mind,"[41] which is not set down here. Therefore it seems that this precept is inappropriately given by Deuteronomy 6.[42]

BUT TO THE CONTRARY there is the authority of Scripture.

I ANSWER THAT IT SHOULD BE SAID that this precept is found to be handed down in different ways, in different places. For as was said,[43] three things are set down in Deuteronomy 6–namely "with your whole heart," "with your whole soul," and "with your whole strength." Two of these things are set down in Matthew 22, namely "with your whole heart" and "with your whole soul"; "with your whole strength" is omitted, but "with your whole mind" is added. But four things are set down in Mark 12, namely "with your whole heart," "with your whole soul," "with your whole mind," and "with your whole power," which is the same as "strength."[44] And these four things are touched upon by Luke 10, for in place of "strength" or "power" is set down "with all your powers."[45] And so a reason should be assigned to all four of these, since if anywhere one of these four is omitted, this is because one of them is understood from the others.

40. Deuteronomy 6.5.
41. Matthew 22.37.
42. See Deuteronomy 6.5.
43. In Article 1 of this Question.
44. See Mark 12.30.
45. Luke 10.27.

One should therefore consider that love (*dilectio*) is an act of the will, which is signified here by "heart" – for just as the bodily heart is first of all the bodily motions, so too the will is the first of all the spiritual motions – and especially with respect to intention of the ultimate end, which is the object of charity. Now there are three principles of action that are moved by the will – namely the intellect, which is signified by "mind" (*mens*); the lower appetitive power, which is signified by "soul" (*anima*); and the executive exterior power, which is signified by "strength" (*fortitudo*) or "power" (*virtus*) or "powers" (*vires*). Therefore we are taught by precept that our whole intention should be directed toward God, which is "with your whole heart" – and that our intellect should be subjected to God, which is "with your whole mind" – and that our appetite should be regulated according to God, which is "with your whole soul" – and that our exterior act should obey God, which is to love God "with your whole strength" or "power" or "powers."

Yet Chrysostom, in *On Matthew*, takes "heart" (*cor*) and "soul" (*anima*) in a sense contrary to what was said.[46] – And in fact Augustine, in *On Christian Doctrine*, Book 1, refers "heart" to thoughts, "soul" to life, and "mind" to intellect.[47] – But certain people say, "with one's whole heart," that is, intellect (*intellectus*); "with one's whole soul," that is, will (*voluntas*); "with one's whole mind," that is, memory (*memoria*).[48] – Or, according to Gregory of Nyssa, the nutritive soul is signified by "heart" (*cor*), the sensitive soul by "soul" (*anima*), and the intellective soul by "mind" (*mens*).[49] This is because we should refer to God the fact that we are nourished, that we sense, and that we understand.

[1]–[3] And from these things the answer TO WHAT WAS OBJECTED is clear.

Article 6. [Whether this precept about the love of God can be kept *in via*.]

One proceeds in this way to the sixth query. IT SEEMS that this precept about the love of God can be kept *in via*.

46. Ps-Chrysostom, *Opus imperfectum in Matthaeum* hom.42, on Matthew 22.37 (PG 56:873).

47. Augustine, *De doctrina christiana* bk.1 chap.22 sect.21 (PL 34:27; CCSL 32:17.29–32).

48. See *Glossa interlinearis* on Matthew 22.37 (Strasbourg 5).

49. Gregory of Nyssa, *De opificio hominis* chap.8 (PG 44:145).

[1] According to Jerome, in *The Exposition of Catholic Faith,* "Cursed is he who says that God has commanded anything impossible."[50] But God has given this precept, as is clear from Deuteronomy 6.[51] Therefore this precept can be fulfilled *in via.*

[2] Furthermore, anyone who does not fulfill the precept sins mortally, since according to Ambrose, sin is nothing other than "a transgression of the divine law and disobedience against heavenly commandments."[52] If, therefore, this precept cannot be kept *in via,* it follows that no one can in this life be without mortal sin. But this is against what the Apostle says, 1 Corinthians 1, "You will be strengthened."[53] And in 1 Timothy 3, "Let them minister, having no crime."[54]

[3] Furthermore, precepts are given for loving human beings on the way to salvation, according to the Psalm: "The precept of the Lord is clear, enlightening our eyes."[55] But a person is directed to the impossible in vain. Therefore it is not impossible for this precept to be kept in this life.

BUT TO THE CONTRARY Augustine says in his book *On the Perfection of Human Justice:* "In the fullness of charity-of-the-homeland, this precept will be fulfilled: 'Love the Lord your God,' etc. For if there is still something of bodily concupiscence, which is bridled by continence, God is not loved entirely with one's whole heart."[56]

I ANSWER THAT IT SHOULD BE SAID that a precept can be fulfilled in two ways—in one way, completely; in another way, incompletely. A precept is fulfilled completely when a person arrives at the end that the preceptor intends, whereas it is fulfilled but incompletely when a person—even if he should not attain the preceptor's end—yet does not withdraw from an ordering to the end. Thus if the leader of an army teaches his soldiers that they should fight, then those who conquer the enemy by fighting, which

50. See Pelagius, *Libellus fidei ad Innocentium papam* (PL 45:1718); ep.1 to Demetrius, chap.16 (PL 30:32).
51. Deuteronomy 6.5.
52. Ambrose, *De paradiso* chap.8 (PL 14:309).
53. 1 Corinthians 1.8.
54. 1 Timothy 3.10.
55. Psalm 18.9.
56. Augustine, *De perfectione justitiae hominis* chap.8 sect.19 (PL 44:300; CSEL 42:17.24–26 to 18.1–3). Augustine's text does not mention "*caritas patriae*"; it reads "in qua plenitudine caritatis praeceptum illud implebitur." "*Caritas patriae*" is not a characteristically Augustinian phrase. It does appear in Cicero and Livy, with a somewhat different meaning.

the leader intends, will fulfill his precept completely. But the soldier whose fighting does not attain victory, but who still does not act against military discipline, will fulfill the precept but incompletely. Now by this precept, God intends that a man should be wholly united to God, since this shall take place in the homeland, when "God will be all in all," as said in 1 Corinthians 15.[57] And so, fully and completely, shall this precept be fulfilled in the homeland. It is, in fact, fulfilled *in via,* but incompletely. And so *in via* one person fulfills it more completely than another – and so much the more as he approaches the completion of the homeland by a certain likeness.

[1] TO THE FIRST ARGUMENT, THEREFORE, IT SHOULD BE SAID that this reasoning proves that the precept can be fulfilled in some way *in via,* though not completely.

[2] To the second it should be said that just as a soldier who fights lawfully but does not conquer is not blamed, nor does he deserve punishment, so too he who fulfills this precept[58] *in via* does nothing against divine love, nor sins mortally.

[3] To the third it should be said that, as Augustine says, in his book *On the Perfection of Human Justice:* "Why should not this perfection be taught to man by precept, although no one has such perfection in this life? For a straight course cannot be run, if one does not know whereto one should run. But how is a person to know this, if it is not shown to him by any precept?"[59]

Article 7. [Whether the precept about the love of one's neighbor is given appropriately.]

One proceeds in this way to the seventh query. IT SEEMS that the precept about love of one's neighbor is given inappropriately.

[1] The love of charity extends to all human beings, even to enemies, as is clear from Matthew 5.[60] But the name "neighbor" denotes a certain kinship, which does not seem to be had toward all human beings. Therefore it seems that this precept is given inappropriately.

---

57. 1 Corinthians 15.28.

58. Some versions read "he who does not fulfill this precept."

59. Augustine, *De perfectione justitiae hominis* chap.8 sect.19 (PL 44:301; CSEL 42:18.9–12).

60. Matthew 5.44.

[2] Furthermore, according to the Philosopher in *Ethics* 9, "friendly sentiments for another arise from friendly sentiments for oneself"[61] – from which it seems that self-love is the starting point (*principium*) for love of neighbor. But a starting point is better than that which comes from the starting point. Therefore a human being should not love his neighbor as himself.

[3] Furthermore, a person loves himself naturally, but not his neighbor. Inappropriately, therefore, is it commanded that a person should love his neighbor as himself.

BUT TO THE CONTRARY Matthew 22 says: "The second precept is like this [the first precept]: You shall love your neighbor as yourself."[62]

I ANSWER THAT IT SHOULD BE SAID that this precept is appropriately handed down, for in it are touched upon both the reason for loving and the manner of love. The reason for loving is touched upon[63] in the naming of "neighbor." This is because we ought to love others out of charity, since they are neighbors to us, both according to the natural image of God and according to the capacity for glory. Nor does it matter whether he is called "neighbor" or "brother," as attested by 1 John 4,[64] or "friend," as attested by Leviticus 19,[65] since by all these things the same affinity is marked out.

The manner of love is touched upon when the precept says "as yourself." This should not be understood to imply that a person should love his neighbor equally as himself (*aequaliter sibi*), but rather like himself (*similiter sibi*). And this in three ways. First, on the part of the end, as someone loves his neighbor on account of God, just as he should love himself on account of God. In this way the love of neighbor is *holy*. – Second, on the part of the rule of love, so that a person does not stoop to his neighbor's level in something evil, but does so only in good things, as he should satisfy his will only in good things, so that his love of neighbor is *just*. – Third, on the part of the reason for loving, so that a person does not love his neighbor on account of his own advantage or pleasure, but for the reason that he wishes his neighbor good, just as he wishes himself good. In this way, his love of neighbor is *true*. For when someone loves his neighbor on account of his

---

61. Aristotle, *Nicomachean Ethics* bk.9 chap.4 (1166a1); bk.9 chap.8 (1168b5).
62. Matthew 22.39.
63. Some versions read "handed down."
64. 1 John 4.21.
65. Leviticus 19.18.

own advantage or pleasure, he does not truly love his neighbor, but rather himself.

[1]–[3] And from this the answer TO WHAT WAS OBJECTED is clear.

Article 8. [Whether the order of charity falls under a precept.]

One proceeds in this way to the eighth query. IT SEEMS that the order of charity does not fall under a precept.

[1] Whoever transgresses a precept does harm. But if one person loves another as much as he should, and loves some other person more, harm is caused to nobody. Therefore he does not transgress the precept. The order of charity, therefore, does not fall under a precept.

[2] Furthermore, the things that fall under a precept are sufficiently handed down to us in sacred Scripture. But the order of charity that is set down above[66] is never handed down to us in sacred Scripture. Therefore, it does not fall under a precept.

[3] Furthermore, order implies a certain distinction. But love of neighbor, with no distinction, is taught by precept when it says "You shall love your neighbor as yourself."[67] Therefore, the order of charity does not fall under a precept.

BUT TO THE CONTRARY whatever God brings about in us by grace, he teaches by the precepts of the law, according to Jeremiah 31: "I will give my law in their hearts."[68] But God causes in us the order of charity, according to Song of Songs 2: "He has ordered charity in me."[69] Therefore the order of charity falls under a precept of the law.

I ANSWER THAT IT SHOULD BE SAID that, as was said,[70] the measure that belongs to the aspect of a virtuous act falls under the precept that is given regarding the virtue's act. Now the order of charity belongs to the very aspect of virtue, since it is taken according to a proportion of love to

66. Question 26.
67. Matthew 22.39.
68. Jeremiah 31.33.
69. Song of Songs 2.4.
70. In Article 4, Reply [1] of this Question.

what is lovable, as is clear from what was said above.[71] So it is clear that the order of charity should fall under a precept.

[1] TO THE FIRST ARGUMENT, THEREFORE, IT SHOULD BE SAID that a person gives more satisfaction to the person whom he loves more. And so, if someone were to love a person less whom he should love more, he would want to satisfy more the person whom he should satisfy less. In this way, there would be harm to the person whom he should love more.

[2] To the second it should be said that the four things to be loved out of charity are expressed in sacred Scripture. For when it is commanded that we should love God with our whole heart, we are given to understand that we should love God above all things. When it is commanded that someone should love his neighbor as himself, love of self is set before love of neighbor. Likewise when it is commanded, 1 John 3, that "we should lay down our soul," that is, our bodily life, "for the brethren," we are given to understand that we should love our neighbor more than our own body.[72] – Likewise, when it is commanded, in the last chapter of Galatians, that "we are to do good especially to those in the household of faith"[73] and in 1 Timothy 5 that he "who does not have care of his own, and most of all those of his household"[74] is blamed – we are given to understand that among our neighbors, we should love more those who are better and those who are closer to us.

[3] To the third it should be said that from the passage quoted, "Love your neighbor," we are given to understand as a consequence that those who are closer to us should be loved more.

71. In Question 26, Article 4, Reply [1], and in Question 26, Articles 7 and 9.
72. 1 John 3.16.
73. Galatians 6.10.
74. 1 Timothy 5.8.

[The Gift of Wisdom]

One should next consider the gift of wisdom, which corresponds to charity. And first, wisdom itself; second, the opposed vice. About the first point, six queries are raised. (1) Whether wisdom should be numbered among the gifts of the Holy Spirit. (2) In what wisdom is, as in a subject. (3) Whether wisdom is only speculative, or also practical. (4) Whether the wisdom that is a gift can be with mortal sin. (5) Whether wisdom is in everyone who has the grace that makes one pleasing. (6) Which beatitude corresponds to it.

Article 1. [Whether wisdom should be counted among the gifts of the Holy Spirit.]

One proceeds in this way to the first query. IT SEEMS that wisdom should not be counted among the gifts of the Holy Spirit.

[1] Gifts are more complete than virtues, as was said above.[1] But virtue is related only to the good, so that Augustine says that "no one makes use of the virtues badly."[2] Much more, then, are the gifts of the Holy Spirit related to the good. But wisdom is also related to evil, for in James 3 a certain wisdom is said to be "earthly, animal, diabolical."[3] Therefore wisdom should not be set down among the gifts of the Holy Spirit.

[2] Furthermore, as Augustine says, "wisdom is knowledge of divine things."[4] But knowledge of divine things, which man can have through his natural [powers], belongs to the wisdom that is an intellectual virtue. Now supernatural knowledge of divine things belongs to faith, which is a

---

1. *Summa* 1a2ae q.68 a.8.
2. Augustine, *De libero arbitrio* bk.2 chap.19 sect.50 (PL 32:1268; CCSL 29: 271.11).
3. James 3.15.
4. Augustine, *De trinitate* bk.14 chap.1 sect.3 (PL 42:1037; CCSL 50A: 423.48–49).

theological virtue, as is clear from what was said above.[5] Therefore wisdom should be called a virtue rather than a gift.

[3] Furthermore, Job 28 says, "Behold the fear of the Lord, which is wisdom itself; and to withdraw from evil, which is understanding."[6] In the Septuagint, which Augustine used, this passage according to the letter reads: "Behold, piety itself is wisdom."[7] But both fear and piety are set down as gifts of the Holy Spirit. Therefore wisdom should not be numbered among the gifts of the Holy Spirit as though it were a gift distinct from the others.

BUT TO THE CONTRARY there is what is said in Isaiah 11: "In him rests the Spirit of the Lord, a spirit of wisdom and understanding," etc.[8]

I ANSWER THAT IT SHOULD BE SAID that according to the Philosopher, at the beginning of the *Metaphysics,* it belongs to wisdom to consider the highest cause, by which one judges of other things most certainly, and according to which all things must be set in order (*ordinare*).[9] Now the highest cause can be taken in two ways: either simply (*simpliciter*) or in some genus. Therefore, he who knows the highest cause in some genus and, by means of that cause, can judge and set in order all things that are contained in the genus, is said to be wise in the genus, as in medicine or architecture, according to 1 Corinthians 3, "Like a wise architect, I have laid the foundation."[10] Now he who knows the highest cause simply, which is God, is called simply wise: so far as he can judge and set in order all things by divine standards (*per regulas divinas*). Now a man follows judgment of this sort by the Holy Spirit, according to 1 Corinthians 2, "The spiritual man judges all things," since as is said in the same place, "The Spirit probes all things, even the depths of God."[11] So it is clear that wisdom is a gift of the Holy Spirit.

[1] TO THE FIRST ARGUMENT, THEREFORE, IT SHOULD BE SAID that "good" is said in two ways. In one way, as what is truly good is simply complete. In another way, something is said to be good according to a certain likeness, for example, "perfect malice," as someone is called

5. *Summa* 2a2ae q.1 a.1 and q.4 a.5.

6. Job 28.28.

7. See Augustine, *De trinitate* bk.12 chap.14 sect.22 (PL 42:1010; CCSL 50: 375.19); bk.14 chap.1 sect.1 (PL 42:1036; CCSL 50A:421.14).

8. Isaiah 11.2.

9. Aristotle, *Metaphysics* bk.1 chap.2 (982a8).

10. 1 Corinthians 3.10.

11. 1 Corinthians 2.15, 1 Corinthians 2.10.

"a good thief" or a "complete thief," as is clear from the Philosopher.[12] And just as regarding the things that are truly good one finds some highest cause, which is the highest good—that is, the ultimate end, through knowledge of which a man is said to be truly wise—so too in evil things there is found something to which other things are referred as to an ultimate end, through knowledge of which a man is said to be wise in doing evil, according to Jeremiah 4, "They are wise, as in doing evil things, whereas they do not know to do good."[13] For anyone who turns away from a due end, it is necessary that he fix some undue end for himself, since every agent acts on account of an end. So if he fixes an end for himself in worldly exterior goods, one speaks of "worldly wisdom"; if in bodily goods, one speaks of "animal wisdom"; if in some pride, one speaks of "diabolical wisdom," on account of his imitation of the devil's pride, of which it is said in Job, "He himself is king over all of the sons of pride."[14]

[2] To the second it should be said that the wisdom which is set down as a gift differs from that which is set down as an acquired intellectual virtue. For the latter is acquired by human zeal, whereas the former is what "descends from above," as is said in James 3.[15] Likewise, wisdom differs from faith. For faith assents to divine truth according to itself, but the judgment that proceeds according to divine truth belongs to the gift of wisdom. And so the gift of wisdom presupposes faith, since "anyone judges well of that which he knows," as is said in *Ethics* 1.[16]

[3] To the third it should be said that just as piety, which belongs to the worship of God, is expressive of faith, so far as by the worship of God we bear witness to faith, so too piety expresses wisdom. And on account of this it is said that "piety is wisdom"—and fear too, for the same reason. For by this it is shown that a man has right judgment about divine things—that he fears and worships God.

Article 2. [Whether wisdom is in the intellect, as in its subject.]

One proceeds in this way to the second query. IT SEEMS that wisdom is not in the intellect, as in its subject.

12. Aristotle, *Metaphysics* bk.4 chap.16 (1021b17).
13. Jeremiah 4.22.
14. Job 41.25.
15. James 3.15.
16. Aristotle, *Nicomachean Ethics* bk.1 chap.3 (1094b27).

[1] For Augustine, in his book *On the Grace of the New Testament,* says that "wisdom is the love of God (*caritas Dei*)."[17] But charity is in the will as in its subject, not in the intellect, as was attested above.[18] Therefore wisdom is not in the intellect as in its subject.

[2] Furthermore, Sirach 6 says that "the wisdom of teaching is according to its name."[19] Now wisdom (*sapientia*) is said to be, as it were, "prudent knowledge" (*sapida scientia*). But this seems to belong to the affections, to which belongs the experience of spiritual pleasures and sweetnesses. Therefore wisdom is not in the intellect, but more in the affections.

[3] Furthermore, the intellective power is sufficiently brought to completion by a gift of understanding (*intellectus*). But regarding that which can be brought about by one thing, it would be superfluous to set down plural things. Therefore wisdom is not in the intellect.

BUT TO THE CONTRARY Gregory says, in *Moralia* 2, that wisdom is opposed to stupidity.[20] But stupidity is in the intellect. Therefore wisdom is too.

I ANSWER THAT IT SHOULD BE SAID that, as was said above,[21] wisdom denotes a certain rightness of judgment according to divine reasons (*rationes*). Now rightness of judgment can occur in two ways. In one way, according to the complete use of reason. In another way, on account of a certain natural affinity with the things about which one is engaged in judging. Just as he who has learned moral science (*scientia moralis*) judges rightly, by an inquiry of reason, of the things that belong to chastity, so he who possesses the habit of chastity judges rightly of the same things by a certain natural affinity with the things themselves. In this way, therefore, to possess right judgment about divine things from an inquiry of reason belongs to the wisdom that is an intellectual virtue. But to have right judgment about these things according to a certain natural affinity with the things themselves belongs to wisdom, according as it is a gift of the Holy Spirit. As Dionysius says, *Divine Names,* chapter 2, Hierotheus is made

17. Augustine, *Epistulae* ep.140 *De gratia Novi Testamenti ad Honoratum* chap.18 sect.45 (PL 33:557; CSEL 44:193.18).

18. In Question 24, Article 1.

19. Sirach 6.23.

20. Gregory the Great, *Moralia* bk.2 chap.49 sect.77 (PL 75:592; CCSL 143: 106.41–42).

21. In Article 1 of this Question. See also *Summa* 2a2ae q.8 a.6.

complete in divine things "not only by learning (*discens*) divine things, but also by experiencing (*patiens*) them."[22] A feeling for things of this sort – a natural affinity for divine things – comes to be through charity, which indeed unites us to God, according to 1 Corinthians 6: "He who adheres to God is one spirit."[23] In this way, therefore, the wisdom that is a gift does in fact have its cause in the will, namely charity. But it has its essence in the intellect, the act of which is to judge rightly, as was attested above.[24]

[1] TO THE FIRST ARGUMENT, THEREFORE, IT SHOULD BE SAID that Augustine is speaking of wisdom with respect to its cause. From this too is taken the name of wisdom, according as it denotes a certain "taste" or "savor" (*sapor*).

[2] So the response to the second objection is clear – or it would be, if this were the sense of the authority cited. This does not seem to be the case, since this reading is not appropriate for anything except to the sense that *sapientia* has in the Latin language. In Greek, however, it is not applicable, and perhaps not in other languages. So it seems better there to take the name of wisdom for its reputation, by which it is commended to all.

[3] To the third it should be said that intellect has two acts, namely to perceive[25] and to judge. To the first act, the gift of understanding (*donum intellectus*) is directed, whereas the gift of wisdom (*donum saptientiae*) is directed to the second act, according to divine reasons. The gift of knowledge (*donum scientiae*), however, proceeds according to human reasons.

Article 3. [Whether wisdom is only speculative, or also practical.]

One proceeds in this way to the third query. IT SEEMS that wisdom is not practical but only speculative.

[1] The gift of wisdom is more excellent than wisdom according as it is an intellectual virtue. But wisdom as an intellectual virtue is only speculative. Much more, therefore, is the wisdom that is a gift only speculative, and not practical.

22. Ps-Dionysius, *Divine Names* chap.2 sect.9 (PG 3:648B; Chevallier 1:104).
23. 1 Corinthians 6.17.
24. *Summa* 1a q.79 a.3.
25. Some versions read "to teach" (*praecipere*).

[2] Furthermore, the practical intellect is about operable things, which are not contingent. But wisdom is about divine things, which are eternal and necessary. Therefore wisdom cannot be practical.

[3] Furthermore, Gregory says in *Moralia* 6 that "in contemplation the origin (*principium*), which is God, is sought, whereas in action we labor under a heavy bundle of necessities."[26] But the vision of divine things belongs to wisdom, to which it does not belong to labor under any bundle, since as Wisdom 8 says, "Her converse has no bitterness, nor her company any tedium."[27] Therefore wisdom is only contemplative, not practical or active.

BUT TO THE CONTRARY there is what is said in Colossians 4: "Walk in wisdom toward those who are without it."[28] Now this belongs to action. Therefore wisdom is not only speculative, but also practical.

I ANSWER THAT IT SHOULD BE SAID that, as Augustine says in *On the Trinity* 12, the higher part of reason is assigned to wisdom, whereas the lower part is assigned to knowledge (*scientia*).[29] Now the higher reason, as he says in the same book, attends to "heavenly reasons" – that is, divine reasons – "both for observing and for deliberating."[30] For observing, according as divine things are contemplated in themselves. For deliberating, according as the higher reason judges of human things by divine things, directing human acts by divine standards. In this way, therefore, wisdom – according as it is a gift – is not only speculative, but also practical.

[1] TO THE FIRST ARGUMENT, THEREFORE, IT SHOULD BE SAID that so far as some virtue is higher, to that degree it extends to more things, as is attested in the *Book of Causes*.[31] So because the wisdom that is a gift is more excellent than the wisdom that is an intellectual virtue,

26. Gregory the Great, *Moralia* bk.6 chap.37 sect.61 (PL 75:764; CCSL 143: 330.181–83).

27. Wisdom 8.16.

28. Colossians 4.5.

29. Augustine, *De trinitate* bk.12 chap.14 sect.22 (PL 42:1009; CCSL 50: 375.7–9).

30. Augustine, *De trinitate* bk.12 chap.7 sect.12 (PL 42:1005; CCSL 50: 367.105). Contrary to Thomas's text, Augustine speaks of "*rationes aeternae*" rather than "*rationes supernae*."

31. *Liber de causis* chap.9 sect.95; chap.16 sect.141. (Compare *The Book of Causes*, trans. Dennis Brand [Milwaukee: Marquette University Press, 1984], 29 and 34.)

inasmuch as it touches God more closely – namely by a kind of union of the soul to God[32] – it has the power to guide us not only in contemplation, but also in action.

[2] To the second it should be said that divine things in themselves are necessary and eternal, yet are the rules of contingent things, which lie beneath human acts.

[3] To the third it should be said that to consider a thing in itself comes first, and only then to compare it with another thing. So what belongs first to wisdom is the contemplation of divine things, which is the vision of principles, and what belongs next is to guide human acts according to divine rules. But neither bitterness nor labor arises in human acts from the direction of wisdom; instead, on account of wisdom, bitterness is turned into sweetness and labor into rest.

Article 4. [Whether wisdom can be without grace, and with mortal sin.]

One proceeds in this way to the fourth query. IT SEEMS that wisdom can be without grace, and with mortal sin.

[1] The saints cannot glory in the things that are had with mortal sin, according to 2 Corinthians 1: "Our glory is this, the testimony of our conscience."[33] But a person should not glory in wisdom, according to Jeremiah 9: "The wise man does not glory in his wisdom."[34] Therefore wisdom can be without grace, and with mortal sin.

[2] Furthermore, wisdom denotes knowledge of divine things, as was said. But someone with mortal sin cannot have knowledge of divine things, according to Romans 1: "They detain the truth of God in injustice."[35] Therefore wisdom can be with mortal sin.

[3] Furthermore, Augustine says in *On the Trinity* 15, speaking about charity: "Nothing is more excellent than this gift of God – it is only this which divides the children of the eternal kingdom from the children of eternal perdition."[36] But wisdom differs from charity. Therefore it does not

32. Some versions read "by a kind of union of spirit of the soul to God."
33. 2 Corinthians 1.12.
34. Jeremiah 9.23.
35. Romans 1.18.
36. Augustine, *De trinitate* bk.15 chap.18 sect.32 (PL 42:1082; CCSL 50A: 507.1–3).

divide the children of the kingdom from the children of perdition. Therefore it can be with mortal sin.

BUT TO THE CONTRARY there is Wisdom 1, which says that "wisdom will not enter the malevolent soul, nor dwell in a body subject to
sins."[37] I ANSWER THAT IT SHOULD BE SAID that the wisdom which
is a gift of the Holy Spirit, as has been said,[38] causes rightness of judgment
about divine things, or about other things by divine standards, out of a certain natural affinity or union with divine things. Which is indeed by charity,
as was said.[39] And so the wisdom of which we are speaking presupposes
charity. Now charity cannot be with mortal sin, as is clear from what was
said above.[40] So it remains that the wisdom of which we are speaking cannot be with mortal sin.

[1] TO THE FIRST ARGUMENT, THEREFORE, IT SHOULD BE
SAID that this should be understood of wisdom in mundane things, or even
[of wisdom] in divine things by human reasons. In this, the saints do not glory,
but rather confess themselves not to have it, according to Proverbs 30: "The
wisdom of men is not with me."[41] Whereas they do glory in divine wisdom,
according to 1 Corinthians 1: "Wisdom has been made for us by God."[42]

[2] To the second it should be said that this reason proceeds from the
knowledge of divine things which is had by the study and inquiry of reason. Which can be had with mortal sin, whereas the wisdom of which we
are speaking cannot.

[3] To the third it should be said that wisdom, though it differs from
charity, nevertheless presupposes it. And by this very fact, it divides the
children of perdition from the children of the kingdom.

Article 5. [Whether wisdom is in everyone who has grace.]

One proceeds in this way to the fifth query. IT SEEMS that wisdom is not
in everyone who has grace.

---

37. Wisdom 1.4.
38. In Articles 2 and 3 of this Question.
39. In Article 2 of this Question, and in Question 23, Article 5.
40. In Question 24, Article 12.
41. Proverbs 30.2.
42. 1 Corinthians 1.30.

[1] To have wisdom is greater than to hear wisdom. But to hear wisdom belongs only to the perfect, according to 1 Corinthians 2: "We are speaking of wisdom among the perfect."[43] Since, therefore, not all who have grace are perfect, it seems that much fewer of those who have grace would have wisdom.

[2] Furthermore, "it belongs to the wise man to set in order," as the Philosopher says at the beginning of the *Metaphysics*.[44] And James 3 says that wisdom "judges without dissimulation."[45] But it is not for all who have grace to judge others or direct them, but only for prelates. Therefore it is not for all who have grace to have wisdom.

[3] Furthermore, "wisdom is granted against folly," as Gregory says in *Moralia* 2.[46] But many who have grace are naturally foolish, as is clear from demented people who are baptized, or those who later fall into dementia without sin. Therefore wisdom is not in all those who have grace.

BUT TO THE CONTRARY anyone who is without mortal sin is loved by God, since he has charity, by which he loves God. Now God loves those who love him, as is said in Proverbs 8.[47] But Wisdom 7 says that "God loves no one except for him who dwells with wisdom."[48] Therefore in all who have grace, being without mortal sin, there is wisdom.

I ANSWER THAT IT SHOULD BE SAID that the wisdom of which we are speaking, as was said,[49] denotes a certain rightness of judgment about divine things – both in observing and in deliberating. Regarding both, people happen upon (*sortiuntur*) wisdom by union with divine things, according to different levels. For some people happen upon it by right judgment, both in the contemplation of divine things and in the direction of human things by divine standards, so far as is necessary for salvation. And for those being without mortal sin, through the grace that makes pleasing, this level is lacking in nothing, since if nature does not lack in necessary things, much less does grace. So 1 John 2 says, "His anointing teaches you

43. 1 Corinthians 2.6.
44. Aristotle, *Metaphysics* bk.1 chap.2 (982a18).
45. James 3.17.
46. Gregory the Great, *Moralia* bk.2 chap.49 sect.77 (PL 75:592; CCSL 143: 106.41–42).
47. Proverbs 8.17.
48. Wisdom 7.28.
49. In Articles 1 and 3 of this Question.

about all things."[50] But certain people receive[51] the gift of wisdom at a higher level – both regarding the contemplation of divine things, so far as they are able to know certain high mysteries and are able to make them clear to others, and also regarding the direction of human things according to divine standards, so far as by these standards, they direct not only themselves, but also others. And this level of wisdom is not common to everyone who has the grace that makes pleasing. Rather, it belongs to the grace given gratuitously, which the Holy Spirit "distributes where it will," according to 1 Corinthians 12: "To one by the Spirit is given the word of wisdom," etc.[52]

[1] TO THE FIRST ARGUMENT, THEREFORE, IT SHOULD BE SAID that the Apostle is there speaking of the wisdom that extends to hidden mysteries of divine things, as is said in the same place: "We speak the wisdom of God, hidden in a mystery."[53]

[2] To the second it should be said that although to direct other human beings, and to make judgments about them, belongs only to prelates, it nevertheless belongs to every person to order his own acts and to judge those acts, as is clear from Dionysius in his letter to Demophilus.[54]

[3] To the third it should be said that demented people who are baptized, just like children, do have the habit of wisdom, according as it is a gift of the Holy Spirit, but do not have the act, on account of a bodily hindrance by which the use of reason is hindered in them.

Article 6. [Whether the Seventh Beatitude corresponds to the gift of wisdom.]

One proceeds in this way to the sixth query. IT SEEMS that the Seventh Beatitude does not correspond to the gift of wisdom.

[1] The Seventh Beatitude is, "Blessed are the peacemakers, for they shall be called the children of God."[55] Now both of these things [peace and sonship] belong directly to charity. About peace, it is said in the Psalm:

---

50. 1 John 2.27.
51. Some versions read "complete."
52. 1 Corinthians 12.8.
53. 1 Corinthians 2.7.
54. Ps-Dionysius, ep.8 to Demophilus, sect.3 (PG 3:1093B; Chevallier 2: 1540).
55. Matthew 5.9.

"Much peace have they, who love your law."[56] And as the Apostle says, Romans 5: "The charity of God is poured forth into our hearts by the Holy Spirit, who is given to us"[57] – who indeed is the "Spirit of adoption of sons, by which we cry, 'Abba, Father!'" as is said in Romans 8.[58] Therefore the Seventh Beatitude should be attributed more to charity than to wisdom.

[2] Furthermore, anything is manifested more by its proximate effect than by its remote effect. But the proximate effect of wisdom seems to be charity, according to Wisdom 7: "Through the nations she carries herself into holy souls; she raises up the friends of God and the prophets."[59] Now peace and the adoption of sons seem to be remote effects, since they proceed from charity, as was said.[60] Therefore the beatitude corresponding to wisdom would need to be determined according to the love of charity, rather than according to peace.

[3] Furthermore, James 3 says: "Wisdom from above is indeed first of all chaste, then peace-making, modest, persuadable, consenting to the good, full of mercy and good fruits, judging without dissimulation."[61] Therefore, the beatitude corresponding to wisdom should not be understood more according to peace than according to the other effects of heavenly wisdom.

BUT TO THE CONTRARY Augustine says, in his book *The Lord's Sermon on the Mount,* that "wisdom is appropriate for peacemakers, in whom there is no motion of rebelling, but only obedience to reason."[62]

I ANSWER THAT IT SHOULD BE SAID that the Seventh Beatitude is agreeably adapted to the gift of wisdom, both as to merit and as to reward. What belongs to merit is said in "Blessed are the peacemakers." Those who are called "peacemakers" make peace, either in themselves or in others. In both cases, the things in which peace is established are driven back to a due order, for peace is the "tranquility of order," as Augustine says, Book 19, *City of God.*[63] Now to set in order belongs to wisdom, as is clear from the

---

56. Psalm 118.165.
57. Romans 5.5.
58. Romans 8.15.
59. Wisdom 7.27.
60. In Question 29, Article 3. See also *Summa* 2a2ae q.19 a.2 ad 3.
61. James 3.17.
62. Augustine, *De sermone Domini in monte* bk.1 chap.4 (PL 34:1235; CCSL 35:10–11.217–19).
63. Augustine, *De civitate Dei* bk.19 chap.13 (PL 41:640; CCSL 48: 679.10–11).

Philosopher, at the beginning of the *Metaphysics.*[64] And so to be peace-making is appropriately attributed to wisdom.

What belongs to reward is said in the clause "They shall be called children of God." For they are called "children of God" so far as they participate in a likeness of the only-begotten and natural son of God, according to Romans 8, "Whom he foreknew to be made conformable to the image of His Son,"[65] who indeed is wisdom begotten. And so by participating in the gift of wisdom, a person attains the sonship of God.

[1] TO THE FIRST ARGUMENT, THEREFORE, IT SHOULD BE SAID that to have peace belongs to charity, but to make peace belongs to ordering wisdom. Likewise, the Holy Spirit is called a "Spirit of adoption" insofar as a likeness of the natural son, who is wisdom begotten, is given to us by the Spirit.

[2] To the second it should be said that this should be understood of uncreated wisdom, which first unites itself to us by the gift of charity, and from this union reveals to us the mystery, knowledge of which is infused wisdom. And so infused wisdom, which is a gift, is not the cause of charity, but rather its effect.

[3] To the third it should be said that, as was already said,[66] it belongs to the gift of wisdom not only to contemplate divine things, but also to regulate human acts. In such direction, the first thing to occur is removal from the evils that are opposed to wisdom, so that fear is said to be the beginning of wisdom, so far as it brings about a withdrawing from evils. Now the last thing is like an end, by which[67] all things are driven back to a due order; this belongs to the aspect of peace. And so James appropriately says that the wisdom that is from above, which is a gift of the Holy Sprit, is "first of all chaste," avoiding as it were the enticements of sin, and "then peace-making," which is the ultimate effect of wisdom—which is why it is set down as a beatitude. The qualities that follow manifest the things by which wisdom leads to peace, and by a fitting order. For the first thing that occurs to a man who withdraws by chastity from sinful enticements is to observe the right measure in everything, so far as he can—with respect to this, wisdom is called "modest." Second, in the things in which he is not self-sufficient, he should listen to the advice of others—and regarding this,

---

64. Aristotle, *Metaphysics* bk.1 chap.2 (982a18).
65. Romans 8.29.
66. In Article 1 of this Question.
67. Reading *quo* for *quod,* following the Piana edition.

wisdom is "persuadable." And these two things belong to a person who seeks peace in himself. Beyond this, a person should make peace with others. This requires, first, that he does not oppose the good of others – and thus wisdom is said to be "consenting to the good." Second, that in relation to his neighbor's defects, he should be compassionate in affect (*in affectu*) and provide help in effect (*in effectu*) – and this is to be "full of mercy and good fruits." Third, it requires a person to concern himself with correcting sins in a charitable manner (*caritative*). This is said to be "judging without dissimulation" – lest while pretending to correct others, a person fill up his hatred.

[On Folly, Which Is Opposed to Wisdom]

One should next consider folly, which is opposed to wisdom. Regarding this point, three queries are raised. (1) Whether folly is opposed to wisdom. (2) Whether folly is a sin. (3) To which capital sin it may be traced.

Article 1. [Whether folly is opposed to wisdom.]

One proceeds in this way to the first query. IT SEEMS that folly is not opposed to wisdom.

[1] It seems that what is directly opposed to wisdom is unwisdom (*insipientia*). But folly does not seem to be the same as unwisdom, since unwisdom seems to be only about divine things, as is wisdom, whereas folly bears on both divine things and human things. Therefore folly is not opposed to wisdom.

[2] Furthermore, one of two opposed things is not a way of arriving at the other thing. But folly is a way of arriving at wisdom, for 1 Corinthians 3 says: "If a person seems to be wise among you in this world, may he become a fool, so that he may be wise."[1] Therefore folly is not opposed to wisdom.

[3] Furthermore, one of two opposed things is not the cause of the other thing. But wisdom is a cause of folly, for Jeremiah 10 says: "Every man has become a fool for his own knowledge"[2] – and wisdom is a kind of knowledge. And Isaiah 47 says: "Your wisdom and your knowledge – these have deceived you,"[3] whereas it belongs to folly to be deceived. Therefore folly is not opposed to wisdom.

[4] Furthermore, Isidore says in the *Etymologies* that "a fool is he who is not moved by ignominy to grief, and who is not moved by harm."[4] But

1. 1 Corinthians 3.18.
2. Jeremiah 10.14.
3. Isaiah 47.10.
4. Isidore of Seville, *Etymologiae,* bk.10 letter "S" sect.246 (PL 82:393; Lindsay lines 8–10). Here Thomas quotes the words but changes their order.

this belongs to spiritual wisdom, as Gregory says in *Moralia* 10.[5] Therefore folly is not opposed to wisdom.

BUT TO THE CONTRARY there is what Gregory says in *Moralia* 2: "The gift of wisdom is granted against folly."[6]

I ANSWER THAT IT SHOULD BE SAID that the name "folly" (*stultitia*) seems to be taken from "numbness" (*stupor*) so that Isidore says in the *Etymologies,* "the fool is he who is not moved, on account of numbness."[7] And folly differs from fatuity (*fatuitas*), as is said in the same place, since folly denotes a sluggishness of heart and deafness of sense,[8] whereas fatuity denotes a total lack of spiritual sense. And so folly is appropriately opposed to wisdom. For "wise" (*sapiens*), as Isidore says in the same place, "is said from 'taste' (*sapor*), since just as the taste (*gustus*) is suited to discriminate the flavors of food, so the wise man is suited for the discernment of things and their causes."[9] So it is clear that folly is opposed to wisdom as a contrary, whereas fatuity is its pure negation. For the fatuous person lacks any sense of judgment, whereas the fool has one, but it is sluggish. The wise person, however, has a sense of judgment that is finely attuned (*subtilis*) and penetrating (*perspicax*).

[1] TO THE FIRST ARGUMENT, THEREFORE, IT SHOULD BE SAID that, as Isidore says in the same place, "unwisdom is contrary to wisdom, because it lacks discrimination and sense."[10] So it seems that unwisdom is the same as folly. Mostly, however, it seems that someone is a fool when he suffers a deficiency in an opinion[11] (*sententia*) belonging to judgment that is applied according to the highest cause. For if a person is lacking in judgment about some small thing, he is not for that reason called a fool.

5. Gregory the Great, *Moralia* bk.10 chap.29 sect.48 (PL 75:947; CCSL 143: 570–71).

6. Gregory the Great, *Moralia* bk.2 chap.49 sect.77 (PL 75:592; CCSL 143: 106.41–42).

7. Isidore of Seville, *Etymologiae,* bk.10 letter "S" sect.246 (PL 82:393; Lindsay lines 8–9).

8. Isidore of Seville, *Etymologiae,* bk.10 letter "S" sect.246 (PL 82:393; Lindsay lines 5–8).

9. Isidore of Seville, *Etymologiae,* bk.10 letter "S" sect.240 (PL 82:392; Lindsay lines 7–9).

10. Isidore of Seville, *Etymologiae,* bk.10 letter "S" sect.240–41 (PL 82:392; Lindsay lines 10–11).

11. Some versions read "deficiency in the chief point (*in summa*)."

[2] To the second it should be said that just as there is a kind of evil wisdom, as was said above,[12] which is called the wisdom of the world, since some earthly good is taken for the highest cause and ultimate end, so too there is a good folly, opposed to this evil wisdom, through which a person scorns earthly things. Of this wisdom, the Apostle is speaking.

[3] To the third it should be said that the wisdom of the world is that which deceives and makes someone a fool in relation to God, as is clear from the Apostle, 1 Corinthians 3.[13]

[4] To the fourth it should be said that sometimes it happens that a person is not moved by harms, because he does not taste earthly things, but only heavenly things. So this does not belong to the folly of the world,[14] but to the wisdom of God, as Gregory says in the same place.[15] Sometimes, however, it happens from this—that a person is simply stupid about all things, as is clear in the demented, who do not discern what is harmful. And this belongs to folly simply.

Article 2. [Whether folly is a sin.]

One proceeds in this way to the second query. IT SEEMS that folly is not a sin.

[1] No sin arises in us from nature. But some people are naturally foolish. Therefore folly is not a sin.

[2] Furthermore, every sin is voluntary, as Augustine says.[16] But folly is not voluntary. Therefore it is not a sin.

[3] Furthermore, every sin is opposed to some divine precept. But folly is opposed to no precept. Therefore folly is not a sin.

BUT TO THE CONTRARY there is what Proverbs 1 says: "The prosperity of fools shall destroy them."[17] But no one is destroyed except for sin. Therefore folly is a sin.

12. In Question 45, Article 1.

13. 1 Corinthians 3.19.

14. Some versions read "this belongs to the folly of the world."

15. Gregory the Great, *Moralia* bk.10 chap.29 sect.48 (PL 75:947; CCSL 143:570–71).

16. Augustine, *De vera religione* chap.14 sect.27 (PL 34:133; CCSL 32:204.5). Compare Alexander of Hales, *Summa Halensis* pt.2 sect.222 (Quaracchi 3:237).

17. Proverbs 1.32.

I ANSWER THAT IT SHOULD BE SAID that folly, as was said, denotes a kind of numbness of the sense in judging, and chiefly about the highest cause, which is the ultimate end and highest good. About this, a person can suffer numbness in judging in two ways. In one way, from a natural disposition, as is clear from the demented. And such folly is not a sin. In another way, so far as a person immerses his senses in earthly things, from which his sense is rendered inept for perceiving divine things, according to 1 Corinthians 2: "The beastly man (*homo animalis*) does not perceive the things that are of the spirit of God,"[18] just as sweet things have no taste for a person whose taste has been infected by a bad humor. And such folly is a sin.

[1] And from this the answer TO THE FIRST THING THAT WAS OBJECTED is clear.

[2] To the second it should be said that although nobody wants folly, a person can still want things that turn out to be foolish, namely to distract his sense from spiritual things and immerse it in earthly things. The same thing also happens in other sins. For the lustful person wants pleasure, without which there is no sin, although he does not simply want sin – for he would want to enjoy the pleasure without sin.

[3] To the third it should be said that folly is opposed to the precepts that are given in relation to the contemplation of truth – as was attested above, when knowledge and intellect were treated.[19]

Article 3. [Whether folly is the daughter of lust.]

One proceeds in this way to the third query. IT SEEMS that folly is not the daughter of lust.

[1] Gregory, *Moralia* 31, enumerates the daughters of lust – and folly is not contained among them.[20] Therefore folly does not proceed from lust.

[2] Furthermore, the Apostle says, 1 Corinthians 3, "The wisdom of this world is stupidity in relation to God."[21] But as Gregory says, *Moralia* 10,

18. 1 Corinthians 2.14.
19. *Summa* 2a2ae q.16.
20. Gregory the Great, *Moralia* bk.31 chap.45 sect.88 (PL 76:621; CCSL 143B: 1610.34–37).
21. 1 Corinthians 3.19.

"the wisdom of the world is to cover the heart with tricks" – which belongs to duplicity.[22] Therefore folly is the daughter of duplicity rather than lust.

[3] Furthermore, a person is chiefly turned by anger to furor and insanity, which belong to folly. Therefore folly arises from anger rather than from lust.

BUT TO THE CONTRARY there is what Proverbs 7 says: "At once he follows her," namely a prostitute, "not knowing that he is drawn like a fool to chains."[23]

I ANSWER THAT IT SHOULD BE SAID that, as has been said already,[24] the folly that is according to sin arises from this – that the spiritual sense is sluggish, so that it is not suited for judging spiritual things. The sense of a person is most greatly immersed in earthly things by lust, which is about the greatest pleasures, which are most greatly absorbed by the soul. And so the folly that is a sin is most greatly born out of lust.

[1] TO THE FIRST ARGUMENT, THEREFORE, IT SHOULD BE SAID that it belongs to folly that a person should have a loathing for God and his gifts. So Gregory numbers two things among the daughters of lust that belong to folly, namely "hatred of God and despair over future times" – dividing folly into two parts, as it were.[25]

[2] To the second it should be said that this passage of the Apostle should not be understood causally, but essentially, since the very wisdom of the world is folly in relation to God. So it is not necessary that anything which belongs to the wisdom of the world should be a cause of this folly.

[3] To the third it should be said that anger by its sharpness especially alters a body's nature, as was said above.[26] So it especially causes the folly that arises from a bodily hindrance. But the folly that arises from a spiritual hindrance, namely from the immersion of the mind in earthly things, arises especially from lust, as was said.[27]

---

22. Gregory the Great, *Moralia* bk.10 chap.29 sect.48 (PL 75:947; CCSL 143: 570.1–2).

23. Proverbs 7.22.

24. In Article 2 of this Question.

25. Gregory the Great, *Moralia* bk.31 chap.45 sect.88 (PL 76:621; CCSL 143B: 1610.35–36).

26. *Summa* 1a2ae q.48 a.2.

27. In the body of this Article.

Essays

Some Paradoxes in Teaching Charity

MARK D. JORDAN

1. Expectations for a Theology of Love

Readers have reached the *Summa of Theology* by Thomas Aquinas expecting to find many different works. They have wanted a seventeenth-century legal codification, an eighteenth-century encyclopedia, a nineteenth-century deductive system, or a twentieth-century collection of exercises in analytic philosophy. The *Summa* is none of those things, but readers cannot discover what it is except by reading it against their own eager projections. Just as a lonely young man will turn any stranger into the fulfillment of cherished fantasies about love, so a community of readers in search of an authority or a system can seize on the *Summa* regardless of the pedagogy that text actually offers.

Readers' expectations are all the more powerful for being both tacit and passionate. It is hard to glimpse their operation, because they work always in advance, conditioning a reader's perception of the whole text. Expectations do sometimes show themselves in their incongruous effects. Nothing seems more obvious for some contemporary readers, for example, than to put Anders Nygren and Thomas Aquinas side by side on a reading list for a course in the theology of love. Yet nothing should be more obvious than the differences in writing love that oppose *Agape and Eros* to the *Summa of Theology*.

Nygren begins his book by announcing a "twofold purpose": "first to investigate the meaning of the Christian idea of love; and secondly, to illustrate the main changes it has undergone in the course of history."[1] Nygren faults his predecessors for spending so little time examining an idea that produced "a revolution in ethical outlook without parallel in the history of ethics." The idea then passed through two "crises," during which the distinctively Christian notion of *agapē* "thrusts itself powerfully to the fore" instead of becoming mired in "alien conceptions." The most important of these counterconceptions has been Platonic *eros*. According to Nygren, Pauline Agapē and Platonic Eros had originally nothing to do with each other, but through history they become increasingly entangled. In some languages, they are now concealed under a single word, like the English "love." Worse, Eros has regularly acted as a "solvent" that undoes the characteristics of Agapē when mixed with it. Nygren's earnest aim is to separate them – philologically, historically, but above all as opposed "fundamental motifs" or "general attitudes towards life." Indeed, differentiation – a sort of chemical separation – is the urgent work: "the most important task for those engaged in the modern scientific study of religion and theological research is to reach an inner understanding of the different forms of religion in the light of their different fundamental motifs." Separation need not imply adjudication. If Eros and Agapē are "still living forces," Nygren's purpose in writing about them is precisely not to render judgments. He means just to clarify their incommensurability.

A reader who wants to resist expectations should see that all of this stands in striking opposition to the questions on charity in Thomas's *Summa*. I am not thinking about the disagreements between Nygren and Aquinas on the alleged dichotomy between Eros and Agapē in early Christian writing. Nor am I thinking about Nygren's facile criticisms of Thomas.[2] I have in mind rather the two texts' opposed conceptions of the tasks of a theology of love. Indeed, it is hard to find a single point of contact between them. Writing on charity, Thomas is studying neither the meaning of an idea nor its history. He is judging the relative adequacy of traditional languages about a divine gift. If he emphasizes that charity is a gift that can be understood only by relying on scriptures, he does not think that it marks a simple "revolution" in ethics. Instead, it comes as the long desired, poorly foreseen fulfillment of ancient human longings. Thomas hardly knows Plato, but he regards Plato's pupil, Aristotle, as a reliable guide to the ethical discoveries of human reason before revelation. While Thomas judges that Aristotelian notions about love or friendship fall far short of the divine virtue of charity, he refuses to treat them as its polar opposites. The Aristotelian notions are garbled anticipations, distorted, and still real teleologies. So Thomas does not mean to separate Aristotle from theology. He hopes instead to use Aristotle pedagogically for accomplishing theology's purposes. If those purposes require judgments of what Nygren calls "values," they need even more the means of helping a reader's attainment of them. For Thomas, theology is written principally neither to study concepts nor to judge values. It is written to shape souls.

I sketch this contrast between Nygren and Thomas on the purposes for writing a theology of love in order to ask: What after all *should* a reader expect from the questions on the virtue of charity in the *Summa*?

2. The Pedagogical Plan of the Questions on Charity

The questions on charity take their place within a teaching project that is Thomas's hope for the *Summa*. He announces his largest purpose as pedagogical simplification: he means to teach "Christian religion" (*Christiana religio*) for "beginners" (*incipientes*) in a way that spares them the "distaste and confusion" provoked by disordered multiplication (1a pr). The *Summa* undertakes to teach "briefly and clearly" only what is useful, according to an appropriate order, and without frustrating duplication. This means in practice that Thomas must trim textual precedents (*auctoritates*) and their explicit or implicit arguments around each topic. He must reduce more significantly the number of topics and then fit them within a helpful frame.

The simplification takes a particular form in the section of the *Summa* that contains the questions on charity. Within a larger consideration of human actions as pilgrimage back to God, the *Secunda Secundae* analyzes their most significant patterns. These are the forms of character and states of life according to which individual acts can be judged in relation to the human end. The analysis brings Thomas face to face with a tangled inheritance of theological writing on virtues and vices, graces and sins. He refuses to add more knots to the tangle. He acknowledges rather that the great temptation for any more detailed moral teaching is to run on endlessly, through every variety of virtue, gift, vice, precept, and counsel, illustrating each with overly abundant cases (2a2ae pr).[3] Instead, Thomas proposes two simplifying principles. First, he unites in a single cluster of questions a virtue, the corresponding gifts, the opposed vices, and the attached affirmative or negative precepts. Second, he sets intellectual virtues aside and traces all of the moral virtues back to three theological and four cardinal. He insists that the vivid depiction of vices – the morose delectation of varieties of destruction – not distend this pattern. Vices must be subordinated to virtues, and they must be distinguished by real differences rather than by accidental ones. Thomas mentions the traditional triplet of sins of the heart, the mouth, and the deed only to reject it – and with it the disorder of moral topics drawn from Peter Lombard's *Sentences* or William Peraldus's *Summas of the Vices and Virtues,* together with all the works that follow their outlines.[4] The reorganization of moral teaching accomplished in *Summa*

2a2ae depends on resisting all secondary classifications, however vivid, in favor of the essential.

What is it to be essential to a moral pedagogy? The topics or authorities that the *Summa* chooses to include are not the elements of a naturally occurring substance or the components of an artifact. They are "essential" (if we want to continue with that analogy) only in relation to a structure of teaching. A topic is essential to teaching by content and by position or placement. For example, a learner must understand something of habit in order to understand virtue, and it is better for a learner to understand something about habit *before* understanding the kind of habit that virtue is.

In the *Summa* itself, Thomas reflects explicitly on the varieties of sequence in learning. There is the *sequence of insight* that Thomas finds well described in Aristotelian logic. It is the teacher's duty, he remarks in one place, to supply the missing middle steps that encourage a student to connect general notions with remembered experiences (1a 117.1). He also recalls the *hierarchy of whole bodies of knowledge,* according to which a learner moves from the liberal arts through the stages of philosophy to metaphysics and then revealed theology. The *Summa* begins just at the moment when a learner realizes that something more is required beyond "philosophical teachings" (1a 1.1). But neither of these senses of pedagogical sequence is specific enough to explain how the teaching on human action actually unfolds in the *Summa.*

The pedagogical sequence of Thomas's questions on virtues and vices cannot be mapped as formalized syllogisms or as completions of speculative knowledge somewhere beyond metaphysics. They unfold rather in the life of a learner who is presumed already to be a Christian in sacramental community and, typically, under vows of earnest striving toward God. The sequence for teaching that kind of learner about moral matters cannot be settled by deductive patterns or schematic hierarchies of knowledge. It requires instead prudential reflection on how inherited moral words might help or hinder a moral progress assumed to be already under way. The pedagogical simplification of the moral part of the *Summa* hopes at least to remove the obstacles of moral misunderstanding that misspeaking can cause.

The *Summa*'s questions on charity show both general and particular intentions of simplification. In these questions, Thomas reduces the customary authorities and their arguments. The reduction is noticeable. Thomas's articles and questions here are rather short by the standards of the *Summa* itself. They are remarkably reduced in comparison with texts by Thomas's predecessors or, indeed, with his own pattern of commentary in the *Scrip-*

tum on the *Sentences.*[5] If they are longer than the corresponding distinctions in Peter Lombard's *Sentences,* they are much more simply organized. Thomas has already separated off the discussion of God's loving to treat it in the *Summa*'s First Part (1a 20).[6] He postpones the discussion of Christ's charity, the Lombard's starting point, into the Third Part, where he will imply that *caritas* is the only theological virtue that Christ possesses (3a 7.1–4). Thomas then sorts what remains of the Lombard's topics around charity, taking special care perhaps to pull out the discussions of the "commandments" (*mandata*) about charity under the heading of the "precepts" corresponding to the virtue.

"Precept corresponding to a virtue" is one of the headings that Thomas uses to reorganize inherited moral writing around the seven virtues. Indeed, the basic order of the questions on charity follows rather strictly the sequence of subtopics Thomas has announced in the 2a2ae's Prologue: there is the virtue (23–33), the vices opposed to it (34–43), the attached precepts (44), and the annexed gift (45, with its opposed vice, 46). Of course, the *Summa* varies the announced pattern. A reader can see this by comparing the treatment of the theological virtues. Charity is the last of these according to the Pauline order (1 Cor 13:13). Paul also calls it the "greatest" (*major* in the Vulgate). Certainly it is the most complex in Thomas. It requires four times as many questions as hope, and more even than faith. The questions are arranged differently in each case. Leaving aside the laconic treatment of hope, a reader should compare the allocation of questions for faith and charity.[7] In faith, one question is given to the virtue's object (1), two questions to its acts (2–3), and four questions to the virtue as habit (4–7), which includes the virtue itself, its cause, and its effects. Both the proportion and sequence are different for charity. There are two questions on the virtue itself (23–24), two more on its objects and their hierarchy (25–26), and then seven questions on the principal act (27) together with its inward and outward effects (28–33). There is another obvious difference in the arrangement of questions. For faith, the gifts of insight (*intellectus,* 8) and knowledge (*scientia,* 9) follow immediately after the discussion of the virtue's effects and before the discussion of opposed vices or entailed precepts (10–15, 16). For charity, the gift of wisdom (*sapientia,* 45) is relegated to the very end, after both the opposed vices (34–43) and the attached precepts (44).

The comparison of the treatment of the two theological virtues shows the flexibility of Thomas's underlying scheme. It should also raise questions about his compositional decisions. The order of the questions on charity suggests that what is most important for a reader to understand about this virtue is the depth and comprehensiveness of its working in or on a human subject. If faith is incomplete cognition, an incomplete anticipation of the beatific vision, charity is a present union with divine life that produces cascading effects. It can be forfeited by serious sin, of course, but it is not mere anticipation of union. It *is* union. While cognition ends with the thing known being somehow in the knower, appetite reaches out to the thing itself. If I know something according to my manner, I want something in *its* manner (27.4 corp). So charity toward God is greater than knowledge of God, especially in the *viator*, the wayfarer still in this life (27.4 ad 2). The incompletion of charity in the present differs importantly from the incompletion of faith. "While knowledge begins from creatures and tends toward God, charity begins from God as from an ultimate end and is drawn toward creatures" (27.4 ad 2).

The difference in the treatment of faith and charity can be appreciated from another direction by noticing their relations to the gifts of the Holy Spirit, which provide another of the "subheadings" in the reorganization of the 2a2ae. The effects of faith must be measured against two gifts that happen to share names with (Aristotelian) intellectual virtues. These two gifts take the place of the inward and outward effects of charity, but they also secure the fundamental contrast between faith and knowledge. By contrast, the gift of wisdom seems less important to the understanding of charity. This is because charity is so plainly a divine gift. For similar reasons, no separate question is devoted to the cause of charity: the virtue's very definition makes its causality clear. Charity is a union with the divine brought about by the divine. That is why charity lasts into the beatific vision, when neither faith nor hope can.

Thomas arranges the questions on charity to emphasize that this theological virtue is a divine infusion acting intimately and pervasively within the subject's present. But then the very exercise of composing the questions provokes an objection. If that is what charity is, what can Thomas hope to add to its gift by writing questions? This objection may be made against writing on any theological virtue – indeed, about any book offering a theology that depends on the inheritance of revelation and the present gift of grace. Thomas himself raises a version of the objection when discussing fraternal correction. He replies, "in all good things to be done, the action of a man is not efficacious unless divine help is present – and yet a man must do what is in him" (33.2 ad 1).[8] Of course, the exhortation for "a man [to] do what is in him" is not a license to ignore divine causality or to pretend to accomplish what no human can. The objection against human teaching is particularly strong with regard to charity because Thomas is so clear about both its infused character and the unusual logic of its increase or decrease. How do you teach a reader about an infused gift that cannot be earned or diminished by action, that can only be accepted and then intensified or forfeited?

"Thus charity is increased only by this – that its subject participates in charity more and more – that is, so far as it is more led back to its act and more subject to its act" (24.5 corp). Charity increases when the subject "dwells more deeply in what it receives." This means that God increases charity by making it more present through a more complete likeness of the Holy Spirit (ad 3). How should human teaching help such a virtue? And if it cannot help, in what sense can it be considered moral education?

3. Exhortation, Admonition, and Loving Vision

In his Prologue, Thomas directs the *Summa* to beginners, *incipientes.* He does not immediately say what he means. Many readers assume that he refers to beginners in the academic study of theology. Leonard Boyle argued, more precisely, that *incipientes* was also a Dominican name for newer members of the order still in need of formation.[9] Both meanings make sense; neither excludes the other. There are still other meanings. Later in the *Summa,* Thomas correlates differences of state or rank in the church with the degrees of charity – that is, with the traditional spiritual division into *incipientes, proficientes,* and *perfecti* (2a2ae 183.4). In the very questions on charity he recalls the triplet differently. The *incipientes* are those who stand on the lowest "step" or "stage" (*gradus*) of charity (24.9). In them, charity has indeed been born, but it still requires nourishment (24.9 sc). Their "main pursuit" or chief study (*studium principale*) is to avoid sin by resisting concupiscence (24.9 corp). Charity must be nurtured in them so that it is not corrupted. They must be helped in their study. Should a reader understand, then, that the function of the *Summa*'s questions on charity is to help someone on the first step of charity to avoid corrupting the virtue?

To address the question, we need to decide what textual features might offer such help. A bit later, while considering whether God should be loved only for God's self, Thomas argues that in a subordinate sense God may be loved on account of other things, "since we are disposed by some other things to make progress in the love of God, for example, by *benefits* (*beneficia*) that we receive from him, or by *rewards* (*praemia*) that are hoped for, or by *punishments* (*poenae*) that through him we strive to avoid" (27.3 corp, emphases added).[10] It is interesting to compare this passage with

Thomas's discussion of the use of promises and threats in the moral teaching of the Old Law (1a2ae 99.6). It is perhaps more important to recognize it as an echo of the traditional teaching on the "modes" or rhetorical motives of theology.

Opening his *Scriptum* on Peter Lombard's *Sentences*, Thomas raises a standard question in medieval exposition: Is the *modus* of proceeding in theology *artificialis*?[11] The question is standard in scholastic Latin but difficult to translate into contemporary English – in part because *modus* has a large range of associations, including with rhetoric and music. So the question can be translated as: Does the way of doing theology resemble the technique of an art? But the question can also mean: Is theological teaching a deliberate and compelling rhetoric? Replying to it, Thomas insists that theology's procedure is artful, then names some of its main modes. In order for theology to do what it must in leading human beings back to a revealing God, Thomas says, it must be prayerful and narrative and metaphorical or symbolic or parabolic. To correct errors it must argue, but to teach morals it must set forth precepts, must warn and promise, must tell examples. It must also set before us objects of true contemplation. The most pertinent modes for assessing the pedagogy of the *Summa*'s questions on charity are those associated with the *instructio morum*, the teaching of morals: *praeceptivus, comminatorius, promissivus,* and *narrativus exemplorum*. The *Secunda Secundae* of the *Summa* regularly discusses precepts as one of the headings of its pedagogical reorganization. It certainly does so in considering the virtue of charity. Yet a reader should also look for the next two modes, warning and promising. To specify these modes with the language about fraternal correction, a reader should look in the *Summa* especially for evocations of benefits received or rewards promised or punishments threatened.

Examples are not hard to find. The *Summa*'s questions on charity describe many of the virtue's benefits. The very enumeration of the three steps of charity immediately asserts that those on the highest step enjoy God (24.9 corp and ad 3). Joy follows from charity, and enjoyment belongs properly to its activity (23.3 ad 2, 27.3 sc, 27.8 ad 1, 28 throughout).[12] Indeed, enjoyment is not so much a benefit following from charity as its quality or atmosphere. That is why Thomas links enjoyment with "participation" in divine life, where "participation" means something like the English "sharing" (23.3 ad 3). Those who live in charity take part in divine actuality, they share in blessedness (23.5 corp, 25.12 corp). If this language seems too abstract to influence a reader's dispositions, Thomas puts alongside it the more concrete language of desire and pleasure. He says that desire by its nature seeks peace, wants to be brought to rest (28.3 ad 2,

29.2). The peace of this world is incomplete; complete peace comes only in the next (29.2 ad 4). Still, whatever real peace can be had here is the effect of charity. The gift of that virtue produces pleasure (23.2 corp). Indeed, it leads one to join a rational feast with God and the angels (25.10 ad 3). The body also shares in this pleasure by a sort of overflowing (*redundantia,* 25.5 ad 2, 25.12 corp). Charity promises all of this in the present, though more fully and finally in the future.

The rhetoric of benefits and rewards is more prominent in these questions than the rhetoric of threat. That balance accords with Thomas's understanding of the pedagogy of the New Law (*lex amoris* as against the Old Law, *lex timoris,* 1a2ae 107.1 ad 2). But there are reminders in the questions on charity of the present and future "punishments" brought by its rejection. The theological mode of promise is complemented by the mode of warning. The greedy selfishness or concupiscence that undoes charity is described as illness and infection (24.10 corp, 25.5 ad 1). It is also, following Augustine, likened to poison (24.10 ad 2). Thomas justifies both curses and executions as responses to those who seem to refuse any education in charity (25.6 ad 2 and ad 3). More significantly, his detailed consideration of the vices opposed to charity is a sort of gallery of individuals and communities that have refused the virtue or forfeited it (34–43). Hatred, despair, envy, discord, polarization, war: these are indeed the "punishments" a reader should recognize and seek to avoid by exercising charity.

Still, Thomas's rhetoric puts the accent on joy and pleasure, on sharing and communion rather than on the separation of pain. A reader can see this in the allusions to the language of excess from Pseudo-Dionysius: according to Thomas, charity "hyper-exceeds the proportion of human nature" (*superexcedat,* 24.3 corp). Whenever it grows, the aptitude for more growth "grows surpassingly" (*superexcrescit,* 24.7 corp). Such poetic-technical terms are confirmed as general lessons: God is infinitely lovable and so exceeds any creature's capacity to love (27.5 corp). The freely given gift of charity "surpasses the power of nature," which Thomas confirms by quoting Paul's eloquent testimony from Romans 5:5 (24.2 sc and corp).

Thomas gathers these rhetorical inducements in passages that approach liturgical poetry, the rhythms of which he sometimes imitates. Consider this: "We must not, however, love the infection of sin and the corruption of its punishment in our body, but rather pant for its removal by a desire for charity" (25.5 corp). This sort of exhortation, striking because brief, shows Thomas's familiarity with the hortatory devices of classical rhetoric and Christian preaching. He belongs after all to an order of preachers, and he writes the *Summa* at least in part to train them.

It is important to recognize these textual features and to appreciate them in relation to the moral pedagogy of the *Summa*'s questions on charity. Still, this section of the text attempts another sort of persuasion, one for which there is no ready-made rhetorical term. Let me call it the persuasion of loving vision. In one place, Thomas remarks that "the passion of love (*amor*) has this characteristic – that it does not arise all at once, but only through an incessant focus (*assidua inspectio*) on the thing loved" (27.2 corp). *Inspectio* implies a visual analogy: "incessant focus" means here uninterrupted view or contemplation. The virtue of charity comes by infusion, not in slow stages of observation. Even so, Thomas applies to charity something like the visual pedagogy of love. Light and fire are the two consistent images for love (24.5 arg 2, 24.10 sc, 24.12 corp, 27.7 corp). They point to a visual physics of love, in which the vision of the beloved draws the lover. "Vision is the cause of love (*dilectio*) – not for the reason that if something is visible, it is lovable (*diligibile*), but rather because we are led by vision to love (*per visionem perducimur ad dilectionem*)" (26.2 ad 1). This might seem a cliché from medieval romances (or modern ones), but Thomas applies it to the Lord's first and great commandment: the love of God and neighbor. He will shortly explain that *dilectio* is the principal act of the infused virtue of charity (27).

While this passage is striking in its emphasis on vision as the occasion for being drawn by love, it is hardly unique in emphasizing that charity implies motion. Divine love is a motion (27.8 corp). Charity entails operations (28.4 corp). Indeed, and of course, the point of virtue is to arrive at God (23.3 corp). Thomas summarizes the whole line of metaphors and analogies when he remarks that a virtue is not an end so much as a way to it (29.4 sc). A *virtus* is a *via*. So Thomas will also console the reader with reminders that not everything has to be done at once – that the seemingly impossible demands of charity can be approached by stages of preparation (as with *praeparatio* and *crisis* in 25.8 corp, 25.9 corp). In all of this, the underlying pedagogical strategy is not only an exhortation by promise and warning, but a clearing away of any obstacles that might block the motion of the lover toward the beloved.[13]

The visual physics of love can remind the reader that one mode of moral instruction in theology seems to have gone missing in this part of the *Summa* – the mode of the exemplary narration (*narrativus exemplorum*). Where do the questions on charity present the object of loving vision? They do not attempt the presentation, because the structure of the *Summa* postpones that work to the final part. According to Thomas, the most effective teaching of the lesson of divine love was undertaken in the divine incarnation. So the pedagogy of the questions on charity must point forward to the pedagogy of the *Summa*'s Third Part.

4. Gospel Narratives as Visions of Love

For Thomas, the Son came into the world principally to make saving truth manifest (3a 40.1 corp, 40.2 ad 1). The canonical Gospels narrate the Christ's manner of life, the *conversatio Christi,* in order to instruct those who read them in various registers. The truths enacted by Christ's way of life are truths with moral effect. His way-of-life is meant to show the range of virtues (3a 35.7 ad 2, *virtuosa conversatio*). Jesus teaches virtue through the form of his life, but also through particular incidents in it. "In his way-of-life the Lord gave an example (*exemplum*) in all things pertaining as such to salvation" (3a 40.2 ad1).

Christ's suffering and death are the culminating episodes of this incarnate pedagogy. The moral education of fallen souls can be brought to completion only in a terrifying example. If the questions on charity diagnose concupiscence as the chief obstacle to the cultivation of the virtue, Thomas's reading of the pedagogy of the Gospels points to what we call in English "hardness of heart." For Thomas, "blindness of mind" is a vice opposed to the gift of insight that he associates with faith (2a2ae 15). He mentions cruelty as a vice opposed to charity, notably in the conduct of war (2a2ae 40.1 corp). "Hardness" (*duritia*) he associates with "wantonness" (*protervia*) as a vicious excess in the charitable act of fraternal correction (2a2ae 33.4 corp). All of these enter into Thomas's understanding of the need for the brutal lesson of an incarnate god's torture and death. Still the more exact name for the vice that delights in crucifying another might be "hate," *odium,* which Thomas describes as the last corruption of the basic human ordering toward mutual love (2a2ae 34.5 corp).

Christ's passion and death are needed for human redemption, but Thomas takes pains to prevent a misunderstanding of their necessity. What is required in order for God to forgive human sin? According to Thomas, the strictest answer is: whatever God decides. God could have provided other means of freeing human beings from the consequences of sin.[14] Indeed, God can forgive injuries done to God without demanding any satisfaction at all (3a 46.2 ad 3). So whatever necessity there is for the passion and death of Jesus is conditional or suppositional. Thomas names three considerations in the divine choice of this form of redemption (3a 46.1 corp). The first has to do with freeing human beings; the second, with Christ's meriting glory through self-abnegation; the third, with what was revealed in Israelite prophecies and prefigurations. The second and third evidently depend on the first. Hebrew scripture foretold the sacrificial death of a savior just because God foreknew that death as the most beneficial for human liberation.

Thomas multiplies arguments for the appropriateness of Christ's passion and death on a cross (3a 46.3–4). Their multiplicity is part of Thomas's argument: given the possible means of redemption, God's choice will fall on the one that draws together many kinds of appropriateness (3a 46.3 corp). All of the considerations are moral in some sense. Indeed, Thomas does not even attempt a comprehensive enumeration of the virtues shown forth in Christ's willingness to suffer. Still, the principal lesson of the passion is about divine love: through Christ's voluntary suffering, human learners can know "how much God loves (*diligat*)" them, so can "be provoked" (*provocatur*) to love God back, "in which consists the completion of human salvation" (3a 46.3 corp). Thomas repeats the lesson several times, returning to the images of fire and light. On the altar of the cross, he says, Christ is burned "with the fire of charity" (3a 46.4 ad 1). The gruesome sight of God crucified displays love and so draws fallen souls in love.

Readers may still wonder why teaching morals requires such violence. Indeed, they may ask whether the violent manner of teaching doesn't undo any intended lesson about love. The doubt is sharpened precisely by the typological considerations. Jesus's passion and death fulfill all of the precepts of the Old Law – moral, judicial, and ceremonial (3a 47.2 ad 1). In particular, Christ's passion fulfills the ceremonial sacrifices of the Old Law (3a 46.10 ad 1). But if it is true that Christ fulfilled the ceremonial precepts given to Israel, it is more importantly true that the precepts were given in anticipation of Christ's fulfillment. Earlier sacrifices were completed in his sacrifice because they were ordained in view of his sacrifice. What remains unexplained is the pedagogy of sacrifice itself – especially the sacrifice of a human being.

In the Third Part of the *Summa*, Thòmas defines a sacrifice as anything appropriate done to honor God for the sake of "appeasing" (*ad eum placandum*, 3a 48.3 corp). The notion of appeasement is connected to an earlier passage in which Thomas tries to explain Christ's death. An objector argues that it is cruelly unjust to hand over an innocent person to suffering and execution. If God handed Jesus over, then God was unjust (3a 47.3 arg 1). Thomas's reply to the argument first emphasizes Jesus's willingness to suffer. God did not hand Jesus over so much as inspire in Jesus-as-human a willingness to suffer for us. Then there comes an interesting addition: "In which is shown also God's severity (*severitas*), who did not wish to remit sin without a penalty" (3a 47.3 ad 1). The addition is striking because Thomas has already argued that the whole human race could have been redeemed if Christ had willed to suffer only slightly, through *una minima passio* (3a 46.5 ad 3). If he chose to suffer more, that was not for sufficiency, but for pedagogy.

In the questions on charity, severity is contrasted with mercy or clemency (2a2ae 32.2 ad 3).[15] Elsewhere, Thomas explains that severity is most technically the part of justice concerned especially with the strict application of punishment (2a2ae 157.2). The technical meaning would seem to fit with the mention of God's severity in choosing a gruesome passion. God's severity is God's refusal to relax the punishment required for sin. Only it must immediately be remembered that God has also set the punishment and, indeed, decided that some punishment must be required. That decision Thomas has explained in terms of love. So God's severity is an aspect or expression of God's love. How can this be? A reader may suddenly remember that Thomas has said something similar when discussing fraternal correction as an act of charity. If the deed of correction shows severity, the proper intention of correction is always mercy (2a2ae 32.2 ad 3). So with the sacrifice of Christ: God's severity in requiring such violent satisfaction is mercy for the hardened condition of fallen human learners. As Thomas explains of fraternal correction: "The removal of our brother's sin belongs more to charity than even the removal of an outward injury, or of a bodily harm" (2a2ae 33.1 corp). God's severity in choosing the crucifixion, far from contradicting love for humankind, carries it to the farthest point.

This illuminating relation between the questions on charity and the narration of Christ's passion may suggest a larger relation and so address a lurking question. I argued before that the relation of vision to love described in the questions on charity pointed forward to Thomas's meditation on the manner of the passion as God's most vivid teaching of love. The absence of the representation of the object of love in the 2a2ae is remedied, at least in part, by the narration of Gospel examples in the Third Part. Yet if Christ's passion is the culmination of the divine pedagogy of love, what is the function of the questions on charity in teaching charity? Why do they precede the discussion of the passion rather than follow it?

One answer is that an earlier analysis of the virtue of charity can help the reader to recognize it in stories about the human life of Jesus the Christ. Having worked through the complete pattern of major virtues and vices in the Second Part, a reader can see them more clearly within the Gospel narration. Indeed, having learned something from the pedagogical structure of the questions on charity, a reader might also be able to appreciate how virtuous is God's manner of teaching. The passion and death of Jesus show God's love in double deed, in Christ's willingness to suffer and in God's choice of the means most likely to bring about the teaching of human observers or readers.

Of course, the reader of the *Summa* is not presumed to be hearing the story of Christ's suffering and death for the first time. On the contrary, Thomas assumes that the reader has heard the story already, many times – that the reader knows it by heart. More: the reader is presumed to have been taken up into the life of Christ by sacramental participation, beginning with a baptism into the Lord's death and resurrection. So the textual relation of the questions on charity and the narrative of love in the passion within the *Summa* does not function in isolation. The "time" of the textual sequence is caught up in the much more complicated temporal relations of an individual life, salvation history, and divine eternity.

Many modern readers come to the *Summa* having heard that its structure illustrates the cosmic pattern of *exitus* and *reditus,* the procession of all things from God that leads to their return. Like so many others, this expectation may become a hindrance. Thomas knows the pattern of *exitus/ reditus* of course. He also knows that it is a theological commonplace, both canonized and standardized in Peter Lombard's *Sentences.* When Thomas invents the *Summa* as a pattern of moral education, he locates the circle of *exitus/reditus* at another and more intimate level. He sees in it not an abstract cosmological pattern, but the pedagogy of the embodied intelligence fallen into sin. That pedagogy has at its central point a severe lesson about how much God has loved any reader of the *Summa* first. The circle of divine love stands before and behind all of love's other circlings – its reflexivity or reciprocity, its seeming entanglement with the self. "Love begins in this other [God] and from there is drawn to other things by way of a certain circular course . . . Love begins from God as from an ultimate end and is drawn toward creatures" (27.4 ad 2). It is drawn by the divine gift of a virtue, but the virtue is given to restore and complete a motion inscribed in the soul at its creation. Thomas's hope for a theology of love is that it can assist the soul in moving – by exhortation or admonition, yet even more by narrating examples of the beloved's prior love.

NOTES

1. Anders Nygren, *Agape and Eros,* trans. Philip S. Watson (London: SPCK, 1953), 27–35, for all of the quotations in this paragraph. I attend to Nygren's

stated purposes, not to the ambiguities or ambivalences of what he actually achieves.

2. Nygren, *Agape and Eros,* perhaps especially 642–45.

3. In what follows, I cite the *Summa* parenthetically by number of part, question, article, and (where necessary) element within the article. Where no part is given, I am referring to the 2a2ae.

4. The triplet *cordis, oris, operis* is applied by Peter Lombard to penance at *Sentences* 4.16.1. In the *Summa "of Br. Alexander,"* the triplet is used as one of the means of sorting classifications of sins (*Summa Halensis* 2.42). In William Peraldus, *Summa of Vices,* the basic division of seven capital sins (which Thomas deliberately subordinates) is supplemented by a lengthy consideration of "sins of the tongue." See Peraldus, *Summa aurea de virtutibus et vitiis* (Venice 1497), ff. 339va–57vb.

5. It is illustrative to try mapping individual articles on charity from the *Summa* onto the corresponding articles in Thomas's earlier commentary on Peter Lombard. To take a simple example: many of the topics in *Summa* 2a2ae 26 correspond roughly to those in *Scriptum* 3.27.2, articles 1–2 and 4. But in composing the *Summa,* Thomas has not only rearranged the order of the earlier articles, while skipping some and altering their proportions, he has also included material from other parts of the *Scriptum* (1.17.1.1, 2.26.4 ad 6, 3.23.3.1 ad 1) and inserted a topic that has no clear parallel anywhere in the *Scriptum* (*Summa* 2a2ae 26.6).

6. This is correlated with a terminological distinction. In the Lombard, *caritas* is applied to both God and humans. In the First Part of the *Summa,* Thomas discussed God's *amor,* not God's *caritas.* He also treated God's mercy (1a 21) as connected to justice rather than to love. In short, separating out divine love allows Thomas to treat human *caritas* within a pattern suitable for virtue infused into humans.

7. Making these comparisons, I rely not on the titles of the questions or articles, but on the divisions of topics by which Thomas introduces each textual segment. So here I rely chiefly on the brief "prologues" to Questions 1 and 23.

8. Thomas has already addressed the complementary version of the question when discussing the cause of faith. There, one "objection" holds that since faith depends on the activity of preachers, it must have a human cause. Thomas replies that all such exterior persuasions are at best inducements – but inducements that may be used by divine grace (2a2ae 6.1 arg 2, corp and ad 2)

9. See Leonard E. Boyle, *The Setting of the Summa theologiae of Saint Thomas* (Toronto: PIMS, 1982), reprinted in *The Etienne Gilson Lectures on Thomas Aquinas,* ed. James P. Reilly (Toronto: PIMS, 2008).

10. It is also important not to overstate the causal relation among inducements, dispositions, and progress in the love of God. As Thomas insists, there is something unpredictable about their interrelation. Like the circumstances of physical growth, they somehow augment the aptitude for charity until the person "breaks out" (*prorumpit*) in greater fervor (24.6 corp).

11. Thomas Aquinas *Scriptum super Sent.* 1.1.5. For the tradition of the discussion of the modes of theology, see M.-D. Chenu, *La théologie comme science au XIIIe siècle* (3rd ed., Paris: J. Vrin, 1957), 40–41 and throughout.

12. Here and in the next two paragraphs, I try to supply exemplary instances of the textual features I describe. I do not pretend to catalogue their every appearance in this section of the *Summa*.

13. A complete enumeration of pedagogical devices in these questions would have to look at many other features, some of them quite small. For example, there are passages in which Thomas performs acts of charity in reading his predecessors (toward Lombard, 23.2 corp; Augustine's Platonic locutions, 23.2 ad 1; Augustine in his own voice, 25.8 corp). Again, Thomas will correct common mistakes in the application of maxims or principles. The crucial notion of love's reciprocity (*reamatio*) appears in a series of "objections" or *argumenta* (23.1 arg 2, 25.2 arg 3, 25.4 arg 2, 25.5 arg 3). The right use of the notion requires a series of adjustments in the reader's sense of it. And so on.

14. See 3a 46.1–2. The principle is reiterated with an explicit back-reference in the discussion of Christ's resurrection (3a 56.1 ad 2).

15. Compare 2a2ae 108.4 ad 1, 157.2 ad 1. In other passages, *severitas* is contrasted with *epikeia,* understood as laxity (120.1 arg 1 and ad 1), with clemency or meekness (157.2 arg 1, ad 1 and ad 2).

Disagreeing in Charity

Learning from Thomas Aquinas

ROBERT MINER

As the most excellent virtue, charity is productive. It diffuses goodness, generating a range of inward and outward effects. These are indicated in Questions 28–33 of the 2a2ae. Among these effects are peace and concord, qualities that seem conspicuously absent from our public discourse. The ever-present human tendency to factionalism proceeds unabated, as attested by our persistent inability to conduct disagreements in a rational and charitable fashion. What might we learn from Thomas Aquinas – and particularly from the questions on charity in the 2a2ae – about the conditions of reasonable and charitable disagreement?

1. Disagreement in Speech: Contention as a Vice

For Thomas to illuminate these conditions, he must have some background account of what constitutes unreasonable or uncharitable disagreement. Such an account may be found in 2a2ae Question 38 on the vice of "contention" (*contentio*). As a vice, contention cannot be a disposition toward oppositional speech as such, since things that are untrue or bad should be opposed. The first thing to consider, Thomas says, is the direction of the speech, its "intention" (*intentio*). If oppositional discourse is directed against (actual) falsehood, it is to that extent praiseworthy. Conversely, if I have no reason to think that something is false, but I speak against it nonetheless – perhaps because its truth injures my pride or prevents me from getting what I want – then my speech is viciously contentious. The second thing to consider is the "manner" of contention, its *modus*. A sharp edge or cutting tone may be required, since efficacious opposition may demand "brisk speech" (*oratio acris*) – or so Thomas suggests (38.1 corp) by citing a passage from the *Rhetorica ad Herennium* (a text falsely attributed to

Cicero by medieval authors). But what distinguishes an appropriately sharp tone from undue harshness? And if a discourse attacks something that is reasonably judged false, why place any limit at all on the sharpness of that discourse?

That a limit is required, Thomas insists. Even the falsest of notions can be opposed in a vicious manner. Sound judgment about oppositional discourse demands that we consider whether its manner (*modus*) is "appropriate both to the persons (*personae*) and to the business at hand (*negotii*)" (38.1 corp). If the manner of discourse is not appropriate, the attacking speech is at least a venial sin, even if the targeted opinion is clearly false. It may be more than venial, depending on how disproportionate the attack. Its lack of proportion does *not* depend upon the degree to which the targeted opinion is false. Thomas does not take some opinions to be so false that they can never be attacked too much, or too harshly. But on what does an attack's disproportionality depend? Thomas notes scenarios where "so much inordinateness arises in contending that a stumbling block (*scandalum*) is generated for others" (38.1 corp). Whether or not the modus of oppositional speech is inordinate, and to what degree, depends in part on how others in the community of hearers are likely to receive it. To underscore the point, Thomas quotes Paul's admonition (at 2 Timothy 2:14) not to contend in words, giving special emphasis to his words: "For [contention] is useful for nothing, except for destroying those who hear it."

Speech directed against what is false must exhibit restraint, lest it constitute a stumbling block for those who might otherwise be receptive to the truth that it means to defend. It might be tempting to codify the restraint: "Eschew any speech that is cutting; always take care to be nice." For small children, some such rule may be appropriate, for example, "If you don't have anything nice to say, don't say anything at all." Self-styled "truth tellers," or others who have the vice of contention, might also benefit from a rule (compare the advice given at *Nicomachean Ethics* 2.9, 1109b1–8). But rules that are suitable enough for the immature or the vicious cannot cover all cases. Accordingly, Thomas recognizes a nonvicious form of contention, a manner of speech that is "an attack on falsehood with a due measure of briskness (*acrimonia*)." Here *acrimonia* bears little resemblance to "acrimony." It corresponds rather to *oratio acris,* as mentioned in the passage from the pseudo-Cicero quoted above. Some things need to be opposed – briskly, but with due proportion and in charity.

How to distinguish between properly sharp opposition and vicious contention? Is there a rule by which such a determination can be made? As we have seen, Thomas gives an important piece of practical advice.

Ask whether your words will be a stumbling block, impeding the motion of its hearers toward the good that you wish for them. Beyond this caution, however, Question 38 gives little indication of a rule by which to tell whether the modus of an oppositional discourse is "appropriate both to the persons (*personae*) and to the business at hand (*negotii*)" (38.1 corp). Thomas's reticence is deliberate. He does not judge a single rule, or a collection of rules, capable of making the necessary discriminations. In one setting, carefully chosen words of opposition may be *oratio acris,* edifying and refuting in a suitable manner. In another setting, the same words may "go beyond what is appropriate to the persons or business at hand," and so exhibit blameworthy contention. Sometimes readers, noting correctly that the 2a2ae treats moral matters in a more particular manner than the 1a2ae, exaggerate the degree of particularity that Thomas attains (or wishes to attain).[1] Thomas identifies the general features of appropriately oppositional speech (a correct *intentio,* a suitable *modus*). He cannot supply a rule enabling us to tell whether any particular speech act, isolated from its context, is an instance of properly sharp opposition or vicious contention. What he can do is provide insight into the deeper causes of unreasonable and uncharitable disagreement.

2. Disagreement at Heart: The Vice of *Discordia*

Contentious speech makes a good starting point, since its occurrence is familiar to us, amply attested in our public culture and our universities.[2] It is so familiar because it lies near the surface of things. Thomas uses a triplet, taken from Peter Lombard, to organize his treatment of the vices opposed to peace: "of the heart, of the lips, and of the deed."[3] By assigning *contentio* to the lips, Thomas evokes its status as an exterior manifestation of a more interior vice. This is the failing of the "heart" (*cor*), appropriately named *discordia,* treated in Question 37. Those unable to disagree rationally and in charity are not merely ignorant of a rule that, if known and followed, would reform their excessive speech. The structure of the questions on the vices contrary to peace indicates a deeper root of contention. Outward contentiousness springs from internal discord.

Like other evils, discord cannot be understood except as the privation of something good. The good condition is *concordia,* the joining of many hearts into one thing—"principally the divine good, and secondarily the good of our neighbor" (37.1 corp). By setting a person against either, discord prevents or undoes the work of charity. Discordant people focus on what they imagine to be their own good, taking it as incompatible with other goods. Such discord *per se* destroys concord, *secundum intentionem* (37.1 corp). Though Thomas begins with the extreme version of discord, he does not dwell on it. Those who sincerely intend to promote the good are vulnerable to another type of discord. Such discord is *per accidens,* because it does not involve a basic error in the will's direction. It arises whenever people agree that both God and our neighbor's advantage should be honored, but disagree about particulars. To questions of the form – "Does this proposed action actually honor God or our neighbor?" or "What would count as loving God or our neighbor?" – they give different answers. Such discord is not itself vicious. It is, Thomas says, neither a sin nor repugnant to charity. Disagreeing about particular ways of loving God or neighbor does not by itself destroy concord. To think otherwise is to give our opinions too much power. The concord that charity brings about, Thomas says (37.1 corp), is not merely a "union of opinions (*unio opinionum*)." It is, more deeply, a "union of wills (*unio voluntatum*)." People of goodwill may disagree. Concord produced by charity is strong enough to withstand deep and serious disagreement about particulars.

Thomas recognizes the possibility of people disagreeing in charity. Though their opinions do not meet, their hearts do. But why does this description seem so notional? Why does it indicate the exception rather than the norm? Why does discord that begins as a difference of opinion, discord *per accidens,* so persistently turn into a division of hearts, discord *per se*? Thomas begins with a sanguine description of discord *per accidens,* saying it is neither sinful nor repugnant to charity. Beyond the sanguine description, he notes two conditions under which disagreement in opinions may become something worse. One is "an error about things that are necessary for salvation"; the other is an insistence on one's own opinions, "administered with an undue doggedness (*pertinacia*)" (37.1 corp). I propose to set the first condition to one side, at least for now, and focus intently on the second. Under what circumstances does appropriate tenacity in argument – holding one's ground, not abandoning one's opinion in the face of the first objection – become inappropriate doggedness?

To address this question, we may turn to Article 2 of Question 37. Here we see Thomas's handling of a trope that he inherits from Gregory the Great: the derivation of discord from "vainglory" (*inanis gloria*). Discord *per se* is not mere disagreement. In its proper sense, the term "denotes a certain coming-apart (*disgregatio*) of wills, namely so far as the will of one person sticks to one thing, and the will of another person sticks to another thing" (37.2 corp). To "stick" to an opinion, in this sense, is to prefer it because it is ours. "But that a person's will should halt at his own object arises from this – that he prefers the things that are his own to the things that are of another" (37.2 corp). Perhaps we have fallen in love with our opinion; perhaps we have come to identify with it. In the domain of opinion-holding, such pertinacity is not simply an act of intellect. It is an act of will, a determination to love one's own simply because it is one's own. To love one's own in this manner – as if the mere fact of its being one's own suffices to make it excellent – is symptomatic of vainglory. Significantly, Thomas portrays both *discordia* and its immediate verbal manifestation, *contentio,* as offspring of vainglory:

> Discord is a daughter of vainglory, because each of the discordants sticks to his own sense of things and neither yields to the other. Now it is proper to pride and vainglory to seek one's own excellence. Now just as some are discordant from this – that they stick in their heart to their own notions (*stant corde in propriis*) – so some are contentious from this – that each one defends in word (*verbo*) that which appears to him. And so, for the same reason, contention is set down as a daughter of vainglory, as discord was. (38.2 corp)

Discord *per accidens* carries with it the danger of turning into discord *per se.* It is not wrong to have one's own opinion about how God and neighbor are best loved. But when we "stick in our heart to our own notions" – insulating them from scrutiny, closing them off to reconsideration – chances are poor that we will remain on the safe ground of disagreement in opinion, discord *per accidens.* Instead, we are likely to move from intellectual affirmation to willful stubbornness, generating the division of wills that is discord *per se.* Such discord weakens our power to see those who hold opinions different from our own as people of goodwill, who love God and neighbor no less than we do. It fosters the tendency to see others not merely as holding doubtful opinions, but as active despisers of God and neighbor. In this way, we come to regard others as perpetuators of discord *per se,* "knowingly and intentionally dissenting from the divine good and the neighbor's good" (37.1 corp), while remaining blind to our own participation in the syndrome.

Vicious factionalism does not arise simply from difference in opinions. It springs from a disunion of wills – and especially an insistence on seeing others who have divergent opinions as willfully opposed to the good. As the most excellent virtue, charity produces concord. Concord includes within itself the capacity for disagreeing rationally and peaceably about judgments that concern human living. As daughters of vainglory, discord and contention work to oppose charity. They do so by polarizing us at a level more basic than the mere holding of divergent opinions. They divide us at heart.

3. Disharmony Within Persons: Failures of Self-Love

Discord brings about a "division of wills" as its proper effect (38.2 ad 3). If there are two discordant parties, the will of either one or both of them must be turned away from the *bonum universale* – the highest good in which all can participate without loss – and toward a lesser particular good. Such a turn requires the mistaken reduction of universal good to what is "one's own," whether this be some finite object of desire or the shadow of one's own opinions. Such reduction may seem to be a function of excessive self-love. Frequently one hears failures of charitable love described in just these terms, for example, "He loves himself too much and others not enough." To move from the language of fixating on what is "one's own" (language used by Thomas himself) toward a diagnosis of the problem as consisting of excessive self-love seems a short step.

Is it a step that Thomas takes? Earlier in the treatment on charity, in the middle of Question 25 of the 2a2ae, Thomas asks whether sinners love themselves too much. His answer: in the proper sense, they do not love themselves at all. They love themselves only by a stunted conception of what they are, reducing themselves to "sensitive and bodily nature" and thus "not rightly knowing themselves (*non recte cognoscentes seipsos*)" (25.7 corp). Losing sight of the universal good, they misidentify their true being with a shell of themselves. Demands imposed by that shell, not to be confused with genuine self-love, are what drive them. Deference to these demands is self-love only "according to the corruption of the outer man" (25.7 corp), Thomas says, invoking Paul's contrast between the *homo interior* and the *homo exterior* at 2 Corinthians 4. A man who genuinely loves himself, by contrast, sets aside the *homo exterior.* He pays no heed to the outer man's persistent reduction of the good to what it knows best, that is, bodily or sensible things. Instead, he loves himself according to *mens rationalis,* whose nature is to desire nothing less than the good that fully satisfies – participation in eternal beatitude. This concern for one's actual well-being, driven by the deepest desire of the inner man, is true self-love. Self-regard as demanded by the outer man is not self-love. It is a parody, a counterfeit that should not be confused with the genuine article.

For Thomas, perpetrators (and therefore victims) of discord *per se* do not love themselves too much. They are not capable of any such thing. The habit of clinging in their hearts to a limited good is perpetuated by a failure to know their own deepest desire. The failure to know this desire does not mean that it is not present. On the contrary, hunger for the universal good remains. Dominance of the *homo exterior* never destroys the *homo interior* but only muffles its voice, which still makes itself heard from time to time by a "gnawing conscience (*conscientia remordens*)" (25.7 corp). Souls caught up in discord are not empowered by true self-love. Their actual condition is a failure to harmonize with themselves. Thomas evokes the internal harmony of those in whom the *homo interior* is sovereign: "They do not suffer dissension of the will in themselves, since their whole soul tends toward one thing" (25.7 corp). By contrast, those who fail in self-knowledge, esteeming primarily their sensitive and bodily nature in accordance with the demands of *homo exterior,* are racked with division. Disdaining spiritual goods, while continuing at some level to desire them, such people find being alone with themselves unpleasant. They cannot fully enjoy "returning to their heart, since they find in that place evil things in the present, past, and future, from which they shrink." Accordingly, they fail to "harmonize with themselves (*sibi ipsis concordant*)" (25.7 corp).

What can we learn from Thomas about disagreeing rationally and in charity? My answer to this question began with his analysis of contention, the vice of speech that most evidently conflicts with rational and charitable disagreement. Since contention is a vice of the lips, it must be grounded in a prior vice of the heart, discord. Question 37 of the 2a2ae stresses discord *between* persons. Placing Question 37 within the fuller context of the questions on charity as a whole, we can readily see that discord between persons presupposes a more fundamental discord *within* a person. The contrary of this more fundamental discord, Thomas holds, is "peace" (*pax*), "a union of desires within a single person who desires" (29.1 corp). A lack of internal peace – a dissension within the appetites – explains more adequately than facile diagnoses of excessive self-love why our communities are so liable to the vices of discord and contention. If we are habitually at odds with others, unable to disagree rationally and in charity, it is likely because we are at odds with ourselves.

4. Is Thomas Himself Contentious?

In proposing that Thomas offers something from which we can learn, so that we might conduct our disagreements better, I may seem perversely oblivious to at least two features of his authorship. First, Thomas tends to strike modern readers as addicted to argument, manifesting the very vice that he deplores. Perhaps he did not engage in the conversational practice of "talking for victory" (as Boswell said about Johnson).[4] But his textual practice insists on portraying legitimate differences of opinion as though they amounted to deficiencies in rationality (excepting, of course, his own magisterial determinations). Second, even if his apparent contentiousness can be explained, does not Thomas remain a theological dogmatist – a man whose doctrinal rigidity prevents him from offering any persuasive teaching about how to disagree reasonably and charitably? In this section, I consider the appearance of Thomas's texts as contentious. A concluding section examines the second, potentially more serious charge of theological dogmatism.

It would be idle to deny that a reader new to the *Summa* is likely to find Thomas contentious. The very form of the disputed Question – of which any *Summa* Article is a stylized abbreviation – seems to imply the essentially contentious character of his discourse. What cannot be denied is his commitment to dialectical argument. As Mark Jordan observes, "Thomas's 'contentiousness' is his being thoroughly dialectical, his wanting to have it out on every point."[5] The analysis of *contentio* in 2a2ae 38 provides one way – I believe a persuasive way – of showing that Thomas is not contentious, but only (as Jordan intimates with scare quotes) "contentious."

One mark of vicious contentiousness is the incapacity to stand back from appearances, to query them. Contentious people insist on maintaining and defending whatever appears to be the case to themselves. Because they "stick in their heart to their own notions," as Thomas says (38.2 corp), they are incapable of submitting themselves to the discipline of questioning. They dislike any process that might require them to modify, qualify, or even reject the particular view with which they are in love. They are stuck in their own idiosyncratic notions, refusing to see them as the provisional approximations – the intellectual shantytowns – that they are.[6] To this entrenched habit, Thomas quietly and persistently enacts an alternative. The procedure of every Article of the *Summa* assumes that opinions begin their lives as appearances, as views to be queried. From the work of sifting through the received opinions, something emerges that transcends the play of appearance and counterappearance featured in the *videtur quod*. This is the "determination," stated in the body of a *Summa* Article. When made well, the determination moves beyond the appearances, not least by accounting for their intelligibility while showing their insufficiency. But only a very hasty reader – or perhaps a zealous disciple who knows something of Thomas's letter while missing his spirit – would conclude that what emerges in the *determinatio* acquires a status transcending appearance as such. Whatever the practice of later readers, Thomas never himself endows his determinations with any such status. On the contrary, he regards any particular determination that he makes as the most pedagogically apt thing to say, "appropriate to the persons or business at hand." It is the best thing that he can say at the time, and therefore provisional. It remains subject to revision – susceptible to enrichment, revisable in the light of new evidence or a change of context. Thomas does not so much say this as show it, weaving it into the procedure and structure of the *Summa*. Frequently what is stated in the body of one Article will reemerge in a later Article, as an appearance to be queried or refined. The *Summa* never claims to reach a point where no more can be said. Far from foreclosing future examination, it actively encourages it.

As the author of the incomplete and unfinished dialectical inquiry that is the *Summa*, Thomas arguably displays more openness and less contentiousness than some proponents of "system" in the modern sense. What may strike a novice reader as contentiousness is actually a willingness to "test everything," without pronouncing any particular human test to be final. To come at the point another way, consider how things would stand if Thomas were to suppose that his own determinations were anything other than provisional. Were he to take this view, he would tacitly expect our reception of his discourse to differ in kind from his own reception of the multiple *auctoritates* that he uses. He would thereby exempt his discourse from the dialectical scrutiny to which he subjects other authors. He would value his own productions as peculiarly excellent, simply because they are his – and thereby exhibit the vice of vainglory. Thomas is undoubtedly many things, not all of them good. But the charge of vainglory is not likely to stick. Humility and a corresponding gentleness, in word and deed, are among his most widely attested traits of character (noted even by adversaries like John Pecham).[7] One must, of course, correct for hagiographical distortions. But such corrections, in my view, do not alter the judgment that Thomas composes his dialectical works from a humble desire to know – as distinct, say, from the desire to enclose the world in an encyclopedic "system," or the habit of starting with a conclusion and then finding arguments to support it.[8]

5. Rational Disagreement and Sectarianism

Let us now turn to the claim about Thomas's theological dogmatism. Does Thomas possess a doctrinal rigidity that prevents him from offering insight about reasonable and charitable disagreement? The question is a serious one. It appears that Thomas judges the denial of certain doctrines, taught by the Roman Catholic Church, to be possible only for people whose wills have turned away from God. He seems to reject the possibility that people of goodwill can hold certain things; he denounces such people as heretical or schismatic. In this way, he contributes to the discord he ostensibly opposes. He increases the difficulty of charitable disagreement. Or so the indictment runs.

In establishing that Thomas is a poor teacher about how to disagree in charity, how far does this indictment go? Let us begin with his conception of heresy. For Thomas, heresy is not simple unbelief; it is not "irreligion" in our sense of the term. Christian belief is a condition of being a Christian heretic: "Heresy is a species of unfaithfulness belonging to those who possess Christ's faith, but who corrupt its dogmas" (2a2ae 11.1 corp). To "corrupt its dogmas," the heretic engages in an act of will, choosing not "the things that are truly handed down by Christ, but the things that his own mind suggests to him" (11.1 corp). Thomas identifies "the things that are truly handed down by Christ" with the articles of faith and the things that follow from the articles, as determined by the Church. If some debatable point regarding faith has not yet been determined by the Church, then one cannot be a heretic about that point. Only when a man "stubbornly rejects" what has been determined by the "authority of the universal Church" (11.2 ad 3) can he be a heretic. Such a man has two chances to repent for his obstinacy. If he persists past two corrections, the Church quits "hoping for his conversion"; it must "provide for the health of others, separating him from the Church by a sentence of excommunication. And it further relinquishes him to secular judgment in order that he be exterminated from the world by death" (11.3 corp).

This chilling passage cannot be ignored by those who wish to read the *Summa* seriously. It is useful to face it, precisely because it suggests that if we are to learn from Thomas about rational and charitable disagreement, we cannot accept his view *in toto*. For Thomas, the question "who counts as a heretic?" is answered by applying a particular criterion, namely, that of fidelity to teachings determined by the Roman Catholic Church. This criterion is plausible if one accepts two background premises: (1) the set of things that "belong to the teachings of Christ" is identical with the set of things taught by the Roman Catholic Church, and (2) acts of contesting that identity, when repeated, necessarily flow from a perverse will, a will turned away from the last end. For reasons whose elucidation is well beyond the scope of this essay, Thomas accepts both premises. We may reject either premise, or both. Certainly contemporary Christians of various descriptions need not follow Thomas in counting dissenters as ill-willed heretics who endanger the salvation of others and merit punishment by death.

It might seem that Thomas's unpalatable answers to the questions "who counts as a heretic?" (any Christian who publicly dissents from Church teaching) and "what should be done with unrepentant heretics?" (they should be excommunicated and killed) are consequences of his fundamental ideas about heresy. This appearance, I think, is specious. I have no desire to rehabilitate the particular language of heresy; it has long since outlived whatever usefulness it had. But charitable reading can see other possibilities. Quoting Isidore of Seville, Thomas notes that "just as 'heresy' is said from 'choosing,' so 'sect' is said from following . . . So heresy and sect are the same" (11.1 ad 3). When Thomas takes on heresy, his deeper intention is to oppose sectarianism. If we oppose the side of Thomas's teaching that ascribes ill-will to those who do not conform to a particular church's teachings—that is, to what we with our post-Reformation eyes cannot help but see as a particular church—we do so because we *agree* with his larger contention that sectarianism is a bad thing.

To make this clearer, let us look once more at Question 38 on contention. In arguing that disputation is not of itself contentious, Thomas uses a courtroom example. An advocate who argues his case, however wrong-headed or materially false that case may be, is not guilty of contention, provided that his arguments are genuinely directed by the intention of attaining justice. When Thomas says that "the person who contends in court is he who attacks the truth of justice" (38.1 ad 3), he means that vicious contention does not consist merely of a weak case, featuring bad arguments. The standard for vicious contention is higher than that. The advocate must be attacking the "truth of justice" itself. He must knowingly make claims that are false and deceitful, or otherwise employ tactics that by their very nature are opposed to justice. Thomas says something similar about doctrinal matters. "The person who contends in disputation is he who *intends* to attack the truth of doctrine" (38.1 ad 3; emphasis mine). A person may propose a wrong or muddled idea about the truth or falsity of some doctrine, but this is different from *intending* to attack the "truth of doctrine" itself. To attack the "truth of doctrine," one has to do something far more radical than question a particular teaching or find oneself unable in conscience to accept it. Regarding the topic in question, one must deny the very possibility of any teaching whatever. Instead, one must hold that the topic serves only as a pretext for the exercise of power, an occasion to fill the vacuum by pure will, since nothing rightly termed a teaching or an illumination of the mind is even possible. Such assertions may well be an intentional attack on the "truth of doctrine." So far as they claim the absolute impossibility of any teaching, such attacks are the actual enemy of reasonable and charitable disagreement over matters difficult to know. Attempts to engage in rational argumentation, by contrast, are attempts to know the truth about something–to rise above the ideological assertions and counterassertions of quarreling sects. Such attempts, so far as they aim at truth and avoid ascribing ill-will to those who see things differently, are the very opposite of sectarian. They are the stuff of disagreements conducted rationally and in charity.

In this way, we can learn from the core of Thomas's opposition to sectarian divisions, even as we reject his particular application of the teaching to heretics. (This proposal bears some analogy to contemporary philosophers who defend Kant's reasoning about the categorical imperative, while denying his particular application of it–for example, to the death penalty.) Thomas's willingness to identify dissenters as ill-willed heretics, and to recommend their death, can and should trouble us. He is too quick to acquiesce in the judgment that all heretics are guilty of mortal sin, voluntarily turning away from God. But what makes it implausible to suppose that heretics deliberately and knowingly turn their will away from God? Why is it more plausible to claim that if they are in fact wrong on some particular point, the explanation lies in ignorance rather than malice? Persuasive answers to these questions will, in my view, draw upon premises and arguments helpfully articulated by Thomas himself.

"We must judge men, not by their opinions, but by what these opinions make of them," writes Lichtenberg.[9] This rule may initially seem to count against Thomas. Do not his opinions lead him to advocate terrifying things? Thomas does hold a number of opinions (and not only about heretics) that are all too characteristic of his time and place and merit our clear-eyed rejection. We can acknowledge that he is not immune to the limitations of time and place (even if Thomas discipleship is sometimes slow to admit it). But do these limitations capture what is most distinctive or interesting about Thomas? Lichtenberg's rule suggests another possibility. Thomas's opinions, even the most objectionable ones, do not reduce his textual practice to that of an arrogant bigot who habitually prefers eristic to dialectic. His lapses, however regrettable, should not obscure the general tendency of his pedagogy toward compassionate and charitable assessment.

A relevant example is available in Question 38 of the 2a2ae, where he interprets Job's declaration "I speak to the Almighty, and I desire to dispute with God" (Job 13:3). *Disputare,* he says, does not mean vicious "contention." Job neither intends to attack, nor does he actually attack the truth. No matter how angry or opposed to God he may seem, his goal is "to inquire." While spirited, his inquiry contains no *inordinatio*. It is difficult to imagine a more charitable interpretation of Job.[10] Nothing prevents us from extending the precedent, even introducing it into domains that might surprise Thomas. That *"might* surprise Thomas," I say – because they might not. Confident utterances regarding "what Thomas would think" about any given topic, were he alive today, are often attempts to claim his authority, attempts that seek to deny or obfuscate their own status as conjectures. We can speculate on what Thomas would make of new evidence and fresh discoveries that were unknown to him. We can conjecture about how he would address questions posed in categories that were not available to him. We can do little more.

In his own practice as an author, Thomas exercises a remarkable dialectical freedom. As heirs of Thomas, we may claim this freedom as our own. We can attempt to emulate the generally high intellectual standards of his discourse. In the process, we can seek to avoid taking those who disagree with us as our enemies. Should someone insist upon regarding us as an enemy, addressing us with contentious speech, we do not have to be drawn into hatred. We can "retaliate" by showing some good sense, sending "a box of confections to get rid of a painful story."[11] By the "completion of charity," we can hope "to draw the enemy into our love" (25.9 corp).

NOTES

1. See (for example) the generally excellent and accessible introduction to the *Summa* by Bernard McGinn: "His treatment here is so detailed that all but the most devoted Thomists may be excused from reading 916 articles that constitute the *Secunda Secundae*" (*Thomas Aquinas's "Summa theologiae"* [Princeton, NJ: Princeton University Press, 2014], 102).

2. For contentious speech in our public culture, it suffices to mention "talk radio." On our universities, these words from Collingwood remain timely: "Philosophers, especially those with an academic position, inherit a long tradition of arguing for the sake of arguing; even if they despair of reaching the truth, they think it a matter of pride to make other philosophers look foolish. A hankering for academic reputation turns them into a kind of dialectical bravoes, who go about picking quarrels with their fellow philosophers and running them through in public, not for the sake of advancing knowledge, but in order to decorate themselves with scalps. It is no wonder that the subject they represent has been brought into discredit with the general public and

with students who have been trained to care less for victory than for truth"
(R. G. Collingwood, *Principles of Art* [Oxford: Oxford University Press,
1938], 106–7).

3. Thomas's simultaneous rejection of the Lombard's triplet as a large-scale
   organizing device (see 2a2ae pr) and his use of it in a more limited context is itself an expression of his way of disagreeing with his predecessors
   charitably.

4. James Boswell, *The Life of Samuel Johnson* (New York: Everyman's Library,
   1991), 374.

5. Mark Jordan, *Ordering Wisdom* (Notre Dame, IN: University of Notre Dame
   Press, 1986), 195.

6. For this vivid way of putting the matter, I remain indebted to conversations
   with Christian Moevs. See also his *The Metaphysics of Dante's Comedy*
   (Oxford: Oxford University Press, 2005), particularly the reflections at 104
   and 189.

7. See Simon Tugwell, O.P., *Albert & Thomas: Selected Writings* (New York:
   Paulist Press, 1988), 264, as well as Jean-Pierre Torrell, O.P., *Saint Thomas
   Aquinas: Volume 1, The Person and His Work*, trans. Robert Royal (Washington, DC: Catholic University of America Press, 1996), 195 (on Pecham) and
   281 (citing Peter of San Felice's comment "Thomas fuit homo . . . mire hu-
   militatis et patientie, adeo quod nunquam aliquem corruscavit aliquot verbo
   ampulloso aut contumelioso").

8. For the *locus classicus* of the claim that Thomas has it all worked out in
   advance, and so possesses "little of the true philosophical spirit," see Ber-
   trand Russell, *The History of Western Philosophy* (London: George Allen &
   Unwin, 1946), 484. For a direct (and witty) confrontation with Russell on
   the point, see Mark T. Nelson, "On the Lack of 'True Philosophic Spirit' in
   Aquinas: Commitment *v.* Tracking in Philosophic Method," *Philosophy* 76
   (2001): 283–96.

9. Georg Christoph Lichtenberg, *The Waste Books,* trans. R. J. Hollingdale
   (New York: New York Review of Books, 2000), 170.

10. In his commentary on Job, Thomas gives an account of noncontentious dis-
    putation, an account that bears comparison to 2a2ae 38. See Jordan, *Ordering
    Wisdom* 66–67.

11. The line about confectionary retaliation derives from Friedrich Nietzsche,
    Ecce Homo, trans. Walter Kaufmann (New York: Vintage, 1967), 228–29.
    For the suggestion that more insight about how to undo or reverse conten-
    tious discourse might come from attending to Thomas's treatment of the
    command to love our enemies, I thank Dominic Doyle.

Is Charity the Holy Spirit?

The Development of Aquinas's

Disagreement with Peter Lombard

DOMINIC DOYLE

Thomas Aquinas's mature presentation of charity in the *Summa of Theology* comes at the end of a lengthy process of theological development. From his earliest, sprawling treatment in his commentary on Peter Lombard's *Sentences,* through his more focused (and ultimately abandoned) second commentary on the same, to his expansive disputed question *On Charity,* which enabled his concise and clarifying reformulation in the *Summa of Theology,* we see a mind in motion, achieving not only a significant breakthrough in the understanding of a central topic in Christian theology but also a historic advance in the systematic organization of theology. This essay focuses on one aspect of Thomas's understanding of love: his refutation of Lombard's identification of charity with the Holy Spirit. By focusing on the back story to this crucial question in the *Summa of Theology,* we gain a deeper appreciation of its value and achievement. In particular, we see Thomas's evolving grasp of how best to articulate the intimate presence of God without diminishing the real activity of the believer. More broadly, by tracing this development we may discover an underlying reason for Thomas's writing of the *Summa of Theology* itself.

1. Peter Lombard's *Sentences*

In his enormously influential *Sentences,* Lombard controversially identifies charity with the Holy Spirit, a claim that, in the words of one commentator, serves as "a cornerstone of his entire theological construction."[1] Lombard's reasoning for the position that the Holy Spirit is the very love by which we love God and neighbor is made in Distinction 17 of Book 1, in the midst of his treatment of the doctrine of the Trinity. It runs as follows:

1. The Holy Spirit is the "love or charity or affection of the Father and the Son," that is, the mutual love between Father and Son that unites them to each other.[2]
2. The sending of God's Spirit brings about in us a spiritual love or charity for neighbor and God.[3]
3. But God is love itself (1 John 4:8), and not just the cause of finite love.[4]
4. Further, the Spirit gives itself, and not merely a gift of something else.[5]
5. Therefore, it is possible to affirm that our spiritual love for neighbor and God is neither simply caused by God nor a mere gift from God, but is God's very Spirit itself in us.

For Lombard, then, the charity that arises in us through the gift of divine love is itself divine. Charity is not just *from* God, it *is* God.[6] The infusion of the Spirit not only causes us to love God and neighbor, but also means that our resultant spiritual love is itself nothing less than the Spirit in us.

As Lombard explores in more detail how this indwelling takes place, it becomes clear that he is not maintaining that the Holy Spirit is the believer's act of loving itself. Rather, the Holy Spirit "is given to us . . . that is, exists in one, in such a way that he makes one a lover of God and neighbor."[7] But at this point some confusion arises. For the claim that the Holy Spirit "makes one a lover of God and neighbor" stands in some tension with the earlier claim that the Spirit is not just the cause of love, but is the love itself. This problem becomes acute when Lombard has to deal with Augustine's authoritative definition of charity—"the motion of the [human] mind toward enjoying God for God's own sake, and oneself and one's neighbor for the sake of God"[8]—for if the Holy Spirit is identified with charity, then the unchanging Spirit would be in motion. Lombard answers this latter problem by arguing that charity is said to be a movement of the spirit only in the sense that it draws the spirit to loving God and neighbor. But this only compounds the confusion noted above as to whether the Holy Spirit is more than just the cause of charity. It also adds a new problem: since the Holy Spirit also moves the mind to believing and hoping, and not just to loving, why not define charity as a movement of the mind to believing and hoping too?

This nest of problems comes to a head in chapter 6, section 8. Here, Lombard attempts to remove the confusion by making explicit a previously implicit but crucially operative distinction between virtue and act. Charity or the Holy Spirit does indeed cause the *acts* of the other virtues, but through the mediation of the *virtues* from which these acts proximately arise. Thus, charity or the Holy Spirit works the act of faith through the virtue of faith.[9] But with acts of love it is different. In this unique case, Lombard argues that there is no mediating virtue through which the Holy Spirit/charity works to bring about acts of love. To the contrary, the Holy Spirit/charity works the act of love through itself, not through the mediation of any virtue. By making explicit the distinction between virtue and act, Lombard has clarified his position: our acts of love are caused by the Holy Spirit, but the very love from which these acts spring is nothing but the Holy Spirit abiding in the believer.

Before considering Thomas's evaluation of this argument, it is important to appreciate the principle at stake for Lombard: safeguarding the intimate presence of the Holy Spirit in the believer. This intimacy is most clearly seen in the arrestingly beautiful conclusion that Lombard draws from his identification of charity with the Holy Spirit: "Whoever loves the very love by which he loves his neighbor, in that very thing loves God, because that very love is God, that is, the Holy Spirit."[10] Lombard can therefore quote approvingly the words of Augustine: "Embrace God who is love, and embrace God in love. . . . For the more holy we are and the more emptied of the swelling of pride, the more we are filled with love; and with what is he filled who is full of love, if not with God?" To which Lombard adds, "By these words, Augustine sufficiently shows that the very love by which we love God and neighbor is God."[11]

2. Thomas's "Parisian Commentary" on the *Sentences*

Like his teacher Albert the Great and his contemporary Bonaventure, Thomas categorically rejects Lombard's position that charity is the Holy Spirit in us, directly moving our acts of love without any intermediary habit.[12] While sympathetic to the principle at stake—the intimate presence of the Spirit in the believer[13]—Thomas nonetheless rejects the identification of charity with the Spirit across his lifetime. His first commentary on Lombard's Distinction 17 begins immediately by dismantling this "cornerstone" of Lombard's theology. By laying out some of the arguments presented here, we can gauge the refinement that takes place in later texts.[14] Distinction 17, Article 1 comprises eight objections, a surprisingly lengthy three-part *sed contra,* and a long *responsio.* The first of the three arguments in the *sed contra* draws upon a metaphysics of participation, arguing that "whatever is received into a thing is received into it according to the recipient's mode." If the finite (human) is to share in some way in the infinite (divine), then that sharing must happen in a finite, and thus created, way – otherwise it would not be a *human* sharing in the divine, and thus no real participation at all. On the basis of this metaphysical analysis, Thomas can assert at the outset that the very structure of participation entails the finite or created nature of charity.

Another argument in the *sed contra* starts from the premise that the saints are more intimately present to God than other creatures and that this more intimate presence involves a real change in the saint, not in God. What, then, does the saint possess that other creatures do not? It cannot be that the saint possesses God in Godself, for otherwise all the just would be assumed into the Holy Spirit, as Christ is assumed into the Word. The saint must therefore possess some *effect* of God. This effect, however, must be more than a mere divine act – otherwise saints who were not acting (for example, who are asleep) would not be holy. This effect must therefore be a habit, that is, an enduring, settled disposition that is the source of the good acts in question.[15]

The *responsio* gives further reasons for affirming that charity must be a habit and not just an act. Citing 1 Corinthians 13, Thomas asserts that the soul's goodness comes from charity. This supernatural goodness must be greater than natural goodness. But natural (or acquired or political) virtues not only make a person act well, they also make a person good. Consequently, charity must not only cause a person to act well, it must also make a person good. Just as all being stems from some inhering form, so the soul's graced being must stem from some informing grace or charity. Similarly, just as any perfect act stems from a power perfected by a habit, so acts of charity, which are perfective by virtue of their meritorious nature, must stem from a created habit in the soul. Since this habit flows from the Holy Spirit as the exemplary cause, there arose the understandable but mistaken elision between the Holy Spirit and the theological virtue of charity.[16]

To defend and elucidate Lombard's position, certain supporters, principally Richard Fishacre, drew a comparison with the phenomenon of light, arguing that just as light itself may be compared to the Holy Spirit itself, so the illumination of an object by that light may be considered as the same Spirit existing in the soul, moving it to acts of charity.[17] But this entails a similar position already rejected in the *sed contra*, namely, that saints would be assumed into the Person of the Spirit. Thomas thus shows in more detail why the assumption of the saint's will into the Spirit is not tenable and, more briefly, that it does not account for the proximate causal power of the human will itself. Consequently, there cannot be a "likeness of the will's act to the Holy Spirit unless there be a likeness of the soul to the Holy Spirit through some form, which is the principle of the act by which we are conformed to the Holy Spirit."[18]

Further refutations and clarifications come in the replies to the eight objections. Three of these objections, which recur in later texts, provide a basis for comparison. The second objection draws on Augustine's claim that just as the soul is the life of the body, so God is the life of the soul. But the soul itself is the form of the body; it does not vivify the body through some mediating form. Therefore, the Holy Spirit should vivify the soul immediately, and not through some mediating habit. To this objection, Thomas replies that God is not the form of the soul insofar as God is that abiding, internal, structuring principle by which the soul lives, as the soul *is* that abiding internal principle by which the body lives. (If God were the form of the soul in this sense, the soul would be divine.) Rather, God vivifies the soul as its exemplary principle by pouring into it the life of grace. This appeal to a differentiated causal explanation recurs in the immediately following discussion of the image of light, which attempts to correct the use of this imagery made by supporters of Lombard's position discussed earlier. Thomas distinguishes the illuminating source of light from the illuminated object that receives the light. The illuminating source (analogous to God) is the *efficient* principle of the shining of the illuminated object. The illuminated object's received light (analogous to charity and grace) is the very *form* by which the object shines. Whatever the merits of this analogy, the point behind it is clear enough: Thomas's insistence on a differentiated account of causation whereby he can assert simultaneously that (1) God is the ultimate source of action and (2) the creature receives the effects of that action into its integral structure (and without thereby merging with the cause).

Thomas's reply to the third objection reinforces this point. The objection argues as follows: since God creates nature without intermediaries, so he re-creates through grace without intermediaries. To which Thomas replies: God creates (that is, gives existence to) things precisely through the conferring of the form by which a thing is the thing it is. This is the formal principle of any thing's natural operation. Likewise, it is fitting that God recreates (that is, restores through grace) by bestowing a form in the souls of the just. This created habit is the formal principle of the soul's graced acts. Again, Thomas is distinguishing the extrinsic efficient source (God) from the internal, abiding principle (the habit of charity) in order to maintain the integrity of both natural and graced life as something that truly belongs to (although by no means is caused by) the creature.

In the response to the fifth objection, this deployment of a differentiated Aristotelian causality is stated more clearly. The objection argues that, because charity bridges the infinite distance between divine and human—making a just person out of a sinner—it cannot be something created and finite but must instead have infinite power. To which Thomas replies: something—for example, a white wall—is said to be "made" in two senses: by the painter who paints it, and by the white paint itself, by which the wall is white. In this case, the painter is the efficient cause, that is, the agent responsible for bringing about the effect; while the white paint is the formal cause, that is, the abiding feature belonging to the wall itself, constituting it as the kind of wall it is (a white one). By analogy, the "making" of a sinner to be joined to God is from God as the efficient cause, and from charity as the formal cause.[19] Thus, while charity is the *effect* of infinite power, it does not possess infinite power in itself—and so it can be finite and created.

Clearly, Thomas seeks to refute Lombard's position by the repeated use of a differentiated account of causality. He has distinguished between *principium efficiens* and *forma ipsius,* and between *principium exemplariter* and *formaliter* (in objection 2); between God *contulit/confert esse* (whether of nature or grace) and *principium formale* (objection 3); and between *per modum efficientis* and *per modum formae* (objection 5). Such differentiation in causal analysis is more broadly applied in the very next distinction's detailed analysis of the four causes in the context of the naming of God ("Whether the Holy Spirit can be called our gift," d. 18, a. 5). In the immediately following *expositio textus* at the end of that distinction, Thomas attempts to gather together the scattered distinctions he drew over several objections in the preceding distinction. "We are '*in* the Holy Spirit' not formally (*formaliter*), but effectively (*effective*); we *exist,* formally, by a created spirit, which is the soul; but by the Holy Spirit we are *holy* both formally and effectively, insofar as through charity, which has as its exemplar the love that is the Holy Spirit, we are formally sanctified, and through this [gift] the Holy Spirit is conjoined to us [as mover]."[20]

It is debatable whether this summary succeeds in fully clarifying the issue. The trajectory of Thomas's argument up to this point had been to distinguish God as the efficient cause of love from the virtue of charity by which we formally love God and neighbor. Here, however, Thomas uses the notions of formality and effectiveness together to name the Spirit's action. While not inaccurate, this move runs against the grain of the previous arguments. We must turn to Thomas's second attempt to comment on Lombard for a more satisfactory resolution.

3. Thomas's Second *Sentences* Commentary, the *Lectura romana*

About a dozen years later, Thomas began work on a new commentary on the *Sentences* for the Dominican *studium* at Rome.[21] Given more freedom over the syllabus in this new teaching venue, Thomas eventually abandoned this second commentary and started composing a more systematic work, the *Summa of Theology*, which aims to present material "according to the order of learning" and not "according to what the exposition of the texts required."[22] The frustration with the *Sentences*'s presentation of the material that prompted this move comes across clearly in the discussion of Distinction 17–seemingly the point at which Thomas abandoned his commentary.[23]

The *Lectura romana* is lucid and succinct. There are only three objections, a two-sentence *sed contra,* and a *responsio* that is half the length of the Parisian commentary's *responsio* plus *sed contra.* Nor is this newfound directness only a matter of brevity. In the very first sentence of the *responsio,* he asserts that "here the Master was deceived"–a charge that Thomas, who rarely repeats himself, makes three times over the course of a single *responsio.*[24]

More importantly, Thomas reframes the context from which he approaches his discussion of Lombard's controversial position. Instead of beginning with the question of whether charity is uncreated, he first asks the logically prior question: "Whether a supernatural light is required in order to love God."[25] That this article has no parallel in Thomas's oeuvre is further evidence that Thomas is straining to adapt the *Sentences* material to his more systematic vision. Clearly, he is trying to impose greater order on the discussion of charity than he found in the *Sentences.* That reframing is further signaled by the *sed contra* of the second Question on the created nature of charity, which states simply that "charity falls into the same category of virtue as faith and hope. But these are created things, therefore charity also is." By recalling how charity belongs to the genus of theological virtues, Thomas underlines his wish to shift the setting of the conversation about charity *from* its tangentially occasioned source within an extended discussion of the Trinity, as it is placed in Lombard's work, *to* a more fitting venue of a discussion of the theological virtues. Clearly, this goal cannot be achieved by continuing the commentary, for there is a manifest contradiction between Lombard's presentation of the material and the logic of its intelligibility. Hence, it invites surmise that it was this issue – of finding a more systematically compelling place in which to discuss the theological virtues – that occasioned Thomas's historic break with the tradition of commenting on Lombard.

Be that as it may, the *responsio* itself reflects this more accurate positioning of the discussion and so can cut all the tangential discussion of the Trinity that cluttered the Parisian version. It also ignores the light analogy advanced by Lombard's supporters, presumably because it can be used ambiguously to support the arguments that an object's illumination by a light source is *either* the direct presence of the source (as Lombard's supporters would have it) *or* the internal possession of the effect of light in the object itself (as Thomas argued).[26] Thomas begins instead in the more direct way by noting the key distinction between act and virtue and, appropriately, by using the examples of faith and charity to illustrate this distinction. He then gives a fuller explanation than he gave in the Parisian commentary of Lombard's position, focusing on the critical section of Distinction 17 in which Lombard was pressed into a corner – chapter 6, section 8. Thomas summarizes Lombard's point here succinctly: "The difference between charity and the other virtues is that the Holy Spirit moves us to the acts of the other virtues by means of the habits of those virtues, whereas the Holy Spirit moves us to the act of charity not by means of any habits, but immediately." From this accurate summary of the heart of Lombard's argument flows a clear statement of the principle at stake: "He would have it that . . . the Holy Spirit itself in the soul took the place of a habit that would move the will" – with the result that grace would not perfect nature, but displace it.

Having summarized Lombard's position and identified the principle at stake, Thomas then advances two reasons for rejecting the position. The first begins by simply stating that "the Holy Spirit dwells in the human person through an effect [of the Spirit – and not immediately in itself]." This argument is effectively similar to the third argument in the *sed contra* of the Parisian version, discussed above. There are, however, seemingly small yet significant differences. Thomas omits the discussion of the will of the saint being united to the *suppositum* of the Holy Spirit itself. He also adds to and qualifies his positive argument. In the Parisian lectures, Thomas argued simply that this effect of the Holy Spirit, charity, must be present as a habit and not just an act; otherwise, sleeping saints would not be any different from those without grace. But in the *Lectura romana,* rather than appealing straight to the "sleeping saint" argument, Thomas explains the issue at stake: "Therefore if the Holy Spirit is not in man except according to the act of love, the Holy Spirit will not be in someone except when he is actually loving–even a man in a state of grace–but at times he is and at times he is not, it would follow [on this position] that he does not always have the Holy Spirit and grace, but at times does and at times does not."[27] Only after establishing this fundamental point does Thomas then appeal to the *reductio ad absurdum* of the sleeping saint.

The second argument for rejecting Lombard's position exhibits the same pattern of substantial agreement with the earlier Parisian text along-side significant reframing. This second argument begins "since the act of love is the noblest act . . . one ought to be disposed in the noblest way to the noblest act." This involves the Holy Spirit not only moving a person to act, but also giving him or her the capacity to act well and easily. Thomas can thus restate more succinctly the argument that was advanced in the meandering *responsio* of the Parisian text: "And therefore we say that, as in the other infused virtues, the Holy Spirit brings about two effects: he moves a man to the act and, beyond this, he gives to the agent the capacity to act well and easily." Crucially, by moving the discussion away from the contrary-to-fact Trinitarian speculation of a quasi-hypostatic union of the will with the Spirit (in which the importance of the proximate causal power of the will was only tangentially mentioned), Thomas here highlights the following critical point: the nobility of the human person as an active par-ticipant in the process of salvation.

By the end of the *responsio,* Thomas need state only once his crucial distinction between causes (which was made several times, in different ways, across many objections in the Parisian text): "And for this reason it is better to say something else [than the Master does]–that from one van-tage charity is the Holy Spirit itself by whom we love God *effectively,* and in this regard it is something uncreated because it is the Holy Spirit itself; yet from a different vantage it is something created, insofar as we *formally* love God with the very charity given to the soul." The initial blunt rejection of Lombard's position gives way to a charitable restatement of the truth that Thomas sees to lie behind Lombard's undifferentiated identification of charity with the Holy Spirit. More importantly, the cumulative effect of the developments in this streamlined Roman text is the more accurate and effective communication of his central point: that God acts toward human-ity not through occasional and arbitrary impositions of an external will, but through an abiding and fitting transformation of human interiority. God's grace does not leave a person unchanged.

4. The Disputed Question *De caritate*

The genre of the disputed question allows a thinker to probe one issue in depth. As a result, Thomas can here give a more searching examination of Lombard's position that issues in deeper analysis of the root divergences between the thinkers. Most likely written around the same time as the *Secunda Pars* of the *Summa of Theology,* this text, along with the disputed question on hope, allowed him to examine carefully the theological virtues that he was about to place at a critical point in his major systematic work.[28] A close look at the disputed question on charity supplies the context for those critical yet sometimes compressed arguments in the *Summa of Theology.*

Turning to the first article, we see that this different genre allows Thomas to return to his original ordering in the Parisian commentary and place the refutation of Lombard's argument at the very beginning of his discussion. In this more detailed exploration, there are twenty-four objections, of which seventeen Thomas is treating for the first time in this text, including four based on opinions taken from Augustine's *De trinitate.*

The *sed contra* restates the same argument that was made in the first part of the Parisian *sed contra,* namely, "whatever is received into something is received in it according to the measure of the receiver. Accordingly, if charity is received in us from God, we must receive it in a finite way, in keeping with our measure."[29] Why does Thomas return to this argument rather than the Roman *sed contra* argument that charity belongs to the genus of theological virtue? Presumably because it is a much stronger argument, whereas the statement that charity belongs to the same genus as faith and hope is more an association than an argument. So then the question shifts: Why was this stronger argument dropped in the Roman version and replaced with a weaker argument by association? I suggest that in his second *Sentences* commentary, Thomas wished to signal clearly that he was detaching his discussion of charity from its accidental occurrence within Lombard's exploration of the Trinity and instead remind his reader that charity is a theological virtue. This obvious but necessary reminder, which displaced the more persuasive argument in the *sed contra* of the previous (Parisian) text, indicates Thomas's dissatisfaction with Lombard's order of presentation. In any case, by the time of *De caritate,* Thomas can deal with charity on its own terms, and not within the constraints of the order in which he happens to find it in the text that he happens to be commenting on. As a result, the *sed contra* can give a more persuasive argument that better sets up the *responsio.*

In the *responsio,* Thomas begins as usual with a summary of Lombard's position but then offers a new and fuller account of his error. He was, Thomas suggests, swayed by "excellentia caritatis, et verba Augustini." Gone is the harsh, repeated accusation that Lombard was deceived. But the more emollient tone cannot hide the fact that in this text Aquinas comprehensively dismantles Lombard's position.

The argument of the *responsio* runs as follows. The natural inclinations and acts of a thing arise from some intrinsic source, that is, from a thing's nature. While natural things can be moved by an exterior source – for example, a stone thrown upward – such movement is clearly not natural for the thing in question. Even God cannot make a stone move upward naturally. If God did infuse the stone with some power to do so by itself, it would no longer be a stone. Its very nature would have changed.

Having established the principle of the integrity of created reality at the level of nature – specifically, regarding the need for an interior source of movement – Thomas then applies that principle to the level of volitional activity, which must likewise arise from an interior principle. Just as God cannot cause a natural thing to be moved naturally by an exterior source, so God cannot cause a person's will to desire voluntarily from an exterior source. Consequently, if a person is to desire an end exceeding his or her nature, then something must be added to that nature such that that desire for a supernatural end arises from an interior source. If this addition of an interior disposition is bypassed, as Lombard would have it, and the will is simply moved by the Holy Spirit directly as an exterior source, then either (1) the consequent act of charity will not exceed human nature, and so will not unite the person to what is above human nature, or (2) it will not be voluntary – which is impossible, because to love something is precisely to want it from an interior source and not have it imposed by an exterior force. Thus, if a human act does not arise from its own form but instead comes from an exterior agent, then the person will be a mere instrument used by God, like an axe wielded by a worker. Furthermore, such a coerced act cannot be meritorious, because only acts that are chosen deserve merit. If acts of love are externally imposed and not internally chosen, then "human merit is entirely eradicated, since love is the root of meriting."[30]

Whereas the Parisian text mentioned merit incidentally in one sentence, here Thomas deals with it centrally and draws out the deleterious consequences of Lombard's position.

Only after these fundamental arguments are made concerning the integrity of the created order – especially the human will – does Thomas advance the secondary argument from fittingness that came first in the Roman commentary. In addition to this change in order that more appropriately reflects the relative importance of the arguments, subtle shifts are made even within the argument. Thomas drops the "sleeping saint" point completely and simply states more clearly the principle that lies behind that *reductio ad absurdum:* that virtuous acts must arise from an interior disposition if they are to have the hallmark of true virtue, that is, be performed readily and with pleasure. Further, Thomas adds that the habit of charity not only allows the act of charity to happen very readily and with great pleasure; it makes all that we do or undergo pleasurable. By this additional argument, Thomas underscores the nature of charity as something that extends comprehensively across all human action, a point he spells out in more detail when he describes charity as the form of the virtues.

Finally, Thomas returns to the parallel between charity and creation as both existing through created forms. The Holy Spirit moves "the soul to the act of love just as God moves all things to their own acts to which they are inclined from their proper form." From this parallel, Thomas concludes the *responsio:* "That is how God arranges all things sweetly, because he gives all things the forms and powers that incline them to what he moves them to, so that they tend to it without compulsion, but of their own accord."[31]

In this conclusion, there is an association between how charity makes all human life pleasurable and how God makes all created life orderly – no shortchanging of the excellence of charity here. The parallel between creation and charity as both involving form, which was primarily treated in objections in the Parisian and Roman texts, here is greatly expanded and stands as the culminating argument of the *responsio.* This nobility accorded to the created form or habit of charity is further supported in Thomas's reply to two objections, which significantly add to his earlier texts. *De caritate*'s objections 2 and 14 argue that the more powerful an agent, the less the need for a tendency in the thing acted upon (objection 2) or an intermediary (objection 14). In earlier texts, Thomas countered this objection by arguing that it was not a matter of God's lack of power, but rather of a need within the soul (Parisian text, response to objection 1). In *De caritate,* however, God's use of a created tendency or intermediary is not a concession to the neediness of the soul, but rather a manifestation of the power of God. Why? Because it is a greater sign of power to create a tendency and bestow a form than just create sporadic acts without giving a more settled, interior disposition to the thing acted upon. As Yves Congar puts it, Thomas certainly affirms an "'Allwirksamkeit Gottes,' but he rejects an '*Allein*wirksamkeit Gottes.' Otherwise, what would it mean to love God with all one's heart, with all one's spirit, with all one's strength?"[32]

De caritate constitutes a significant advance from the earlier commentaries that were bound to Lombard's *Sentences*. Its powerful argument in the *responsio* is more or less repeated in the *Summa*. But, as we will see shortly, important shifts and refinements still occur in that last text. The most important of these changes concerns the interpretation of Augustine and so we must first consider *De caritate*'s set of objections that deal with various passages from *De trinitate,* for, as Thomas observed at the outset, Lombard was led astray by *verba Augustini.*

Thomas presents four objections that draw on passages from Augustine. Here, for the first time, Thomas deals with the full force of Augustine's argument that pushed Lombard to his radical position. Surprisingly, Thomas did not consider any of these passages before in his treatment of this topic, even though the arguments they forward were decisive for Lombard. The first of these objections (objection 4) quotes Book 8 of *De trinitate:* "If people love their neighbor, it follows that they love this love itself. But God is love, and so it follows that they love God especially." To which Thomas's objection adds, "Therefore, charity is not something created, but is God himself."[33] The next three objections rebut the rejoinder that "God is the love by which we love our neighbor by being love's cause" by arguing that God is love essentially, not just causally. Thomas's reply to the fourth objection argues: "It is true that the love by which we love our neighbor is God, but this does not rule out that over and above this uncreated love we also have a created love by which, as a formal principle, we love."[34] While true, such a reply is weak insofar as it does not account for how we can properly talk about the simultaneous presence of uncreated and created charity in the same subject, nor why any created charity is needed if God in Godself is with us. The response to objection 7 brings more clarity to this confused situation. It makes the argument (directly about the act of charity but applicable to the habit also) that "in perceiving the act of loving in ourselves, we are observing in ourselves a participation in God, since God is love."[35] *Mutatis mutandis,* one can argue that in inferring that a person possesses the habit of charity (from the presence of the act), that person is aware of an abiding participation in God; but this is because God is love, not because God is the actual habit of charity in the person.

In this set of objections, which respond to Augustine for the first time, Thomas is struggling to engage Augustine's arguments without succumbing to Lombard's conclusion. By the final objection of this set (objection 7), he seems to have struck on an appropriate response that identifies the source of the misunderstanding in the nature of participation language. In the *Summa,* this problem is addressed head on in the very first objection and more satisfactorily resolved.

5. Charity in the *Summa of Theology*

The first objection in the *Summa*'s question "Whether charity is something created in the soul" (2a2ae 23.2 arg 1) refers to the same passage from Augustine's *De trinitate* (8.5.10) that was quoted in the first of *De caritate*'s four objections dealing with Augustine (objection 4, quoted above). To that argument that God is love, it adds the argument from *De caritate*'s objection 6 that God is so essentially, not just causally. Into this single objection of the *Summa,* Thomas compresses what was strewn across four objections in *De caritate.* In his reply, he jettisons the inconclusive suggestion that the presence of uncreated charity need not exclude the possession of a created habit. Instead, he expands on the central insight of the argument he introduced at the end of his set of four replies dealing with Augustine in *De caritate,* namely, that our love is a certain participation in God and not God itself. Thomas develops this argument by drawing parallels between, on one hand, our love and, on the other, our wisdom and goodness. The argument runs as follows. God's essence is as much wisdom and goodness as it is love. But we have no problem saying that the wisdom and goodness by which we are formally wise and good (that is, which constitute us as wise and good) share in God's wisdom and goodness, without drawing the radical conclusion that the wisdom that is in us has merged with God's uncreated wisdom, or that our created goodness is identical with God's uncreated goodness. Similarly, therefore, the love by which we formally love our neighbor and God is our participation in divine love, not something identical with God in Godself that displaces our humanly possessed love.

Having made this argument, Thomas can then identify the source of the confusion: "This mode of speaking is customary among Platonists, in whose teachings Augustine was trained. By not paying attention to this, some have been led through his words to an occasion of error" (23.2 ad 1). Perhaps this explains why Thomas did not use the compelling argument from participation in the *sed contra,* as he had done in the Parisian commentary and *De caritate,* but instead cited Augustine's own definition of charity: "the motion of the mind toward enjoying God for God's own sake (*On Christian Doctrine* 3.10). By this move, Thomas shrewdly draws the solution to the problem from the same place as its cause–*verba Augustini*–thereby showing that Augustine's words at their most relevant point for this discussion–that is, in their very definition of charity–support his interpretation, not Lombard's (since what is in motion cannot be divine). In any case, by dealing with Augustine in the first objection, Thomas flags early on the source of the problem in misleading interpretations of an authoritative figure; and, in the *sed contra,* he leaves no room for ambiguity in how Augustine should be interpreted when it comes to understanding charity.[36]

In the second objection, we see the final significant change from earlier texts. This objection, which we have seen before in the Parisian commentary (objection 2) and *De caritate* (objection 1), draws an analogy of proportion between <God : soul :: soul : body> to argue for the unmediated presence of God in charity. In his earlier replies to this objection, Thomas denied that God is the form of the soul and argued instead for another relationship of God to soul–that of origin or source. Before we come to the *Summa*'s reply in the question on charity, we must first note that Thomas deals with the very same objection in the questions on grace from the 1a2ae. As he considers "whether grace is anything in the soul," Thomas provides in more detail his reasoning for the position he takes: "God is the life of the soul through the mode of an efficient cause, but the soul is the life of the body through the mode of a formal cause. But there is not any medium between form and matter, because the form through itself informs the matter or the subject. But an agent informs the subject not through its own substance, but through the form that it causes in the matter" (1a2ae 110.1 ad 2).

Thomas has thus tightened the terminology of God's causal relation to the soul from exemplary cause (in the Parisian text) or moving principle (in *De caritate*) to efficient cause. More significantly, he gives an explanation instead of the convoluted and ambiguous image of light. Form is the very organization or structure of matter itself. As a result, there can be no intermediary between a thing's form and its matter. Indeed, "form reaches to the innermost recesses of that which it informs and *vice versa.*"[37] By contrast, an efficient cause of a thing–that is, the agent that is responsible in part or whole for the existence of the thing–informs or shapes or structures the thing not through its (the agent's) own substance directly (as form does), but by acting upon and even bringing about the very form of the thing. To put it loosely, formal cause refers to the *arrangement in* matter, efficient cause refers to the *arranging of* matter. Hence, an efficient cause requires an intermediary – the form – by which it arranges or forms the matter. Thus, in this question on grace in the 1a2ae, Thomas has given a more precise and philosophically rigorous explanation for his position.

Turning to the question on charity in the 2a2ae, the very same objection arises but is met with a reply that brings a significant theological development. The reply runs as follows: "In terms of efficient cause (*effective*), God is the life of both the soul through charity and the body through the soul; but in terms of formal cause (*formaliter*) charity is the life of the soul, as also the soul is the life of the body. Therefore it can be concluded from this that just as the soul is immediately united to the body, so charity is immediately united to the soul" (23.2 ad 2). Note that Thomas here states at the outset that God is the efficient cause of the life of *both* the soul (through charity) and the body (through the soul). By thus reframing the debate with a reminder of the universality of divine efficient causality, Thomas can underscore the role of formal causality, for such a universally efficient Source does not have to intervene sporadically and directly to cause a person to love, but instead can mediate love through an abiding form that befits the recipient. Specifically, Thomas can now affirm that charity is formally the life of the soul in the way that the soul is the life of the body, thereby altering one of the terms in the analogy of proportion from which the objection arose, such that it now stands as <charity : soul :: soul : body>. From this reconceived analogy, Thomas can extend his argument beyond the negative conclusion – that God is not the vivifying form of the soul and so charity is not uncreated – and add a decisive positive conclusion – that charity, the gift and effect of God's love in us, is as intimately united to the soul as the soul is to the body. This is a significant development in Thomas's discussion of this topic. The infusion of God's love into a person is not only something that is humanly possessed in a way that fully accords with the integrity of created human nature, as Thomas has all along argued against Lombard's position, but it is also something that is profoundly, extensively, and immediately present to the soul in a proportionally similar way to how the soul is present to the body.[38] This love, the effect of the Holy Spirit in the believer, has an intimately ordering influence that is coextensive with the totality of what makes a person a living being capable of rational freedom.[39] It is therefore unpersuasive to argue that Thomas's position represents a move away from Lombard's more spiritual theology by "decoupling . . . the cardinal virtues from the theological virtues" and creating "a space for a philosophical ethics in which moral judgments can be made outside the spiritual realm."[40] To the contrary, Thomas provides a more than adequate safeguard to the principle at stake that was so important for Lombard – the intimate presence of the Spirit in a person – for charity is the most noble effect of the gift of the Spirit, and it is as closely bound to the soul as the soul is to the body.

Freed from the constraints of commenting on the *Sentences,* and supplied with the thorough analysis of Thomas's contemporaneous disputed questions, the *Summa* can embed a detailed discussion of the theological virtues at the heart of its tripartite structure, between the *Prima Pars* on God and creation and the *Tertia Pars* on Christ, sacraments, and eschatology. Within the *Secunda Pars,* which treats a person's return to God through the exercise of rational freedom, the theological virtues stand as the bridge between the 1a2ae's general considerations of human action, which culminate in two external principles – instruction through God's law and help through divine grace – and the 2a2ae's specific considerations of human acts insofar as they arise through the intrinsic principles of virtue transformed by that divine grace. Placed at the start of the 2a2ae, the treatment of the theological virtues, culminating with charity, describes in detail the spiritual transformation of human agency that is the Christian context for understanding and practicing the cardinal virtues.

6. Concluding Reflections

Tracing the evolution of Thomas's refutation of Lombard sheds light on a key question in the *Summa*. It allows us to see a thinker coming to grips with an important theological disagreement with ever-greater insight and precision; grappling to find the appropriate venue in which to give the best systematic expression of a major theological idea; removing all needless criticism of an interlocutor's faults and focusing instead on the understandable sources of confusion; and identifying and saving the principle at stake that the interlocutor wished to defend.

If, for Lombard, the principle at stake was the intimate presence of the Holy Spirit, for Thomas, it was safeguarding divine transcendence[41] and, increasingly as his thought matured, affirming at the same time the integrity and nobility of created acts, especially the freedom of the human will. In fact, this study shows a key example of Thomas's growing realization that these two claims are different sides of the same coin, for the more one preserves the radical distinction between Creator and creation, the more one creates space, as it were, for created causality. Remove created causality from the divine-human relationship at its highest point, and human participation in divine love becomes unintelligible.

No doubt, both Lombard and Thomas share the same goal of affirming God's intimate presence in charity. But whereas Lombard sought to achieve that goal by displacing a humanly possessed habit with the immediate presence of the Spirit, Thomas sought instead to affirm the virtue of charity as the most intimate and indeed empowering effect of the Spirit. At the heart of this disagreement lie differing approaches to the elusive task of trying to articulate the relationship between infinite and finite through the use of participation language. Since the very notion of participation inevitably entails systematic imprecision (as the perennial conflict of interpretation over *verba Augustini* shows), it is no surprise that Thomas came to see the need for firmer control of this aspect of the discourse.

But more than that, by the time of the *Summa,* he reconfigured the very order of his presentation to emphasize a person's active role in charity. No longer does the refutation of Lombard's bold move come first, as it had done in all but one of Thomas's treatments of charity up to this point. Instead, Thomas now begins with his far bolder and startlingly original move: the description of charity in terms of friendship. While the exploration of this position would require a separate essay, it is worth concluding that here, in his greatest and most systematic work, Thomas opened his treatment of charity with the highest human experience – friendship – and (revised in the light of Christian revelation) employed it to describe humanity's most significant relationship with God.[42] Rather than beginning with a theological disagreement, Thomas began with his consistently held view that the most noble human experience between people serves as the basis for conceiving the highest human relation to the divine. By initiating his discussion of charity in terms of friendship, Thomas at once affirmed Lombard's principle of the intimate presence of God – for what is closer to a person than his or her friends? – and encompassed that affirmation within his profound appreciation for the dignity of human nature as something truly able to share in divine life.[43]

NOTES

1. Aage Rydstrøm-Poulsen, *The Gracious God: "Gratia" in Augustine and the Twelfth Century* (Copenhagen: Akademisk, 2002), 470. (See pp. 390–476 for a discussion of the varied reception of this minority claim in subsequent medieval theology.)

2. Peter Lombard, *The Sentences, Book 1: The Mystery of the Trinity,* trans. Giulio Silano (Toronto: Pontifical Institute of Medieval Studies, 2007), d. 10, chap. 1.2 (58).

3. Romans 5:5 states that "the charity of God is poured forth into our hearts by the Holy Spirit, who is given to us," and 1 John 4:13 affirms that the giving of the Spirit brings the believer into God's intimate presence: "By this we know that we abide in him and he in us, because he has given us of his Spirit."

4. Lombard, *Sentences 1* d. 17, chap. 3.

5. See Lombard, *Sentences 1* d. 14, chap. 2 for this identification of Giver and gift (trans. Silano 74–75).

6. Lombard, *Sentences 1* d. 17, chap. 3. For an alternative (and often criticized) interpretation of Lombard's position, which is animated by the wish to defend him against the charge of "pantheistic substitution of divine virtue for human capacity," see Marcia Colish, *Peter Lombard,* vol. 1 (New York: Brill, 1994), 260–63, at 263. Note the absence in Colish of a discussion of the crucial section in Lombard, *Sentences 1* d. 17, chap. 6.8.

7. Lombard, *Sentences 1* d. 17, chap. 4.3 (trans. Silano 92).

8. Quoted by Lombard, *Sentences 1* d. 17, chap. 6.6 (trans. Silano 96). The quotation comes from Augustine, *De doctrina christiana* 3.10.

9. Although Lombard does not say so explicitly, he seems to be drawing on Galatians 5:6, "faith working through love."

10. Lombard, *Sentences 1* d. 17, chap. 1.2 (trans. Silano 88).

11. Lombard, *Sentences 1* d. 17, chap. 3, quoting from Augustine, *De trinitate,* bk. 8, chap. 7.10 (trans. Silano 89).

12. Albertus Magnus, *Commentarii in I Sententiarum,* d. 17, A, a. 1, in *Opera Omnia,* vol. 25, ed. A. Borgnet (Paris: Vives, 1893), 461–66. Bonaventure, *Commentaria in quator libros Sententiarum Magistri Petri Lombardi,* I, d. 17, a. 1, q. 1, in *Opera Omnia,* vol. 1 (Quaracchi , 1882), 292–94. For a study of these three authors, see A. Stevaux, "La doctrine de la charité dans les commentaires des Sentences de Sainte Albert, de Sainte Bonaventure et de Sainte Thomas," *Ephemerides Theologicae Lovanienses* 24 (1948): 59–97.

13. For Thomas, the issue is not the indwelling of the Spirit, which he affirms, but the displacement of a created habit, which he denies. On the affirmation of the presence of the Spirit, see Thomas Aquinas, *Scriptum super libros Sententiarum Magistri Petri Lombardi,* I (hereafter *In I Sent.*), d. 17, q. 1, *expositio textus:* "along with the gift of charity, the Holy Spirit himself is also given, inasmuch as he is said to dwell in the creature in a new way by a new likeness of himself being in it." Unless stated otherwise, all translations of this text are from St. Thomas Aquinas, *On Love and Charity: Readings from the "Commentary on the Sentences of Peter Lombard,"* trans. Peter

Kwasniewski, Thomas Bolin, and Joseph Bolin (Washington, DC: Catholic University of America Press, 2008), 29; compare *Summa of Theology* (hereafter *ST*) 1a 43.3 ad 1.

14. As I advance this argument of a positive development in Thomas's position, it will become clear why I do not share Franz Zigon's premise that the (first) *Sentences* commentary "provides the basis for the whole investigation" of the subsequent texts. "Der Begriff der Caritas beim Lombarden, und der hl. Thomas," *Divus Thomas* 4 (1926): 404–24, at 411–12. For a refutation of Zigon's position, see Johann Stufler, "Petrus Lombardus und Thomas von Aquin über die Natur der caritas," *Zeitschrift für katholische Theologie* 51 (1927): 399–408, esp. 402.

15. As Thomas notes later on, without this claim it is unintelligible to talk about a person's growth in charity. *In I Sent.* d. 17, q. 2, a. 1, ad 1.

16. An exemplary cause refers to that form or pattern in the agent that is imitated by the effect.

17. For a discussion of the *quidam* to whom Thomas is responding, see Geertjan Zuijdwegt, "'Utrum caritas sit aliquid creatum in anima': Aquinas on the Lombard's Identification of Charity with the Holy Spirit," *Recherches de Théologie et Philosophie médiévales* 79.1 (2012): 39–74, esp. 46–59.

18. *In I Sent.* d. 17, q. 1, a. 1 corp (trans. Kwasniewski, *On Love and Charity* 12).

19. For a precursor of this appeal to the Aristotelian distinction between formal and efficient causality, see the discussion of Simon of Tournai in Rydstrøm-Poulsen, *Gracious God*, 435–49, and the position of an anonymous early scholastic *Sentences* commentator quoted in Artur Landgraf, *Dogmengeschichte der Frühscholastik*, vol. I/1 (Regensburg: Pustet, 1952), 228, and the later and better known position of Philip the Chancellor (ibid., 236). Langraf also quotes Simon of Tournai's use of the wall/painter imagery (ibid., 232).

20. *In I Sent.* d. 18 *expositio textus* (trans. Kwasniewski, *On Love and Charity,* webnote 34, http://cuapress.cua.edu/res/docs/thomasaquinas-suppmaterials. pdf). Note the addition in the translation (the final square brackets) that seeks to communicate Thomas's point more explicitly than Thomas himself affirms.

21. On the authenticity of this work, see Thomas Aquinas, *Lectura romana in primum Sententiarum Petri Lombardi,* ed. Leonard Boyle and John Boyle (Toronto: Pontifical Institute of Medieval Studies, 2006), which includes John Boyle's "Introduction," 1–69.

22. *ST* 1a pr (translations from the *ST* are my own). It seems that Thomas abandoned his *divisio textus* and *expositio textus* in this second commentary, which "may indicate that Thomas is less interested in commenting on the

Liber sententiarum itself and more interested in addressing the theological substance of the book" (Boyle, "Introduction," 11).

23. Strangely, Thomas did comment on one further distinction, no. 23, skipping over the intervening distinctions. John Boyle suggests that "most likely, Thomas taught these articles but without change" (Boyle, "Introduction," 6). Why? "Perhaps, as Thomas neared the end of the year . . . like many teachers, he found himself pressed for time. He now moves selectively in the final stretch, selecting distinctions and topics, repeating his own Parisian *Scriptum* verbatim" (ibid.). Against this position, it is worth noting M. Michèle Mulchahey's reconstruction of Thomas's teaching in Rome, in *"First the Bow Is Bent in Study . . ." Dominican Education Before 1350* (Toronto: Pontifical Institute of Medieval Studies, 1998), 303, which conjectures that the first year's *lectio prima* was *I Sententiarum* (ca. 57,000 words) compared with the third year's *lectio prima* on *ST,* 1a, qq. 75–119 (ca. 153,000 words). Thus, if Boyle is correct, Thomas would have lectured during the first year on just over a third of the amount of material that he lectured on during the third year, but still ran out of time in the first year's lectures. Assuming Mulchahey's reconstruction is reliable, this explanation seems unlikely. And so we are back to the strange coincidence that invites surmise: Thomas more or less abandons his *Sentences'* commentary at the very place not only of sharp disagreement with Lombard's explicit argument (which could be addressed through more commentary), but also of a deeper frustration with the more serious and systemic questions concerning structure (which can be addressed only by a comprehensive reordering of the material).

24. The directness may also be a function of this text's status as (most likely) a student's *reportatio*.

25. His answer affirmatively, "love follows knowledge, since nothing is loved unless it is known," and this prior knowledge is given through faith. Thomas Aquinas, *Lectura Romana* d. 17, q. 1 corp, and on faith, ad 3 (trans. Kwasniewski, *On Love and Charity* 59–60).

26. One could argue that this streamlining of the second *Sentences* commentary stems also from the fact that Thomas no longer deals with the arguments of Lombard's supporters since they were no longer widely held (see Zuijdwegt, *"Utrum caritas,"* 58). If it seems coincidental that the light analogy and the Trinitarian discussions were both subject to the same fate of a decline in popularity at the same time, this could well be because they were both tentative speculations of Richard Fishacre that were successfully refuted in Thomas's detailed criticism in his first commentary (as suggested by Zuijdwegt in email correspondence). This historical-contextual argument does not conflict (and in fact harmonizes) with the systematic point – that Thomas judged these

arguments of Lombard's supporters to be irrelevant to a direct engagement with the substance of Lombard's position. We are thus seeing the progress of an argument over time and can locate that development within the trajectory of a maturing author laying aside tangential material to focus on the truly relevant and compelling points demanding treatment.

27. Aquinas, *Lectura Romana* d. 17, q. 1, a. 2 corp (trans. Kwasniewski, *On Love and Charity* 62).

28. Thomas had already treated faith in detail in one of his earliest theological works, the Commentary on the *De trinitate* of Boethius and in his later *Compendium*. Also, it is worth noting that Thomas made an important breakthrough in his treatment of hope through an analogous appeal to differentiated causality, specifically, by affirming that hope is a theological virtue not only because it tends toward God as final cause (the Goal), but also because it relies upon God as efficient cause (the Helper). See Dominic Doyle, *The Promise of Christian Humanism: Thomas Aquinas on Hope* (New York: Crossroad, 2010), 85, including note 458. Thus, whereas in his treatment of charity, Thomas distinguished efficient cause and formal cause (and emphasized formal cause) in order to preserve charity as a theological *virtue* (that is, as an excellence belonging to the person), in his treatment of hope, Thomas distinguished final cause and efficient cause (and emphasized efficient cause) in order to preserve hope as a *theological* virtue (that is, as a gift given by God). This comparison is a good example of his flexible deployment of Aristotelian terms for theological ends.

29. *De caritate* a. 1 sc; Thomas Aquinas, *Disputed Questions on Virtue,* trans. Jeffrey Hause and Claudia Murphy (Indianapolis, IN: Hackett, 2010), 99–100.

30. *De caritate* a. 1 corp; *Disputed Questions* 101.

31. *De caritate* a. 1 corp; *Disputed Questions* 101–2.

32. Yves Congar, "Aimer Dieu et les hommes par l'amour dont Dieu aime?," *Revue des Études augustiniennes* 28 (1982), 97.

33. *De caritate* a. 1 arg 4; *Disputed Questions* 96.

34. *De caritate* a. 1 ad 4; *Disputed Questions* 102.

35. *De caritate* a. 1 ad 7; *Disputed Questions* 102–3.

36. Lombard's selective use of Augustine is noted by Congar, "Aimer Dieu?" at 91–93.

37. *In I Sent.* d. 27, q. 1, a. 1 ad 4 (trans. Kwasniewski, *On Love and Charity* 124).

38. Earlier, Thomas suggested that while God is the efficient cause of charity, a person "in some sense stands in relation to charity as a material cause receiving it." *In I Sent.* d. 17, q. 2, a. 1 ad 4 (trans. Kwasniewski, *On Love and Charity* 37). A little later, Thomas expresses the same point as follows: "The

active cause of charity is God, while the receptive cause is the rational creature." *Lectura Romana* d. 17, q. 2, a. 4 corp (trans. Kwasniewski, *On Love and Charity* 76). Shortly before the passage in the *ST* under consideration here, Thomas argued more directly that "natura comparatur ad caritatem . . . sicut materia ad formam" (2a2ae 2.9). What is new in the *ST* passages under consideration here is that Thomas brings this analogy involving form/matter (and more specifically, soul/body) to bear upon the discussion of created charity.

39. While Thomas all along argued that charity is the form of the virtues, he came to interpret that claim less along the lines of *forma exemplaris* and more as *causa efficiens formae,* as argued by Michael Sherwin, *By Knowledge and by Love: Charity and Knowledge in the Moral Theology of St. Thomas Aquinas* (Washington, DC: Catholic University Press of America, 2005), 192–201. Thus, the claim that charity is the form of the virtues does not coincide with the analogy Thomas introduces here between charity's relationship to the soul and the soul's relationship to the body. Also, it is important to stress that Thomas is using an analogy of proportion. He is not claiming that charity is the form of the soul, but that something of its intimate presence to the soul can be evoked by a consideration of the soul's immediate and extensive presence to the body.

40. Philipp Rosemann, *"Fraterna dilectio est Deus:* Peter Lombard's Thesis on Charity as the Holy Spirit," in *Amor amicitiae: On the Love That Is Friendship,* ed. Thomas Kelly and Philipp Rosemann (Leuven: Peeters, 2004), 435.

41. "Howsoever much one approaches to the likeness of God, one always stands infinitely apart from him." *In I Sent.* d. 17, q. 2, a. 4 sc (trans. Kwasniewski, *On Love and Charity* 48).

42. For the historical factors accounting for why Lombard did not use the notion of friendship to describe charity, see G. G. Meersseman, "Pourquoi le Lombard n'a-t-il pas conçu la charité comme amitié?," in *Miscellanea Lombardiana* (Novara: Istituto Geografico de Agostini, 1957), 165–74, esp. 168. Systematic reasons for why Thomas's position entails the rejection of Lombard's position would need to include the consideration that friendship involves a stable relationship with a "second self," not the sporadic operation of God's self that displaces the highest virtue of the human self.

43. I am grateful to Joseph Bolin, John Boyle, Daria Spezzano, and Geertjan Zuijdwegt for their insightful comments on an earlier draft of this essay.

Righteousness and Divine Love

Maimonides and Thomas on Charity

JEFFREY A. BERNSTEIN

What is it we do when we give to the poor or needy? What do we understand ourselves to accomplish when we perform a charitable act, such as making a monetary donation? In such an act, are we supposed to give up to or beyond our means? Does the performance of this act come naturally to us or by an external impetus? If the latter, does the impetus to perform this act have the character of a duty, obligation, or law? And whom does the charitable act most benefit – the giver or the receiver? The individual or the community? Finally, does the concept of charity most properly refer to a deed, a virtue, or a condition? When we inquire into what "charity" means, these are some of the questions we find lying in wait.

Given pervasive concerns over social and economic inequalities, the obvious starting point for such an inquiry is, perhaps, to hold that charity is first and foremost a good act that benefits primarily the impoverished recipient. This construal is so obvious, finding support in both Jewish and Christian religious traditions, that one can easily assume its presence, value, and status in Judaism and Christianity to be identical.[1] In a world saturated with gross inequalities, this construal may have a distinct practical value. But while both traditions do emphasize the charitable deed, it would be a mistake to view this similarity as the final word on the matter. In fact, the charitable deed gains a specific conceptual significance when viewed against the backdrop of the different religious and philosophical contexts pertaining to Judaism and Christianity. In order to better understand the concept of charity that underlies the charitable deed – and where we ourselves may stand in relation to such a deed – it is helpful to present the Jewish and Christian understandings of charity in the manner of a dialogue between the two traditions. In proceeding thus, we begin to understand the resources that each tradition brings to our own (self-)understanding of the above questions.

One exemplary place to begin this general dialogue is with the particular dialogue between the twelfth-century Jewish Andalusian philosopher and rabbi Moses ben Maimon (Maimonides) and the thirteenth-century Christian theologian and philosopher Thomas Aquinas. Both thinkers lay the fundamental philosophical and theological (or, in Maimonides's case, jurisprudential) groundwork for their respective religions. Moreover, Thomas examines and responds to Maimonides's positions in his own work. A sense of great respect that Thomas had for Maimonides can be gleaned from his assessment of Maimonides's view that the heavenly spheres exhibit intelligence and possess intellective soul: "This view has no value even though Rabbi Moses proposes it."[2] While Thomas's engagement with Maimonides focuses largely on metaphysics and natural philosophy, the extension to jurisprudential/theological issues is not a stretch.[3] This is particularly true because Thomas views theology as a completion of – but not a break with – the philosophical endeavor.[4] To anticipate the ensuing discussion, we can say this much at the outset: Maimonides understands charity (*tzedakah*) as the virtue of righteousness, the capacity for which belongs (in principle) to all human beings naturally, whereas Thomas understands charity (*caritas*) as an infused virtue that completes and perfects the manifold natural virtues by means of a gratuitous divine dispensation. By proceeding through discussions of (1) the terminological contours of tzedakah and caritas, and (2) the religious contours of Maimonides's and Thomas's differing conceptions into (3) a deeper philosophical examination of their respective views (particularly their differing relations to the thought of Aristotle), we can begin to understand their strengths, limitations, and possible interactions. This, in turn, gives us a greater capacity for understanding the charitable act itself.

1. Tzedakah and Caritas

A great deal can be gleaned simply from a consideration of the Hebrew and Latin terms of which "charity" serves as the conventional translation. I would argue, in fact, that the entire religious constellations of Judaism and Christianity (dealt with in the next section) are announced in the terms "tzedakah" and "caritas." Before proceeding directly to the texts of Maimonides and Thomas, therefore, I provide a brief discussion of the two terms.

Tzedakah, the feminine form of *tzedek* ("justice"), derives from the root *tz-d-k* that refers (in the Hebrew Bible) to a quality or capacity extending from God, by means of which all individuals (rulers and/or subjects) and communities are able to perform good actions.[5] As a quality or capacity, tz-d-k is a potency that requires actualization as a deed; it is not simply the deed itself. As an extension from God to anyone willing or able to actualize it, tz-d-k is a quality or capacity originating from something like a natural process of divine emanation, to speak in the terms of medieval Neoplatonism.[6] Applicable to both the individual and communal levels, tz-d-k is as much a political quality or capacity as it is a conventionally religious one (that is, one involving one's personal relationship to God). It is this natural and political root quality that forms the linguistic basis for the dual relationship of tzedek and tzedakah. That tzedakah is simply a modified form of the Hebrew word for justice is fully in keeping with the natural and political character of the root word tz-d-k; for no one denies that justice – in either its punitive or its reparative sense – is anything other than natural and political (irrespective of whether it originates in the divine). Given its derivation from tz-d-k and its kinship with tzedek, therefore, we can see that tzedakah also carries these senses. Joseph Telshukin makes this point, laying particular emphasis on the political sense: "*tzedakah* derives from the word *tzedek,* which means 'justice' . . . Judaism regards someone who gives *tzedakah* as acting justly, and one who does not as acting unjustly."[7]

Insofar as a deed of tzedakah is brought to completion or made actual, it enters the realm of eternity. As Telshukin puts it: "When we give money to charity . . . we retain permanent possession of the good deed we performed; no one can ever take this from us. Therefore, paradoxically, the only money we possess forever is the money we give away."[8] In referring to tzedakah within the context of giving and retaining money, Telshukin brings to light another aspect of Jewish "charity" in its relation to justice: it operates (like justice) within a paradigm of relationality and exchange. We perform acts of tzedakah because they help people; through the act of helping people, we ourselves are helped. The relational context of these acts reminds one of Aristotle's view that "the friend is another self,"[9] a view that finds similarly broad resonance in the Talmud as well. This explains why the biblical sources refuse to simply limit deeds of tzedakah to the poor. Leviticus 19:9–10 implores the Israelites to leave harvest (fallen to the ground) for the poor and the wanderers. Similarly, Deuteronomy 26:12 commands the Israelites to give 10 percent of their annual produce, every three years, to the wanderer, the sojourner, the orphan, and the widow. Poverty, widowhood, losing family are conditions that can befall anyone. We help the needs of others because we might also (at some point) be the others in need of help.

In its relational aspect, tzedakah is "not only measured by concrete efficacious action. It also involves the subjective response of sympathy—listening and sharing in the pain of the person in need," as David Hartman and Tzvi Marx put it.[10] This, again, involves not only individual acts but also their relation to and effect upon the community. Nowhere perhaps is this communal dimension clearer than in the otherwise paradoxical decision (in Tractate *Peah* 8:9 of the Jerusalem Talmud) concerning the quandary over what to do with money found on a person recently deceased. The answer provided is that in such a situation, one must act charitably even concerning deceitful persons; were it not for such persons, hesitancy over giving tzedakah (when asked for it) would be a punishment. Put differently, even deceivers help people make the kinds of distinctions necessary for the sustainment of communities. The deed of tzedakah, then, is bound up with the capacity to know both (1) when to give and not to give (for example, to the genuinely poor and to deceivers) and (2) that such decisions are bound up with always changing circumstances. This prudential reasoning is an aspect of the virtue of tzedakah—a virtue that is naturally available for acquisition. So while tzedakah refers first and foremost to deeds, these deeds become *understandable* in a Jewish context insofar as they exhibit the virtue of tzedakah. This means that, while tzedakah is (especially for Maimonides) the most important virtue, its importance is different in *degree*—not in *kind*—from the other virtues.[11]

Since my aim is to distinguish between the Jewish and Christian conceptions of charity, it might be helpful to seek a felicitous translation of "tzedakah." Joshua Haberman bids us to look back to the connotations that were absorbed, over time, by the word "tzedek" (justice): (1) fidelity to the covenant, (2) truth, (3) possessing of integrity, and (4) wholeness (being without blemish). For Haberman, the adequate translation of tzedek in the collective light of its connotations is "righteousness": "Righteousness, as illustrated in biblical and rabbinic usage, is morality in its totality of the moral ideal in all spheres—private, social, and religious."[12] As one might expect, given the just character of charitable deeds in Judaism, "righteousness" is also perfectly able to render tzedakah. (One finds this translation, for example, in Robert Alter's magisterial ongoing translation of the Hebrew Bible, as well as in the more standard translation by the Jewish Publication Society.)[13] But how are we to understand "righteousness" in this context? It may help to remind readers of Hillel's statement, in the Mishnaic Tractate *Avot* 2:5 (here paraphrased) in which the relational and just character of good works is raised to the level of an ethical imperative: in a world devoid of humans, strive to be human. In performing acts of righteousness, we do not bestow something gratuitous upon the poor and the needy. Rather, we raise them up; in being so raised, the poor and the needy are brought to our level. In being brought to our level, an injustice is *made right*. Righteous acts are important because they help to make the world right. Charity, understood as righteousness, is fundamentally reparative.

"Caritas" is the Latin Vulgate translation of the Greek term *agapē*–that is, love of God. Considerations of the term, therefore, can very well begin with 1 John 4:16–17: "God is charity, and whoever abides in charity abides in God and God in him. In this the charity of God is brought to perfection among us." Insofar as one can remain in love, love contains a continuous temporal dimension. It is something other than a momentary act; it is a state or condition. Thus, charity (in a Christian context) is just this condition of love. And insofar as this condition is the human instantiation of a divine exemplar–that is, Christian love is (however imperfectly) the same love that God has for creation–it is a properly religious condition. In his first papal encyclical, *Deus caritas est,* Pope Benedict XVI elaborates on this conception of love in 1 John: "Being Christian is not the result of an ethical choice or a lofty idea, but the encounter with an event, a person, which gives life a new horizon and a decisive direction . . . [God's love] is the love which God lavishes upon us and which we in turn must share with others . . . [it is] the love which God mysteriously and gratuitously offers to man."[14] Insofar as caritas is neither an idea nor a decision, but rather an encounter with God (through the personage of Jesus Christ), it falls outside the realm of natural capacity and/or experience. It is, in some sense, the product of a special revelation.[15] And insofar as this offering is gratuitous, it is in no sense deserved. In this respect, caritas operates on a different (and higher) level than justice and reciprocity do.

Have I drawn too stark a contrast between natural capacity and the grace provided through faith?[16] Surely caritas (and its central place in Catholic social doctrine) has some relation to the natural order, else it would risk a lapse into Gnosticism. Benedict XVI elaborates: "Faith enables reason to do its work more effectively and to see its proper object more clearly . . . [the aim of Catholic social doctrine, therefore] is simply to help purify reason and to contribute, here and now, to the acknowledgement and attainment of what is just."[17] Far from being an escape from this world, caritas helps to direct the natural faculties toward their proper (if never humanly attainable) object in God's actual love. Unlike tzedakah, however, acts of caritas are not principally aimed at repairing a sick world. They are, rather, an attempt to bring the natural world closer to perfection by spiritually supplementing it. And this direction toward the proper cannot be achieved by human means alone: "Love – *caritas* – will always prove necessary, even in the most just society. There is no ordering of the State so just that it can eliminate the need for a service of love."[18] Without this divine supplement, any individual or institution is open to the co-opting and corrupting influence of sin (for this reason, Paul construes true righteousness, in Galatians 3:11, to be possible only in the light of faith). In the language of Matthew 5:17, one could say that caritas aims to fulfill nature rather than abolish it.[19] As a condition given gratuitously through Christian faith, caritas must also make a natural appeal to reason if it is to provide the aforementioned direction to humans. As Robert Sokolowski explains, "Christian faith thus elevates, heals and perfects reason, but it also appeals to reason, because faith presents a message and a truth that is to be understood, not just a law that is to be obeyed."[20]

Insofar as caritas becomes accessible in the world by means of understanding, it is not properly approached by means of a *jurisprudential* explanation of law, but rather by means of a *theological* explanation of the divine Word. Such a theological explanation makes use of philosophical argumentation in order to indicate both (1) how nature/reason is related to grace/faith and (2) how the former is limited in relation to the latter: "The theological virtues of faith, hope and charity are best presented not just by themselves but in contrast with the natural virtues, which we understand spontaneously from our natural experience; the theological virtues are best brought out by showing how they go beyond natural human agency."[21] While we may be able to love our neighbor, we have no natural experiential frame of reference for loving God. Insofar as caritas brings together both love of neighbor and love of God (as proclaimed by Jesus),[22] it more accurately (or less inaccurately) represents the full range of God's actual love. If caritas is "divine love" as understood by Christian theology, then human acts of charity express a love (of God, self, and neighbor) whose exemplar is God's love of the created order.

2. Divine Law and Divine Word:
The Different Religious Backgrounds

If Christianity understands righteousness without faith as (in Pauline terms) a curse, and if Judaism understands the gratuity of love as being overly arbitrary, how can the two traditions begin to dialogue? As I mentioned at the outset, the terms "tzedek" and "caritas" announce the different religious backgrounds pertaining to Judaism and Christianity. I will speak in general terms about these backgrounds in order to frame my discussion of Maimonides and Thomas in particular.

As traditionally understood, Judaism (whatever else it has become over the millennia) is a religion based in divine law. This means that it aspired to be, in the words of Ernest Fortin, an "all-inclusive social order . . . regulating every segment of men's private and public lives and precluding from the outset any sphere of activity in which reason could operate independently of the divine law."[23] This view, while correct in itself, needs some qualification. If Judaism were simply based on divinely revealed law – that is, if the word "torah" were understood, in the manner of the Greek New Testament, as "nomos," as conventional, humanmade law or custom – then traditional Judaism would amount to nothing other than a sham theodicy.[24] In fact, the word "torah" means "teaching." The Torah refers to the entirety of divine teaching in the Hebrew Bible and the normative rabbinic tradition.[25] Differently stated, after God gave Moses the law (both the "written law" of the Torah and the "oral law" of the Mishnah) on Sinai, it was (and is) up to the Jewish people to understand, interpret, and apply it in changing historical situations. For this reason, the highest science in Judaism (as in Islam) is jurisprudence.[26]

Why the need in Judaism for interpretation and application? It hardly needs to be said, but also cannot be emphasized enough, that the God of Judaism is radically transcendent. Such transcendence resonates deeply with Aristotle's statement in the *Nicomachean Ethics* that friendship between a god and a human is impossible because it would admit of too great a degree of separation.[27] Because God remains radically transcendent, Judaism's only recourse to understanding God's teaching is through communal interpretation of the Torah and rabbinic writings. It is therefore less correct to say that Jews are the "people of the Book" than it is to intimate that they are people of the Text. But if interpretation and application of law is the burden (or joy) that Judaism has to bear, its analogy in Christianity is to the divine *logos* as presented in Jesus Christ. As mediator, Jesus brings God's words directly to humans. As a result, Thomas's thinking displays a qualified break with Aristotle's notions about the impossibility of friendship between the gods and human beings. Since "there is a sharing of some kind between man and God, according as he shares his blessedness with us, it is necessary that upon this sharing some friendship be founded" (2a2ae 23.1 corp).[28] This friendship, for Thomas, just is caritas (23.1 corp; 24.2 corp). The event of incarnational mediation becomes the proper "object" of Christian interpretation and understanding in order that people can be taught how to live their earthly lives so as simultaneously to be directed toward their ultimate supernatural end.[29]

In this respect, a logos of God and what relates to God becomes for Christianity a necessary intellectual science. Such a logos (especially for thinkers like Thomas) must necessarily make use of philosophy in order to explain, to the extent possible, God's word. That such an explanation is circumscribed by natural limits simply means that one must be precise regarding what can and cannot be known philosophically (that is, naturally). Indeed, Thomas articulates both sides of this theological dialectic. While knowledge of God in this life admits only of divine "thatness" and not "whatness," still "even in the present life it is possible for us to arrive by reasoning at a full knowledge of some divine things. But even though we can have knowledge of them, and some persons actually achieve it, faith is still necessary. And this for the . . . reasons given by Rabbi Moses."[30] Put differently, one can understand up to a point (perhaps up to the point at which one is open to receiving the gift of faith), but not beyond. For this reason, philosophy is properly the "handmaiden" of theology. Also worthy of note in this passage is Thomas's respectful incorporation and interpretation of Maimonides. In referring to his *Guide of the Perplexed,* I. 33 (as Maurer holds), Thomas gives the impression that Maimonides argues that faith (in the Christian sense) is necessary for the understanding of God. The point for Maimonides, however, is not theological. He is concerned with the attempts at understanding the foundations of the Torah by people whose intellectual capacities are not prepared to do so. His concerns are therefore motivated by concerns over the stability of the Jewish community.

I can express this dichotomy between Thomas's apparent openness and Maimonides's apparent sternness in the following way: Christianity has historically had relatively few problems assimilating the discipline of philosophy. Thomas's *Summa of Theology* acquired an authority in Catholic theology far beyond what Maimonides's *Guide* had in Judaism.[31] As Leo Strauss notes, "the first article of the *Summa* deals with the question as to whether the sacred doctrine is required besides the philosophical disciplines: Thomas, as it were, justifies the sacred doctrine before the tribunal of philosophy. One cannot even imagine Maimonides opening the *Guide,* or any other work, with a discussion of the question as to whether the Halakha (the sacred Law) is required besides the philosophical disciplines."[32] In other words, philosophy (in medieval Judaism and Islam) was seen as inherently hostile to divine law and was thus viewed, at best, with suspicion. Strauss could have mentioned Maimonides's veiled reference to Aristotle in *Eight Chapters* (the introduction to his commentary on Tractate *Avot*): "Hear the truth from whoever says it. Sometimes I have taken a complete passage from a text of a famous book. Now there is nothing wrong with that, for I do not attribute to myself what someone who preceded me said. We hereby acknowledge this and shall not indicate [the author] . . . Identifying the name of such an individual might make the passage offensive to someone without experience and make him think it has an evil inner meaning of which he is not aware. Consequently, I saw fit to omit the author's name, since my goal is to be useful to the reader."[33] As with the aforementioned passage from the *Guide,* Maimonides is concerned to make right an inherently difficult communal situation in accordance with the religious (or better, religio-political) strictures of his day. Thomas seeks to provide for his readers the same gift of intellectual and spiritual charity that he manifests in his philosophical and theological writings.

I have touched on the differences between a religion based in divine law and one based in divine word. I have also noted the difference between the suspicion of philosophy by jurisprudence and the incorporation of philosophy by theology. A further question remains: Why does tzedakah appear so "worldly" and caritas so "otherworldly"? One needs to give an (at least provisional) answer to this question in order for a genuine dialogue to occur between Maimonides and Thomas on charity. The answer, for our purposes, is straightforward. What Christianity construes as "original sin," Judaism sees as a legal transgression. Put differently, there is no theological necessity in Judaism for viewing the exile from the garden of Eden as an historical event, a fall from perfection which brings about a condition that gets transmitted throughout the generations. It is, at most, an exile that explains the human processes of giving birth, working, and dying. In sharp contrast, the reality of the fall (for Christianity) is what necessitates the Incarnation as the gratuitous event that manifests divine grace and love. A discussion of Maimonides's and Thomas's particular construals of the Adam and Eve story far exceeds the purview of this essay. But their respective understandings of charity do in fact follow the trajectories set by the distinction between (1) living in a natural world that (by dint of particular actions) can be made either healthy or sick and (2) living in a fallen realm that can be made good only by divine grace.

It is precisely the temporarily infirm character of the world, coupled with its natural ability for mending, that lies behind Maimonides's classification of the eight degrees concerning acts of tzedakah (as enumerated in the *Mishneh Torah*). These are (from best to worst): (1) forming a business partnership with–or providing a gift or loan for–a person in need; (2) personally giving in a way such that the giver and the recipient do not know each other; (3) personally giving in a way such that the giver has knowledge of the recipient, but not the other way around; (4) personally giving in a way such that the recipient knows the giver, but not the other way around; (5) personally giving with one's "own hand" before being asked; (6) giving with one's "own hand" after being asked; (7) giving less than is fitting for the recipient, but doing so graciously; and (8) giving "morosely."[34]

Notable in this list is the relative deemphasis on charitable attitude. Giving "morosely" is still giving and thus still meritorious; even in occupying the lowest level of righteousness, one is still righting an injustice. In this way, even the meanest individual who gives contributes to mending the community and world. In so construing righteousness, Maimonides shows the political character of righteous deeds – they help largely irrespective of one's inner disposition. "Largely," however, is not the same as "completely." Maimonides also notes that a righteous act of giving that is performed both ill manneredly *and* "with downcast looks" has "lost all the merit of the action even [if the giver] should give [the recipient] a thousand gold pieces."[35] In attempting to coordinate (1) the actual value of the deed with (2) the way the deed was accomplished and (3) the way the deed might be experienced, Maimonides brings to light an interesting and subtle question: Can a charitable deed be done in such a problematic manner that it harms more than it heals? Maimonides answers in the affirmative, when it is a question of shaming the recipient. In this instance, shame is detrimental because, far from raising up the poor and needy, it pushes the recipient down farther. Instead, he holds that one should show sympathy for the recipient's plight.[36] Once one considers the issue of shame, it becomes clear why Maimonides ranks lending to the needy above simply giving to them: "[Lending money to the poor] is a greater and more weighty obligation than [giving money to the poor] . . . for the poor beggar, whose need compels him to ask openly for alms, does not suffer such acute distress in doing so as one who has never yet had to do it, and whose need is for help which will save him from disclosing his poverty."[37] It is, in other words, the *suffering* accompanying shame that presents a stumbling block toward the health of the individual or community in question. When Maimonides calls on givers to "ease [the] position" of the person in need,[38] he is speaking in psychological as much as material terms. It is the consideration of the wholeness of the individual or community – both the material and the psychological well-being – that renders tzedakah capable of signifying "the seed of Abraham," establishing "the Throne of Israel," and upholding "the true religion."[39]

But if nature – and with it, human nature – is corrupted, it becomes difficult to see how any such giving (even if prescribed by divine teaching and commandment) is possible. For Thomas, the situation of charitable acts is thus part of the larger problem articulated by Augustine – the problem of whether humans can by their own power overcome their fallen nature.[40] It is here that Thomas argues for the necessity of grace. If corrupted human nature is conditioned by sin, then charitable giving is from the outset subject to the temptations of greed and pride. After the expulsion from the garden of Eden, the possibility to know the good (let alone to will and act on it) can no longer have the status of a natural capacity. For Thomas, uncorrupted nature needed infused virtues only in order to accomplish the supernatural good. Corrupted nature, however, needs such virtues in order to accomplish both the natural and the supernatural good. This means that legal and political ordinances aimed at producing justice fall far short of their intended outcome: "in the state of corrupted nature man cannot fulfill all the divine commandments without healing grace" (1a2ae 109.4).[41] This is so not only for the substance of the acts, but also for the "mode of acting, i.e., their being done out of charity" (1a2ae 109.4). For sinful human nature, neither the acts themselves nor the way they are undertaken is possible without divine grace. The divine love that is caritas is possible only if one "presupposes a gratuitous gift of God, who moves the soul inwardly or inspires the good wish" (1a2ae 109.6).[42]

The emphasis on divine grace in no way means that Thomas lacks an appreciation for justice (*iustitia*) and the legal-political context in which it occurs. Building upon Aristotelian foundations, Thomas holds justice to be "the habit whereby one with a constant and perpetual will renders to others what is due them" (2a2ae 58.1).[43] The appreciation of the virtue of justice actually leads Thomas to claim an analogous relation between them. Both the legal form of iustitia and caritas can be construed as "virtue in general":

It is in [this] sense . . . that we say that legal justice is virtue in general, namely, insofar as legal justice directs the acts of other virtues to its end, which is to induce all other virtues by commanding them. For as we can call charity virtue in general insofar as charity directs the acts of all virtues to the divine good, so also we can call legal justice virtue in general insofar as legal justice directs the acts of all virtues to the common good. Therefore, as charity, which regards the divine good as its object, is essentially a special virtue, so also legal justice is essentially a special virtue insofar as legal justice concerns the common good as its object. (2a2ae 58.6)[44]

Nonetheless, it remains the case that justice (like the other natural virtues) is subordinate to caritas.[45]

Differently stated, the one-to-one correspondence between iustitia and caritas has a decisively vertical and not horizontal relationship. Justice is a natural virtue and can undergo corruption; divine love is incorruptible. From the horizontal standpoint of natural and unaided reason, however, caritas (as a form of goodness) is imperceptible outside of the acts that express it. Such acts cannot themselves be the visible markers of goodness, given that (as we saw with Maimonides) they can be done in accordance with varying attitudes. Unaided reason can never simply determine when a charitable act is being done with a charitable disposition. For this reason, according to Hannah Arendt, there is always a tension between the Christian conception of goodness and the infused virtues that express it (such as caritas) and the political order: "When goodness appears openly, it is no longer goodness, though it may still be useful as organized charity or an act of solidarity . . . whoever sees himself performing a good work is no longer good, but at best a useful member of society or a dutiful member of a church."[46] This is yet another way of stating that Thomas's account of caritas attempts to give both (1) a rational articulation of something that exceeds reason and (2) a rational articulation of the limits of reason. Keeping this in mind may help readers understand Maimonides's and Thomas's respective accounts of charity, along with the different ways in which they incorporate Aristotle's thought.

3. How to Begin to Incorporate Aristotle: Maimonides's and Thomas's Conceptions of Charity

Medieval philosophers of all three monotheisms faced an interesting and stark dilemma: how to make use of the insights of Greek philosophy without violating – or seeming to violate – the foundation of their religions. Maimonides, as I already mentioned, was compelled to make reticent use of Aristotle in his texts. Such reticence is due to the fact that Aristotle's thought undergoes only minimal revision in the texts of Maimonides. Thomas, on the other hand, never fails to cite "the Philosopher" – yet his usage is not without its own conflict. Because of the Pauline and Augustinian contours of Catholic Christianity in the Middle Ages, Thomas had to incorporate Aristotle in a manner that could be reconciled with original sin/fallen nature and divine grace. He had to subordinate Aristotelian philosophy within a framework of rational theology.[47] Consideration of this difference leads to a number of interesting situations: (1) in order to remain true to the Pauline and Augustinian theological conception of fallen nature and original sin, Thomas must adopt a different (less Platonic and Aristotelian) definition of justice than Maimonides, one that severs the connection between justice and charity; (2) whereas Thomas remains quite true to certain aspects of Aristotle's moral vision when it comes to the natural virtues, such a vision undergoes a reversal within the context of the theological/infused virtues; (3) within the theological context, a particular moment of Aristotle's physical reflections becomes paradoxically applicable for Thomistic caritas.

One of the reasons that Maimonides refuses to cite his sources in the *Eight Chapters* is that the first four chapters of the text[48] are largely a summary of the first three chapters of Aristotle's *Nicomachean Ethics*. That is, Maimonides seeks to use Aristotle's account of the acquisition of moral virtues (through education and habituation to the mean) in order to best promote the capacity for obeying the 613 commandments in the Torah. Similarly, acquisition of the moral virtues is understood as propaedeutic to acquisition of the rational virtues, thus preserving the same order of virtue as contained in the *Nicomachean Ethics*. This priority is largely replicated in the discussion of tzedakah in the *Guide of the Perplexed:* "The word *tzedakah* is derived from *tzedek,* which means justice; justice being the granting to everyone who has a right to something, that which he has a right to and giving to every being that which corresponds to his merits . . . the fulfilling of duties with regard to others imposed upon you on account of moral virtue, such as remedying the injuries of all those who are injured, is called *tzedakah* . . . when you walk in the way of the moral virtues, you do justice unto your rational soul, giving her the due that is her right . . . I refer to the virtue of faith."[49] Here, moral virtue is again an outgrowth (or alternative manifestation) of justice – both to other people and to one's self (in the form of one's rational soul). Faith, however one understands this term for Maimonides, is consequent upon acquisition and performance of tzedakah and not the other way around. If "faith" amounts to the justice accorded to the rational soul, it would be no exaggeration to hold that it expresses the acquisition of true opinions about the foundations of Mosaic law.[50] Through justice, then, comes righteousness and ultimately faith. And in good Aristotelian fashion, this form of righteousness is illustrated by a medical metaphor: a remedy. (It is relevant to note that Maimonides was himself a medical doctor.) One's soul or city is not corrupt; it is sick.

Thomas cannot abide by this, because his conception of justice subtly differs from that of Maimonides. Where Maimonides (following Plato and Aristotle) defines justice as the giving to someone what is theirs by right according to merits, Thomas holds that "justice (*iustitia*) signifies a certain equality, as the very name indicates, since we commonly speak of equal things being exactly right (*ius*)" (2a2ae 57.1). Maimonides's conception of justice, based on merit and capacity, entails that not everyone has the same capacity for acquiring the rational virtues or having faith. In redefining "justice" so that it refers to a situation of full equality rather than one involving merit, Thomas places everyone on the same acquisitional level. That level, understood within the theological contours of Catholic Christianity, is marked by fallen nature. Justice on its own, therefore, cannot be the basis of charity – understood as divine love – because fallen/corrupted nature is always plagued by sin. This transformation either raises a conflict with the political character of justice (as Plato and Aristotle understood it)[51] or (in keeping with Arendt's point) "de-justifies" the political realm. Either way, it is clear that for Thomas, justice cannot be the basis for divine love. If everyone is equal, then everyone is equally obstructed by original sin. The corruption of human nature will also threaten to de-elevate the virtue of mercy (*misericordia*) on Thomas's account. That is, insofar as the "wretchedness" (2a2ae 30.1) of the needy can infect the one who sympathetically possesses (and acts upon) the virtue of mercy, this virtue must be accompanied by divine love in order for it to exceed the purview of sin.

From the standpoint of natural and unaided reason (which knows nothing about original sin), this does not amount to a problem. But from a theological standpoint, it is a large problem indeed, one that actually calls for the reversal of priority between the intellectual life and the moral life. Thomas's approach is to present a rational argument from the theological standpoint. That is, he shows how this standpoint can discursively "touch" the standpoint of natural reason even though his argument is predicated upon an assumption not demonstrable by natural reason. One sees this approach in Thomas's characterization of the work of intellect and understanding:

The intellect's work is completed when what is understood is in the one who understands. And so the nobility of the intellectual work is observed according to the intellect's measure . . . Now things that are below the soul, exist in the soul in a nobler way than they are in themselves, since what is contained is in the container according to the mode of the container . . . But things that are above the soul exist in themselves in a nobler way than they exist in the soul. And so regarding things that are below us, cognition is nobler than love, which is why the Philosopher in *Ethics* 10 prefers the intellectual virtues to the moral virtues. But regarding things that are above us, love – and chiefly love of God – is to be preferred to cognition. (2a2ae 23.6)

Although this argument deals specifically with the priority of one theological virtue over another (caritas over faith), for our purposes, the point becomes clear: the Aristotelian order of virtue (intellect being higher than morality) is preserved in the natural realm, but reversed when it comes to love of God. In this case, infused practicality (as it were) is higher than natural cognition – let alone natural virtues like justice. As intimated in the first section, the condition of theological virtue preserves, but completes, the order of nature. This is a reversal similar to the one discussed in the previous section concerning whether or not there can be friendship with God. From the standpoint of natural unaided reason, the degree of difference (à la Aristotle) is too great. From the theological standpoint, however, God gratuitously lessens the degree to allow for such (Aristotelian) friendship to occur.

It would, perhaps, not be surprising for Aristotelian metaphysics to exert some influence over Thomas's handling of ethical matters; metaphysics, after all, is the "divine science." Nonetheless, it is somewhat audacious for Thomas to include reflections from the *Physics* in his discussion of caritas, particularly in light of Augustine's rebuke in *Confessions* 4.16 of those who use Aristotle to measure the physical magnitude of God. For Thomas, to say that all the virtues depend on caritas (2a2ae 23.4) is to say that it exhibits a simple and indivisible unity that becomes differentiated only through the partial expressions of the other virtues. So when Thomas argues that caritas is in fact a simple form, he calls *Physics* 6.2 to his defense: "A simple thing added to a simple thing does not make something greater, as was proved in *Physics* 6. Therefore, charity is not increased by addition" (2a2ae 24.5 sc). It is unproblematic to hold that caritas, as the ultimate infused virtue, exhibits a simple and indivisible unity. Why, however, does Thomas draw from a passage in Aristotle dealing with physical magnitudes? Paradoxically, it is by returning to Aristotle's *Physics* that one finds an answer: "every magnitude is divisible into magnitudes . . . neither a line nor a surface nor, in general, anything continuous can be indivisible . . . [because] the indivisible will turn out to be divisible."[52] The point is a dialectical one: nothing with magnitude – that is, nothing based on natural experience – is indivisible; caritas, as a divine gift, does not belong, in any sense, to nature; therefore, caritas is simple. If one of the aims of Thomas's account of caritas is to indicate its own natural limits, then (ironically) Aristotle's *Physics* is excellent source material.

This essay has sought to give a sense of the different religious and philosophical approaches to charity embodied by two of the most important philosophers of the medieval period. From Maimonides, one gains the insight that charity is a virtue extending beyond the mere individual to a larger whole (be it the community, the polis, or the world). From Thomas, one sees the utter fragility of the charitable attitude. That is, whether or not one shares Thomas's theological background, such an attitude does not appear to be simply present in individuals at birth. The continuance of the debate over the source (law or faith?) and origin (nature or grace?) of charity attests to the abiding import of the questions I posed in the beginning. They will continue to be asked.

NOTES

1. In this context, see Gary A. Anderson, *Charity: The Place of the Poor in the Biblical Tradition* (New Haven, CT: Yale University Press, 2013), 2, 54, 109.

2. Thomas Aquinas, O.P., *Questions on the Soul (Quaestiones de Anima)*, trans. James H. Robb (Milwaukee: Marquette University Press, 1984), 122 (question 8, response 19). For Maimonides's statement, see *The Guide of the Perplexed* 2.5, in Moses Maimonides, *The Guide of the Perplexed*, vol. 2, trans. Shlomo Pines (Chicago: University of Chicago Press, 1963), 259–261.

3. For two exemplary texts that illustrate this possibility, see David Burrell, *Knowing the Unknowable God: Ibn Sina, Maimonides, Aquinas* (Notre Dame, IN: Notre Dame University Press, 1986), and Idit Dobbs-Weinstein, *Maimonides and St. Thomas on the Limits of Reason* (Albany: State University of New York Press, 1995).

4. See Mark D. Jordan, "Theology and Philosophy," in *The Cambridge Companion to Aquinas*, ed. Norman Kretzmann and Eleonore Stump (Cambridge: Cambridge University Press, 1993), 232–51. For a view opposed to Jordan's, see Dobbs-Weinstein, *Maimonides and St. Thomas*, 168–69.

5. Michael Zank, "Justice," in *The Cambridge History of Jewish Philosophy: The Modern Era*, ed. Martin Kavka, Zachary Braiterman, and David Novak (Cambridge: Cambridge University Press, 2012), 709.

6. Alexander Altmann, "Maimonides and Thomas Aquinas: Natural or Divine Prophecy?," *AJS Review* 3 (1978): 7–8.

7. Rabbi Joseph Telshukin, *A Code of Jewish Ethics, Vol. 2: Love Your Neighbor as Yourself* (New York: Bell Tower, 2009), 156 (transliteration modified).

8. Telshukin, *Code of Jewish Ethics*, 170.

9. Aristotle, *Nicomachean Ethics* 1166a31, trans. Robert C. Bartlett and Susan D. Collins (Chicago: University of Chicago Press, 2011), 194. On the

352   Jeffrey A. Bernstein

resonance of Aristotle's view in the Talmud, I thank Alan Avery-Peck for bringing this point to my attention.

10. David Hartman and Tzvi Marx, "Charity," in *Contemporary Jewish Religious Thought: Original Essays on Critical Concepts, Movements, and Beliefs,* ed. Arthur A. Cohen and Paul Mendes-Flohr (New York: The Free Press, 1987), 49.

11. Thus, Moore's gloss on the rabbinic Jewish conception of tzedakah – that is, that almsgiving (and deeds of loving-kindness) are equal to all the other commandments of the law – has to be understood as expressing a horizontal relation between tzedakah and other virtues rather than a vertical (and transcendent) relation. See George Foot Moore, *Judaism in the First Centuries of the Christian Era: The Age of the "Tannaim,"* vol. 2 (Cambridge: Cambridge University Press, 1962), 171.

12. Joshua O. Haberman, "Righteousness," in *Contemporary Jewish Religious Thought: Original Essays on Critical Concepts, Movements, and Beliefs,* ed. Arthur A. Cohen and Paul Mendes-Flohr (New York: The Free Press, 1987), 833.

13. One also finds this connection with justice in the Oxford English Dictionary definition of the word "righteousness": "the state or quality of being righteous or just."

14. Pope Benedict XVI, *God Is Love (Deus caritas est)* (San Francisco: Ignatius Press, 2006), 7, 9.

15. In this context, I follow Hans Urs von Balthasar's indication in "Love as Revelation," chap. 6 of *Love Alone Is Credible,* trans. D. C. Schindler (San Francisco: Ignatius Press, 2004), 83–98.

16. In this respect, my reading follows Altmann, "Maimonides and Thomas Aquinas" 9. For a cogent reading arguing the closer proximity of nature and grace (particularly as it concerns prudence), see Robert C. Miner, "Non-Aristotelian Prudence in the *Prima Secundae*," *Thomist* 64 (2000): 419–20.

17. Benedict XVI, *Deus caritas est* 67.

18. Benedict XVI, *Deus caritas est* 69. For an articulation framed in a more "existentialist" manner, see Karl Rahner, "Thomas Aquinas on the Incomprehensibility of God," *Journal of Religion* 58 (1978): 117–18.

19. See Jaroslav Pelikan, *The Christian Tradition: A History of the Development of Doctrine. Vol.3: The Growth of Medieval Theology (600–1300)* (Chicago: University of Chicago Press, 1978), 285.

20. Robert Sokolowski, *Christian Faith and Human Understanding: Studies on the Eucharist, Trinity, and the Human Person* (Washington, DC: Catholic University of America Press, 2006), 304. See also Etienne Gilson, *The Chris-*

tian Philosophy of St. Thomas Aquinas, trans. L. K. Shook (Notre Dame, IN: Notre Dame University Press, 1956), 343.

21. Sokolowski, *Christian Faith and Human Understanding,* 303.

22. Benedict XVI, *Deus caritas est* 8.

23. Ernest L. Fortin, *Classical Christianity and the Political Order: Reflections on the Theologico-Political Problem,* ed. J. Brian Benestad (Lanham, MD: Rowman & Littlefield, 1996), 154.

24. Marvin Fox, *Collected Essays on Philosophy and on Judaism,* ed. Jacob Neusner (Lanham, MD: University Press of America, 2003), 202.

25. Fox, *Collected Essays,* 202.

26. Fortin, *Classical Christianity,* 154. See also Moore, *Judaism,* 162, 181.

27. Aristotle, *Nicomachean Ethics* (1159a6–7), trans. Robert C. Bartlett and Susan D. Collins (Chicago: University of Chicago Press, 2011), 175.

28. All parenthetical references to the questions on charity (2a2ae 23–46) are to the translation contained in this volume.

29. On this point, see Gilson, *Christian Philosophy of St. Thomas Aquinas,* , 349.

30. Thomas Aquinas, *De trinitate* q.3 a.1 corp, in Thomas Aquinas, *Faith, Reason and Theology,* trans. Armand Maurer (Toronto: PIMS, 1987), 66.

31. One would have to go to Maimonides's explicit legal work, *Mishneh Torah,* to find a proper analogue. But the *Mishneh Torah* has rarely been mistaken for a philosophical text.

32. Leo Strauss, *Persecution and the Art of Writing* (Chicago: University of Chicago Press, 1952), 19–20.

33. Maimonides, *Ethical Writings of Maimonides,* ed. Raymond L. Weiss and Charles Butterworth (New York: Dover, 1975), 60–61.

34. Maimonides, *Book of Seeds (Sefer Zera'im), Mishneh Torah,* in *A Maimonides Reader,* ed. Isadore Twersky (West Orange, NJ: Behrman House, 1972), 136–37.

35. Maimonides, *Book of Seeds,* 136.

36. Maimonides, *Book of Seeds,* 136.

37. Maimonides, *Book of Divine Commandments,* vol. 1, trans. Charles B. Chavel (New York: Soncino, 1967), 211.

38. Maimonides, *Book of Divine Commandments,* 211.

39. Maimonides, *A Maimonides Reader,* 135. Cf. Moshe Halbertal, *Maimonides: Life and Thought,* trans. Joel Linsider (Princeton, NJ: Princeton University Press, 2014), 270.

40. See Alasdair MacIntyre, *Whose Justice? Which Rationality?* (Notre Dame, IN: University of Notre Dame Press, 1988), 205.

41. Translations of passages in the 1a2ae are as printed in *Introduction to Thomas Aquinas,* ed. Anton C. Pegis (New York: Modern Library, 1948). On the need

of virtues for attaining both the natural and the supernatural good, see 1a2ae 109.2 and MacIntyre, *Whose Justice?*, 181–82.

42. While the acceptance of divine grace is a free act, Thomas also holds that it can take place only via the soul's being prompted by God. Dobbs-Weinstein argues that such grace as infuses gifted human beings is really the agent intellect becoming actualized in them through which the natural virtues like justice and reason can be regained. See Dobbs-Weinstein, *Maimonides and St. Thomas*, 168.

43. This passage, as well as others appearing in the questions on justice and prudence in the 2a2ae, are quoted from Thomas Aquinas, *On Law, Morality and Politics*, 2nd ed., trans. Richard J. Regan (Indianapolis: Hackett, 2002), 106.

44. Thomas Aquinas, *On Law, Morality and Politics*, 114.

45. Dobbs-Weinstein argues that this subordination is more a matter of theological/doctrinal emphasis than of philosophical views (*Maimonides and St. Thomas*, 169). Differently stated, from the standpoint of natural reason, Maimonides and Thomas are in agreement as to the capacities of the moral virtues. Thomas's break from Maimonides (and Aristotle), in this respect, can only be substantiated on the basis of the theological framework in which Thomas's philosophical remarks occur.

46. Hannah Arendt, *The Human Condition* (Chicago: University of Chicago Press, 1958), 74. See also 53–54.

47. See MacIntyre, *Whose Justice?*, 165, 188–89. Compare Harry Jaffa, *Thomism and Aristotelianism* (Chicago: University of Chicago Press, 1952), 187.

48. See *Ethical Writings of Maimonides*, 61–74.

49. Maimonides, *Guide of the Perplexed* 3.53 (trans. Pines, 631; transliterations slightly altered). One interesting question follows from this: Is Maimonidean ethical activity such as tzedakah (1) ultimately a rejection of Aristotle insofar as, given via divine emanation, it is characterized by excess (see *Guide* 3.54, 632–38) or is it (2) better thought as a kind of Aristotelian magnanimity? For the first possibility, see Dobbs-Weinstein, *Maimonides and St. Thomas*, 182. For the second, see Kenneth Hart Green, *Leo Strauss and the Rediscovery of Maimonides* (Chicago: University of Chicago Press, 2013), 164.

50. A discussion of the difference between true opinions and demonstrative philosophy exceeds the limitations of this essay. Let it be said in passing that Maimonides is here concerned about the upholding of the Mosaic law with or without a demonstration of its veracity.

51. See Zank, "Justice," 710.

52. Aristotle, *Metaphysics* (232a23, 233b16–19), trans. Hippocrates G. Apostle (Grinnell, IA: Peripatetic Press, 1980), 107, 110.

Grace-Perfected Nature

The Interior Effect of Charity in Joy, Peace, and Mercy

SHERYL OVERMYER

In the first question on the virtue of charity, the "most excellent" of all the virtues (2a2ae 23.6), Thomas strikes a climactic note within the *Summa*'s moral part. The question's cornerstone is the Aristotelian notion of friendship, read in light of the words of Jesus at the Last Supper: "Now I will not call you servants . . . but my friends" (John 15:15). Moving from Aristotle to Jesus, Thomas suggests that our natural understanding of human friendship forms the basis for understanding our friendship with God.

As Thomas traces the return of the rational creature to the end, throughout the *Summa* and especially in the questions on charity, readers may discern a pattern founded upon a fundamental continuity between nature and grace.[1] When speaking of our nature, Thomas includes the natural powers given to human beings to achieve the human good. When speaking of grace, he notes additional principles divinely added to humans to share in divine nature. To speak of a continuity between nature and grace in friendship, then, is to claim that natural friendships, as we find them in the world, enjoy a goodness that somehow carries over into "a certain friendship with God" (23.1 corp). Thomas traces a similar continuity in other contexts, for example, the relation between human love and divine love, or the relation between the cardinal virtues and the theological virtues.[2] Even as we are perfected in grace, nature enjoys an integrity of its own. For all of this, Thomas would not have us underestimate the remarkable differences between ordinary friendship and friendship with God, human love and divine love, cardinal virtue and theological virtue. Seen through a theological lens, the friendship, love, and virtue within our natural reach are limited. We need the power of charity to transform our activities. We need an efficient cause to redirect our actions toward our ultimate end of union with God. Thus beyond the principle of continuity, Thomas proposes another principle: the fundamental discontinuity between nature and grace. Indeed, according to one interpretive tradition, this second principle of discontinuity is more basic and comparatively greater.[3]

These principles mutually condition one another, as reflected in the relationship between love and charity. Often we are tempted to think of charity as simply pushing our natural loves farther along their original path. Charity seems like "natural love plus some." Thomas would regard this as an underestimation of charity. In his account of the interplay between nature and grace, charity keeps our natural loves intact, even strengthening them (continuity) while inviting us to a *new* love with a *new* object, God (discontinuity).[4] "It is the nature of love," Thomas writes, "to transform the lover into the object loved. And so if we love God, we ourselves become divinized."[5] Charity is transformative.

For Thomas, the virtues lie at the center of the rational creature's return to God. Perhaps surprisingly, he asserts that they do not suffice by themselves. The work of the Holy Spirit is so complex as to require an additional grammar: the gifts, beatitudes, and fruits of the Holy Spirit (1a2ae 68–70). Together with the virtues, the vocabulary of gifts, beatitudes, and fruits describes the newness and fullness of the life in charity. Thomas structures the whole of the 2a2ae around ordered relationships between virtues, gifts, and beatitudes.[6] Much remains to be said about Thomas's treatment of the gifts, beatitudes, and fruits – in part because so little has been said in the past.[7] By the sixteenth century, with the increasing prominence of casuistry, the Questions on the fruits, beatitudes, and gifts of the Holy Spirit were omitted from the transmission of the *Summa* altogether.[8]

In this essay, I examine three Questions from the 2a2ae: Question 28 on joy, Question 29 on peace, and Question 30 on mercy. Each of these Questions further works out the transformation by grace set out in Question 23. Joy, peace, and mercy mark a gratuitously new orientation of our basic loves, desires, pleasures, and sorrows. Grace perfects what seems most human about us – our natural inclination to love.

1. Joy and the Opposed Vices of Acedia and Envy

The affection of joy is an affection of the highest kind: the exaltation of the embodied creature in charity. This theme is sounded near the beginning of the moral part of the *Summa,* where Thomas hints at the ultimate unity of joy and beatitude: "The essence of beatitude consists in an act of the intellect, whereas what pertains to the will is an act of delighting that is consequent to this beatitude. Accordingly, in *Confessions* 10 Augustine says that beatitude is 'rejoicing in the truth' (*gaudium de veritate*) because the act of rejoicing is the consummation of beatitude" (1a2ae 3.4).

In Question 28 of the 2a2ae, Thomas provides a brief but ample consideration of "spiritual joy" (*spirituale gaudium*). Charity is the virtue that perfects our will; spiritual joy is the affection that expresses this completion. Of the eleven basic passions considered in the 1a2ae, joy comes closest to pleasure (*delectatio*). While pleasure denotes any kind of resting in the possession of a perceived good, joy is a special kind of pleasure, one that follows upon and participates in reason. Like love, desire, and pleasure – passions of the concupiscible power – the affection of joy is neither good nor bad absolutely, but only by its relation to intellect and will. The affection is not inherently good, Thomas holds, since demons experience joy after a fashion (1a2ae 64.3 ad 1). The defining feature of "complete" or "true" joy is that it participates in right reason. The deeper its participation, the more it shows itself to be a fruit of the Spirit at work in the soul, accompanying the cultivation of the theological virtues.

As an effect of charity, joy refines and perfects our loves. Yet joy is not the effect of love alone. Joy is the effect of love of God, well-ordered desire, *and* rational pleasure. The cause of joy is charity. Without charity, we cannot have true and complete joy. Such joy takes its object as God and is therefore "spiritual joy." In its complete form, spiritual joy goes beyond natural joy; it is the culmination of all our loves, the cessation of all our restless desires, and the satisfaction of true delight. Read in conjunction with Question 23, Question 28 suggests both that natural joy is the basis for understanding spiritual joy *and* that the difference between natural and spiritual joy is not one merely of degree, but a difference in kind – a qualitative difference. "Now charity is love of God, whose good is immutable, since he is his goodness. And from the very fact that God is loved, God is in the one who loves him by his noblest effect, according to 1 John 4: 'He who abides in charity, abides in God, and God in him.' And so spiritual joy, which is had over God, is caused by charity" (28.1 corp).

Spiritual joy is first made available to us in this life, here and now. It will not, however, be complete in this life. Thomas gives several reasons for this. One reason is inescapable, grounded in our being as embodied creatures: "For as long as we are in the body, we are wandering away from the Lord" (2 Corinthians 5:6; quoted at 28.1 arg. 1). Another reason is sin. We can look to ourselves first. Charity prompts us to sorrow over our past sins, as well as those of others. In loving our neighbors, charity prompts us to grieve over their sins and share in their sufferings. This may suggest the counterintuitive conclusion that the more holy and joyful a person is, the more she or he feels sorrow. (Indeed, in Question 30 on mercy, Thomas insists on the abiding role of sorrow in this life.) Here Thomas describes our journey in this life, with a note of sorrow detectable even in the writing: "Although in the exile of this wretchedness we participate in the divine good in some fashion, by knowledge and love, the wretchedness of this life nevertheless hinders us from complete participation in the divine good – how it will be in the homeland. And so this sorrow, by which a person mourns over the delay of glory, belongs to the hindrance of participation in the divine good" (28.2 ad 3).

This passage helps us understand why Thomas thinks that joy in this life must be "incomplete" (*imperfecta*). We await completion of joy in the next life, free from sin and suffering. As the joy of the "homeland" (*patria*) – a fuller enjoyment of the Triune life – it is certain. Faith in things unseen is no longer necessary, because in the *patria* we will see the object of faith. Hope too is no longer necessary, because we fully enjoy the union that was previously anticipated (28.1 ad 3). To rejoice in the presence of God, with no taint of sorrow or evil, would seem to be pure joy that Thomas calls "complete" (*perfecta*).

The distinction between complete joy and incomplete joy does not, however, exhaust the possibilities. Only God's joy is complete, absolutely speaking. Thomas underscores this point, arguing that since only God's joy is infinite, only God's joy is worthy of the infinite goodness of God. Though we can enter into this joy – Thomas cites Matthew 25:21, "Enter into the joy of your Lord" (28.3 corp) – it remains that relative to God, our joy is incomplete, particularly in this life. "So long as we are in this world," Thomas writes, "the motion of desire does not come to rest in us, because it still remains that we draw nearer to God by grace" (28.3 corp). In the next life, all of our desires come to rest, making our joy complete and abundant. Thus does Thomas frame our crossing over from this life to the next as an invitation to greater participation in the life of God. All are invited, and some will have greater joy than others, on account of their fuller participation in divine blessedness. Throughout Question 28, the language of "participation" designates our joy as a sharing in God. By connecting our joy to God's joy, Thomas suggests that human perfections are not entirely unlike the divine. At the same time, however, he does not lose sight of the essential difference between God's joy and ours.

Directly opposed to joy stand two vices: acedia (Question 35) and envy (Question 36).[9] Acedia is a species of sorrow, namely sorrow over the divine good. We may understand this as apathy about the ultimate end. This sorrow feels like an oppressive burden on the soul, weighed down by sadness. It is implicitly a rejection of true joy. Acedia's physical manifestations, though conspicuous, are not acedia itself but its effects. The vice of acedia is a soulful pain, an aversion from the good to which the will consents – and so rooted more in the intellectual than in the sensitive appetite.[10] Curiously, it can drive us toward laziness, despondency, and boredom, on the one hand, or mad frenetic activity – a condition of distracted restlessness – on the other.[11]

Acedia springs from a rejection of God's love extended in friendship to us. It manifests itself as a habitual reluctance and resistance to love in the way that charity commands. Though the sorrow of acedia is directly over divine good, it also brings about sorrow over genuine particular goods. Those afflicted by acedia withdraw from the network of loving relationships animated by charity – from God, others in God, and even themselves. It is fitting, therefore, that thirteenth-century Christians construed acedia as a capital vice contrary to the sacrament of charity, the Eucharist.[12] The body of Christ as given in the Eucharist incorporates Christians physically and spiritually into Christ's body and the life of the Triune God. The remedy for acedia is nothing less than conversion. Its cure requires a reorientation of the whole person – passions, actions, intellect – back toward God in love.[13]

In Question 36, Thomas turns from acedia to envy (*invidia*), describing it as sorrow over our neighbor's good. Envy is "*always* depraved," writes Thomas, "as the Philosopher says in *Rhetoric* 2, since it grieves over that in which one should rejoice – namely, our neighbor's good" (36.2 corp; emphasis added). As a vice, envy involves a judgment of the worthiness of the good itself alongside one's own comparative worth. Thomas's account of envy illuminates the process by which love (for our neighbor, ourselves, God) turns into hatred (of our neighbor, ourselves, *and* God), severing the bonds of love. Though properly a vice, acedia is also experienced as a passion. It is a species of sorrow, felt when a person is weighed down by sadness as she or he apprehends the good of another. Even as a passion, Thomas maintains, there is no good way to feel envy. It is one of the few passions that is morally evil in itself (1a2ae 24.4 corp). As a passion, envy occurs first at the sentient level. If it remains there, it is a venial sin. But if reason consents to the passion, it becomes a mortal sin, a "complete motion" of appetite that ranks among the capital vices. A certain kind of envy is among the gravest sins: "namely, envying the grace of one's brother, according as a person grieves over the very increase of God's grace, and not only over his neighbor's good. So it is set down as a sin against the Holy Spirit" (36.4 ad 2).

2. True Peace and Apparent Peace

In the 1a2ae, Thomas explicitly connects joy and peace: "Joy necessarily follows upon the love of charity (*amor caritatis*). For every lover rejoices at being joined with the beloved. But charity always has God, whom it loves, present, according to 1 John 4:16 ['He who abides in charity, abides in God, and God in him']. So what follows from charity is joy. Moreover, the completion of joy is peace" (1a2ae 70.3 corp). In Galatians 5:22–23, Paul writes that charity is the prime source of beatitude. Extending Paul's logic, Thomas turns to peace as a fruit of the Holy Spirit and a beatitude. He treats not only the fruits of the Holy Spirit (for example, joy), but also the fruits that have reached their full maturity and perfection in beatitude (for example, peace).

Thomas's invocation of blessedness recalls his treatment of the ultimate end in Questions 1–5 of the 1a2ae. Thomas takes "the Beatitudes" to mean the acts of the virtues and the gifts of the Holy Spirit working in coordination. Nothing is better, he holds, than to live the life of the virtues and of the gifts in this excellent way. Such activity gives us a share in beatitude now and, as it were, an assurance of future beatitude. For example, "Blessed are the peacemakers, for they shall be called the children of God" (Matthew 5:9).[14] Because we are sometimes tempted to think of peace as merely a restful state, or a simple lack of activity, it is important to clarify Thomas's scriptural understanding of peace. Doing so points to another idea of peace, which might be called "restful activity."

In Question 29, Thomas distinguishes between kinds of peace in terms that recall the vocabulary of "incomplete" and "complete" joy. First, he distinguishes between peace and mere concord. Concord is a sort of external peace where one person's appetites are in accord with another's. Since this condition can obtain among any group of people, the good or the wicked, "complete peace" must according to Thomas denote something "over and above this union" (29.1 corp). Next, he extends the meaning of peace; he does so by moving beyond external peace between multiple people to internal peace within a single person. Internal peace would have one's appetites, sensitive and rational, cooperate. Such peace provides a firm and abiding foundation for external peace, so much so that internal peace appears as the ground for external peace as such. The combination of internal and external peace, the "peace of all things," is alone worthy of being called "peace."[15] This peace is complete peace, the peace of beatitude.

Thomas distinguishes a range of conditions that claim to be peace, according to the worthiness of their objects. What he calls "true peace (*vera pax*)" is aimed at a true and complete (*perfecta*) good. Only the true good can bring our appetites to rest. This peace is characteristic of good human beings, in relation to good things. Another peace is what he calls "apparent peace (*apparens pax*)" (29.2 ad 3). Apparent peace is aimed at an apparent good and characterized by restlessness. Its objects, Thomas says, leave us wanting: "Every evil, though it may appear good in some respect, so that it brings appetite to rest in some respect, nonetheless has many defects, from which the appetite remains restless and disturbed" (29.2 ad 3).

Thomas sets *vera pax* alongside its false counterpart, *apparens pax.* The distinction seems related to the contrast drawn earlier in the *Summa* between the true virtue of the holy, on one hand, and the false virtue of *infideles,* on the other (1a2ae 65.2). He knows Augustine's gloss on Romans 14:23: "All that is not of faith is sin," as well as his observation: "Where cognition of the truth is lacking, there is false virtue even in good behavior" (quoted at 1a2ae 62.2 corp). Thomas does not want simply to oppose Augustine on the issue. Indeed, he wants to affirm Augustine's judgment that certain virtues are false in the order of supernatural merit. But there is an apparent problem here, since he is likewise committed to something other than strict condemnation of the "virtue" of *infideles.* Accordingly, Thomas moves toward a more complex and conciliatory solution in the 2a2ae, proposing a threefold distinction between true and complete virtue, incomplete virtue, and false appearances of virtue (23.7 corp).[16] He sets up conceptual leeway by allowing two possibilities for *infideles:* false virtue and incomplete virtue. If the acts of the *infideles* proceed from a lack of charity, their acts are sinful, symptomatic of "false virtue." This would coincide with Augustine's conviction. If, however, the acts refer to some other gift of God, they may be acts good of their kind, though not fully good. Without reference to the principal and ultimate good, these habits are true but incomplete virtues. By leaving open two possible descriptions of the habits of *infideles,* Thomas gives due acknowledgment to Augustine while transcending the dichotomy.

Thomas's conceptual innovation gives us resources for thinking more deeply about the distinction between "complete (*perfecta*) peace" and "incomplete (*imperfecta*) peace." The only peace we know in this world – that is, incomplete peace – seems to lie somewhere between complete and apparent peace. It remains, however, that Thomas does not in Question 29 further develop the distinction between true and false peace. In not doing so, his explicit treatment of peace remains closer to Augustine's. As one might expect, Thomas concludes by agreeing with Augustine. Any peace we might attain in this world, he holds, is a pale comparison to the peace of the next world. The peace we know here is constantly disturbed by "certain repugnant things both within and without" (29.2 ad 4).

Peace is a proper effect of charity, according to Thomas. Does this imply, as the third objector wonders, that those who lack grace – the so-called "gentiles" – are incapable of peace (29.3 arg 1)? We might suppose that in speaking of "gentiles," Thomas means to include anyone who maintains an idolatrous conception of God, including many members of the Church. Thomas's reply to the argument confirms this impression: "No one lacks the grace that makes one pleasing except on account of sin, from which it happens that a person is turned away from his due end, erecting the end in something undue. And according to this, his appetite does not adhere principally to the true final good, but to apparent good. And so on account of this, without the grace that makes one pleasing, there cannot be true peace, but only apparent peace." (29.3 ad 1). Neither pagans nor sinners, so far as they are pagans or sinners, can realistically hope for anything more than apparent peace.

Since peace is not only a fruit but also a beatitude – that is, virtue in its *completion* – there are a host of ways to fall short. The vices opposed to peace in Questions 37–42 of the 2a2ae are as diverse as they are familiar: discord, contention, schism, war, quarreling, and sedition. In Question 40, Thomas casts war (*bellum*) in a light that might be unfamiliar to us – the illumination granted by its placement in the larger context of its offense against the beatitude of peace. As a vice, war is the inevitable result of our passions run amok. On the societal level, we are desperate for peace, so much so that we seek war to attain it. We really want the peace in which nothing is opposed to our own will (see 29.2 ad 2). On the individual level, even just war inflicts moral injury upon those who are party to it. That is to say, the inner tranquility characteristic of peace is, psychodynamically speaking, the absence named in casualties of war who are diagnosed with posttraumatic stress disorder.[17] Quarreling (*rixa*), the vice treated at Question 41, Thomas understands as "a kind of private war," waged by an inordinate will (41.1 corp). Sedition – the last of the six vices opposed to peace – resembles both war and quarreling in its contrariness to the unity and peace of the multitude. It is unique in that it is not characterized by multitude against multitude (as is war) or person against person (as is quarreling), but parts against parts. Sedition opposes justice and the common good, fragmenting the people and the commonwealth held up as ideals in Augustine's *City of God.* In sum, schism, war, quarreling, and sedition are all deeds defined by opposing the unity found in peace.

It would be remiss to portray peace as the result of charity alone, for peace enjoys an especially intimate relationship with a gift of the Holy Spirit: the gift of wisdom. As one interpreter puts it, "wisdom from one point of view is more important even than charity in effecting peace."[18] Thomas writes that charity is the efficient cause of peace whereas wisdom is its formal cause: "To *have* peace belongs to charity," whereas "to *make* peace belongs to ordering wisdom" (45.6 ad 1). The gift of wisdom enables us to judge rightly about things of God. It complements infused prudence. How does wisdom lead to peace? Thomas uses James 3:17 to indicate how wisdom charts a route to peace (45.6 ad 3). The wise avoid the enticements of sin, observe the mean in all things, and listen to the advice of others. Thus the wise find peace in themselves through calm appetites. The wise also consent to the good of others. They do what they can to bolster others' good, practice the spiritual and corporal works of mercy, and treat their neighbor with charity and prudence in fraternal correction (45.6 ad 3). Thus wisdom forges peace with others. Of special note is how wisdom alongside charity demonstrates a cooperation that Thomas envisions in the harmony of all of a person's powers—wisdom has its cause in the will, but its essence in the intellect (45.2 corp).

As we find ourselves in the world, we are broken: at war with others and with ourselves. The dark irony is that this too is due to our love. Augustine writes in *De trinitate:* "For the soul, loving its own power, slips onwards from the whole which is common, to a part, which belongs essentially to itself. And that apostatizing pride, which is called 'the beginning of sin,' whereas it might have been most excellently governed by the laws of God, if it had followed him as its ruler in the universal creature, by seeking something more than the whole, and struggling to govern this by a law of its own, is thrust on, since nothing is more than the whole, into caring for a part; and thus by lusting after something more, is made less."[19] We love to choose a part over the whole, something less over something more. Given our restless internal strife, external peace seems fantastical. We need external help to bring those parts together in unity. This external help, given in the Holy Spirit, enables us to undertake our activity in the harmonious unity we know as joy. As an effect of charity, peace reverses our natural tendency toward destruction, as displayed by the vices that opposed peace.

3. Mercy as Virtue and Effect of Charity

Thomas begins Question 30 by telling us that "mercy" (*misericordia*) is named from having one's heart (*cor*) with the poor and those in distress (*miserum*). We speak of this as mercy, compassion, or perhaps pity. Thomas understands "compassion" (*compassio*) as a heartfelt response of sadness with another in suffering, literally "feeling passion with" (*cum + passio*). Yet this alone falls short of *misericordia* as a virtue, which demands more than fellow feeling. Augustine writes: "Mercy is compassion in our heart for the wretchedness of another, by which we are certainly compelled to help him, if we are able to do so."[20] Therefore mercy adds the habitual compulsion to help, as one interpreter puts it, "the settled disposition to *do something,* or more precisely the connatural inclination that *I must do something*" (emphasis in original).[21] And as Thomas inherits it, especially in the wake of Aristotle, pity carries connotations of compassionate condescension.[22] Notions of condescension are inimical to *misericordia* because charity establishes equality among all. Thus we make our peace with "mercy." The word "mercy" has roots in classical Latin, *merces:* "wages, bribe, rent, price, or commodity." For postclassical Latin, the term comes to mean "the reward of heaven."[23] As both a passion and a virtue, mercy is a complex phenomenon. Question 30 brings out and clarifies these complexities.

It is difficult to overstate the theological significance of mercy. The doctrine of God and doctrine of creation in the *Prima Pars* stand as background for Thomas's specific treatment of mercy as an effect of charity in the *Secunda Pars.* From the outset, God's work of creation is overwhelmingly determined by his overabundant goodness; he cannot but reveal himself as infinite mercy. "Mercy," Thomas writes in the *Prima Pars,* "appears in every work of God as its first source."[24] Only on this basis, he holds, are creatures able even to begin making any claims to justice. (In the first Question of the *Tertia Pars,* Thomas reads the fittingness of the Incarnation in the same light, that is, as an ongoing work of mercy.) As a continuation of God's original event of love, God draws all creatures back to himself, in mercy. Thus the Christian accounts of creation and redemption are interpreted as one. The Scriptures are the history of God's relationship with us in mercy. Mercy is the eternal origin of world history, as well as salvation history. As Walter Kasper writes, "everything stands in and under its sign."[25] Mercy is God's fundamental posture toward us in unexpected, unmerited, gratuitous love.

God's answer of mercy comes to us even before we know what question to ask. Not only does Jesus speak of God's mercy as revealed in the Old Testament, explaining it by comparisons and parables, but above all he makes mercy incarnate.[26] "Mercy is an indispensable dimension of love; it is as it were love's second name," writes John Paul II, "and, at the same time, the specific manner in which love is revealed and effected vis-à-vis the reality of the evil that is in the world, affecting and besieging man, insinuating itself even into his heart and capable of causing him to 'perish in Gehenna.'"[27] The good news in Christ is divine mercy *for all*. The sum total of our story is mercy, not sin. In becoming one with Christ, we are made a new creation. "This corresponds," concludes John Paul II, "not only to the most profound truth of that love which God is, but also to the whole interior truth of man and of the world which is man's temporary homeland."[28] If divine mercy corresponds to our greatest transformation, it also affirms who we were always meant to be. Thus Herbert McCabe writes that we need "not only to be forgiven from sin but to be divinised from simple creaturehood."[29]

Because mercy surpasses human nature so greatly, Thomas calls it a gift of the Holy Spirit and a new infused virtue. As an infused *moral* virtue, mercy turns our love of God toward our neighbor's suffering. By focusing on the wretchedness of the person in pain, mercy adds a new aspect to charity. Thomas gives exceedingly high praise to mercy: "Among all the virtues that pertain to one's neighbor, mercy is the most preferable, even as its act is preferable. For to supply the defect of another, so far as the other has a defect, belongs to the higher and better" (30.4 corp). In mercy we see the highest point of the Christian life, as it expresses itself in outward works. For "it belongs to mercy that it overflows to others, and, what is more, that it alleviates the defects of others. And this belongs most of all to the higher. So to be merciful is set down as proper to God" (30.4 corp). It remains, however, that for us charity is the great virtue. The reason is that mercy is only as good as its possessor, whereas charity makes its possessor good by binding the possessor to God. Only in and through love of God can we undertake his likeness in activity; only in and through God can we show mercy.

This bold claim raises the question of whether there are kinds of mercy that are not so directly connected to the divine. Alasdair MacIntyre observes that Thomas "treats *misericordia* as one of the effects of charity, and, since charity is a theological virtue, and the theological virtues are due to divine grace, an incautious reader might suppose that Aquinas does not recognize it as a secular virtue. But this would be a mistake."[30] Mac-Intyre characterizes Thomas's *misericordia* as a virtue that goes beyond the ordinary boundaries of communal life. Thomas can furnish an example supporting MacIntyre's point in his treatment of the Ninevites, an example that at first blush would not seem to offer much hope: "It is a natural law that one should repent of the evil one has done," he writes, "by grieving for having done it, and by seeking a remedy for one's grief in some way or another, and also that one should show some signs of grief, even as the Ninevites did, as we read in Jonah 3. And yet even in their case there was also something of faith which they had received through Jonas' preaching" (3a 84.7 ad 1). Thus we ought not be surprised to find "something of mercy" everywhere. The fecundity of Thomas's thought allows him to acknowledge other kinds of mercy, even if they fall short of the mercy that is properly an effect of charity. Indeed, Thomas uses the names of many virtues analogously, mentioning (for example) that there is even charity of various kinds: charity itself, perfect charity, imperfect charity, false charity, etc. (23.7 corp).[31] God alone constitutes the *ratio* of virtue; other meanings are secondary and derivative (23.3 corp). The question of how MacIntyre's "secular" *misericordia* should be understood remains open. But Thomas himself would not want to grant mercy without charity the status of true mercy, simply speaking. Here Thomas follows Paul: "If I should distribute all my goods to feed the poor, and if I should deliver my body to be burned, but have not charity, it profits me nothing" (1 Corinthians 13:3).

In a gesture intimating the inner coherence of the best life, Thomas grants that mercy has close but complicated relationships with joy, peace, and justice. Mercy exceeds both joy and peace in terms of the interior effects of charity. For "joy and peace add nothing over and above the aspect of good that is the object of charity. And they do not require any virtues other than charity" (30.3 ad 3). Mercy, in contrast, is not only born of love but turns that love specifically toward the wretchedness of another person. Thus in the sense that joy and peace go beyond the beginning of charity, in bringing that love to completion, so too mercy goes beyond charity's beginning, in likening our love most to God's. Mercy is, in fact, inclined to increase joy and peace.

So too mercy surpasses justice. This might sound odd because we are tempted to think of mercy and justice at odds with one another in cases where just punishment is foregone for leniency. (We might do well to think of those instances – above all, our own – when we deserved punishment but received mercy.) Thomas parses this distinction by considering God's mercy and justice in Question 21 of the *Prima Pars* as a context for our mercy, treated at 2a2ae 30. God is primarily and fundamentally oriented toward us in love and mercy. In this relationship he owes us nothing – that is, we have no claims of justice on him. But justice is not lost, for as Thomas says, "justice is a fitting accompaniment of his goodness" (21.1 ad 3). As Yves Congar observes, "mercy is not opposed to justice. Mercy does not suspend justice; rather, mercy transcends it; mercy is the fulfillment of justice."[32]

In the questions on charity, the reader sees justice and mercy come together in Thomas's conviction that spiritual and bodily works of mercy are our *imitatio Dei,* and not merely optional deeds that crown an already holy life. They are given to us as acts of virtue to fulfill the law of love, according to a measure of justice. These constitute the good life we must lead.[33] We only begin by addressing the works of mercy in their traditional form: feed the hungry, give drink to the thirsty, clothe the naked, offer hospitality, visit the sick, ransom the captive, and bury the dead; teach the ignorant, counsel the doubtful, console the grieving, correct the sinner, forgive injuries, bear with those who trouble and annoy us, and pray for all of the living and the dead. (Thomas rehearses this familiar list at 32.2 ad 1.) Quoting Basil, Thomas stresses the mandatory nature of works of mercy: "It is the bread of the hungry that you withhold, the cloak of the naked that you lock in a chamber, the shoe of the barefoot that in your keeping withers away, the money of the needy that you take to bury. Wherefore you bring harm to as many as you give help."[34] The seriousness of omission is underscored in cases of extreme need, where "a person sins mortally if he omits to give a good of mercy" (32.5 ad 3).

Rather than stop at this point, we should include the miseries that are a part of our daily news digest – all insults to human dignity, cultural poverty, addiction, chronic and painful disease, serious mental illness, abuse of every kind, the inner turmoil of despondency and despair, systemic moral evils, casualties of war.[35]

Given the pattern established in the treatment of joy and peace, we are tutored to expect that mercy will have a litany of specific vices directly opposed to it. Yet Thomas neglects to name a single one. Since Thomas is a master architect, it seems unlikely that he merely made a mistake. Robert Miner proposes one possible explanation for this strange omission:

> As long as we are human, we can suffer, and suffer with another. Since compassion is so tightly bound up with our humanity, it is nearly impossible to eliminate the precondition of *misericordia* as a virtue. Even if we are in the grip of any number of vices, we remain capable of

experiencing another's distress as our own. There is no single vice that destroys the possibility for compassion as such. The appropriate term for a person whose capacity for compassion has been utterly destroyed is not "vicious" but "inhuman." Inhumanity is not the name of a vice. It indicates something that (for members of the species homo sapiens) is much worse than a vice; it names a condition in which neither human vices nor human virtues are possible.[36]

Inhumanity is not a specific failure but a categorical insult to the *imago Dei*. Nothing goes more against the grain of the doctrines of God, creation, Incarnation, and redemption. The whole genus of unforgivable sin is summed up in a total, utter lack of mercy.[37]

Suffering and vulnerability are part of who we are. There is hardly a more realistic statement about how we naturally are, despite all of our straining against it.[38] We tend to exaggerate the intellectual aspects of the *imago Dei*. We are tempted to think that supernatural perfection entails renouncing our humanity and aggrandizing our sense of divinity. Instead, Thomas tells us that our dignity lies in receiving and giving mercy, as exemplified by Christ, who elevates us to friendship with God. As the perfect image of God, Christ reveals to us what it is to be human in God's merciful humanity. Our merciful response to suffering is precisely how we image God.

4. Becoming More Human

The interior effects of charity, as set out in Question 28 on joy, Question 29 on peace, and Question 30 on mercy, are all charity's work. Yet charity does not leave the other virtues behind. Faith, hope, prudence, and justice all play an essential role in our perfection; indeed, they make significant appearances in these questions. By contrast, the virtues of fortitude and temperance do not seem to enter significantly into them. This is because fortitude and temperance perfect the sensitive appetite, while joy, peace, and mercy as effects of charity belong more clearly to rational appetite. The thesis I venture is that their relationship is more one of beginning and completion. Fortitude and temperance begin the work that charity transforms and brings to completion in joy, peace, and mercy.

In an analogous manner, the work of charity does not stop with the infused virtues but is made complete in these same fruits and gifts. By their very definition, the fruits and gifts of the Holy Spirit are special actions, reminding us that the fullest life is not possible without further divine help.

God acts in both the infused moral virtues and the fruits and gifts, but the infused moral virtues work according to a human mode, whereas the fruits and gifts work through a divine mode. The virtues perfect our human nature in grace, while the fruits and gifts more directly image God in grace-perfected nature.[39]

Questions 28–30 are a high point of the *Summa*. In attending to charity's perfection in the fruits of the Holy Spirit and beatitudes, we find Thomas affirming the sense that passions are integral to our perfection. If we leave the "lower" sensitive appetite behind, we are not complete, since the higher requires the participation of the lower. Charity's work includes all of our powers, including our passions. One of Thomas's gifts to us is his insistence that the perfected *imago Dei* is a passionate creature full of joy, peace, and mercy. In these three, Thomas shows how charity takes root in the animal part of our being and comes to liken us more to God than any other virtue. These are hardly the only effects of charity, for Thomas clarifies that charity is the root and end of *all* the gifts, fruits, and beatitudes (23.8 corp; 45.6 ad 2). For Thomas, abundant divine goodness transforms and perfects our ordinary human ways of desiring, delighting, and sorrowing. God would have us changed unto his likeness. In so doing, we do not become other than we are. Rather, we become more *human*.

NOTES

1. Servais Pinckaers argues that Thomas's adaptation of Aristotelian analyses is a testament to the fundamental harmony between reason and revelation, in "The Sources of Ethics of St. Thomas Aquinas," in *The Pinckaers Reader: Renewing Thomistic Moral Theology,* ed. John Berkman and Craig Steven Titus (Washington, DC: Catholic University of America Press, 2005), 3–25.

2. See Michael Sherwin, *By Knowledge and by Love: Charity and Knowledge in the Moral Theology of St. Thomas Aquinas* (Washington, DC: Catholic University of America Press, 2005), 204–38.

3. See the Fourth Lateran Council: "Between the Creator and the creature so great a likeness cannot be noted without the necessity of noting a greater dissimilarity between them," in Heinrich Denzinger, ed., *The Sources of Catholic Dogma,* trans. Roy J. Defferrari (St. Louis: Herder, 1957), 171n432.

4. See Rudi te Velde, *Aquinas on God: The "Divine Science" of the Summa Theologiae* (Burlington, VT: Ashgate, 2006), chap. 6. Te Velde expounds upon two recurring and fundamental principles of Thomas's theology: *gratia praesupponit naturam* and *gratia perficit naturam, non tollit* (see esp. 150–55).

5. Thomas Aquinas, *Collationes in decem preceptis,* in "Les *Collationes in de-cem praeceptis* de Saint Thomas d'Aquin, édition critique avec introduction et notes," *Revue des Sciences Philosophiques et Théologiques* 69 (1985): 26–29.

6. Thomas integrates the powers of the human person, rather than eschewing the acquired virtues for a model of perfection centering on infused virtues, gifts, and fruits alone. Here my view differs somewhat from Andrew Pinsent, "The Gifts and Fruits of the Holy Spirit," in *Oxford Handbook of Aquinas,* ed. Brian Davies and Eleonore Stump (Oxford: Oxford University Press, 2012), 475–90, and Pinsent, *The Second-Person Perspective in Aquinas's Ethics: Virtues and Gifts* (New York: Routledge, 2012).

7. To underscore this point, while Thomas's own *Quaestio disputata de caritate* shares several arguments with the *Summa*'s treatment of charity, it does not share the mature substance of 2a2ae 28–43 and 45–46.

8. Servais Pinckaers, *The Sources of Christian Ethics* (Washington, DC: Catholic University of America Press, 1995), 254–65.

9. Rebecca DeYoung writes about the history of these vices in the Christian tradition, along with the interpretive difficulties they present. See her "Resistance to the Demands of Love: Aquinas on the Vice of *Acedia,*" *The Thomist* 68 (2004): 173–204, and "Aquinas on the Vice of Sloth: Three Interpretive Issues," *The Thomist* 75 (2011): 43–64.

10. Thomas Aquinas, *De Malo* 11 q.1 corp.

11. For an extended treatment of modern boredom, see Nicholas Lombardo, *The Logic of Desire* (Washington, DC: Catholic University of America Press, 2010), 259–71.

12. Siegfried Wenzel, *The Sin of Sloth: Acedia in Medieval Thought and Literature* (Chapel Hill: University of North Carolina Press, 2012), 56, cited in DeYoung, "Resistance to the Demands of Love," 200.

13. DeYoung, "Resistance to the Demands of Love," 196.

14. See 2a2ae 45.6, in which Thomas asks whether the Seventh Beatitude corresponds to the gift of wisdom.

15. Here Thomas cites Augustine, *De civitate Dei* 19.13.

16. For a clear exposition of this article, see Eberhard Schockenhoff, "The Theological Virtue of Charity," in *The Ethics of St. Thomas Aquinas,* ed. Stephen J. Pope (Washington, DC: Georgetown University Press, 2002), 251.

17. See Jonathan Shay, *Achilles in Vietnam: Combat Trauma and the Undoing of Character* (New York: Scribner, 1995) and *Odysseus in America: Combat Trauma and the Trials of Homecoming* (New York: Scribner, 2003). Thanks to Michael Baxter for these references.

18. Frances McMahon, "A Thomistic Analysis of Peace," *The Thomist* 1 (1939): 190.

19. Augustine, *De trinitate* bk.12 chap.9 sect.14 (PL 42:1005–6); *A Select Library of Nicene and Post-Nicene Fathers of the Christian Church,* vol. 4, ed. P. Schaff and H. Wace (Reprint, Peabody, MA: Hendrickson, 1994), 160.

20. Augustine, *De civitate Dei* 9.5, cited at 2a2ae 30.1 corp. Walter Kasper argues that Augustine and Thomas come closer to Aristotle's interpretation of compassion than to Platonism or Stoicism (*Mercy* [Mahwah, NJ: Paulist, 2014], 22–23). Kasper also contrasts Augustine and Thomas with later thinkers on mercy, including Rousseau, Lessing, Hegel, Kant, and a host of postmoderns (23–33). For two treatments that contrast Aristotelian pity with Thomist *misericordia,* see Anthony Keaty, "The Christian Virtue of Mercy: Aquinas' Transformation of Aristotelian Pity," *Heythrop Journal* 46 (2005): 181–98, and Guy Mansini, "Mercy, 'Twice Blest,'" in *John Paul II and St. Thomas Aquinas,* ed. Michael Dauphinais and Matthew Levering (Ann Arbor, MI: Sapientia, 2006), 75–100.

21. Miguel Romero, "The Call to Mercy: *Veritatis Splendor* and the Preferential Option for the Poor," *Nova et Vetera* 11 (2013): 1215.

22. Alasdair MacIntyre recognizes this feature of the term "pity" and opts for the Latin *misericordia,* though not without speaking just a few pages earlier of "the virtue of taking pity" (*Dependent Rational Animals* [Chicago: Open Court, 1999], 123 and 121, respectively). MacIntyre's arguments elsewhere explain precisely the trouble here. This is the proliferation of moral language as fragments of a conceptual scheme, parts of which now lack the context in which they originally found their significance.

23. Definition "mercy, n. and int." Oxford English Dictionary online, www .oed.com.

24. 1a 21.4; see also 2a2ae 30.1. For more on the relation between God's impassibility and mercy, see Thomas Weinandy, *Does God Suffer?* (Notre Dame, IN: University of Notre Dame Press, 2000).

25. Kasper, *Mercy,* 98. See Kasper's study of the coherence of God's mercy, graciousness, and fidelity in *Mercy,* chap. 3.

26. John Paul II, *Dives in misericordia* (1980), §§2, 5.

27. John Paul II, *Dives in misericordia* (1980), §7.

28. John Paul II, *Dives in misericordia* (1980), §13.

29. Herbert McCabe, O.P., *God Still Matters* (London: Continuum, 2002), 7.

30. MacIntyre, *Dependent Rational Animals,* 124. I am slow to agree that Aquinas recognizes it as a "secular virtue," if only because Thomas seldom uses *secularus* and never *virtus seculara.*

31. See the many "approximations" of mercy in Kasper, *Mercy,* chap. 2.

32. Yves Congar, "La misericorde: Attribut soverain de Dieu," *Vie spirituelle* 106 (1962): 380–95, as interpreted by Kasper in *Mercy,* 23.

33. In contrast, as Pinckaers notes (*Sources of Christian Ethics,* 263), sixteenth-century writers tend to interpret even the *Summa* as a morality of obligation, in which these movements of the Holy Spirit are flourishes for the spiritual elite.

34. Basil the Great, *Homilia in illud dictum evangelii secundum Lucam,* sect.7, on Luke 12:18 (PG 31:275), quoted at 2a2ae 32.5 ad 2.

35. For the inner logic of expanding the works of mercy as various forms of poverty, see Kasper, *Mercy,* 143–44.

36. Robert Miner, "The Difficulties of Mercy: Reading Thomas Aquinas on *Misericordia,*" *Studies in Christian Ethics* 28 (2015): 70–85.

37. See Matthew 12:32 and 2a2ae 14.

38. Although realistic, it may appear as contentious when judged by the set of illusions concerning independence and sovereignty cultivated by so much of the Western intellectual tradition. MacIntyre offers his *Dependent Rational Animals* as a corrective, esp. ix–9.

39. Romanus Cessario attributes later clarifications to the seventeenth-century Dominican John of St. Thomas in *Christian Faith and the Theological* Life (Washington, DC: Catholic University of America Press), 162–69.

Works Cited

Buytaert: John Damascene. *De Fide Orthodoxa.* Ed. E. M. Buytaert. St. Bonaventure, NY: Franciscan Institute Press, 1955.

CCSL: *Corpus Christianorum, Series Latina.* Turnhout: Brepols, 1953.

Chevallier: *Dionysiaca.* Ed. Philippe Chevallier. Paris and Burges: Desclée de Brouwer, 1937–.

CSEL: *Corpus Scriptorum Ecclesiasticorum Latinorum.* Vienna, 1866–.

Grottaferrata: Peter Lombard. *Sententiae in IV Libris Distinctae.* 3rd ed. Grottaferrata: Collegium S. Bonaventurae, 1971–1981.

Lawless: *Augustine of Hippo and His Monastic Rule.* Oxford: Clarendon, 1987.

Lindsay: Isidore of Seville. *Isidori Hispalensis Episcopi Etymologiarum sive Originum.* Ed. W. M. Lindsay. Oxford: Clarendon, 1911.

Mansi: *Sacrorum conciliorum nova et amplissima collectio . . .* Ed. I. D. Mansi. Paris: H. Welter, 1901–1927.

PG: *Patrologiae Cursus Completus, Series Graeca.* Ed. J.-P. Migne. Paris, 1841–1864.

PL: *Patrologiae Cursus Completus, Series Latina.* Ed. J.-P. Migne. Paris, 1841–1864.

Quaracchi: Alexander of Hales. *Summa Theologica,* also known as *Summa Halensis.* Quaracchi: Collegium S. Bonaventurae, 1924–1928.

Richter-Friedberg: *Corpus Iuris Canonici.* Ed. A. L. Richter and E. Friedberg. Leipzig: B. Tachnitz, 1922.

Strasbourg: *Glossa ordinaria* and *Glossa interlinearis.* From the version in *Biblia latina cum glossa ordinaria Walafridi Strabonis aliorumque et interlineari Anselmi Laudunensis.* Strasbourg: Adolf Rusch for Anton Koberger, not after 1480.

Scriptural Citations

For reasons of space, Questions 32 and 33 on works of mercy and fraternal correction are not included in this book. Translations of these Questions are available online at http://yalebooks.com/aquinasloveandcharity, so the scriptural citations for those Questions are included here.

Old Testament

Genesis 2.24	26.11 arg 1
Genesis 3.16	32.8 arg 2
Genesis 26.21	41.1 arg 2
Genesis 37.2	33.7 arg 2
Exodus 19.13	33.4 arg 1
Exodus 20.8	40.4 arg 1
Exodus 20.12	26.8 sc
Exodus 20.12	34.3 ad 1
Exodus 22.18	25.6 arg 2
Exodus 32.27	39.2 arg 1
Leviticus 19.17	44.3 ad 3
Leviticus 19.18	44.7 corp; 25.4 sc; 25.9 corp; 26.4 sc
Leviticus 20.9	26.6 sc
Numbers 16.26	39.4 sc
Numbers 16.30	39.2 arg 1
Deuteronomy 6.5	27.5 sc; 27.5 corp; 44.2 arg 2; 44.4 sc; 44.5 arg 1 & arg 3; 44.6 arg 1
Deuteronomy 10.12	25.1 arg 1
Deuteronomy 23.18	32.7 arg 2
Deuteronomy 25.2	39.2 arg 1
Deuteronomy 30.20	23.2 arg 2
Joshua 6.4	40.2 ad 2
Joshua 8.2	40.3 sc
1 Samuel 14.1	38.1 arg 3

2 Samuel 6.6–7	33.4 arg 1
2 Samuel 19.6	25.8 arg 3
2 Kings 17.20	39.2 arg 1 & ad 1
1 Esdras 4.19	39.2 ad 1
2 Esdras 4.17	24.9 ad 2
3 Esdras 4.36, 39	34.1 arg 2
Tobit 4.9	32.10 sc
1 Maccabees 2.41	40.4 sc
Job 5.2	36.1 ad 3; 36.3 sc
Job 13.3	38.1 ad 4
Job 28.28	45.1 arg 3
Job 31.2	32.3 arg 3
Job 33.15	33.7 ad 1
Job 35.7	31.1 arg 1
Job 39.32	38.1 arg 4
Job 41.25	45.1 ad 1
Job 42.7	38.1 arg 4
Psalms 6.3	33.6 arg 1
Psalms 9.18	25.6 arg 3
Psalms 10.6	25.7 sc
Psalms 10.8	25.6 ad 3
Psalms 18.9	44.6 arg 3
Psalms 34.13	32.3 arg 2
Psalms 36.1	36.2 corp
Psalms 49.21	25.7 corp
Psalms 57.11	25.6 ad 3
Psalms 68.10	36.2 arg 3
Psalms 72.2	36.2 corp; 43.5 ad 3
Psalms 72.3	36.3 ad 3
Psalms 72.28	23.7 corp; 27.6 ad 3
Psalms 73.23	34.1 sc
Psalms 81.4	40.1 corp
Psalms 100.8	25.6 arg 2
Psalms 102.5	28.3 corp
Psalms 105.1	23.5 ad 2
Psalms 106.18	35.1 corp
Psalms 118.113	25.6 arg 1
Psalms 118.165	29.3 sc; 43.5 corp; 45.6 arg 1
Psalms 119.5	28.2 arg 3
Psalms 124.1	43.5 corp

Psalms 138.22	25.6 ad 1
Psalms 144.9	30.2 arg 1; 30.4 arg 3
Psalms 147.3	29.2 ad 4
Proverbs 1.32	46.2 sc
Proverbs 4.2	32.3 corp
Proverbs 6.16	37.1 ad 2
Proverbs 6.19	37.1 ad 2
Proverbs 7.22	46.3 sc
Proverbs 8.8	34.3 arg 1
Proverbs 8.17	45.5 sc
Proverbs 9.8	33.6 sc
Proverbs 10.12	25.8 arg 1; 41.2 arg 4
Proverbs 12.26	26.4 arg 2
Proverbs 15.18	37.2 arg 1; 41.2 sc
Proverbs 17.19	41.2 arg 5
Proverbs 18.6	41.2 arg 3
Proverbs 18.24	28.8 arg 1
Proverbs 24.15	33.2 ad 4
Proverbs 25.21	25.9 corp
Proverbs 27.4	30.2 ad 3
Proverbs 27.6	32.2 ad 3
Proverbs 29.2	36.2 arg 2
Proverbs 28.25	41.2 arg 2
Proverbs 29.22	41.2 sc
Proverbs 30.2	45.4 ad 1
Ecclesiastes 7.14	33.2 arg 1
Song of Songs 2.4	26.1 sc; 44.8 sc
Song of Songs 8.6	24.10 sc
Wisdom 1.4	45.4 sc
Wisdom 1.13	25.6 ad 3
Wisdom 2.24	36.4 ad 2
Wisdom 7.27	45.6 arg 2
Wisdom 7.28	45.5 sc
Wisdom 8.1	23.2 corp
Wisdom 8.7	23.7 sc
Wisdom 8.16	28.2 sc; 45.3 arg 3
Wisdom 9.15	25.5 ad 1
Wisdom 11.17	39.4 corp
Wisdom 11.25	25.3 arg 1
Wisdom 14.22	29.2 ad 3

Sirach 6.23	45.2 arg 2
Sirach 6.26	33.2 sc; 44.3 ad 3
Sirach 7.29	26.10 arg 3
Sirach 9.14	26.9 corp
Sirach 12.4, 6	31.2 arg 2; 32.9 arg 1
Sirach 13.19	26.2 arg 2
Sirach 17.18	32.4 sc
Sirach 21.2	35.1 arg 4
Sirach 29.13–15	32.4 corp
Sirach 30.24	30.1 ad 2
Isaiah 11.2	45.1 sc
Isaiah 28.28	25.11 sc
Isaiah 32.17	29.3 arg 3
Isaiah 47.10	46.1 arg 3
Isaiah 48.22	29.1 sc
Isaiah 58.3	40.4 arg 2
Isaiah 59.2	27.4 arg 3; 28.2 ad 2; 39.1 arg 1
Jeremiah 4.22	45.1 ad 1
Jeremiah 9.23	45.4 arg 1
Jeremiah 10.14	46.1 arg 3
Jeremiah 15.19	25.6 ad 4
Jeremiah 17.5	25.1 arg 3
Jeremiah 31.33	44.8 sc
Ezekiel 34.4	39.4 arg 2
Daniel 2.11	23.1 arg 1
Daniel 4.24	32.1 arg 2; 32.5 arg 1
Hosea 6.6	30.4 arg 1
Micah 7.6	26.7 ad 1
Nahum 1.9	39.4 arg 3

New Testament

Matthew 5.5	28.1 arg 2
Matthew 5.9	29.4 arg 2; 45.6 arg 1
Matthew 5.19	34.4 sc
Matthew 5.39	40.1 arg 2
Matthew 5.40	43.8 arg 4
Matthew 5.42	32.3 sc
Matthew 5.44	23.1 arg 2; 25.8 sc; 25.9 arg 2 & sc; 31.4 arg 1; 44.7 arg 1

Matthew 5.46	27.7 arg 1
Matthew 6.18	32.9 arg 2
Matthew 7.3	33.5 corp
Matthew 7.6	40.3 corp; 43.7 arg 2
Matthew 7.12	40.3 ad 3
Matthew 7.18	43.2 arg 2
Matthew 9.10	25.6 arg 5
Matthew 9.36	30.1 ad 1
Matthew 10.28	32.2 arg 1
Matthew 10.34	29.2 arg 3; 37.1 ad 2; 40.1 ad 3
Matthew 10.36	26.7 ad 1
Matthew 12.7	30.4 ad 1
Matthew 15.12	43.1 sc; 43.6 arg 1
Matthew 15.14	43.7 corp
Matthew 16.23	43.2 arg 2; 43.5 arg 1
Matthew 18.6	43.4 arg 2; 43.5 sc
Matthew 18.7	43.2 arg 1
Matthew 18.15	33.1 arg 1; 33.7 sc & corp; 33.8 corp
Matthew 19.6	26.11 corp
Matthew 19.21	32.6 sc
Matthew 22.30	25.10 corp
Matthew 22.38	44.1 corp
Matthew 22.37–39	25.2 arg 1; 26.4 sc; 44.7 sc
Matthew 22.40	44.3 sc
Matthew 25.15	24.3 arg 1
Matthew 25.21	28.3 corp
Matthew 25.35	32.2 arg 1
Matthew 25.41	32.5 sc
Matthew 26.52	40.1 arg 1; 40.2 sc
Mark 9.49	29.2 arg 4; 29.4 arg 1
Mark 12.30	44.5 corp
Luke 3.14	40.1 sc
Luke 6.36	30.4 arg 3
Luke 6.38	28.3 corp
Luke 10.27	44.5 corp
Luke 11.41	32.5 corp
Luke 12.4	32.2 arg 1
Luke 14.12	31.3 arg 1; 32.3 arg 2
Luke 14.26	25.6 corp; 26.2 sc; 26.7 arg 1; 34.3 arg 1; 44.2 arg 3

Luke 16.9	32.7 arg 1; 32.9 arg 2
Luke 21.3	32.4 arg 3
Luke 21.4	32.10 corp
Luke 22.24	38.1 arg 1
John 3.8	24.3 sc
John 4.42	27.3 ad 2
John 7.23	40.4 corp
John 14.6	34.1 arg 2
John 14.21	24.12 sc; 27.8 corp
John 15.13	26.5 arg 3
John 15.15	23.1 sc
John 15.24	34.1 sc
John 17.3	24.12 sc
John 24.11	28.3 sc
Acts 5.3	33.7 arg 2
Acts 5.29	33.7 ad 5
Acts 15.37	29.3 arg 2
Acts 15.39	37.1 arg 3
Acts 23.6	37.1 arg 2
Romans 1.18	45.4 arg 2
Romans 1.20	27.3 arg 2
Romans 1.30	34.3 arg 2
Romans 1.32	40.2 arg 3
Romans 2.1	33.5 sc
Romans 3.8	33.6 arg 3
Romans 5.5	24.2 sc
Romans 6.13	25.5 corp
Romans 6.23	24.2 corp; 24.12 sc
Romans 7.5	34.5 arg 2
Romans 7.8	43.1 ad 4
Romans 7.24	25.5 arg 1
Romans 8.15	45.6 arg 1
Romans 8.29	45.6 corp
Romans 8.38	43.5 ad 2
Romans 9.3	27.8 arg 1
Romans 12.1	27.6 arg 3
Romans 12.12	28.1 arg 3
Romans 12.15	28.2 arg 1; 30.2 corp
Romans 12.19	40.1 arg 2
Romans 13.4	40.1 corp

Romans 13.8	44.2 arg 4
Romans 14.13	44.3 ad 3
Romans 14.15	43.3 sc; 43.8 arg 3
Romans 14.17	28.1 sc
Romans 14.21	43.1 arg 5
Romans 15.1	32.2 corp
Romans 15.37	29.3 arg 2
Romans 16.6	26.10 arg 3
1 Corinthians 1.8	44.6 ad 2
1 Corinthians 1.9	23.1 corp
1 Corinthians 1.10	44.3 ad 3
1 Corinthians 1.30	45.4 ad 1
1 Corinthians 2.6	45.5 arg 1
1 Corinthians 2.7	45.5 ad 1
1 Corinthians 2.9	28.3 corp
1 Corinthians 2.10	45.1 corp
1 Corinthians 2.14	46.2 corp
1 Corinthians 2.15	45.1 corp
1 Corinthians 3.3	38.2 arg 1
1 Corinthians 3.8	27.7 arg 3
1 Corinthians 3.10	45.1 corp
1 Corinthians 3.18	46.1 arg 2
1 Corinthians 3.19	46.1 ad 3; 46.3 arg 2
1 Corinthians 4.16	43.5 corp
1 Corinthians 6.7	43.8 arg 4
1 Corinthians 6.17	27.4 arg 2; 45.2 corp
1 Corinthians 6.18	35.1 ad 4
1 Corinthians 8.1	38.2 arg 3
1 Corinthians 8.10	43.1 ad 2
1 Corinthians 8.12	43.4 arg 3
1 Corinthians 8.13	43.8 ad 3
1 Corinthians 9.13	43.8 arg 5
1 Corinthians 11.3	32.8 ad 2
1 Corinthians 11.19	43.2 ad 1
1 Corinthians 11.26	40.2 corp
1 Corinthians 12.8	45.5 corp
1 Corinthians 12.11	24.3 corp
1 Corinthians 12.31	24.4 corp; 43.7 ad 4
1 Corinthians 13.3	23.7 sc; 32.1 arg 1; 32.1 arg 1; 32.10 corp
1 Corinthians 13.4	23.4 arg 2; 25.4 arg 3; 31.2 arg 3

1 Corinthians 13.5   26.4 arg 3

1 Corinthians 13.6   27.2 arg 1

1 Corinthians 13.12   27.4 arg 1 & sc

1 Corinthians 13.13   23.4 sc; 23.6 sc

1 Corinthians 14.1   36.2 corp

1 Corinthians 14.33   29.1 arg 3

1 Corinthians 14.40   43.6 corp

1 Corinthians 15.28   26.13 arg 3; 44.6 corp

1 Corinthians 16.14   23.4 arg 2; 24.1 arg 3

2 Corinthians 1.12   45.4 arg 1

2 Corinthians 2.7   35.1 corp

2 Corinthians 3.17   44.1 arg 2

2 Corinthians 4.16   25.7 corp

2 Corinthians 5.4   25.5 ad 1

2 Corinthians 5.6   28.1 arg 1 & ad 1

2 Corinthians 6.11   24.7 ad 2

2 Corinthians 6.17   25.6 arg 5 & ad 5

2 Corinthians 7.10   35.3 sc

2 Corinthians 8.13   32.10 arg 3

2 Corinthians 9.10   24.5 arg 3

2 Corinthians 10.4   40.2 ad 1

2 Corinthians 12.14   26.9 arg 1; 31.3 arg 4

2 Corinthians 12.20   42.1 sc; 42.2 sc

Galatians 2.11   33.4 arg 2 & ad 2

Galatians 2.14   43.6 arg 2

Galatians 5.6   23.6 arg 2

Galatians 5.17   29.1 corp

Galatians 5.20   29.4 arg 3

Galatians 5.21   37.1 sc; 38.1 sc; 41.1 sc

Galatians 5.22   28.4 corp

Galatians 5.26   36.2 sc; 44.3 ad 3

Galatians 6.2   32.2 corp; 33.1 arg 3

Galatians 6.10   31.2 sc; 44.3 ad 2; 44.8 ad 2

Ephesians 3.17   23.8 arg 2

Ephesians 3.19   24.2 ad 2

Ephesians 4.5   23.5 sc

Ephesians 4.7   24.3 corp

Ephesians 5.1–2   33.7 arg 1

Ephesians 5.28, 5.33   26.11 arg 2 & sc

Ephesians 6.1   32.8 arg 3

Philippians 1.17	38.1 arg 2
Philippians 1.23	25.5 arg 1; 28.2 arg 3
Philippians 3.12	24.7 sc; 24.8 arg 1
Philippians 3.20	23.1 ad 1
Philippians 4.4	28.2 corp; 28.4 arg 3; 44.3 ad 2
Colossians 1.9	28.3 ad 3
Colossians 1.12	24.3 ad 1
Colossians 2.18	39.1 corp
Colossians 3.12	30.4 sc
Colossians 3.14	27.6 arg 1
Colossians 4.5	45.3 sc
Colossians 4.17	33.4 ad 2
1 Thessalonians 2.18	43.5 arg 2
1 Thessalonians 5.22	43.1 ad 2
1 Timothy 1.5	23.4 ad 3; 23.7 arg 2; 24.2 arg 3; 44.1 corp
1 Timothy 1.6	39.1 ad 3
1 Timothy 3.10	44.6 ad 2
1 Timothy 4.8	30.4 arg 2; 32.5 ad 4
1 Timothy 5.1	33.4 corp
1 Timothy 5.8	26.7 sc; 32.6 arg 3; 32.9 sc; 44.8 ad 2
1 Timothy 5.20	33.7 corp
2 Timothy 2.4	40.2 corp
2 Timothy 2.14	38.1 sc & corp
2 Timothy 3.1–2	25.4 arg 3
Titus 2.9	32.8 arg 4
Philemon v. 7	32.3 arg 3
Hebrews 12.14	44.3 ad 2
Hebrews 13.16	30.4 ad 1; 32.1 arg 3
James 3.15	45.1 arg 1 & ad 2
James 3.17	45.5 arg 2; 45.6 arg 3
James 4.1	41.2 arg 1
1 John 1.8	24.8 arg 2; 33.5 arg 3; 43.5 arg 2
1 John 2.9	34.3 sc
1 John 2.10	24.5 arg 2
1 John 2.27	45.5 corp
1 John 3.4	33.1 ad 1
1 John 3.9	24.11 arg 1
1 John 3.14	23.2 arg 2; 36.3 corp
1 John 3.15	34.4 arg 1
1 John 3.16	44.8 ad 2

1 John 3.17	32.1 sc
1 John 3.18	25.9 arg 1; 32.5 corp
1 John 3.20	27.5 arg 2
1 John 4.10	27.8 arg 2
1 John 4.16	28.1 corp
1 John 4.20	26.2 arg 1
1 John 4.21	25.1 sc; 27.8 corp; 44.2 sc; 44.7 corp
Revelation 2.4	24.11 sc
Revelation 22.3–4	23.1 ad 1

Nonscriptural Citations

Citations from Aristotle and Augustine are listed first, in alphabetical order of textual title. Citations of other ancient and medieval texts follow, in alphabetical order of author.

Aristotle

Metaphysics

bk.1 chap.2 (982a18)	45.5 arg 2, 45.6 corp
bk.1 chap.2 (982a8)	45.1 corp
bk.2 chap.2 (994b13)	24.7 arg 1
bk.2 chap.4 (1001b8)	24.5 sc
bk.5 chap.11 (1018b9)	26.1 corp
bk.4 chap.16 (1021b17)	45.1 ad 1

Nicomachean Ethics

bk.1 chap.1 (1094a12)	23.4 ad 2
bk.1 chap.2 (1094b10)	39.2 arg 2
bk.1 chap.13 (1102a9)	31.4 arg 1
bk.2 chap.1 (1103b3)	31.4 arg 1
bk.2 chap.3 (1105a9)	27.8 arg 3
bk.2 chap.4 (1105b31–6a2)	35.1 arg 1
bk.2 chap.5 (1106a3)	30.3 arg 1
bk.2 chap.6 (1107a1)	23.3 corp; 23.4 ad 1
bk.2 chap.6 (1107a12)	33.2 corp
bk.2 chap.7 (1107a28)	30.3 arg 4
bk.2 chap.7 (1108a35)	30.3 arg 2
bk.3 chap.2 (1111b5)	30.3 arg 1
bk.3 chap.2 (1112a14)	30.3 arg 1
bk.3 chap.2 (1111b26)	24.1 ad 3

bk.3 chap.6 (1114a32)	24.11 corp
bk.4 chap.1 (1120a24)	32.1 arg 4
bk.4 chap.1 (1121a17)	32.6 arg 2
bk.4 chap.1 (1122a10)	32.7 arg 2
bk.5 chap.2 (1130a19)	43.3 arg 2
bk.5 chap.11 (1138b8)	30.1 ad 2
bk.6 chap.2 (1139a23)	30.3 arg 1
bk.6 chap.3 (1139b15)	23.7 arg 3
bk.6 chap.5 (1140a25)	33.1 arg 2
bk.6 chap.7 (1141b8)	33.1 arg 2
bk.6 chap.9 (1142b31)	33.1 arg 2
bk.6 chap.13 (1144b26)	23.4 ad 1
bk.7 chap.12 (1144a8)	33.1 ad 2
bk.7 chap.12 (1153a28)	34.6 corp
bk.7 chap.13 (1153b1)	34.6 corp
bk.7 chap.14 (1154b2)	35.4 ad 2
bk.8 chap.1 (1155a3)	23.3 arg 1; 23.3 ad 1
bk.8 chap.1 (1160b8)	42.2 ad 3
bk.8 chap.1 (1160b9)	34.2 sc; 39.2 arg 3
bk.8 chap.2 (1155b21)	23.1 arg 3
bk.8 chap.2 (1155b28)	23.1 arg 2; 25.4 arg 2
bk.8 chap.2 (1155b29)	25.2 arg 3
bk.8 chap.2 (1155b31)	23.1 corp
bk.8 chap.3 (1156a7)	23.1 arg 3; 23.5 arg 3
bk.8 chap.4 (1157a18)	23.1 arg 3
bk.8 chap.5 (1157b13)	24.10 corp
bk.8 chap.5 (1157b15)	35.4 ad 2
bk.8 chap.5 (1157b19)	23.1 arg 1; 25.3 corp; 25.10 arg 3
bk.8 chap.6 (1158a23)	35.4 ad 2
bk.8 chap.7 (1158b33)	26.10 corp
bk.8 chap.8 (1159a12)	27.1 arg 2
bk.8 chap.8 (1159a16)	25.1 arg 2
bk.8 chap.8 (1159a16)	27.1 ad 2
bk.8 chap.8 (1159a27)	27.1 sc
bk.8 chap.8 (1159a28)	27.1 corp
bk.8 chap.12 (1161b1)	23.5 corp
bk.8 chap.12 (1161b19)	26.9 corp
bk.8 chap.12 (1161b21)	26.9 arg 2
bk.8 chap.12 (1162a24)	26.11 arg 3
bk.8 chap.12 (1165a17)	26.8 corp

bk.8 chap.13 (1162b21)	23.3 ad 1
bk.8 chap.14 (1163b18)	31.3 ad 4
bk.9 chap.2 (1164b27)	31.3 ad 3
bk.9 chap.3 (1165b13)	25.6 ad 2
bk.9 chap.4 (1166a1)	25.4 corp
bk.9 chap.4 (1166a1)	26.3 arg 1; 44.7 arg 2
bk.9 chap.4 (1166a3)	25.7 corp; 27.2 arg 3; 27.2 ad 3; 31.1 sc; 30.2 corp
bk.9 chap.4 (1166a7)	29.3 corp; 30.2 corp
bk.9 chap.5 (1160b30–32)	27.2 sc
bk.9 chap.5 (1160b33)	27.2 corp
bk.9 chap.5 (1167a3)	27.2 sc; 27.2 corp
bk.9 chap.5 (1167a4)	26.2 arg 1
bk.9 chap.6 (1167a22)	29.3 ad 2
bk.9 chap.7 (1167b17)	26.12 sc; 26.12 corp
bk.9 chap.7 (1168a25)	26.10 arg 2
bk.9 chap.8 (1168b5)	25.4 corp; 44.7 arg 2
bk.9 chap.8 (1169a2)	26.5 ad 1
bk.9 chap.12 (1171b29)	26.2 arg 1
bk.10 chap.2 (1172b9)	34.6 corp
bk.10 chap.3 (1094b27)	45.1 ad 2
bk.10 chap.6 (1176b19)	35.4 ad 2
bk.10 chap.7 (1177a12)	23.6 ad 1
bk.10 chap.8 (1178a9)	23.6 ad 1

On Generation and Corruption

bk.1 chap.5 (320b30)	24.5 arg 1
bk.1 chap.20 (729a10)	26.10 arg 1
bk.2 chap.4 (738b23)	26.10 arg 1

On the Heavens

bk.1 chap.1 (268a12)	24.9 ad 1
bk.1 chap.11 (281a11)	23.3 arg 2

On the Soul

bk.3 chap.9 (432b5)	24.1 ad 2

De baptismo contra Donatistas

1.1	39.3 arg 1
6.5	39.3 arg 2; 39.4 arg 1

De catechizandis rudibus

4.7	26.12 arg 1; 27.1 arg 3

De civitate Dei

1.9	33.2 arg 3 & ad 3; 33.3 ad 1; 43.7 ad 3
2.21	42.2 corp
9.5	30.3 sc & corp
14.5	30.1 corp
14.28	25.7 arg 1
15.22	23.4 arg 1
19.11	29.4 sc
19.12	29.2 sc; 40.1 corp
19.13	29.1 arg 1; 29.2 corp; 45.6 corp

De correptione et gratia

15.46	33.2 ad 1

De cura pro mortuis gerenda

3.5	32.2 ad 1

De diversis quaestionibus LXXXIII

36.1	24.8 arg 2; 24.10 arg 2 & ad 2

De doctrina christiana

1.4	27.3 sc
1.5	27.3 sc
1.22	26.2 arg 3; 26.3 sc; 26.6 arg 2; 44.2 arg 2
1.23	25.5 sc; 25.12 corp; 44.3 ad 1

1.26	25.10 arg 1
1.27	26.2 arg 3; 26.5 sc; 26.6 arg 2
1.28	26.6 arg 1; 31.2 arg 1; 31.3 sc; 32.9 corp; 33.2 ad 4
1.30	25.6 sc; 25.10 sc
1.32	26.9 ad 3
3.10	23.2 corp

De dono perseverantiae

14	24.11 corp

De Genesi ad litteram

4.3	27.6 arg 3
8.12	24.10 arg 3; 24.12 corp

De libero arbitrio

2.19	45.1 arg 1

De mendacio

15.25	33.7 arg 2

De moribus ecclesiae catholicae

1.8	27.6 arg 2 & ad 2
1.11	23.3 sc

De natura boni contra Manicheos

3	27.6 arg 1

De perfectione justitiae hominis

5.11	23.4 arg 3
8.19	44.6 sc & ad 3

De sermone Domini in monte

1.4	45.6 sc
1.19	40.1 ad 2; 43.8 ad 4
1.20	32.3 sc; 43.8 corp
2.10	33.5 corp
2.24	24.11 corp

De trinitate

8.7	23.2 arg 1; 24.11 arg 2; 25.2 sc
10.1	27.4 arg 1
10.2	27.4 arg 1
12.7	45.3 corp
12.12	36.3 arg 1
12.14	45.1 arg 3; 45.3 corp
13.5	30.1 corp
14.1	45.1 arg 2 & arg 3
14.27	46.2 arg 2
15.17	23.2 arg 1
15.18	24.11 arg 1; 45.4 arg 3

De vera religione

48.93	26.13 arg 1

Enchiridion ad Laurentium seu de fide, spe et caritate

4.12	34.4 sc
19.73	25.8 arg 1; 27.7 arg 2

Epistolae

28.3	43.6 ad 2
78.6	33.7 corp
82.2	33.4 ad 2
118.3	25.5 ad 2
138.2	40.1 sc & ad 2
140.18	45.2 arg 1
167.15	23.4 arg 1

189.6	40.1 ad 3; 40.3 arg 2
211.11	33.8 arg 4 & ad 1 & ad 3
211.12	26.4 ad 3
211.14	35.6 ad 3
211.15	33.4 sc & ad 3

In Ioannis Evangelium tractatus

tr.32 on John 7.39	37.2 arg 2
tr.74 on John 14.16	24.4 sc
tr.83 on John 15.12	25.12 arg 1

Quaestiones Evangeliorum

2.34	32.7 ad 1

Quaestiones in Heptateuchum VII

6.10	40.1 corp; 40.3 sc

Sermones ad populum

82.4	33.2 sc & ad 4; 33.7 sc
82.7	33.7 corp; 33.8 arg 1
113.1	32.9 arg 2
113.2	32.7 sc & ad 1; 32.8 sc

Tractatus in epistolam Ioannis

tr.5 on 1 John 3.9	24.8 sc; 24.9 sc
tr.9 on 1 John 4.18	24.2 ad 3; 27.3 arg 3

Ancient and Medieval Authors Other than Aristotle and Augustine

Ambrose

DE OFFICIIS

1.7	26.8 arg 2
1.29	40.3 corp
1.30	32.9 ad 2; 32.10 arg 1 & 2, ad 2 & 3

DE PARADISE

chap.8   39.1 arg 2; 44.6 arg 2

EXPOSITIO EVANGELII SECUNDUM LUCAM

7.245   32.7 ad 1

SERMONES

81/84   32.5 corp & ad 2; 32.7 arg 3

Ambrosiaster

IN EPISTOLAM I AD TIMOTHEUM

On 1 Timothy 4.8   30.4 arg 2; 32.8 arg 1

IN EPISTOLAM B. PAULI AD CORINTHOS PRIMAM

On 1 Corinthians 8.2   23.8 sc

Basil the Great

HOMILIA IN ILLUD DICTUM EVANGELII
SECUNDUM LUCAM

On Luke 12.18   32.5 ad 2

TWENTY-FOUR SERMONS ON MORALS

serm.6 "On Avarice"   32.7 ad 1

Bernard of Clairvaux

ON LOVING GOD

chap.1   27.6 sc

Cicero

ON FRIENDSHIP

chap.20 & chap.61   29.3 corp

Ps-Cicero

RHETORICA AD HERENNIUM

4.15   38.1 corp

Cyprian

EPISTOLAE AD ANTONIANUM PARS ALTERA

sect.24   39.3 sc

Dionysius the Areopagite (= Ps-Dionysius)

CELESTIAL HIERARCHY

4.3   31.3 corp

DIVINE NAMES

1.5   27.4 corp
2.9   45.2 corp
4.4   34.1 arg 3
4.10   24.2 arg 1; 25.7 arg 3; 34.1 arg 1
4.12   25.4 corp; 27.5 arg 2; 29.3 ad 3; 31.1 ad 1
4.23   25.11 arg 1
11.1   29.1 arg 2; 29.2 arg 1 & sc & ad 1

EP.8 TO DEMOPHILUS

sect.1   33.4 corp
sect.3   45.5 ad 2

Frontinus

STRATAGEM

1.1   40.3 corp

Glossa Interlinearis

On Matthew 1.2   24.2 ad 3; 25.1 arg 3; 27.3 arg 3
On Matthew 18.8   43.1 arg 1

On Matthew 18.16   33.8 ad 3
On Matthew 22.37   44.5 corp

Glossa Lombardi

On Psalms 106.18   35.1 corp
On Romans 1.29   38.1 corp
On Romans 9.3   27.8 ad 1
On 1 Corinthians 13.3   32.10 corp
On 2 Corinthians 7.13   32.10 ad 3
On 2 Corinthians 12.20   42.1 corp; 42.2 arg 1
On Galatians 2.11   33.4 arg 2
On Galatians 2.14   33.4 ad 2
On Galatians 5.20   41.1 corp
On Philippians 3.12   24.7 sc; 24.8 ad 1
On 1 Timothy 4.8   30.4 arg 2

Glossa Ordinaria

On 1 Samuel 14.1   38.1 arg 3
On Proverbs 9.8   33.6 sc
On Matthew 5.44   25.9 sc
On Matthew 18.16   33.1 arg 1
On Luke 22.24   38.1 ad 1

Gratian

DECRETALS

1.47.8 can.8   32.5 ad 2
2.23.1 can.6   40.1 corp
2.23.5 can.44   39.4 arg 3
2.23.8 can.7   40.2 arg 2
2.23.8 can.9   40.2 arg 4
2.23.8 can.10   40.2 arg 3
2.24.3 can.14   33.3 sc

Gregory IX

DECRETALIUM

5.1.24	33.7 arg 3

Gregory of Nyssa

DE OPIFICIO HOMINIS

chap.8	44.5 corp

Gregory the Great

HOMILIAE IN EVANGELIA

1.9	32.2 sc
1.11	26.2 ad 1; 27.3 arg 1
1.14	40.2 arg 1
1.17	25.4 arg 1; 44.3 corp
2.30	24.11 arg 3; 25.9 arg 3; 26.8 ad 3
2.34	28.2 arg 2; 30.1 ad 1; 30.2 ad 3

MORALIA IN IOB

2.49	45.2 sc; 45.5 arg 3; 46.1 sc
5.46	36.1 arg 1 & ad 3; 36.2 arg 4; 36.4 arg 2 & ad 2
6.37	45.3 arg 3
8.42	33.6 sc
10.29	46.1 arg 4 & ad 4; 46.3 arg 2
22.11	36.2 corp
25.11	34.2 ad 1 & ad 3
31.13	43.8 corp
31.45	34.5 sc; 34.6 sc; 35.2 sc; 35.4 arg 2, sc, & ad 3; 36.4 arg 2, arg 3, sc, ad 1; 37.2 sc; 38.2 arg 2 & sc; 41.2 arg 4 & sc; 42.1 arg 3; 46.3 arg 1 & ad 1

ON EZEKIEL

1.17	43.7 sc

REGULA PASTORALIS

3.1   24.6 arg 3

Isidore

ETYMOLOGIAE

8.3   39.1 corp
10, "R"   41.1 arg 1
10, "S"   42.1 arg 1; 46.1 arg 4, corp, & ad 1

QUESTIONS ON THE OLD TESTAMENT

On Deuteronomy, chap.16   35.4 arg 3

SENTENTIAE

2.37   35.4 arg 3; 36.4 ad 1
3.32   33.5 sc

Jerome

EPISTLES

ep.53   23.1 arg 3

ON EZEKIEL

bk.13 on Ezekiel 44.25   26.10 sc; 26.12 arg 3

ON MATTHEW

bk.2 on Matthew 12.26   37.2 arg 3
bk.2 on Matthew 15.12   43.1 sc
bk.3 on Matthew 7.3   33.5 corp
bk.3 on Matthew 16.23   43.2 arg 2
bk.3 on Matthew 18.6   43.4 arg 2; 43.5 sc
bk.3 on Matthew 18.15   32.2 corp; 33.7 corp
bk.3 on Matthew 18.16   33.8 ad 3

ON PAUL'S LETTER TO TITUS

On Titus 3.10	39.1 ad 3

John Cassian

DE INSTITUTIS COENOBIORUM

5.1	36.4 ad 1
10.1	35.1 arg 2
10.25	35.1 arg 3 & arg 4
19.2	35.3 arg 3

John Chrysostom

ON COMPUNCTION

bk.1	27.8 ad 1

ON MATTHEW

hom.60	33.8 ad 3

Ps-Chrysostom

OPUS IMPERFECTUM IN MATTHAEUM

hom.10 on Matthew 5.19	34.4 sc
hom.17 on Matthew 7.4	33.5 corp

John Damascene

ON THE ORTHODOX FAITH

2.4	34.3 arg 3
2.14	30.1 sc; 35.1 corp; 36.1 sc; 36.2 arg 2

Leo the Great

SERMONES

tr.60 chap.4	24.12 arg 2

Origen
HOMILIAE IN CANTICUM CANTICORUM
hom.2 on Song of Songs 2.4   26.9 sc; 26.10 corp

ON FIRST PRINCIPLES
1.3   24.12 arg 1

ON JOSHUA
hom.7   33.3 arg 1

Pelagius (Pope)
LETTER TO VICTOR AND PANCRATIUS
39.1 arg 1

Peter Lombard
SENTENCES
bk.1 d.17   23.2 corp
bk.2 d.3 chap.2   24.3 arg 3

Rabanus Maurus
DE ECCLESIASTICA DISCIPLINA
bk.3, "De acedia"   35.1 corp

Sallust
DE CONIURATIONE CATILINAE
chap.51   30.3 arg 1
chap.54   32.3 ad 2

Urban II (Pope)
COUNCIL OF PIACENZA
chap.10, q.1   39.3 arg 3

Valerius Maximus

FACTORUM ET DICTORUM MEMORABILIUM

bk.4 chap.7   26.8 arg 1

Vegetius

EPITOMA REI MILITARIS

bk.1 chap.9   40.1 arg 4

William of Auxerre

SUMMA AUREA

pt.3 tr.24. q.5   33.8 ad 1